THE MEDIA AND AUSTERITY

The Media and Austerity examines the role of the news media in communicating and critiquing economic and social austerity measures in Europe since 2010. From an array of comparative, historical and interdisciplinary vantage points, this edited collection seeks to understand how and why austerity came to be perceived as the only legitimate policy response to the financial crisis for nearly a decade after it began.

Drawing on an international range of contributors with backgrounds in journalism, politics, history and economics, the book presents chapters exploring differing media representations of austerity from UK, US and European perspectives. It also investigates practices in financial journalism and highlights the role of social media in reporting public responses to government austerity measures. They reveal that, without a credible and coherent alternative to austerity from the political opposition, what had been an initial response to the consequences of the financial crisis, became entrenched between 2010 and 2015 in political discourse.

The Media and Austerity is a clear and concise introduction for students of journalism, media, politics and finance to the connections between the media, politics and society in relation to the public perception of austerity after the 2008 global financial crash.

Laura Basu is a research fellow in the Department of Media and Communications, Goldsmiths, University of London and at the Institute for Cultural Inquiry, Utrecht University. She is the author of *Media Amnesia: Rewriting the Economic Crisis* (2018).

Steve Schifferes was the Marjorie Deane Professor of Financial Journalism at City, University of London from 2009 to 2017, where he directed a new MA in Financial Journalism. He is the co-editor of *The Media and Financial Crises: Comparative and Historical Perspectives* (2014). As a BBC economics journalist for 20 years, he covered many financial and economic crises around the world.

Sophie Knowles is a senior lecturer and programme leader in journalism at Middlesex University. She has been a researcher at Murdoch University, Australia; City, University of London, and the University of Cambridge, UK. She has written on the reporting of financial crises in financial news and has published work in journals such as *Journalism Studies*.

Routledge
Taylor & Francis Group

LONDON AND NEW '

First published 2018
by Routledge
2 Park Square, Milton Park, Abingdon, Oxon OX14 4RN

and by Routledge
711 Third Avenue, New York, NY 10017

Routledge is an imprint of the Taylor & Francis Group, an informa business

British Library Cataloguing-in-Publication Data
A catalogue record for this book is available from the British Library

Library of Congress Cataloging-in-Publication Data
A catalog record for this book has been requested

ISBN: 978-1-138-89730-4 (hbk)
ISBN: 978-1-138-89731-1 (pbk)
ISBN: 978-1-315-17891-2 (ebk)

Typeset in Bembo
by Apex CoVantage, LLC

Printed and bound by CPI Group (UK) Ltd, Croydon, CR0 4YY

CONTENTS

FOREWORD

The UK vote to leave the EU in 2016 and the election of Donald Trump in the same year have been widely seen as emblematic of an increasingly corrupted public sphere. The building blocks of a more democratic information age were, it seemed, riddled with misinformation and mendacity. The digital media system, with it capacious archives, was permeated by both brilliance and bullshit – with no obvious means to tell one from the other. After the optimism of the Arab Spring, digital activism and the careful construction of a galaxy of information networks, we had, it seemed, degenerated into the bitter acrimony of post-truth politics and fake news.

It is, of course, right to be concerned about the rise of social media rumour-mongering and political campaigns underpinned by bold-faced lies. But *The Media and Austerity: Comparative Perspectives* offers a critical but less cataclysmic account of the current state of media and public understanding. The downgrading of expertise and the creation of mythic narratives did not begin with Brexit or Donald Trump, nor is it simply a symptom of social media excess. In the chapters that follow, we can see a more profound set of structural conditions emerge, one in which traditional media allowed a grand but highly skewed narrative to shut down debate and limit the public imagination.

This comes against a backdrop of concern about the ability of media to communicate enough accurate information for people to form independent and informed judgements. A survey in the United States in 2010 (Ramsay, et al. 2010) was a stark demonstration of the extent of public misunderstanding of basic economics. According to the US Congressional Budget Office, by the third quarter of 2010, President Obama's fiscal stimulus legislation had increased the number of full-time equivalent jobs by between two and five million. But only 8% of Americans were aware of this (while 20% said that economists thought the fiscal stimulus had actually *reduced* the number of jobs). Even more remarkably, most Americans were entirely unaware of the way in which the stimulus package impacted their own tax bills. Federal taxes were reduced for almost all American households, and yet only 10% of Americans knew this. Nearly four times as many (38%) thought their taxes had actually *gone up*.

President Obama's fiscal stimulus policy (much like Gordon Brown's in the UK) was quickly stymied by political opposition as austerity politics gained a grip across both Europe and the United States. But if the financial crash of 2008 was one of the defining moments of the 21st century thus far, *The Media and Austerity* shows how poorly its causes and consequences have been communicated and understood.

The crash – based on mistaken, unchecked assumptions about financial packages being bought and sold – revealed the cracks in an economic system fuelled by the monetised abstractions of the finance sector and lightly regulated consumer capitalism. It also showed how dependent these lucrative private businesses were on government when things went wrong. The scale of the failure was such that we might have imagined that it would have led to a shift in the great political balancing act between public and private sectors. Public money after all, was required to bail out the misdemeanours of private finance. We needed more public intervention in financial regulation, not less.

Yet, as the chapters in this book reveal, the crisis met with a paradoxical political response. Rescuer became villain as the consequence became the cause. Scrutiny turned away from *private* finance towards *public* finance, from addressing flimsy models of private profiteering to an all-encompassing concern about public debt. A crisis caused by the ill-informed hubris of the *private* financial sector thereby paved the way for an onslaught on the *public* sector – one already struggling under the weight of an aging population and rising public expectations.

This remarkable turnaround was profoundly political. The financial crisis was undoubtedly a moment for the political left to address the manifest failures of lightly regulated capitalism. It was a time to ask hard questions of those on the right who had been cheerleaders for a lack of regulation and who championed an unerring faith in the private sector – and yet this moment evaporated almost before it began. Instead, the capitalist crash of 2008 paved the way for a right-wing economic policy to shrink the state and increase dependence on the private sector.

Behind *The Media and Austerity* is a political story of breath-taking opportunism in which the right outmanoeuvred the left. The right's strategy was to divert attention away from the failures of the private financial sector (and, indeed, their part in it) and make the issue one of excessive public spending on public services. While this matched an ideological desire to shrink the size of the state, it was so audacious as to be almost implausible. It was built on the shaky premise that instead of creating more robust regulatory structures to prevent a repeat of the 2008 crash, governments should simply build up surpluses to be ready to bail out the system when it failed. By this rather skewed logic, ultimate culpability for the financial crisis lay with governments who spent too much on public services when they should have been saving money to bail out a lightly regulated banking sector. This should have been a difficult idea to sell – and yet our scrutineers in the news media did not treat this political response with the scepticism it probably deserved. On the contrary, they abandoned their critical faculties and went along with – and indeed promoted – this partial and highly partisan version of events. For the privately owned, highly partisan, right-leaning sections of the press, this was to be expected. They were happy to offer up a few sacrificial bankers to appease popular outrage, but generally kept quiet about more systemic failures. Their political imperatives, as ever, trumped any journalistic instincts to ask too many questions about a poorly regulated private sector (of whom, as we saw with the reaction to the subsequent 2011–2014 Leveson enquiry into the behaviour of the UK press, they are fully paid-up members). But for the broadcast media, the inability to focus on the causes of the financial crisis and allow themselves to be so easily diverted is, without doubt, a significant lapse of public service journalism.

This was not simply a failure to hold responsibility to account. Once blame has been redirected, the macroeconomic conventional wisdom set in place by the politics of austerity was, at best, questionable. For many economists, the post-2008 recession was precisely the wrong time to focus on government debt. Indeed, with interest rates so low, one of the few public policy levers available to boost economic growth (and, therefore, tax revenues which might later be used to reduce government debt) was to *increase* public spending. While some economists briefly flirted with austerity, the consequent slow growth across Europe led to a macroeconomic consensus *against* a focus on deficit-reduction at the expense of growth.

In media coverage, however, a very different narrative emerged. This was notably the case in the UK, where the focus quickly turned away from banking regulation towards the need to pay off government debt as quickly as possible. By this measure, the Labour government, which held power from 1997–2010 despite a decade of carefully managed economic growth, were to blame for the financial crisis, *not* because of their failure to regulate the financial sector (to avoid excessive speculative risk-taking) but for spending too much on public services. Basic macroeconomics – that cuts in spending would suppress economic growth and reduce the public finances still further – were displaced by the folksy wisdom that economies were like households that needed to save for a rainy day.

When the UK economy finally emerged from a period of sluggish growth – happily for the Conservative-led government, in time for the 2015 General Election – most economists saw this as a recovery that had been delayed by the politics of austerity. But in the dominant media narrative – what Simon Wren-Lewis refers to as 'mediamacro' – this was seen as a *vindication* of austerity politics. After sensible stewardship of the public finances, the story went, the economy was finally returning to health.

It is, of course, appropriate for this narrative – one promoted by the government of the day – to get a good airing. But for this to be presented with so little questioning – especially given the weight of economic evidence – was neither informative nor politically impartial. It allowed the Conservative Party to portray itself as the party of economic competence while traducing the public about the Labour Party's record – a narrative that remains uncontested to this day, and firmly entrenched in public opinion surveys.

The consequence of a short-term focus on the repayment of debt (at the expense of economic growth) is, of course, felt more acutely in poorer countries like Greece, where austerity is imposed to appease political concerns even if it results in weakening the Greek economy (and hence delaying the repayment of debt). But when journalists use the folksy 'economy as household' metaphor as their principal way to explain the Greek debt crisis, it allows, once again, the politics of austerity to become conventional wisdom.

The Media and Austerity encourages journalists to rethink the ways in which economic policy is reported. This involves reflecting the range of economic expertise that exists outside the City of London, as well as explaining basic economics in ways that avoid simplistic and misleading metaphors. It also asks those committed to impartiality to be aware of the ways in which economics has been politicised – to be aware, for example, that a short-term focus on the repayment of debt was as much a political strategy as an a economic one. Given the state of public understanding on these issues, the stakes for a healthy democracy could scarcely be higher.

Justin Lewis,
Cardiff University

Reference

Ramsay, C., Kull, S., Lewis, E., and Subias, S. (2010) *Misinformation and the 2010 Election: A Study of the US Electorate*, University of Maryland, Program on International Policy Attitudes. Available at: http://drum.lib.umd.edu/bitstream/handle/1903/11375/Misinformation_Dec10_rpt.pdf?sequence=4&isAllowed=y

ACKNOWLEDGEMENTS

There are many people and organisations whom we need to thank for making the production of this volume possible. Laura Basu's contribution has been funded by a Marie Skłodowska-Curie fellowship at the Cardiff School of Journalism, Media and Cultural Studies, supported by Professor Justin Lewis. She would like to thank Justin and all her colleagues at the School.

Steve Schifferes would like to thank the Department of Journalism, City, University of London, for supporting this project through the provision of generous sabbatical leave. He would also like to thank his major funders, the Marjorie Deane Foundation for Financial Journalism, for continuing support over the past eight years for the MA in Financial Journalism.

Sophie Knowles would like to thank the Media Department at Middlesex University for the support and time she needed to complete this project and in particular would like to thank her PhD supervisor and now colleague, Gail Phillips.

The editors also would like to acknowledge the support of Cardiff University and City, University of London, in organizing the original conference on *the Media and Austerity* that took place at City in May 2016 and inspired this volume.

The editors thank all the contributors for their outstanding scholarship and dedication across a range of disciplines and perspectives.

We are saddened to report that one of our authors, Richard Roberts, Professor of Contemporary History at Kings College London, died suddenly while this volume was in the process of production. Dick was an outstanding scholar who made contributions to a wide range of topics in UK financial history, and who had a deep understanding of the important role played by the financial press. He was also a treasured collaborator with one of us as co-editor of a previous volume in this series (S. Schifferes and R. Roberts, editors, *The Media and Financial Crisis*, Routledge, 2015). We dedicate this volume to his memory.

Finally, no book of such depth and complexity could have been completed without the love and support of our families, to whom we are all deeply grateful.

TABLES

FIGURES

NOTES ON CONTRIBUTORS

Ángel Arrese is Professor of Marketing and of Economic and Business Journalism at the University of Navarra, Spain. He has published widely on economic and business news and has been a member of the Editorial Board of the *Journal of Media Economics* and *The Journal of Media Business Studies*. He is author of *Economic and Financial Press* (2001), *La prensa económica* (2002), and *Fundamentos de Periodismo Económico* (2011), all published by EUNSA (Editiciones Universidad Navarra, Pamplona, Spain).

Stefan Bauchowitz holds a PhD in Development Studies from the London School of Economics. His work and research focus on the role of oil and mining industries in developing countries. He is also interested in public opinion and polling.

Mike Berry is a Senior Lecturer at Cardiff University's School of Journalism, Media and Cultural Studies. He is author of five books including *Bad News from Israel* (Pluto, 2004) and is currently working on a book on media coverage and public understanding of economic news.

Adam Cox is a Senior Lecturer at the University of Roehampton, where he is co-convenor of the undergraduate journalism programme. A former senior editor for Reuters, he has reported extensively on financial market activity, policy and economic events in Europe, the United States and Asia, and co-authored a book on European Monetary Union (EMU). His current research is focused on financial policy-making and the media's role in agenda-building.

Aeron Davis is Professor of Political Communication and co-director of the Political Economy Research Centre (PERC) at Goldsmiths, University of London. He has published extensively on business and financial journalism and public relations. His work crosses media sociology, political communications and economic sociology. He is the author of *Public Relations Democracy* (Manchester University Press, 2002), *The Mediation of Power* (Routledge, 2007), *Political Communications and Social Theory* (Routledge, 2010) and *Promotional Cultures* (Polity, 2013).

Christian Fuchs is Professor at the University of Westminster, where he is the director of the Westminster Institute of Advanced Studies and of the Communication and Media Research Institute. He is editor of the journal *tripleC: Communication, Capitalism & Critique* and an executive board member of the European Sociological Association.

Iñaki Garcia-Blanco is a Senior Lecturer at the Cardiff University School of Journalism, Media and Cultural Studies. He is interested in the relationships and interplays between the media and democratic politics. He has carried out research funded by the BBC Trust, the UNHCR and the European Commission. His work appears in journals including *Media, Culture & Society*, *Journalism Studies* and *Feminist Media Studies*.

Max Hänska is a Senior Lecturer at De Montfort University. His work explores the role of digital technologies in political communication and citizen journalism, and the impact of communication on our political decision-making. He holds a PhD in Media and Communications from the London School of Economics.

Niko Hatakka is a doctoral candidate at the Centre for Parliamentary Studies at the University of Turku, Finland. His research focuses on online right-wing populist publics and their interaction with institutionalized politics and the media. His work has been published in journals such as *New Media & Society* and *Discourse & Society*.

Anne Kaun is an Associate Professor at the Department for Media and Communication Studies at Södertörn University, Stockholm. Her research combines archival research with interviews and participant observation to better understand changes in how activists have used media technologies and how technologies shape activism in terms of temporality and space.

Maria Kyriakidou is a lecturer at the Cardiff University School of Journalism, Media and Cultural Studies. Her work focuses on the intersection between media, politics and globalisation. Her work on cosmopolitanism, media events and the mediation of distant suffering appears in journals such as *Media, Culture & Society*, the *International Journal of Communication* and the *European Journal of Communication*.

Justin Lewis is Professor of Communication at the Cardiff University School of Journalism, Media and Cultural Studies, and Dean of Research for the College of Arts, Humanities and Social Sciences. He has written widely about media, culture and politics. His books include *Constructing Public Opinion* (Columbia University Press, 2001), *Citizens or Consumers: What the Media Tell Us about Political Participation* (Open University Press, 2005) and *Beyond Consumer Capitalism: Media and the Limits to Imagination* (Polity, 2013).

Maria Francesca Murru is Lecturer in Sociology of Media and Communication at Università Cattolica di Milano, Faculty of Political and Social Sciences. Her research interests focus on online public spheres and mediated civic participation. She is currently engaged in research projects dealing with mediated civic literacy and emergent publics.

Yiannis Mylonas is Assistant Professor at the Media Department of the National Research University Higher School of Economics in Moscow. His latest publications include *The 'Greferendum' and the Eurozone Crisis in the Danish Daily Press* (with Matina Noutsou; *Race and Class*, 2017, 59(3): 51–66) and "Liberal Articulations of the 'Enlightenment' in the Greek Public Sphere" (*Journal of Language and Politics*, 2017, Vol 16 (2): 195–218).

Heinz-Werner Nienstedt is Professor Emeritus at the Johannes Gutenberg-University, Mainz, Germany. From 2002 to 2015 he held the chair for Media Management at the Department of Communication in Mainz. Before that he worked for 20 years in leading executive positions in the media industry. His academic background is in economics and econometrics, and his research covers media marketing and media industries. He participated in the project titled "The Euro Crisis in the Media" led by the Reuters Institute for the Study of Journalism at Oxford University.

Richard Roberts was the director of the Institute for Contemporary British History and Professor of contemporary history at Kings College London. He was co-editor with Steve Schifferes of *The Media and Financial Crises: Comparative and Historical Perspectives* (Routledge, 2015). He wrote extensively on financial history, including a history of HSBC (*The Lion Wakes*, co-authored with David Kynaston, Profile Books, 2015), *Saving the City: The Treasury and the 1914 Banking Crisis* (Oxford University Press, 2014), and *When Britain Went Bust: the 1976 IMF Crisis* (OMFIF, 2016). His most recent publication is *Six Days in September: Black Wednesday, Brexit, and the Making of Europe* (co-authored with Bill Keegan and David Marsh, OMFIF, 2017).

Richard Thomas is a Senior Lecturer in Journalism at Swansea University. His research considers the news coverage of a range of economic, business, financial and political issues. His work has been published in a range of international journals, and his book with co-author Stephen Cushion examines the media coverage of political elections (Polity Press, 2018).

Simon Wren-Lewis is Professor of Economic Policy at the Blavatnik School of Government at Oxford University. He began his career as an economist in H.M. Treasury. In 1981 he moved to the National Institute of Economic and Social Research, where he became head of macroeconomic research, developing the Institute's domestic and world models. His critique of the media coverage of macroeconomics is found in his widely read blog *mostly macro*.

INTRODUCTION

The media as messenger

Laura Basu, Steve Schifferes and Sophie Knowles

It appears that from both left and right, the concept of austerity is now under attack, and the media are seen to share some of the blame. It is no coincidence that the new political landscape created by the election of Donald Trump in the US, the rise of nationalist populism across Europe, the UK's decision to leave the EU (Brexit) and the surprisingly strong showing by the left-wing Labour leader Jeremy Corbyn in the 2017 General Election, all have been accompanied by alarm over 'fake news' and attacks on the legitimacy of the mainstream media. These seismic political shifts are the latest manifestations of the political and economic turmoil unleashed by the global economic crisis of 2007–8, and the failure by governments to develop an alternative response that would improve the lives of ordinary citizens. The political turmoil reaching across continents can be linked to the global economic crisis and the policies implemented in response to it. While austerity is now, finally, being challenged, the debate about a new economic paradigm to replace it is just beginning.

The central question this volume seeks to answer is what role the media has played in the construction of austerity as the only legitimate narrative to frame the response to the financial crisis for nearly a decade since it first began. The authors address different aspects of the subject, come from a range of disciplines, and adopt different theoretical approaches and methodologies. However, they all explore the connections between the media, politics and society, in relation to what can been seen as phase two of the global economic crisis that continues to affect the lives of millions in what has become known as the Age of Austerity.

The approach is multi-disciplinary and comparative, with perspectives from across the UK, the Eurozone, Scandinavia, the US and Australia. We concentrate mainly on Europe and the UK, where the politics of austerity assumed its most political dynamic. We do, however, look at the way the US media acquiesced in Wall Street's attempt to roll back new banking regulations designed to avert a future financial crisis, which is now bearing fruition under the Trump administration (Chapter 13).

Austerity is of course not a new concept, and its meaning has morphed and changed shape over time. In earlier centuries, philosophers and the Church taught that it was a personal virtue to live one's life in moderation. It was the rise of the modern state, and its growing role in the economy in the 20th century, particularly in an age of total war, which put austerity on the political agenda and made it synonymous with cutbacks in government spending. Britain's first austerity plan arose in the aftermath of the huge increase in government debt during the First World War. Following World War II, 'austerity' had a different meaning: it was the restriction of private consumption, for example through rationing, to provide the government resources to rebuild the economy and create the welfare state. In the post-war years, when Keynesianism dominated economic thinking in the US and UK, Germany rebuilt its war-torn economy on yet another view of austerity, known as 'ordoliberalism', with a conservative approach to government borrowing, a fear of inflation, and economic growth based on a rules-based approach and cooperation between government, business and labour. This view shaped Germany's response to the Eurozone crisis and ensured that it would embrace economic orthodoxy, rejecting budget deficits as a way of expanding the economy, and try to enforce it on other member states (Blyth, 2013).

The deregulation of global financial markets from the 1980s added another layer of vulnerability to governments who were increasingly dependent on financing their budget deficits through international borrowing on bond markets. The fear of the bond market reaction played a major role in pushing governments to cut spending in May 2010 both in Britain and in the weaker members of the Eurozone (Greece, Portugal, Spain and Ireland).

Ten years after the financial crash it is perhaps difficult to remember the sense of sheer panic accompanying the meltdown in the major world financial markets that centred on New York and London in September 2008. Governments responded initially with massive bailout packages and fiscal stimulus to keep their economies afloat, combined with tougher regulation of banking, which led to large public deficits. Despite these measures, the crisis continued to deepen and expanded to incorporate the Eurozone in 2010, when it became clear that many Eurozone countries in southern Europe also had huge and rapidly growing public sector deficits, causing private capital markets to withdraw funding. The intervention by the 'Troika' – the European Commission (EC), European Central Bank (ECB) and the International Monetary Fund (IMF) – offering financial support in return for deep cuts in public spending, exacerbated the crisis. Now, a decade after the crisis, many of these economies have barely recovered to the level they were before the crisis, and personal household incomes have not recovered.

There was widespread resistance to austerity from an early stage in the shape of the populist global Occupy movement. More recently we have seen resistance linked to social democratic political parties such as Syriza in Greece, Podemos in Spain, the UK Labour Party under Jeremy Corbyn, as well as Bernie Sanders' insurgent campaign for the US Democratic presidential nomination in 2016. A more powerful political response, however, has been the rise of nationalist "authoritarian populism" (Hall, 1983), as people's fear and anger over their financial struggles have been harnessed into anti-immigration and protectionist projects, which have grown in strength in northern and eastern Europe, threatening conventional political parties in France, Germany, Sweden, the Netherlands, Hungary and Poland, among others.

Such protest against established economic order and anti-immigrant rhetoric means it is more important than ever to understand how austerity became the dominant response to the economic crisis, and the role the media have played in both communicating it to the public and giving voice to resistance against it. In turn, it is also critical to understand the impacts these economic conditions have had on media practice and content. To do this, and to be able to represent the various ways austerity and the role of the media have been analysed since the crisis began, the book is divided into four sections. Parts 1 and 2 look at how austerity and opposition to it have been covered by the mainstream media, first in the UK and then in continental Europe. Part 3 examines how the crisis has affected the political economy of media and journalistic practice; and Part 4 considers how social media intersects with the rise of social and political movements on both the left and the right.

In addressing these issues, the volume raises a series of key questions that go to the heart of debates about media's role within democracy. How have the news media framed the crisis and possible responses to it? Whose interests have these framings served? How heterogeneous and pluralistic has coverage of austerity and the crisis been? Whose voices get heard? What material and ideological factors have influenced the coverage? What role has media coverage played in policy? What have been the effects on different publics? What is the relationship between the political economy of (social) media and wider economic processes behind the crisis such as financialisation and marketisation? How have both anti-austerity movements and far-right politicians used social media in relation to the crisis and austerity? What have been the interactions between mainstream and social media when it comes to the crisis?

The UK experience

The UK's shift to austerity is a central part of our story. Containing a global financial hub (Norfield, 2016), London was one of the epicentres of the 2008 crash. Unlike many Eurozone countries, the UK was not forced to impose austerity by supranational authorities but chose to adopt this path unilaterally when a new coalition government was formed in 2010, led by the Conservative Party. The coalition zealously pursued austerity policies that aimed to reduce the government deficit to zero and sharply cut back the role of the state in the economy, an approach that was continued when the Conservatives won power on their own in the 2015 General Election. Arguably, the shifting of blame for austerity and its negative effects on living standards to the effects of immigration and EU policies, as promoted by pro-leave politicians and much of the media, contributed to the UK's momentous decision in 2016 to leave the European Union.

The first two chapters in the UK section explore the ways austerity has been framed by the mainstream media over several years. They show that, just as the crisis is constantly morphing, narratives about the crisis have been slippery and they have shifted over time. In Chapter 1, Steve Schifferes and Sophie Knowles carry out a longitudinal study of how the crisis was portrayed from 2010 to 2015 through the prism of key political and economic commentators from the UK quality press, particularly focusing on the lead-up to the Tory election victory in 2015. Following their earlier work (Schifferes and Knowles, 2015) on the establishment of the austerity narrative in the run-up to the 2010 election, they point to the limited discussion about the underlining human and social consequences of austerity, and the lack of any debate on alternative paths, despite the deteriorating economic situation. In Chapter 2, Laura Basu tracks the development of the UK news coverage of the economic crisis in its different mutations over eight years. She argues that continual reframings of the crisis led to 'media amnesia' in which all the lessons of the crash and the failure of orthodox economics were forgotten. Instead, using framing analysis, she shows how the media legitimised policies that redistributed resources towards the rich, through austerity measures on one hand, and supply-side measures such as corporation tax cuts on the other. As Mike Berry shows in Chapter 3, a critical factor in the framings and reframings of the crisis – and the shaping of journalistic content generally – are the sources journalists turn to for information (see Hall, 1978; Philo, 1995). Berry tackles this issue in his chapter through the prism of media reporting of the UK public sector deficit, whose reduction was the key metric of the government's austerity programme. He finds that political and financial elites dominated coverage, so that news reproduced a very limited range of opinion on the implications of and potential strategies for deficit reduction. This analysis is complemented by focus group research which examines how audiences have reacted to the media coverage of the deficit and what should be done about it.

While these chapters discuss the lack of a sustained discussion of alternative policies to austerity, and the gap between elites and the experience of ordinary people in mainstream news, they also raise what is becoming a central issue in the Age of Austerity: growing inequality. Who pays the price of economic adjustment and who benefits from any economic growth? This issue IS tackled directly in Chapter 4, which asks how beneficial economic growth is if the proceeds are distributed mainly to the rich. Richard Thomas examines how growth and inequality were presented on two of the UK's most watched TV news bulletins – on ITV and

BBC – before and after the crisis. He finds that economic growth is rarely, if ever, associated with redistribution that would share its gains across all sections of society. As long as influential news platforms do not 'join the dots' in terms of growth, poverty and inequality, such issues may not gain sufficient momentum among the public to impact on the policy agenda.

Austerity and its media construction, however, is not new; Chapter 5 provides much-needed historical context in Britain's long history of battles over austerity. The debates in the media in earlier austerity drives are very instructive in understanding how the debate has unfolded in the present day. Richard Roberts, in Chapter 5, looks at the way the media shaped the first major debate on austerity in the UK – the Geddes Axe of 1922, a proposal by a government-sponsored committee of businessmen to cut public spending across the board by 20% to pay down the war debt accumulated during the First World War. The press played a key role in both promoting the austerity drive, and later, in helping to limit its effects, when some influential government departments and lobbies seized on the cuts as unfair and unwise – especially in education and the military.

The media also played a critical role when Labour governments in the UK were forced by international pressure to cut back public spending, in 1931 and again by the IMF in 1976. The 1931 cuts were generally backed by the press on 'patriotic' grounds (Roberts, 2015, p. 249) and in both cases damaged the credibility of the ruling Labour Party, causing a split in the party in 1931 and seriously damaging its claims to economic competence in the run-up to the election of Margaret Thatcher as Prime Minister in 1979 (Needham, 2015, p. 266).

Continental perspectives

Part 2 of the book takes us from the UK to the European continent, which has been the site of what Bank of England chief economist Andy Haldane has called part two of the crisis, beginning in 2010 – with part one being the 2007–8 financial crash itself (Stewart, 2015). The Eurozone crisis has involved radical austerity and privatisation packages imposed across much of Europe, both voluntarily by governments, and through external pressure from the Troika. The southern European states have been among the hardest hit, especially Greece, which has lost 25% of its GDP. There has been widespread resistance to austerity in the Eurozone, by ordinary citizens and social movements, left-wing political parties and a re-energised extreme right.

Chapters 6 and 7 present findings from a large-scale content analysis of the Euro crisis carried out under the auspices of the Reuters Institute for the Study of Journalism. These chapters address the issues of consensus and divergence in the media coverage of the Eurozone crisis. Heinz-Werner Nienstedt in Chapter 6 analyses how the press in six European countries framed three basic issues related to the Euro crisis in 2012: its fundamental causes, the immediate political and economic responses, and broader long-term responses. He finds that these three issues were reported very differently both within and between countries, and they corresponded to current political and economic debates between Eurozone countries. While there are big differences in the narratives of the big northern countries – France, Germany and the UK – there are smaller ones between the crisis countries of Greece, Italy and Spain. Ángel Arrese in Chapter 7 looks specifically at support for austerity measures across the European media, and analyses the results both for countries and by type of publication (with the financial press sharing a pro-austerity consensus cross-nationally). He finds significant differences between Eurozone countries in the North and South and between different publications with different audiences and political agendas, thus giving a more nuanced picture of press coverage.

While Chapters 6 and 7 provide cross-country and comparative analysis, Chapters 8 and 9 home in on two of the epicentres of the Eurozone crisis: Greece and Spain. Maria Kyriakidou and Iñaki Garcia-Blanco in Chapter 8 examine the nature of the mainstream media coverage of two political parties – Syriza in Greece and Podemos in Spain – that have mobilised civic indignation against the wide embrace of austerity policies. They show that in both countries the left-wing parties were predominantly constructed by the mainstream press as a threat to political stability and their anti-austerity policies were portrayed as extreme. In this way, they argue, newspaper coverage contributed to the legitimisation of the imposed austerity policies and neoliberal narratives of the Euro crisis. Yiannis Mylonas in Chapter 9 examines how race and class discourses intersect in German news coverage of the Euro crisis in Greece. He shows that German media have offered an 'Orientalist' framing, blaming the cultural and moral failures of Greece's 'national character' for the crisis. In this way, harsh policies – such as permanent austerity measures – were legitimised for Greece. Taking a critical theory approach, he argues that the German media, through using intersecting "culturalist" and classist discourses about Greece, have served a project of intensified capital "accumulation by dispossession" (Harvey, 2011) in the post-crisis period. In this way, Mylonas raises the relationships between neoliberalism and neo-nationalism that are currently of growing concern.

Journalistic practice and the crisis

In Part 3, we shift focus from a discussion of the framing of the crisis and austerity to the media practices that result in those framings – practices that have themselves been impacted by the crisis and austerity cuts. In a sense, many of the chapters in the Parts 1 and 2 address the media's role in what Colin Crouch (2011) has called "the strange non-death of neoliberalism" since the crisis. Several of the chapters in this section explore how and why the media have played such a role. In Chapter 10, Aeron Davis gives a long-term perspective on how economic, business and financial news reporting has changed since the 1970s. Focusing on an evolving business model of production, he traces the processes by which economic news content has become increasingly narrow and defined in restrictive, elite and financialised terms – thus taking us back to issue of the lack of plurality of views. Ultimately, in addition to limiting the critical role the press might have played in the run-up to the financial crisis of 2007–8, the dependence on elite sources also limited the discussion of alternatives to neoliberalism in the post-crisis world. Davis suggests that this has contributed to the Brexit vote and a wider public rejection of the ruling political and economic elites.

Simon Wren-Lewis argues in Chapter 11 that one aspect of this elite dominance was the emergence of 'media-macro', a narrow and biased view of the economic policy choices facing the UK promulgated by the press. In this narrative, austerity was the only macroeconomic policy choice, despite the evidence from a wide range of academic economists that this approach was clearly not working and delaying the recovery. In trying to explain this development, he suggests that media correspondents were not confident enough to seek out alternative views and were subject to group think where they continued to make the same assumptions about the right direction for economic policy despite evidence to the contrary. He also points to the way the UK press used negative developments in the Eurozone, especially in Greece, to justify the need for continued austerity in the UK, despite their limited relevance to the real situation in the UK.

In Chapter 12, Sophie Knowles presents findings from interviews with financial journalists in the UK, US and Australia. Through her analysis of the interview material, she connects some trends in finance journalism – such as reporting optimistically during boom times and on 'free market' policies – with broad economic factors impacting professional journalism generally. This is a contribution to the understanding we now have of the modus operandi of financial journalists and on-going debates about the extent to which journalism is currently in a state of crisis (Dahlgren, 2009; Franklin, 2014). The neoliberal phase of capitalism that produced the economic crisis has also put multiple strains on the profession of journalism. The traditional, advertising-based business model for news is under threat from reduced revenues (Freedman, 2010), while the 24/7 production process directly impacts the quality of reportage (Davies, 2009). The suggestion is that individual journalists are hard-pressed to find and to report on alternative economic paradigms to discuss, especially when conflicts of interest between business and media further impede the ability to develop a critique that may damage the free market.

Adam Cox asks, in Chapter 13, whether the US media have been complicit in the continuation of a policy paradigm promoting deregulated financial markets as the optimum state of affairs, despite the most cataclysmic crisis since the 1930s. His chapter considers the way the media responded to the growing pressure from Wall Street to repeal and undermine the Dodd-Frank Act, which was introduced to ensure stricter regulation of banks in the United States after the financial crisis. He argues that the media coverage paved the way for the Republican administration of Donald Trump to proceed to dismantle Dodd-Frank. Through content analysis, he looks at the paradigms used by journalists to understand the banking crisis, and shows how quickly the critique of the banking sector was replaced with the earlier paradigm of neoliberal deregulation, helped and abetted by the limited expertise of most journalists in this area and their vulnerability to reframing by financial and right-wing political elites – with a number of parallels to Laura Basu's analysis in

Chapter 2. He suggests the notion of paradigm survival is important for under-standing media behaviour and the media's effects on financial policy, highlighting the links between the media, policy and elite opinion.

Social media, social movements and the crisis

Part 4 introduces the role of social media in communicating the crisis with a broad and deep structural critique, looking at the contradictory roles social media can play both as media of protest, on both left and right, and a huge and growing sector of the commercialised economy. In Chapter 14, Christian Fuchs illuminates how the social media industry stands in the context of the crisis economy, which in turn has implications for its targeted advertising business model. The debate around 'Twitter revolutions' is contextualised in these terms. Fuchs connects the political economy of social media with the ideologies to be found there, presenting initial empirical findings about the phenomenon of 'red scare 2.0' in the context of austerity Britain. As Fuchs points out, the kinds of attacks Labour Party leader Jeremy Corbyn and other left-wing public figures face have a long pedigree (Herman and Chomsky, 1988). He shows how anti-socialist ideology attacking Jeremy Corbyn is played out and challenged on Twitter. With his contribution, Fuchs shows how social media are in complex ways embedded into the contradictions of capitalist society, econ-omy, politics and ideology.

As Anne Kaun and Maria Francesca Murru explain in Chapter 15, a powerful strand of media theory connects social movements – including those arising out of the current crisis – with social media, encapsulated in the concept of 'Twitter revolutions', also explored by Fuchs. Concepts such as networked protests (Castells, 2012) and connective action (Bennett and Segerberg, 2013) focus on the new organizational structures that result from digital-enabled peer production mecha-nisms. In their most optimistic form, these theories argue that social media can play a radically democratising role in society, connecting people horizontally and allow-ing anyone with an internet-enabled device to have a voice. While Max Hänska and Stefan Bauchowitz take up these ideas in Chapter 17, Kaun and Murru aim to reconnect to a large body of research engaging with representations of protest movements that they claim have lately been overshadowed by the dominant focus on the role of digital and social media in mobilizations. Using the case studies of Occupy Latvia and Occupy Sweden, they adopt a narrative approach to show how the Occupy protests have been reshaped by the press in Latvia and Sweden.

Social media have also been important to the rise of right-wing populism, as explored in Chapter 16. Niko Hatakka analyses how politicians from the UK Independence Party and the Finns Party in Finland have remediated and reframed mainstream journalism on Facebook. Meaning is never fixed, and can be encoded, decoded and re-encoded to meet different ends. In this way, online news flow on economic crises – even when highly elite-driven – can become reattributed to support the growing popularity of nationalist-populist political movements. He concludes that minor slants in the salience of certain news frames can be disproportionally utilised by populist parties, as frames prone to populist and anti-establishment rhetoric are not only easily magnified but also bridged to support more sinister political objectives such as far-right opposition to immigration.

In the final chapter, Max Hänska and Stefan Bauchowitz investigate questions of transnational social media activism, and probe the possibility of social media contributing to a European public sphere, through their analysis of the #ThisIsA-Coup hashtag that emerged during Greece's 2015 tough bailout negotiations with the EU. In July 2015, Greece's anti-austerity Syriza government held an historic referendum urging its supporters to reject the bailout conditions that the EU was demanding. Although the government won a resounding 'oxi' – 'no' to more austerity – it was later forced by economic pressures which threatened the collapse of its banking sector to reverse course. The struggle between the Greek government and the Troika (the EC, IMF and European Central Bank) was encapsulated in the hashtag #ThisIsACoup, which rapidly spread across Europe for those who wanted to express support for Greece's stance. Based on a unique dataset of ca. 450,000 tweets, the chapter geo-maps the emergence of the hashtag in the days after the referendum. Hänska and Bauchowitz argue that the way #ThisIsACoup cascaded across Europe illustrates that national boundaries are more porous on social media than they are for broadcast media – while the extent to which the hashtag was discussed in traditional media also demonstrates the agenda-setting potential of this form of hashtag activism. These questions around a European public sphere are becoming increasingly urgent as the European Union risks fragmenting and even disintegrating in the face of unresolved immigration and economic crises, and the withdrawal of one of its largest member states, the UK.

Media, austerity and democracy

As Justin Lewis suggests in his foreword to this volume, 'fake news', though a worrying phenomenon in relation to the current rise of nationalism, is not new, and it is not divorced from the wider issues surrounding journalism at stake in this volume. 'Fake news' implies its other: 'real news' – and 'real news' is presumably the kind of conventional, mainstream news offered by the likes of the *New York Times,* BBC, CNN, the *Financial Times* and so on. However, 'fake news' has arisen and has been able to flourish in a context in which the public no longer trusts 'real news', especially in relation to the economy (Schifferes, 2015). As many of the chapters in this book show, the public may have good reason to be sceptical of the role of the media in failing to present alternatives to austerity. The same economic processes resulting in the 'mother of all crises' have also had a profound impact on journalism, leading to restructuring of news industries internationally (see Chapters 10, 12 and 14). This restructuring has in many cases led to a narrowing of the pool of sources and perspectives, and the further dominance of elite voices promulgating "free market" ideology (see Chapters 10, 11, 12 and 13). This in turn has encouraged media frames that have legitimised the kinds of policies that helped cause the crisis in the first place – which are escalating inequality, and in some cases are associated with extreme forms of nationalism (see Chapters 1–4, 8 and 9). These framings often also delegitimise those resisting austerity (see Chapters 8 and 15). Media frames that are narrow and dictated by elites have a long and complicated history (see Chapter 5), certainly in the UK.

Coverage of austerity, however, is not uniform across countries or across the media's political spectrum (see Chapters 6 and 7). Social media, meanwhile, play multiple and contradictory roles when it comes to social change (see Chapters 14, 16 and 17), and interact with mainstream media in complex ways (see Chapter 16). It is the responsibility of media scholars to probe the boundaries between 'fake news' and 'real news', and what this means for the ways our societies are organised, especially during times of instability. The persistence of the austerity frame long after the crisis began is a sign that the media have failed to play their proper role in enabling a broader debate in the public sphere. It remains to be seen whether the rise of social media, the weakening of establishment elites, and the growing economic and political instability will lead to another paradigm shift – and if so, what direction it will take. In understanding the past, present and potential future roles of media in the on-going crisis, media scholars have much that is positive to contribute to that change.

References

Bennett, W. L., and Segerberg, A. 2013. 'The logic of connective action: Digital media and the personalization of contentious politics'. *Information, Communication & Society*, 15(5), pp. 739–768.

Blyth, M. 2015. *Austerity: The history of a dangerous idea*. Oxford: Oxford University Press.

Castells, M. 2012. *Networks of outrage and hope: Social movements in the internet age*. Cambridge: Polity Press.

Crouch, C. 2011. *The strange non-death of neoliberalism*. Cambridge: Polity.

Dahlgren, P. 2009. The troubling evolution of journalism. In: Zelizer, B. (ed.), *The changing faces of journalism*. Oxon: Routledge.

Davies, N. 2009. *Flat earth news*. London: Vintage.

Franklin, B., 2014. 'The future of journalism'. *Journalism Practice*, 8(5), pp. 469–487.

Freedman, D., 2010. The political economy of the "new" news environment. In: Fenton, N. (ed.), *New media, old news*. London: Sage.

Hall, S. 1983. The great moving right show. In: Hall, S., and Jacques, M. (eds.), *The politics of Thatcherism*. London: Lawrence & Wishart.

Hall, S., Critcher, C., Jefferson, T., Clarke, J., and Roberts, B. 1978. *Policing the crisis*. Hampshire: Palgrave Macmillan.

Harvey, D. 2011. *The Enigma of capital*. London: Profile Books.

Herman, E. S., and Chomsky, N., 1988. *Manufacturing consent*. New York: Pantheon.

Needham, D. 2015. 'Goodbye, great Britain'? The press, the Treasury, and the 1976 IMF crisis. In: Schifferes, S., and Roberts, R.(eds.), *The media and financial crises: Comparative and historical perspectives*. Oxon: Routledge.

Norfield, T. 2016. *The City*. London: Verso.

Philo, G. (ed.). 1995. *Glasgow media group reader, volume 2*. London: Routledge.

Roberts, R. 2015. The pound and the press, 1919–1972. In: Schifferes, S., and Roberts, R. (eds.), *The media and financial crises: Comparative and historical perspectives*. Oxon: Routledge.

Schifferes, S., 2015. Why the public doesn't trust the business press. In: Schifferes, S., and Roberts R. (eds.), *The media and financial crises: Comparative and historical perspectives*. Oxon: Routledge.

Schifferes, S., and Knowles, S. 2015. The British media and the 'first crisis of globalization'. In: Schifferes, S., and Roberts, R. (eds.), *The media and financial crises: Comparative and historical perspectives*. Oxon: Routledge.

Stewart, H., 2015. Beware the global financial crisis, part III. *The Guardian*, 22 September. Available at: www.theguardian.com/business/2015/sep/18/beware-the-global-financial-crisis-part-iii

PART I
The UK experience

1

THE UK NEWS MEDIA AND AUSTERITY

Trends since the global financial crisis

Steve Schifferes and Sophie Knowles

Introduction

Our previous study (see Schifferes and Knowles, 2014), based on a content analysis of key commentators in the years from the 2008 financial crisis to the 2010 General Election, showed how the foundations of the Liberal-Conservative Coalition government's austerity policy were laid in the debate during the preceding two years. Austerity was not a policy unique to this government, and earlier crises, from 1922 to the 1975 International Monetary Fund (IMF) crisis, had led to public spending cuts (Burk and Cairncross, 1992; Roberts, 2016). What was unprecedented was the length of time that austerity has persisted as the central policy framework 10 years after the financial crisis began.

This chapter looks at how leading commentators in the UK quality press supported or criticised the austerity policy despite growing evidence that it was not working or delivering higher living standards to ordinary citizens (Resolution Foundation, 2017). We find that the terms of the debate, while fluctuating at times, barely shifted despite some challenges to the prevailing ideology. Using the methodology from our 2014 study, we examine the views of influential opinion formers who had the power to shape this debate: from 2012, when austerity was virtually unchallenged, to the run up to the 2015 General Election, narrowly won by the Conservatives on an austerity agenda. With this in mind, we wanted to see how the quality press reflected the terms of this debate. Did they offer different terms, options and alternatives to austerity? While the nature and coverage within the tabloid press is perhaps easier to predict, we look at a cross-section of the quality press, which we hoped would represent a broader and more nuanced debate. We, therefore, explore the way in which the quality press framed the debate on austerity in the lead-up to the narrow and unexpected Conservative victory in the 2015 General Election.

In particular, we ask in our study:

- How has the quality press been framing and contributing to the contours of the debate surrounding austerity as an economic policy?
- Are there continuing trends that have continued in the debate since the 2008 financial crisis, or are there departures since the Coalition government took power in 2010?
- What effect did changing economic and political circumstances have on the debate?

Literature review

In the wake of the 2008 financial crisis, the media's relationship with the financial sector has been widely criticised for being too cosy and uncritical (Lewis and Thomas, 2014; Mair and Keeble, 2009); too dependent on a narrow range of sources it uses for information (Knowles et al., 2016; Manning, 2013; Picard et al., 2014); and wedded to narratives that have been shown to have a free-market bias (Davis, 2014; Schiffrin and Fagan, 2012). The crisis, which at first centred on the collapse of the financial system, metamorphosed into a broader debate on the role of the state that was resolutely political in tone and ideological in nature.

During economic crises, public opinion has been shown to shift to both the right and to the left (Blekesaune, 2007; Stevenson, 2001). However, most studies show that it is the way the debate is framed by elites and mediated by the media that has the most decisive influence on shaping political views (Marx and Schumacher, 2016; Murdock and Gripsrud, 2014). This is true despite the rise of social media as an alternative channel of communication. A study of a discussion of austerity on Twitter during the 2015 election campaign shows that although there is a lack of mainstream news media presence, it is still the mainstream media that dictates the debate, as the volume of Tweets peak whenever the topic is mentioned offline, for example in news articles or talk shows (Ragnedda and Ruiu, 2017).

A number of studies show the strength of the neo-liberal, pro-austerity agenda in the British press. One study suggests that although the inevitability of austerity was challenged by the press in the months immediately after George Osborne announced his first budget in 2010, ultimately, little was found in the way of alternatives to what was proposed (Fairclough, 2016). The *Guardian* newspaper was the only publication to stand out as being against the 'unnecessary pain' of cuts to welfare payments.

This press attitude was paralleled by declining support for welfare spending among the general public (see Harkins and Lago-Ocando, 2016, for a discussion of the historical roots of this attitude in the UK). By 2015 the British Social Attitudes longitudinal survey found support for increasing taxes and spending more on health, education and social benefits had fallen from 63% in 2002 to 37% by 2015, and support for more spending on the poor was even lower (Taylor and Taylor-Gooby, 2015). This survey shows Labour supporters tend to support welfare payments, while Conservative supporters do not – a gap that has widened in recent times. Another survey, of 3,500 adults in the UK (Marx and Schumacher, 2016), confirms that political affiliation is a more likely predictor of support for welfare than income levels. It also shows the power of media frames in shaping public attitudes. When shown articles that emphasize debts and deficits rather than inequality, there is lower support for welfare payments. Conversely, after looking at news articles reporting poor economic prospects, there is generally support for generous unemployment benefit.

In this chapter we trace the way that media commentators have shaped the post-2010 debate on austerity, and to what extent they have reinforced or questioned the narrative of the Coalition government. As the literature review demonstrates, the media play a particularly key role at a time of paradigm shifts, by either questioning or reinforcing the case for a new economic or social policy (Dean, 2013; Lippmann, 1922; Mirowski, 2013; Parsons, 1989).

The austerity debate

For the purposes of this chapter, it is important to understand what we mean by 'austerity'. We therefore review the changing meaning of austerity in 20th-century Britain. The literature on austerity shows that attempts to cut back public spending have a long history, beginning with the 1922 Geddes Axe which was responding to the increased government spending in World War I (see Roberts, Chapter 5 in this volume). In the 1940s austerity took on a different meaning as the attempt to curb *private spending* to help fund the welfare state in strained economic circumstances (Kynaston, 2007).

In the 1970s, the IMF demands that the UK cut public spending to avoid a run on the pound fundamentally damaged the credibility of the Labour government and helped Mrs Thatcher's Conservatives to electoral victory in 1979 (Burk and Cairncross, 1992; Roberts, 2016). These cuts to public spending, however, were temporary and not entirely driven by ideology.

The paradigm shift that followed the election of Margaret Thatcher in 1979 has been labelled 'neo-liberalism', and involved a much broader shift away from state provision to free-market capitalism. It included privatisation of state industries, the sale of council housing, big tax cuts for higher earners and the liberalisation of financial markets. Austerity was now just one weapon in shrinking the state. But it was this objective that emerged as the fundamental driving force in the 2010–15 austerity drive.

Austerity first emerged as the key response to the sharp rise in government debt due to the financial crisis in the run-up to the 2010 General Election. The economic competence of the Labour Party came under increasing attack, and by October 2009 most commentators had endorsed the Conservative's austerity agenda (Schiffers and Knowles, 2014). Although the Conservatives did not win the election outright, they were able to form a coalition with the Liberal Democrats on a platform of implementing austerity to save the UK economy as the Eurozone appeared to be deteriorating into chaos (D'Ancona, 2013; Kavanagh and Cowley, 2010; Wring et al., 2011).

After the Coalition took office, the new chancellor, George Osborne, seized the opportunity to shape the austerity narrative and blame Labour for the austerity that was now needed. His narrative – that the deficit was caused by Labour overspending – was simple and powerful. Labour's mistake was "the failure to fix the roof while the sun was shining" (as Goerge Osborne himself put it in his 2010 conference party speech), which had put the British economy and the British government in such dire straits. This went unchallenged for many months, as Labour fought an internal leadership battle and then appointed a Shadow Chancellor who appeared to advocate 'austerity lite'. The power of George Osborne's argument came to dominate the debate for years to come and shows the importance of establishing a clear and simple narrative.

Methodology and findings

Building on the methodology of our previous research, we draw from a data set of 290 articles from 10 commentators from six quality publications – the *Telegraph*, *Financial Times (FT)*, *Economist*, *Independent*, *Times*, and *Guardian* – from August 2012 to May 2015. This paper tracks the mediation of austerity by key economic and political commentators (dubbed the 'commentariat') in the quality UK press in the years since the first austerity policies were introduced, in order to measure their persistence over time (see Appendix 1 for the full list of commentators). We deliberately chose both political and economic commentators to reflect the nature of the debate. We were particularly interested in how another looming General Election, in 2015, affected the coverage. Our content analysis focused on the following themes: the debate around austerity; its relation to inequality; how the financial crisis was described; and who was to blame (see Appendix 2 for a note on the methodology). Our aim was to be able to characterise the nature of the political and economic discourse around the Coalition's austerity policy.

Key findings

We find the same broad trends still in existence as in our earlier study: a preoccupation with the financial crisis and who is to blame, a lack of alternatives and information from the parties, and an economic debate seen through the prism of politics:

- The crisis, from 2012–2014 is consistently framed as having been caused by profligate spending and incompetent economic management in the boom years – in essence providing a rationale for continued austerity. In 2013 the debate broadens to include blame of the financial system generally.
- There is still scepticism about whether the politicians are being honest with the electorate over the budget estimates and the size and effect of the cuts.
- Few of the commentators, with the exception of Martin Wolf (*FT*) and Larry Elliott (*Guardian*), have any suggestions for alternatives to cuts to public spending to reduce the deficit.
- For the most part, the discourse does not look at the consequence of austerity for poverty and household income.

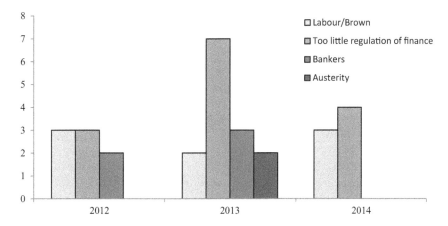

FIGURE 1.1 Blame for causing and prolonging the financial crisis

Two years after the election of the Coalition government, we find that the legacy of the financial crisis is still a dominant theme in the framing of austerity. Figure 1.1 shows that the pattern of who is to blame for the financial crisis does vary over time. While Labour and Brown receive a share of blame in 2012 and 2013, the debate broadens to blame the crisis on deficient economic policies and a lack of regulation of the financial sector in later years. The spike in discussion about financial regulation in 2013 is probably related the new measures being implemented to curb the banks, including the Vickers report suggesting the splitting of their retail and wholesale operations.

Looking at the words used to frame the debate, we find that the crisis rhetoric is dominant (something also found in Knowles et al., 2013). After just two years in power, and four years since the apogee of the crisis, the words are still emotive: 'financial crisis'; 'excesses of the credit boom'; 'banking crisis'; 'recession'; 'global meltdown'; 'credit crunch'; 'double and triple-dip recession'; 'economic crisis'; 'global economic crisis'; 'crisis in light-regulation capitalism'; 'a daunting economic crisis'; and 'a mind-boggling financial crisis'. Thus the focus is on the seriousness of the crisis and implicitly on the need to continue current policies.

Changes in attitudes to austerity over time

There were some important changes in the pattern of coverage over time, and we divided the period that we covered into three distinct phases.

- In the first phase, up to August 2013, there is some debate about the wisdom of austerity but the discussion is dominated by the legacy of the financial crisis itself and few alternatives emerge.
- An inflection point occurs toward the end of 2013 around the time that nascent economic recovery is detected, at which point a strong majority renew their support for austerity on the grounds that it has worked.

- There is another turn at the end of 2014 as the election campaign really begins. Wolf and Elliott particularly start to write about the campaign and economic recovery in terms that discuss inequality and the costs of austerity.

Taking the medicine: 2012–mid 2013

Attitudes towards austerity among key commentators were mixed and fluctuated during our study period, as Figure 1.2 shows, but, by and large, support for austerity outweighed concerns over its effects. It is also noticeable that negative commentary is framed by the unpopularity of the Coalition government, the state of the housing market and the weak indicators of economic growth – not by the impact of austerity measures on the poor. Support for austerity ranges between publication and commentator but, as Figure 1.2 shows, is at a high level until February 2014.

The discussion surrounding austerity since 2010 is fairly mixed between both support and criticism from across the commentary landscape, but there is still strong support for austerity measures in this first period. While Jeremy Warner, business columnist at the *Telegraph*, admits – and one of the earliest in the data set to do so – that economic growth is minimal while living standards are 'squeezed', he still focuses on the deficit and the fact that "Despite all this, Britons are still living well beyond their means, spending far more than they earn on world markets" (August 10, 2012). Meanwhile, also writing in August, Philip Stephens, political commentator at the *FT*, points to "austerity without obvious purpose" and splits within the Coalition government itself (August 31).

During this first period, it is Martin Wolf, economics commentator at the *FT* and Steve Richards, political columnist at the *Independent*, who are the only commentators who are vehemently against austerity – with Wolf drawing from Keynesianism and Richards frequently drawing a link between the Tory cuts and Thatcherism.

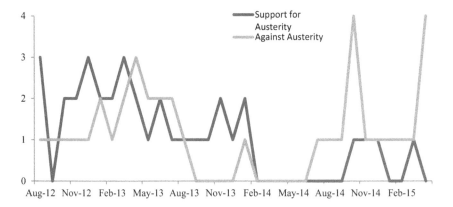

FIGURE 1.2 Positive vs negative descriptions of austerity

In contrast, Hamish McRae, economics commentator at the *Independent*, continues with his support for austerity: "Everyone is cutting budget deficits. The politics vary. Here, it's about correcting the huge deficit that the Coalition inherited" (October 10, 2012). Meanwhile Steve Richards refers to the art of Tory populist rhetoric used to project cuts as kindness in a way that Margaret Thatcher did:

> Cameron spoke up. Like Margaret Thatcher did when she more cautiously sought to reshape the state, Cameron hit upon a populist language . . . The argument was especially well developed in relation to his welfare reforms – cuts projected as an act of kindness.
>
> *October 11, 2012*

Meanwhile Jeff Randall, while business commentator at the *Telegraph*, presented a contrary and favourable view of the Tory party. He believes the Tories have been receiving unfair criticism from 'Armageddonists': "Following the hubris of 'no more boom and bust' and nemesis of a credit – crunch, they [Armageddonists] seek catharsis in a claim that George Osborne's austerity is unnecessarily harsh, economically illiterate; a rerun of Thatcherism, destined to end in catastrophe" (October 29, 2012).

Going in to 2013, pundits follow the same lines. McRae provides a rationale for inequality – cutting the deficit, of course (January 23, 2013) – while Wolf refers to tightening across the Eurozone as something that might be necessary for some countries, but not all: effectively it should not be a one-size-fits-all approach (27 February, 2013). Wolf provides – and is one of the only to do this during this period – an outline of a different policy approach that investigates why the non-financial corporate sector is growing, and encourages the government to borrow at the 'once in a lifetime' rates of interest, invest in structural reforms, recapitalise banks and cut only when the economy is growing.

Daniel Finkelstein, political commentator at the *Times*, supports deficit cutting, highlighting a lack of a need for an alternative: "So even if there were a decisive policy argument for a completely different economic approach (and, as it happens, I do not believe that there is), politically it would be curtains for the Government" (March 20, 2013). Randall also continues to support cuts – and frames the issue as he did during the height of the crisis by focusing on the need to restructure the welfare state. Richards continues to demonize the Tories, arguing that Cameron is not as political adept as Thatcher, who would have known when enough was enough with cuts (April 11, 2013). This sentiment is shared by Wolf, drawing his inspiration from Keynes, he underscores badly timed cuts: "The UK Treasury considers John Maynard Keynes to be an idiot. He famously said that 'the boom, not the slump, is the right time for austerity'" (May 24, 2013).

While there is overall support for austerity still, the variation within publications (i.e. Warner and McRae) and between economic and political perspectives (i.e. Wolf and Finkelstein) indicates the mixed picture and debate that was provided by the commentariat.

A false dawn? Austerity August 2013–July 2014

The words used to describe the crisis continue in their variation. This period is, however, clearly as emotive as the one before, with the following descriptions used: 'Eurozone crisis', 'UK's housing crisis', 'financial crash of 2008', 'a frightening economic crisis', 'credit crunch', 'the recession', 'the deepest recession since the Second World War,' 'the worst recession in living memory', 'the mother and father of a recession' and 'the great recession'.

But, as economic recovery begins to set the terms of the debate, which shift slightly, we detect an inflection point in the nature of the debate. Towards the end of 2013, it appears that a nascent economic recovery in the UK may be underway. As Figure 1.3 shows, there is a sharp upturn in the belief that the recovery is on the way from the third quarter of 2013 – an upturn that disappears until 2015.

Paradoxically, this is taken as a sign not that austerity needs to end, but that it has been successful. At the end of the year, in October, McRae highlights signs the economy is growing and asks those who were pessimistic about Tory cuts to admit the policy has been effective, while the crisis is now described as a "post-crisis" by Wolf (April 16, 2014). The debate broadens, as there is more praise for Tories, subsequently more acceptance of cuts, and a look at the impact of cuts that have been deepening inequality. Even Richards reports with less vehemence about the Tories, and Osborne in particular, who he thinks is starting to get involved in the regulation of markets and is moving "leftwards in response to changing times" (November 25, 2014). However, there is now more focus on the consequences of austerity, and particular in growing inequality.

Those articles that refer to inequality more directly come mostly from Larry Elliott and Jeremy Warner – with Elliott speaking with members of the public about the pain they are experiencing and Warner lamenting policies that are benefitting those at the top and not the larger majority: "The money – printing of

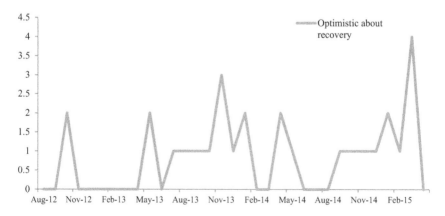

FIGURE 1.3   Optimistic about recovery

the past five years has been hugely redistributive, greatly benefiting the asset – rich at the expense of the asset – poor, and borrowers at the expense of small savers" (November 15, 2013).

It is in January that the terms of the debate continue to broaden and we finally start to see a factoring-in of inequality (see Figure 1.4).

Elliott conflates inequality with cuts and austerity and outlines potential economic policy improvements (and there are many):

> An all-party consensus to tackle poverty rather than simply tactics for rewarding "hard-working families"; macro-economic policies geared to full employment; a higher minimum wage; legislation to make it easier for trade unions to organise; a mass programme of house building; an industrial strategy to rebuild Britain's manufacturing base, including the nurturing and protection of sectors seen as crucial to future growth; a full-blooded assault on the tax dodging activities of the feral rich; and tougher price curbs on oligopolies.
>
> *January 13, 2014*

Richards expresses a more nuanced version of the debate – how economic recovery has been uneven and will benefit the more privileged sections of society. Referring to the help-to-buy-scheme, he argues that any economic recovery has piggy-backed on a housing boom which benefits property owners and will leave young people out in the dark and paying high rents (25 May, 2014).

Meanwhile Elliott highlights some of the pain that people have experienced from cuts. He travels around the country to speak with members of the public and

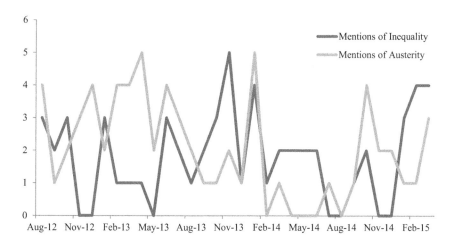

FIGURE 1.4   Mentions of austerity vs mentions of inequality

★All mentions of austerity included, both for and against, and also not just the word 'inequality' (which incidentally was not frequent), but any mention of low wage growth, low productivity, and inequality of any kind, i.e the North/South divide in England, were coded here.

highlights the deepening poverty caused by the austerity agenda: "Recessions scar. Years of slump, flat lining and wage-increase-free recovery have bequeathed a sense of unease. . . . Welcome to Britain in the age of insecurity" (June 17, 2014).

So, we see by the end of this period some of the early optimism for austerity policies is beginning to wane, and the terms of the debate broadening to include discussions about the shakiness of the recovery, the uneven (re)distribution of wealth and deepening inequality.

The politics of inequality and austerity: August 2014–May 2015

In the run-up to the General Election, the terms of the debate begin to change to put more emphasis on context of growing inequality as put forward by the Labour Party. Most of the discussion about an uneven recovery appears toward the end of 2014 and in the months before the election, although there is still optimism that the economy is now growing (see Figure 1.3). Words used to describe the crisis drop off. Words/terms used now include: 'the three months ending in October 2008', 'the month the global system had its near-death experience', 'the 2008/09 down-turn', 'financial crash of 2008' and 'persistence of the recession'.

By early 2015, there is sharp shift towards discussion of inequality as opposed to austerity (see Figure 1.4)

In the months before the 2015 election we see those commentators who have so far been against further austerity (Richards, Warner, Stephens and Elliott) describing a shift toward anger and resentment coming from the press and the public alike.

Elliott discusses an economy that is slowing and stagnant and living standards that are setting the terms of the election campaign (October 16, 2014). While Stephens at the *FT* describes a "rage against austerity" that is influencing the Scottish referendum campaign (October 24, 2014). The same day Warner writes of the

> continued erosion in living standards, the most obvious manifestation of these failings is in the public finances. Britain's fiscal consolidation is once more going seriously awry. . . . Bizarrely for a Government that virtually invented the language of fiscal "austerity", the Coalition finds itself with one of the biggest continuing deficits in Europe.
>
> *October 24, 2014*

Richards echoes Elliot's concerns about further austerity – a concern he says is shared even by "normally supportive newspapers":

> Even some of the normally supportive newspapers wonder whether Osborne has gone too far with his deep spending cuts. Cameron and Osborne have been taken by surprise at the reaction to their plans and are therefore having to re-state or subtly alter their positions quickly rather than enjoy some

pre-Christmas applause before moving on to the final act, the election campaign that begins in January.

30 October, 2014

Wolf discusses on the entrenchment of inequality since the economic crisis that "undermine[s] the ability of young people to afford housing and so form families" (9 January, 2015). This view is reaffirmed by Elliott on January 26, as he goes further to say that inequality is the root of secular stagnation:

> After six years of low interest rates and quantitative easing, the obvious conclusion is that the threat of secular stagnation is not going to be tackled by macroeconomic measures alone. Structural reform is needed. But not the sort that involves pay cuts, a weakening of collective bargaining and austerity.
>
> *26 January, 2015*

Just weeks before the election in the *FT* Wolf outlines the mixed picture – a "stunning" jobs performance but a collapse in productivity and living standards (19 March, 2015). Meanwhile, Stephens highlights the lack of economic competence in all camps, a lack of public trust, and a media system that ignores big questions about investment and productivity:

> To read the Conservative and Labour manifestos is to imagine the biggest challenge facing Britain over the next five years is whether the government balances the budget in 2018 or 2020. Putting aside more urgent economic, security or social problems, the numbers are all nonsense. They do not add up. And the politicians wonder why voters have lost faith.
>
> *April 15, 2015*

This is echoed again on the same day by McRae, a commentator who has been optimistic about a continuation of austerity, who highlights economic incompetence and lack of discussion of bigger questions:

> First, there is the focus on the minutiae of taxing and spending rather than the huge numbers – and huge decisions – in public finance. Second, the emphasis is on inputs rather than outputs: how much more is to be spent rather than how well it is to be spent. Third, it ignores the great uncertainties facing the next government.
>
> *April 15, 2015*

The optimism about deficit-cutting and austerity policies generally that so characterised the 2010 election is no longer universally endorsed by the quality press in the run-up to the 2015 Election. However, there is still scepticism that politicians during the 2015 election campaign are being honest with voters, and criticisms that they failed to explain the details of their policy and communicate the wider economic picture to voters. In the end, the partial shift in the tone of the debate on austerity came too late for the Labour Party, which seemed incapable of laying out its alternative to austerity (Chang, 2014).

During the campaign, the inability of Labour Party leader Ed Miliband to explain his economic policy towards the deficit fatally weakened Labour's already fragile reputation for economic competence. Ironically, the strength of opposition to austerity by Liberal Democrat supporters (after their party embraced austerity during their years in the Coalition government) led to the loss of many seats to the Conservatives. In Scotland, the tough anti-austerity stance of the Scottish Nationalist Party (SNP) contributed to the collapse of the Labour Party vote in Scotland which it had dominated for many years (Cowley and Kavanagh, 2016; Geddes and Tong, 2015).

Discussion and conclusion

There is little doubt that the majority of media commentators supported and legitimised the austerity narrative put forward by the Coalition government in 2010. This was a product of several factors: the clear need for action in the early years of the crisis when the deficit was growing exponentially; the fears of contagion from the continuing drama of the Euro crisis, which was putting the market for government bonds across Europe in turmoil; and the deep recession caused by the financial crisis.

The puzzle is why these factors continued to shape the debate in the UK for so long when many of the factors driving austerity fell away. It took quite a while for the commentariat to look beyond the simple narrative they had constructed to the more complex realities of the UK economy. Just as in the run-up to the 2008 crisis, we can see the power of group think and confirmation bias among economic journalists, who found it difficult to challenge the government narrative,

One important factor in explaining the lack of economic debate over austerity was that the debate was seen through the prism of politics, not economic analysis. The distinguished former BBC economics correspondent during the financial crisis, now political editor at ITN, Robert Peston, says that the lack of diverse voices led to coverage that was "unfair and distorted" As he explains:

> Certainly the media was keener on austerity than what you might say proper economists and that is intriguing. I think it's quite hard to explain other than to say that the coverage tended to be led by political journalists many of whom don't know very much about economics, and secondly, business journalists became much more powerful relative to economic specialists. So it may simply be that the voice of proper knowledgeable trained economists within the media just diminished because you had the rise and rise of business journalism and much of it was seen through the prism of politics rather than economics.
>
> *Interview with Knowles, 2016*

Another key problem was the lack of a credible alternative policy put forward by the Labour Party to challenge austerity. Labour both failed to challenge the Coalition mantra of Labour being the party of profligate public spending (something which New Labour under Blair and Brown has neutralised – 'prudence with a purpose'); it also failed to agree what its alternative narrative was. Larry Elliott, the economics editor of the *Guardian* and one of the leading critics of the government's approach, explained at a public debate on the Media and Austerity in May 2016 at City University how difficult it was to propose alternatives which didn't have the backing of a major political party. (See: www.city.ac.uk/events/2016/may/beyond-the-crisis-the-media-and-austerity.)

Since our research was concluded, there are signs that the obsession with austerity in British politics may be on the wane. The 2016 Brexit referendum and the strong showing of the Labour Party, running on an anti-austerity platform in the 2017 General Election, suggest austerity may be losing its appeal to many voters, and new explanations for falling living standards, such as immigration, are becoming more salient. How this will be resolved is still uncertain, but it is likely that again the press – and particularly the commentariat – will play a key role in shaping the outcome.

References

Blekesaune, M. 2007. 'Economic conditions and public attitudes to welfare policies', *European Sociological Review*, 23(3), pp. 393–403.

Blyth, M. 2013. *Austerity: The history of a dangerous idea*. Oxford: Oxford University Press.

Burk, K., and Cairncross, A. 1992. *Goodbye, great britain: The 1976 IMF crisis*. New York: Yale University Press.

Chang, H-J. 2014. 'Framing the austerity debate'. Paper given to St. Catharine's Political Economy Seminar Series, University of Cambridge, 3 December. Available at: www.politicaleconomy.group.cam.ac.uk/Podcasts-vodcasts

Cowley, P., and Kavanagh, D. 2016. *The British General Election of 2015*. London: Palgrave Macmillan.

D'Ancona, M. 2013. *In it together: The inside story of the Coalition government*. London: Viking.

Davis, A. 2014. Financial insider talk in the City of London. In: Murdock, G., and Gripsrud, J. (eds.), *Money talks: Media, markets, crisis*. Intellect: Bristol. pp. 29–44.

Dean, M. 2013. *Democracy under attack: How the media distorts policy and politics*. Bristol: The Policy Press.

Fairclough, I. 2016. 'Evaluating policy as argument'. *Critical Discourse Studies*, 13(1), pp. 57–77.

Geddes, A., and Tong, J. 2015. *Britain votes 2015*. Oxford: Oxford University Press.

Harkins, S, and Lago-Ocando, J. 2016. "How Malthusian ideology crept into the newsroom: British tabloids and the coverage of the 'underclass'", *Critical Discourse Studies*, 13(1), pp. 78–93.

Kavanagh, D., and Cowley, P. 2010. *The British General Election of 2010*. London: Palgrave Macmillan.

Knowles S., Philips, G., and Lidberg, J. 2016. 'Reporting the Global Financial Crisis: A longitudinal tri-nation study of mainstream financial journalism'. *Journalism Studies* 18(3), pp. 322–340.

Knowles, S., Phillips, G., and Lidberg, J., 2013. 'The framing of the global financial crisis 2005–2008: A cross-country comparison of the US, UK, and Australia'. *Australian Journalism Review*, 35(2), pp. 59–72.

Kynaston, D. 2007. *A world to build: Austerity Britain, 1945–48*. London: Bloomsbury.

Lewis, J., and Thomas, R. 2014. More of the same: News, economic growth and the recycling of conventional wisdom. In: Murdock, G., and Gripsrud, J. (eds.), *Money talks: Media, markets, crisis*. Intellect: Bristol. pp. 81–100.

Lippmann, W. 1922. *Public opinion*, New York: Palgrave Macmillan.

Mair, J., and Keeble, R. 2009. *Playing footsie with the FTSE: The great crash of 2008*. London: Abramis.

Manning, P. 2013. 'Financial journalism, news sources, and the banking crisis'. *Journalism*, 14(2), pp. 173–189.

Marx, P., and Schumacher, G. 2016. 'The effect of economic change and elite framing on support for welfare state retrenchment: a survey experiment'. *Journal of European Social Policy*, 26(1), pp. 20–31.

Mirowski, P. 2013. *Never let a serious crisis go to waste: How neoliberalism survived the financial meltdown*. London: Verso.

Murdock, G., and Gripsrud, J. (eds.). 2014. *Money talks: Media, markets, crisis*. Intellect: Bristol.

Parsons, W. 1989. *The power of the financial press: Journalism and economic opinion in Britain and America*. New Brunswick, NJ: Rutgers University Press.

Picard, R., Selva, M., and Binonzo, D. 2014. 'Media coverage of banking and financial news'. Oxford: Reuters Institute for the Study of Journalism.

Ragnedda, M., and Ruiu, M. 2017. *UK General Election 2015: Dealing with austerity*. Newcastle University Working Paper.

Resolution Foundation. 2017. *The living standards audit 2017*. London: Resolution Foundation.

Roberts, R. 2015. 'Inventing austerity: The 1922 geddes axe'. Inaugural Lecture, Kings College London 11 June Available at: www.kcl.ac.uk/sspp/Inaugural-Lectures/Inaugural-Lecture-Professor-Richard-Roberts.aspx.

Roberts, R. 2016. *When Britain went bust: the 1976 IMF crisis*. London: OMFIF.

Schifferes, S., and Knowles, S. 2014. The British media and the 'first crisis of globalization'. In: Schifferes, S., and Roberts, R. (eds.), *Media and financial crises: Comparative and historical perspectives*. London: Routledge, pp. 42–58.

Schiffrin, A., and Fagan, R. 2012. 'Are we all Keynesians now? The US press and the American Recovery Act of 2009'. *Journalism: Theory, Practice & Criticism*, 2(14), pp. 151–172.

Sheffield Political Economy Research Institute (SPERI). 2014. *Neoliberalism, austerity, and the UK media*. Brief no. 18. Available at: speri.dept.shef.ac.uk/wp. . . /12/brief18-neoliberalism-austerity-and-the-UK-media.pdf.

Taylor, E., and Taylor-Gooby, P. 2015. Benefits and welfare. In: Ormston, R., and Curtice, J. (eds.), *British Social Attitudes: The 32nd Report*. London: NatCen Social Research, available online at: www.bsa.natcen.ac.uk.

Wring, D., Mortimer, R., and Atkinson, S. (eds.). 2011. *Political communication in Britain: The leader debates, the campaign and the media in the 2010 General Election*. London: AIAA.

Appendices

Appendix 1. List of commentators, beat, and number of articles collected

Commentator	Beat	No. Articles
The Economist	Economy, politics, business	26
Larry Elliott	Economics	19
Daniel Finkelstein	Politics	32
Hamish McRae	Economics	32
Jeff Randall	Business	12★
Steve Richards	Politics	31
Philip Stephens	Politics	29
Jeremy Warner	Business	26
Patrick Wintour	Politics	20
Martin Wolf	Economics	27

★Randall left the *Telegraph* for Sky in 2009 on a more permanent basis, reflecting the lower number of articles.

Appendix 2. Note on methodology

The data set consisted of 290 articles from 10 commentators from six quality publications – the *Telegraph*, *Financial Times*, *Economist*, *Independent*, *Times* and *Guardian* – from August 2012 to May 2015. Words used to collect the articles corresponded with those used for our 2013 study: 'recession', 'credit crunch', 'market crash', 'meltdown', 'downturn', 'financial crisis', 'austerity', 'cuts', 'budget deficit', 'Cameron', 'Osborne', 'Ed Balls', 'Miliband' and 'Carney'. We coded the articles under the following themes: debate around austerity; inequality; words used to describe the crisis; and any blame still framing the crisis. Articles were collected from Factiva for each commentator for every month within the time frame. On occasion, none were available, and this is reflected in the number gathered. The news articles were treated as single units for analysis and sections were highlighted and coded if they were at all relevant to be placed within any of the themes.

2

MEDIA AMNESIA AND THE CRISIS

Laura Basu

> The total market system does not merely gloss over its own history; to a great extent it even erases it. 'Homo economicus' has as it were the same perception of time as a small child
>
> *Kurz, 2009, p.30*

It is widely thought that Labour lost the 2015 UK election partly because voters believed it had crashed the economy in 2008 by spending too much public money. In the words of Labour politician Margaret Beckett, the party could not overcome "the huge myth it was overspending by a Labour Government that caused the crisis" (Islam, 2016). Likewise, the 'debt crises' across southern Europe are blamed on profligate governments or even the corruption and laziness of the people themselves. A global banking meltdown caused by the dynamics of neoliberal capitalism somehow morphed into public debt crises caused by swollen public sectors. This is remarkable not only because of the historical reality of the global financial crisis but because that crisis was *all over the news* at the time. How has history been so quickly rewritten, and what might this mean for formulations of solutions to the economic problems?

This chapter explores the twists and turns of the UK news coverage of the economic crisis in its different mutations over a period of eight years. It shows that, as the crisis has developed from banking meltdown to recession to public debt crises, it has been repeatedly reframed. These reframings – with information added and lost each time – have helped legitimise the same kinds of policies that helped cause the crisis in the first place, including cuts to social spending on one hand and 'business friendly' supply-side measures such as corporation tax cuts, privatisation, and deregulation on the other. The reframings amount to a kind of 'media amnesia' that has ideological effects, serving the interests of certain social groups (Philo, 2011, p. 104). Although the forgetful quality of news has often been remarked upon (see Bagdikian, 2004, p. 106; Starkman, 2009), it has not yet been the subject of sustained analysis. The chapter starts with some context to the crisis, then describes the research on which the chapter is based, before unravelling some of the ways the crisis has been framed over time and what this has meant for which crisis-responses are legitimised and which are excluded.

The crisis

Economists of different stripes see the events of 2008 not only as a financial crisis but as a crisis of neoliberalism – a term used to describe a form of capitalism beginning in the 1970s and still ongoing (Stiglitz, 2010; Varoufakis, 2015; Screpanti, 2014). The neoliberal phase of capitalism is characterised by economic liberalisation, financialisation, and globalisation – the accelerated movement of goods and capital around the world. Cuts to the social state (now known as austerity) have been central to neoliberalisation (McNally, 2011, p. 45). So have 'supply side' measures, reforms targeted at structures of production and ownership associated with 'trickle down' theory (Screpanti, 2014, p. 112; see Richard Thomas, Chapter 4 in this volume, for more on trickle down), such as tax cuts for the wealthy, privatisation, and deregulation. At the same time, workers' movements were attacked, leading to 'flexiblisation' of workforces and falling or stagnating wages. These processes were a reaction to problems in the previous form of capitalism, which, after two decades of buoyancy, had led to falling profitability and crisis. For many political economists, neoliberal policies were designed to restore profitability to capital by transferring resources upwards (see McNally, 2011). Inequality, which had been falling in many places since the early-mid twentieth century, began to rise (Piketty, 2014, pp. 25–6). The combination of falling wages and corresponding rising household debt, complex financial products based on the debt, and the trade and 'financial imbalances' associated with globalisation, culminated in 2007–2008 in the "mother of all crises" (Harvey, 2011, p. 7).

If the 2008 crisis was a crisis of neoliberalism, it might be expected that governments have responded to counter those trends. However, governments have actually escalated neoliberal reforms, through both austerity and supply side measures. In the UK, following an initial period of Keynesian stimulus under Labour, after the 2010 election the new coalition government began implementing radical reforms. By 2015, the government had cut £35 billion ($45 billion) in public spending (Gentleman, 2015). Councils had seen 40% reductions in their funding. A further £12 billion ($15 billion) reduction in working age benefits (Gentleman, 2015) was planned. On the other hand, the government wanted to 'boost growth' through a raft of suppy side measures designed to show that 'Britain is open for business' and thus encourage businesses to invest. Those announced in 2011 included a cut in corporation tax to 23%, tax reliefs for small and medium size enterprises, the loosening of planning controls, and the removal of £350 million ($450 million) of regulations on businesses. These kinds of measures were extended in every budget thereafter. Notably, the 2012 budget saw a cut in the top rate of income tax, and corporation tax was cut further in 2012, 2013, 2015, and 2016. Similar kinds of measures in the eurozone are discussed in Part 2 of this volume.

The study

The research aimed to analyse the mainstream media coverage of the crisis in its different manifestations over time. It sampled items from five UK outlets: the *BBC News at Ten*, and the news and comments sections of the *Guardian, Telegraph, Sun,* and *Mirror* newspapers. These five cover the most popular form of news in the UK (*BBC News*) plus the broadsheet and tabloid newspapers leaning left and right with the highest circulations (Ponsford, 2017; see Basu, 2018 for more detail on each of the outlets' ownership structure and political stance). Table 2.1 breaks down the sample by outlet and section.

Two one-week periods per year were selected for analysis. One was always the week of the budget in the UK – when the government announces its tax and spending plans for the year and reveals the state of the economy. In 2010 and 2015 there were two budgets because of the elections, and in these cases both were analysed. The other week covers the events of the crisis that received the most media attention. These include, for example, the run on Northern Rock, the collapse of Lehman Brothers, the official entrance of the UK into recession, the first Greek bailout, the 2012 Spanish bailout, and the 2015 referendum on Greece's bailout conditions. An extra week was included in 2008 due to the sheer amount of coverage. During these periods, not only items referring to the specific events mentioned but also items on any aspect of the crisis were included, such as stories on the Cyprus savings levy, or reports on falling living standards or rising inequality. The sample thus gives a broad sweep of the coverage over the past eight years.[1]

LexisNexis was used to gather the newspaper items from the selected weeks. An initial word search was not used. Instead, all news items from the selected publications, sections, and time periods were first scanned manually to discover which economic problems associated with the crisis gained the most attention. These were: the global financial crisis, the recession, the UK deficit, the eurozone crisis, and UK falling living standards and rising poverty and inequality. All items with those foci were then subjected to analysis.

The study was a framing analysis (Entman, 1993; Kitzinger, 2011). It analysed which economic problem was the main focus of each news item, which explanations were offered for that problem, and which possible responses were mentioned to the problem. Note was taken of whether each explanation and response was endorsed by the news item, rejected by it, or mentioned more-or-less neutrally. For example, a response was considered as neutral if it was either mentioned simply as a measure that was being implemented or proposed without expressing any value judgement, or if evaluation of the measure by the news item was balanced, giving

TABLE 2.1 News items by outlet and section

	Guardian	*Telegraph*	*Sun*	*Mirror*	*BBC News*	*Total*
News	332	235	64	116		747
Comments	118	72	38	22		250
Total	450	307	102	138	136	**1133**

both positive and negative views equally. A response was considered as endorsed either if the journalist explicitly supported a measure (more common in comments pieces) or if positive views on the measure were cited without being balanced by negative views. A response was also considered as endorsed if an opinion was expressed as a fact (e.g. "austerity is necessary"). Responses were considered as rejected in the inverse way. When in doubt, the default category was 'neutral'. This kind of categorisation necessarily misses nuances and important aspects of content such as how stories are structured. Closer analysis of individual items was able to capture those aspects.

Framing the crisis: explanations

Figure 2.1 gives a snapshot of the top six causes mentioned in all the outlets of all the economic problems, combined in three different weeks. This is a rather crude way to present the findings, as it doesn't show the continuous development over time and therefore gives a less nuanced account of the crisis coverage. It also does not capture differences in coverage between the different aspects of the crisis, for instance in the way the Eurozone crisis was treated versus the UK deficit or recession. However, given the limitations of space, this is a good way to express the overall findings of how the coverage has developed (see Basu, 2018 for a book-length exploration).

The first striking detail is the light areas that represent 'none given': in 48.9% of all the media items no explanation whatsoever was given, and this increases over

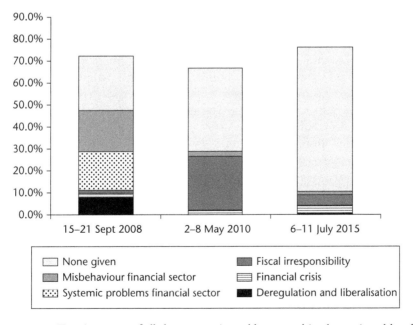

FIGURE 2.1 Top six causes of all the economic problems combined mentioned by all outlets in three periods

time. Apart from that, we see that between the 15th and 21st September 2008, at the height of the meltdown when banks were toppling like dominoes, the main explanations for the problems were badly behaving bankers and systemic problems with finance, such as sub-prime mortgages, banks' business models, or complex financial products. Explanations rooted in the preceding years and decades of deregulation, liberalisation, and globalisation – i.e. neoliberalism – were the third biggest category of explanations at this time. Commentator Tony Parsons (2008, p. 13) wrote in the *Mirror*:

> this was once a country where people built things, and made things. . . . Then Thatcher arrived and proclaimed that the jobs where people got their hands dirty were old-fashioned. . . . That kind of casino capitalism, a culture of unfettered and unapologetic greed, has brought us to this wretched point.

The two small strips show that the 'fiscal irresponsibility' frame – the idea that public overspending caused the problems – was already present in fledgling form, and the financial crisis itself was sometimes given as an explanation for the wider economic downturn, which had already begun.

Jump forward to the 2nd–8th May 2010. This was during the UK General Elections and also the first bailout of Greece. By this time the causes of the crisis have been almost completely reconfigured. In an increasing number of items no explanation at all was given. But the most striking thing is that 'fiscal irresponsibility' as an explanation for the 'debt crises' in the Eurozone and the UK deficit and weak growth comprises 24.4% of the explanations given. A piece in the *Sun* opined, "We are trillions in debt and still borrowing as much as we raise in tax to pay for a bloated welfare state and a ballooning army of unemployed. . . . Huge sums of precious cash have been squandered" (Kavanagh, 2009, p. 8). Even an analysis piece in the *Guardian* referred to "Labour's misguidedly optimistic spending plans in 2005–7" and Labour's "excessive borrowing" (White, 2010, p. 7). The southern European countries, meanwhile, were described as "fiscal miscreants", "fiscal sinners" (Traynor, 2010a, p. 1), "profligate member states" (Traynor, 2010b, p. 3), and "'spendthrift econom[ies]'" (*Mirror*, 2010, p. 17). Meanwhile, the financial crisis was fading from memory, making up 2.2% of explanations. The 'greedy bankers' explanation is also only 2.2% – and the systemic problems with the financial sector and the neoliberal form of capitalism that caused *them* have completely disappeared. The timeline of the crisis is being erased and rewritten; its causes forgotten and misremembered.

Skip forward again to the 6th–1st July 2015. This was during both the British Conservative Party's 'emergency budget' after it had won the 2015 election and Greece's historic referendum on the austerity conditions of its bailout. The Eurozone economy was still on shaky ground and the UK, though officially in 'recovery', was growing slowly. The government was continuing to make much of the deficit. By this point, explanations were barely given at all.

Framing the crisis: possible responses

Figure 2.2 gives a snapshot of the same three weeks, this time showing the possible solutions that were mentioned most frequently to all the economic problems combined, by all the outlets. This graph shows only the possible responses mentioned, not which stance the items took towards them – that will be explored in the following sections. This graph instead gives an idea of which options have received the most media attention, and therefore which ones are likely to have dominated and structured the public debate. In the week from September 2008, when the financial system was in meltdown and explanations centred around the financial sector and "casino" capitalism, the biggest categories of solutions were likewise focused on the banks: bank bailouts and regulating finance. These responses were both overwhelmingly endorsed across the outlets.[2]

Fast forward to the week from May 2010, and the vast majority of possible responses getting media attention were austerity measures, comprising 55.5% of the possible responses mentioned. This makes sense given the way the problems were explained: if the problems were caused by public profligacy, reducing public

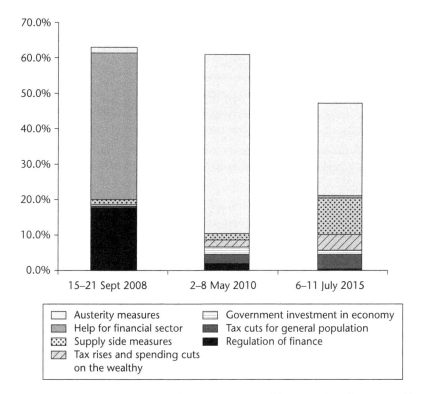

FIGURE 2.2   Top seven responses to all the economic problems combined mentioned by all outlets in three periods

spending is a logical solution to focus on. Moving to July 2015, the two biggest categories of possible solutions were austerity on the one hand and supply-side measures on the other (we will briefly discuss the other possible responses mentioned later on). Again, this can be said to 'make sense'. If the roots of the crisis in neoliberal capitalism are forgotten, it is less illogical that further neoliberal measures in the form of austerity and supply-side measures are the ones getting attention.

Austerity

Tables 2.2 and 2.3 show the stances on austerity and supply side measures by outlet. Austerity was controversial. While the *Telegraph* and the *Sun* endorsed tax rises and spending cuts on the general population much more frequently than rejecting them, the *Guardian* and especially the *Mirror* rejected austerity more often than endorsing it. In the *Sun*, Trevor Kavanagh (2009, p. 8) wondered during the 2009 budget:

> Will [then-Chancellor] Mr Darling do the right thing and slash state spending? . . . Painful cuts will have to be made – including to the sacred NHS. It would be an act of vandalism to leave this mess to fester for another year.

On the other hand, an item in the *Mirror* referred to the coalition government's 2010 'emergency budget' as "a budget from hell" and "a savage axe-and tax package

TABLE 2.2 Mentions of austerity as possible solution to all problems combined. Percentages show proportion of mentions endorsed, rejected or mentioned neutrally by outlet.

Outlet	Endorsed	Rejected	Neutral	Total
Telegraph	59 (38.3%)	8 (5.2%)	87 (56.5%)	154
Sun	26 (45.6%)	5 (8.8%)	26 (45.6%)	57
BBC News	19 (19.4%)	2 (2.0%)	77 (78.6%)	98
Guardian	40 (12.4%)	90 (28%)	192 (59.6%)	322
Mirror	3 (3.8%)	56 (71.8%)	19 (24.4%)	78

TABLE 2.3 Mentions of supply-side measures as possible solutions to all problems combined. Percentages show proportion of mentions endorsed, rejected, or mentioned neutrally by outlet.

Outlet	Endorsed	Rejected	Neutral	Total
Telegraph	52 (80%)	0 (0.0%)	13 (20%)	65
Sun	23 (79.3%)	0 (0.0%)	6 (20.7%)	29
BBC News	12 (33.3%)	0 (0.0%)	24 (66.7%)	36
Guardian	24 (20.9%)	31 (27.%)	60 (52.2%)	115
Mirror	14 (46.7%)	8 (26.7%)	8 (26.7%)	30

which will take £40billion from the economy and hit the poor and pensioners hardest" (Roberts, 2010, pp. 4–5).

The *BBC News,* though mandated to be impartial and balanced, endorsed austerity (usually implicitly) 19.4% of the time, and rejected it only 2% of the time. The *BBC News,* like other outlets, often framed austerity as "painful but necessary", sometimes by suggesting that the Chancellor had no choice but to cut spending. For example, former political editor Nick Robinson referred to "A politician in a straight[sic] jacket", claiming that "The chancellor doesn't have many cards to play" (BBC, 2013). 'The markets' were also repeatedly invoked as a reason why cuts were necessary. In one segment, former economics editor Stephanie Flanders explains: "The Chancellor will want to please voters with his budget tomorrow, but he needs to speak to another audience as well: the City investors who are lending the government a quarter of what it needs to pay its bills" (BBC, 2010). The fact that these 'markets' were in many cases the same financial institutions that caused the crisis in the first place was almost entirely forgotten. In the entire sample of 1,133 items, this was only recollected twice – both times in the *Guardian.*

The press coverage across the sample at first glance appears quite balanced, with the right-wing sections supportive of austerity and the left-wing sections opposed. However, as we have seen, austerity still dominated the coverage, meaning that other possible solutions did not get such sustained or in-depth attention. On top of that, the *logic* of austerity was often accepted even when an item was critical, especially in the *Guardian.* For example, in a comments item on Spain, the *Guardian's* economics editor Larry Elliott (2012, p. 6) gave the case for Keynesian growth measures as opposed to more austerity: "[Spanish prime minister] Rajoy's argument is that he already has IMF-style structural reforms in place, so a further package of austerity would amount to overkill. He is absolutely right about that". Note that Elliott is opposed to more austerity measures but endorses the argument that Spain already has an austerity package in place so doesn't need any more. Spain had a very low debt-to-GDP ratio prior to the 2008 financial crisis. Its problems were squarely located in the private sector, in a property bubble (Blyth, 2013, p. 65) – and its bailout was explicitly differentiated from the others by being a bank bailout, not a sovereign bailout. Why, then, would any austerity at all be appropriate?

Moreover, arguably, some form and level of austerity was accepted even in the *Guardian* and perhaps the *Mirror.* Indeed, at a key moment in time, during the budget before the 2010 General Election, the *Guardian's* content mix endorsed austerity more frequently than rejecting it – endorsing it 21.4% of the time and rejecting it 14.3% of the time. Even after the election, when the new coalition government were bringing in 'swingeing' cuts, the 'painful but necessary frame' was used by some. Polly Toynbee (2010, p. 33), in an opinion piece savaging the budget, nevertheless conceded that "frugality is undoubtedly necessary, but people will turn against all cuts if they go far further and deeper than absolutely essential." Some cuts, it is assumed, are "absolutely essential". This kind of acceptance of 'austerity lite' continued in the run-up to the 2015 election, encapsulated in then–Labour leader Ed Miliband's sound bite of "too far too fast". During the budget-week before the 2015 election, the *Guardian's* content mix again endorsed austerity more frequently than rejecting it (see Basu, 2018, 2017).

The last, crucial point about the framing of austerity is that, even in items very critical of austerity in the left-leaning press, austerity was never rejected outright, not even in the *Mirror*. The view that there should be no cuts at all, or later that they should be completely reversed, was mentioned only ten times – mostly in quotes from Syriza in relation to Greece. It was endorsed *zero* times. Thus, the endorsement of austerity at key moments early on, the acceptance of the logic of austerity even when specific measures were rejected, and the failure to ever reject austerity outright, meant that the left-wing press were arguably endorsing 'austerity lite'.

Supply-side measures

As can be seen in Table 2.3, supply-side measures were much less controversial than austerity. They were consistently endorsed in the *Telegraph* and *Sun*, and endorsed much more frequently than rejected in the *Mirror*. The *BBC News,* again mandated to be impartial, endorsed these measures 33.3% of the time, and rejected them zero times. Only the *Guardian* items rejected these reforms more frequently than endorsing them, and still endorsed them fairly regularly.

When it came to tax cuts for business, tax cuts for top earners, privatisations, and deregulation, comments pieces in the *Telegraph* repeatedly urged the government to go even further. One piece demanded a total reorganisation of the UK economy towards the private sector: "the growth strategy we need requires a complete restructuring of our economy. It means dismantling large parts of the state apparatus and transferring resources to the private sector, where they would generate better value and enhance competitiveness" (Heffer, 2011, p. 20). The idea here is that the public sector is a problem and that private enterprise and "competitiveness" are what is good for "growth": key facets of neoliberal ideology (see Hall, 2011).

The least contested supply-side measures were the corporation and other business tax cuts. The coverage of these across outlets took for granted the idea that what's good for business is good for everyone – another key facet of neoliberal ideology (Hall, 2011). A news report in the *Guardian* (Treanor, 2011) repeated one of the Chancellor's sound bites – that Britain would be "carried aloft by the march of the makers" – and featured no less than five business representatives praising the corporation tax cuts and deregulatory measures balanced by zero critical voices. The BBC has a business editor whose job it is to represent the voice of the business community. In the news coverage of each year's budget, an entire segment is devoted to doing this. There is no equivalent segment by a labour editor or a communities editor that might give opposing views. The business perspective is thus built into the structure of *BBC News* coverage of the budget. Interestingly, supply-side measures were mentioned far less frequently in relation to the Eurozone crisis than in relation to the UK, often only euphemistically referred to in passing as "structural reforms" or simply "reforms". This is despite the fact that in some cases these measures have been quite radical (see Laskaridis, 2014).

On the other hand, there were comments pieces and reports in the *Guardian* that rejected the "pro-business" view, and that even tried to provide a counter-framing. In July 2015, the *Guardian* featured an exposé on 'corporate welfare' by senior economics commentator Aditya Chakrabortty. Based on research by Kevin Farnsworth at York University, the piece claimed that the UK pays out £93 billion ($120 billion) a year in corporate welfare – meaning a combination of tax benefits (£44 billion/$57 billion a year), direct and indirect subsidies, and grants and insurance, advocacy and advice services (Chakrabortty 2015). The framing of supply-side measures as 'welfare' turns on its head simultaneously narratives that scapegoat the poor to justify austerity and those that justify giving money to the rich in the name of growth. In one opinion piece in the *Guardian* there was even a recollection that it was these kinds of reforms that helped cause the economic problems in the first place. Seumas Milne (2012, p. 32), who became Labour's Director of Communications under new leader Jeremy Corbyn, complained:

> The solution to every problem turns out, like a broken record, to be privatisation. Nothing, it seems, has been learned from the failure of an economic model that brought us to the brink of breakdown. For the urbane ideologues now running the show, this crisis has become a ready-made opportunity to shrink the state, shock-doctrine style, and hand over yet more ready-made markets to corporate monopolies.[3]

Despite these instances of resistance, however, with the help of media amnesia and misremembering, these kinds of measures have been largely legitimised in the coverage.

The causes of media amnesia

The factors behind this media forgetting and misremembering are those influencing coverage more broadly and with which media scholars have been busy for decades. Three major factors are: journalistic values and professional routines; the political partisanship of the British press and the orientation towards politics more generally; and the economic conditions of journalism.

Firstly, news values privileging event over process and effect over cause lead to a chronic lack of historical context (see Glasgow Media Group, 1995). In the age of 24/7 multi-platform 'fast news', this has led to an extreme situation where history is being erased and rewritten at "warp speed" (Le Masurier, 2015, p. 139). Indeed, *history is being rewritten while it is happening*.

Secondly, the fact that the British newspapers editorially align with political parties during elections, that their senior staff often have close ties with politicians, and more broadly that media brands' 'public idioms' associate them with similar kinds of values as the main parties, means that the kinds of explanations or solutions getting into the coverage are those offered by the main political parties. The explanations or lack thereof largely reflected which party was able to take control of the narrative.

Labour failed to offer a clear counter-narrative to the Conservative line that Labour overspending was to blame for the crisis and that is why it began to dominate in the media coverage. Similarly, all major parties were offering a version of austerity and until 2015 the Labour Party did not forcefully attack supply-side measures. Likewise, if we look at the other possible solutions represented in the graph in Figure 2.2 – tax rises on the wealthy, tax cuts for the general population, and Keynesian government investment – these were all moves either announced by the government or proposed by the opposition. Thus, the way the crisis was remembered to an extent reflected the way memory was used strategically by politicians to justify the policies they wanted to pursue. The *BBC*, on the other hand, is not aligned with any political party. However, its news coverage is led by what takes place in the corridors of power and rarely explores positions outside those offered by elites in any sustained way. This also applies more broadly to the mainstream media, for which politicians and other officials tend to be "primary definers" of events no matter which party the outlet is aligned with (Hall et al, 1978, p. 58). By far the biggest category of sources mentioned in the media items sampled for this study was politicians and other officials, making up 50.9% of sources cited.

Thirdly, the neoliberal restructuring of capitalism described in this chapter has had an impact on journalism (see Sophie Knowles, Chapter 12 in this volume, for more on this). It has led to increasing concentration of media ownership, which many feel has had a direct or indirect affect on content (see Freedman, 2014, p. 53). Furthermore, the quest for profit has led to cost-cutting on one hand and revenue-raising through 'infotainment' on the other. Cost-cutting has put immense pressure on journalists, resulting in 'churnalism', whereby journalists are churning out stories without being able to check them properly, provide thorough explanation, or seek out a wide range of sources that might provide alternative explanations or solutions to the economic problems (Davies, 2009). Infotainment in this context means an extreme form of simplification at the expense of proper explanation or solutions offered by non-elite social groups. Thus, in terms of the economic factors impacting content, we could say that *the same factors causing the crisis are those that lead to its amnesiac reporting*.

Conclusion

The economic crisis provides an opportunity to study the news coverage of a phenomenon in an ongoing way over time – few other phenomena have remained in the media eye constantly for so many years on end. Studying the coverage of the ever-mutating crisis in this way has found that the narrative of the crisis keeps changing, with information forgotten and misremembered with each re-framing. This forgetting has had ideological effects. It has served to legitimise certain kinds of crisis-responses – the kinds that helped caused the crisis in the first place, and that transfer resources upwards. Media amnesia has in some instances been intentional and in others reproduced passively.

Austerity is only slowly reducing deficits at great human cost. Supply-side measures have not led to business investment: indeed business are hoarding cash or spending it on share buybacks and dividends (see Smith, 2016, p. 293). Meanwhile, none of the options getting media attention face the question of whether an economic model based on infinite growth is even viable for human life on Planet Earth (see Lewis and Thomas, 2015 and Richard Thomas, Chapter 4 in this volume). However, inequality continues to rise (see Corlett and Clarke, 2017; Oxfam, 2017). Important projects for media scholars will be to continue analysing what role the media are playing in the crisis now that it has morphed into widespread political turmoil, and to continue searching for solutions to the problems facing journalism that lie behind media amnesia. The deep link between the conditions of the crisis and the conditions of media amnesia will mean that a joined-up approach is required. The quote by Robert Kurz at the start of this chapter suggests that amnesia is a feature of capitalism itself. If media forgetting is a key site of that amnesia, perhaps resisting media amnesia and insisting on thorough, pluralistic explanations for the ongoing crisis could help form a basis on which to develop ideas for more rational ways of allocating resources.

Notes

1 For a longer discussion of the sampling, see Basu, 2018.
2 The bank bailouts and regulation are not the focus here, but are explored elsewhere (see Basu, 2018). In terms of who have benefited from the emergency responses to the crash, Sayer writes, "*The bailout is itself a huge transfer of wealth from the majority of society to those at the top*" (2015, p. 231, original emphasis).
3 A distinction has been made between privatisation when framed as a supply-side measure in the sense of boosting investment and growth and privatisation when framed as part of austerity – to reduce public spending, or when privatisation is done by the back door as with the NHS. Privatisation is counted as a supply-side measure only in the former case.

References

Bagdikian, B. H. 2004. *The new media monopoly*. Boston, MA: Beakon Press.
Basu, L. 2017. 'Living within our means: The UK news construction of the austerity frame over time'. *Journalism*, first published 22 June.
Basu, L. 2018. *Media, austerity, crisis*. London: Pluto Press.
BBC News at Ten, 20 March 2013.
BBC News at Ten, 23 March 2010.
Blyth, M. 2013. *Austerity*. Oxford: Oxford University Press.
Chakrabortty, A. 2015. The £93bn handshake. *Guardian*, 7 July.
Corlett, A., and Clarke, S. 2017. Back to the '80s. *Resolution Foundation*, [blog] 1 February.
Davies, N. 2009. *Flat Earth news*. London: Vintage.
Elliott, L. 2012. Eurozone's mood music is still downbeat. *Guardian*, 11 June.
Entman, R. 1993. 'Framing: Toward clarification of a fractured paradigm'. *Journal of Communication*, 43(4), 51–58.
Freedman, D. 2014. *The contradictions of media power*. London: Bloomsbury.

Gentleman, A. 2015. Austerity cuts will bite even harder in 2015. *Guardian* [online]. Available at: www.theguardian.com/society/2015/jan/01/austerity-cuts-2015-12-billion-britain-protest

Hall, S. 2011. 'The neo-liberal revolution'. *Cultural Studies*, 26(5), pp. 705–728.

Hall, S., Critcher, C., Jefferson, T., Clarke, J., and Roberts, B. 1978. *Policing the crisis*. Hampshire: Palgrave Macmillan.

Harvey, D. 2011. *The enigma of capital*. London: Profile Books.

Heffer, S. 2011. Reputations are built on actions, not the half-truths of spin doctors. *Telegraph*, 23 March.

Islam, F. 2016. Why Labour lost election: by Margaret Beckett. *Sky News* [website]. Available at: http://news.sky.com/story/why-labour-lost-election-by-margaret-beckett-10144153

Kavanagh, T. 2009. Only you can save us all now, Darling. *Sun*, 20 April.

Kitzinger, J. 2011. Framing and frame analysis. In: Devereux, E. (ed.), *Media studies*. London: Sage. pp. 134–161.

Kurz, R. 2009. *Schwarzbuch kapitalismus. Ein abgesang auf die marktwirtschaft*. 2nd ed. Frankfurt am Main: Eichborn. Translation by Josh Robinson.

Laskaridis, C. 2014. *False dilemmas*. London: Corporate Watch.

Le Masurier, M. 2015. 'What is slow journalism?'. *Journalism Practice*, 9(2), pp. 138–152.

Lewis, J., and Thomas, R. 2015. More of the same. In: Murdock G., and Gripsrud, J. (eds.), *Money talks*. Bristol: Intellect.

McNally, D. 2011. *Global slump*. Oakland: PM Press.

Milne, S. 2012. 'Osborne is stuck in a failed economic model, circa 1979'. *The Guardian*, 21 March.

Mirror, 2010. 'Merkel: All Europe at risk'. *The Mirror*. 6 May.

Oxfam, 2017. 'Just 8 men own same wealth as half the world'. *Press release*, 16 January.

Parsons, T. 2008. 'So many suffer for the grimy greed of a few'. *Mirror*, 11 October.

Philo, G. (ed.). 1995. *Glasgow media group reader, volume 2*. London: Routledge.

Philo, G. 2011. News content studies, media group methods and discourse analysis. In: Devereux, E. (ed.), *Media studies*. London: Sage. pp. 101–133.

Piketty, T. 2014. *Capital in the twenty-first century*. London: Harvard University Press.

Ponsford, D. 2017. 'Print ABCs'. *Press Gazette*, 23 January.

Roberts, B. 2010. 'The VAT trap'. *The Mirror*, 23 June.

Sayer, A. 2015. *Why we can't afford the rich*. Bristol: Policy Press.

Screpanti, E. 2014. *Global imperialism and the great crisis*. New York: Monthly Review Press.

Smith, J. 2016. *Imperialism in the twenty-first century*. New York: Monthly Review Press.

Starkman, D. 2009. 'Power problem'. *Columbia Journalism Review*, May/June. Available at: http://archives.cjr.org/cover_story/power_problem.php

Stiglitz, J. 2010. *Freefall*. New York: Norton.

Toynbee, P. 2010. 'Public backing for cuts will dissolve when reality strikes'. *Guardian*, 26 June.

Traynor, I. 2010a. 'Euros 110bn aid deal agreed to stop Greek meltdown'. *Guardian*, 3 May.

Traynor, I. 2010b. 'Greece in turmoil'. *Guardian*, 6 May.

Treanor, J. 2011. 'It's pretty good news, say business leaders as Osborne springs surprise corporation tax cut'. *Guardian*, 24 March.

Varoufakis, Y. 2015. *The global Minotaur*. London: Zed Books.

White, M. 2010. 'Glossary of Osbornese'. *Guardian*, 22 June.

3

AUSTERITY, THE MEDIA AND THE UK PUBLIC

Mike Berry

Introduction

This chapter examines how the UK press and public service broadcasting reported the sharp increase in the public deficit in 2009 and the subsequent debates around austerity. Although the post 2008 surge in sovereign debt was an international phenomenon, in Britain it was particularly significant, with research suggesting concerns over the public finances were a key factor in both the 2010 and 2015 Conservative General Election victories (Ashcroft, 2010; Hunter, 2015). This chapter focuses on how the rise in the deficit was explained, assessed and what solutions were put forward to address it. The chapter also examines how the public understood these issues through the use of a series of focus groups conducted in 2009. As will be demonstrated, the media strongly influenced the way the public viewed the deficit and what steps could be taken to mitigate it.

However, before presenting the primary data, this chapter will first examine the factors behind the rise in the UK deficit and the range of debate on when and how to reduce it. This provides the spectrum of opinion that journalists could draw on and shows which perspectives were present and which were absent in news accounts. The chapter will then provide details of the methodology before discussing the findings of the content analysis and audience research.

What caused the rise in the deficit?

The proximate cause of the large rise in the UK deficit (and debt) post 2007 was the contraction in the tax base created by the slowdown in the economy following the banking crisis in 2008 (see Table 3.1). From the beginning of 2008 to the end of 2009, income tax fell in absolute terms by 4.5%, national insurance by 4.9%, VAT by 13.1%, corporation tax by 22.7% and stamp duty by 44% (IFS, 2012a).

TABLE 3.1 UK public accounts 2003–2010 in billions

Year	Government Revenue	% Change year/year	Government Expenditure	% Change year/year
2003	423.4	6.9	467.1	8.4
2004	453.2	7.0	509.4	9.1
2005	487.8	7.6	541.6	6.3
2006	518.9	6.4	568.3	4.9
2007	549.2	5.8	602.9	6.1
2008	536.3	−2.3	653.6	8.4
2009	516.1	−3.8	686.3	5.0
2010	555.3	7.6	706.5	2.9

Source: IFS, 2012a, 2012b

The sharp falls in corporation tax were concentrated in the financial sector, which had become one of the economy's key sources of corporate profits and tax revenues (Engelen et al., 2011). At a deeper level, the recession and subsequent rise in the deficit were caused by deleveraging following the collapse of asset bubbles (Koo, 2011). Prior to the crisis, economic growth had become increasingly reliant on consumer spending underpinned by ever-higher levels of household debt, much of which was funded by mortgage equity release (Engelen et al., 2011). However, the banking crisis led to a contraction in credit issuance and a fall in residential property values. This weakened consumer spending and business investment leading to a sharp contraction in the tax base.

The debate on policy options

The deterioration in the public finances led to a debate on both the pace and means of deficit reduction. Some on the right argued the deficit posed such a threat to the economy it should be reduced quickly (Lilico et al., 2009; Taylor et al., 2009). Without accelerated deficit reduction, it was argued, Britain faced interest rate rises, currency devaluations and a possible bailout from the International Monetary Fund (IMF). However, this was contested by those who claimed the recovery was fragile and it was necessary to run large deficits in the midst of a recession (Hutton, 2009; Krugman, 2009a; Reich, 2009; Neild, 2010). These commentators also argued that deficits posed little immediate threat to macroeconomic stability and should only be reduced when the economy had recovered and interest rates were close to their historic average (Krugman, 2009a, 2009b)

As well as timing, there was also a debate about how to reduce the deficit. Some argued for pro-growth policies involving state investment and a broader industrial activism (Chang, 2010). Others advocated cuts to public spending. Some on the right claimed higher public spending would reduce growth by 'crowding out' private investment, which would also be deterred by the prospect of future tax increases (Lilico et al., 2009; Taylor et al., 2009). Another option was increased taxation. This could involve rises in regressive taxes such as VAT and/or the standard rate of tax. Alternatively, higher earners could be targeted through increases in the top rate of income tax or the removal of the ceiling on national insurance contributions (IPPR, 2009). Other options included introducing land or wealth taxes (e.g. Centreforum, 2009; IPPR, 2009; Philo, 2010), eliminating tax relief on company borrowing (e.g. Sikka, 2009), levying a financial transactions tax (e.g. Conway, 2009; PCSU, 2009) or reducing tax evasion and avoidance (PCSU, 2010, p. 9).

Methods

Content studies

This research used thematic content analysis. This is a method which has been used by the Glasgow Media Group to analyze such diverse areas as industrial news, food scares, risk and war/conflict reporting (Glasgow Media Group, 1976, 1980, 1982, 1985; Philo, 1995a, 1995b, 1999). The method is based on the assumption that in any contested area there will be competing ways of explaining events or issues. These explanations are linked to particular interests which seek to explain the world in ways that justify their own position. The purpose of a thematic analysis is to map which explanations are featured in news accounts and which are absent. The research also examined patterns of source access in order to assess who was seen as a credible voice and contributed to public debate.

Newspaper sample[1]

The sample consisted of 166 articles taken from six national newspapers (*The Guardian*, *Daily Telegraph*, *Daily Mail*, *Daily Express*, *The Sun* and *The Mirror*) in the first eight months of 2009. The newspapers were selected because they were high circulation and represented all three segments (broadsheet, mid-market and tabloid) of the UK national newspaper market

Television sample[2]

The sample consisted of 25 bulletins from the *BBC News at Ten* taken from same period as the press sample. The *BBC News* was selected because it remains a mass audience bulletin with regular audiences of between four and five million viewers (BARB, 2015).

Audience studies[3]

Sixteen focus groups were conducted with a total of 56 participants. These consisted of nine groups from Glasgow, three groups from Coventry, two groups from Surrey and two groups from Warwickshire. The research used naturally occurring groups where rapport could be established quickly (Kitzinger, 1994). Most groups were mixed gender but varied by occupation, age, income and social class.

Amongst others, there were groups of child care workers, engineers, janitors, pensioners, manual workers, the unemployed and employees of a development charity. The groups were not intended to comprise a statistically representative sample from which probabilistic statements about the wider population could be inferred. Rather they were intended to generate qualitative data about structures of audience understanding and belief.

Results of the thematic content analysis

Who gets to speak?

Table 3.2 shows the range of sources featured in the sample.[4] The most striking finding is the similarity in the range of sources across print and broadcasting. All media source heavily from the two main parties and City sources. Organisations which primarily advocate free market policies – such as the International Monetary Fund (IMF), Organisation for Economic Co-operation and Development (OCED), Confederaion of British Industry (CBI) and Institute of Directors – were also heavily accessed across the sample.

The *BBC News* sourced heavily from the two main parties – who were carefully balanced – and to a lesser degree the Liberal Democrats. The next most prominent *BBC News* source was the Institute for Fiscal Studies, which was treated as both the authoritative voice on fiscal analysis and a key definer of solutions for reducing the deficit. However, what was missing from all media in the sample was the regular presence of left-of-centre commentators or economists who were skeptical of austerity policies.

What caused the crisis?

As noted earlier, the proximate cause for the rise in the deficit was the collapse in the tax revenues, whilst the deeper cause was deleveraging and the subsequent impact on consumer spending and business investment. As can be seen in Table 3.3, *BBC News* and most newspapers do identify the key role of falling tax revenues in the widening the deficit.

However, it is noticeable that this explanation was significantly less prominent in the *Telegraph* than the *Guardian* and doesn't appear at all in the *Sun*. In contrast, the false claim that the rise in the deficit was caused by Labour overspending appears regularly in the right-wing press but infrequently in the left-of-centre titles or on the BBC:

> Until Gordon Brown accepts he must bring the public finances back under control ending the profligacy of recent times the Labour Government is going to face a far harder task in selling its bonds.
>
> *Daily Mail, 26 March 2009*

TABLE 3.2 Top eight sources in BBC and press reporting (proportion of reports featuring each source)

BBC News	Telegraph	Guardian	Mail	Express	Sun	Mirror
Conservatives 64%	Conservatives 30%	Conservatives 27%	Conservatives 32%	Conservatives 35%	Labour 64%	Conservatives 29%
Labour 64%	City sources 28%	City sources 27%	City sources 32%	Labour 25%	Conservatives 18%	Labour 29%
LibDems 40%	Labour 12%	Labour 25%	Labour 24%	City sources 25%	City sources 18%	LibDems 14%
IFS 36%	IMF 12%	LibDems 14%	BOE 15%	Taxpayers' Alliance 15%	CBI, IOD 18%	City sources 14%
City sources 25%	ONS 10%	CBI, IOD 11%	IMF 10%	CBI, IOD 15%	IMF 9%	BOE 14%
BOE 25%	CBI, IOD 10%	BOE 11%	ONS 7%	LibDems 5%	Taxpayers' Alliance 9%	ONS 14%
OECD 12%	BOE 8%	IFS 11%	Ratings agencies 5%	IMF 5%	IFS 9%	D.Blanchflower 14%
IMF 12%	Ratings agencies 6%	ONS5 8%	CBI, IOD 2%	ONS 5%	ONS 9%	- - - - -

TABLE 3.3 Explanations for the rise in the deficit (proportion of reports featuring each explanation)

Explanation	BBC News	Telegraph	Guardian	Mail	Express	Sun	Mirror
Fall in tax revenues	24%	12%	27%	42%	25%	0%	29%
Benefit bill rising in recession	12%	8%	11%	17%	5%	0%	0%
Bank bailouts	20%	10%	14%	24%	15%	18%	43%
Maintaining demand in recession	4%	2%	5%	0%	5%	9%	0%
Labour overspending/profligacy	4%	14%	3%	17%	50%	18%	0%
Global financial/economic crisis	4%	4%	3%	5%	0%	0%	0%

> The extent of Gordon Brown's mishandling of the economy is now plain for all to see. He borrowed like a man possessed in the boom years when he should have been paying off debt.
>
> *The Express, 22 July 2009*

The broader structural issue about the deficit being a consequence of Britain's reliance on an economic model based on increasing household debt is completely absent from all coverage.

Size and consequences of the UK deficit

The UK had entered the 2008 recession with an internationally and historically low debt burden. though it has subsequently risen to approximately the same level as the EU average (Clark and Reed, 2013; Keep, 2018). Furthermore, most UK government debt was long dated (the longest in the developed world) and held domestically (Aldrick, 2009; Conway, 2013). Writing in the newsletter of the Royal Economic Society, Neild commented:

> Today's ratio of debt to GDP does not look abnormal, let alone alarming. . . . Our deficit – the one figure picked out by the Chancellor – is high, but our debt to GDP is average and our tax ratio is low. Our good corruption score indicates that we are capable of raising tax or cutting expenditure. . . . One would conclude that some action was needed, but not that there were any grounds for alarm.
>
> *Neild, 2010, p. 12*

A very different picture was visible in the press, where discussion of the deficit was infused with fear appeals and apocalyptic language, some examples of which are reproduced in Table 3.4.

On the *BBC News*, descriptions of the deficit from the most accessed sources were also dramatic:

> Mervyn King: We are confronted with a situation in which the scale of the deficit is truly extraordinary.
>
> *BBC News at 10, 24 June 2009*

TABLE 3.4 Descriptions of the public finances

Newspaper	Descriptors of the public finances
Telegraph	"Debt disaster" (19 June 2009) "horrendous fiscal burden" (23 April 2009), "gargantuan" (23 April 2009), "monstrous burden" (23 April 2009), "a crisis . . . almost unprecedented outside wartime (23 April 2009), "catastrophic" (23 April 2009)
Guardian	"Horrifying" (23 April 2009), "colossal black hole" (23 April 2009), "public finances are in meltdown" (19 June 2009) "plunging into the abyss" (April 23 2009) "staggering levels of public debt" (20 February 2009)
Mail	"Borrowing needs are escalating exponentially" (26 March 2009), "terrifying" (20 February 2009), "the most poisonous inheritance imaginable" (23 April 2009), "catastrophe" (23 April 2009), "public finance bloodbath" (23 April 2009), "titanic" (5 January 2009) "extremely scary" (23 April 2009)
Express	"A full blown economic emergency" (22 July 2009) "off the Richter scale" (20 February 2009), "nightmarish" (23 April 2009), "epic scale of Labour"s debt crisis" (23 April 2009), "horrific" (23 April 2009), "the brink of meltdown" (26 January 2009)
Sun	"Ruinous" (26 March 2009) "perilous" (7 May 2009), "frightening" (7 May 2009), "off the Richter scale" (20 February 2009), "truly astronomical" (20 February 2009)
Mirror	"extraordinary level of public debt" (25 June 2009) "the highest amount since records began in 1993" (20 May 2009)

> David Cameron: The scale of our deficit is truly horrific and we need to act on that and act on that now.
>
> *BBC News at 10, 2 April 2009*

Such language was then picked up and endorsed by journalists:

> Stephanie it is obvious that no governing party will be able to escape the full horror of these finances?
>
> *BBC News at 10, 10 June 2009*

When international and historical comparisons were made, (see Table 3.5) they were mostly negative – especially in the right-wing press – and there were very few articles which featured the counter-arguments outlined earlier. Press accounts also featured false accounts of Britain's debt and deficit:

> The International Monetary Fund forecast that by next year Britain will have the highest level of Government debt of any of the top 20 economies in the WORLD.
>
> *Sun, 20 March 2009*

> These latest official figures show that Britain's financial state is now far, far worse than countries such as Greece or Italy, which we have traditionally

looked down upon and sneered at for their profligacy. Italy's indebtedness, though frightening, stands at little more than 100 per cent of GNP. Ours stands at twice that percentage and may well not be sustainable in the long term.

Daily Mail, 20 February 2009

At times the *BBC News* also featured questionable accounts of the public finances by presenting Britain's borrowing in nominal terms, rather than in relation to GDP:

The national debt has hit a new record of just under £800 billion.

BBC News at Ten, 21 July 2009

Now with unprecedented levels of borrowing and debt.

BBC News at Ten, 22 April 2009

Across the press and broadcasting, six dangers were identified in relation to the deficit: Britain might lose its AAA credit rating, foreign creditors might stop buying UK gilts, sterling could fall sharply, interest rates could rise, the IMF might have to bail out Britain and the UK could go bankrupt. As can be seen in Table 3.5, these arguments were used extensively, particularly in the *Daily Telegraph*, *Daily Mail*, *Express* and *Sun*. Such warnings appeared less frequently on the *BBC News*, but were still much more prominent than counter-arguments, and were sometimes endorsed by journalists. This meant that the difference between *BBC News* and

TABLE 3.5 Assessments of the public finances (proportion of articles featuring each assessment)

Assessment	BBC News	Telegraph	Guardian	Mail	Express	Sun	Mirror
Unfavourable historical/ international comparisons	28%	70%	59%	87%	95%	82%	57%
Favourable historical/ international comparisons	4%	4%	14%	10%	0%	9%	0%
Deficit dangers – bankruptcy – not able to sell debt – IMF coming – Internet rates will rise, sterling to fall, may lose AAA rating	33%	70%	51%	73%	70%	91%	43%
Counter-arguments to deficit dangers – not going bust now, can sell debt at moment, IMF not coming etc.	8%	10%	27%	10%	5%	9%	14%

press reporting was often one of tone and tenor, rather than perspective. So for instance, a number of newspaper articles argued Britain could go bankrupt:

> This is a time when Britain stands on the brink of bankruptcy, with the Government's debts expected to reach an unprecedented £1.5trillion.
>
> *Daily Mail, 5 January 2009*

> Labour reverts to type and bankrupts Britain.
>
> *Headline – Daily Express, 23 April 2009*

On the *BBC News* such warnings came from pro-austerity European politicians, City analysts, the Bank of England and the financial markets. These perspectives were then echoed by reporters and framed the contours of debate within which policy was discussed:

> Journalist: Now is the Prime Minister listening to those siren voices in Europe who are so concerned? Is he listening to the Governor of the Bank of England? Is it the markets he's worried about? The answer is probably all of the above. . . . Mr Brown recalled to the meeting he addressed this morning that a Treasury official had written on [John Maynard] Keynes' work: inflation, extravagance, bankruptcy. The same warnings are being heard today and whether he likes it or not, the Prime Minister is having to listen.
>
> *BBC News at Ten, 25 March 2009*

However, what was missing from *BBC News* reports was the opposing perspective, highlighted earlier, of macroeconomists who questioned whether deficits would lead to interest rate rises and sterling depreciation, let alone inflation or bankruptcy. Whilst BBC coverage lacked the strident editorialising seen in the press, it still operated within a framework which stressed the necessity of pre-emptive austerity to placate the financial markets.

How to respond

As can be seen in Table 3.6, the overwhelming consensus on how to respond to the crisis focused on the need to enact austerity policies. These included cuts to public spending – especially public sector wages and pensions – increases in regressive forms of taxation such as the basic rate of income tax or VAT, and increases in the retirement age. Across all newspapers, austerity measures were presented as unavoidable:

> The deterioration in the public finances means the winner of the next General Election - which has to take place by next summer – will have no choice but to slash public spending and hike taxes.
>
> *Daily Mail, 22 July 2009*

TABLE 3.6 How to reduce the deficit (proportion of articles featuring each solution)

Solution	BBC News	Telegraph	Guardian	Mail	Express	Sun	Mirror
Cut public spending /raise retirement age/ raise regressive taxation/ cut public sector pay, wages and staff	72%	56%	38%	63%	70%	73%	42%
Increase income tax on high earners	12%	12%	15%	14%	13%	18%	0%
Improve efficiency in public sector	16%	4%	5%	2%	15%	0%	0%
Scrap NHS computers, Quangos, ID cards, Trident	4%	6%	5%	10%	5%	9%	0%
Increase taxes on non-doms	0%	2%	0%	0%	0%	0%	0%
Introduce Land/ Property/ Wealth/ Financial Transaction taxes	0%	0%	3%	0%	0%	0%	0%
Crack down on tax evasion/ avoidance	0%	2%	8%	0%	0%	0%	0%
Invest for growth – house building etc.	8%	0%	8%	0%	0%	0%	0%

> Cuts and tax rises: there is no other way.
>
> *Headline – Daily Telegraph, 25 June 2009*

> We must freeze or even cut the cost of keeping six million state workers on the public payroll – or be abandoned by international creditors. There can be no sacred cows. The NHS budget has trebled in ten years. It must accept real cuts. So must every other Whitehall and town hall budget.
>
> *Sun, 6 July 2009*

On the *BBC News* 73.4% of total text which dealt with potential solutions was devoted to arguments discussing cuts to public spending or regressive tax increases. Arguments in favour of cuts were made by opposition politicians, Bank of England representatives, and institutions such as the Organisation for Economic Co-operation and Development (OECD) and IMF. On occasions, journalists claimed they would explore the "options" for reducing Britain's "massive debt" but these consisted of different varieties of austerity. For instance:

> Journalist: British workers might have to put off their age of retirement to help repay the country's massive debt. That is one option proposed by independent think-tank . . . Their report lays out three stark alternatives for bringing their debt level down. Government could cut all public spending by 10% in real terms or it could raise the basic rate of tax by 15p or it could raise the state retirement age to 70 by 2023.
>
> *BBC News at Ten, 6 May 2009*

Discussion of raising taxes on high earners was entirely devoted to the rise in the top rate of income tax in the April 2009 budget, which the right-wing press argued would harm entrepreneurship, investment and jobs. On the *BBC News*, City sources and 'wealth creators' argued the tax would be largely avoided and thus raise little extra revenue. Alternatives to regressive taxation or spending cuts were almost completely absent from news accounts. There was a single line mentioning property taxes in a *Guardian* article which noted the "perverse" concentration on cuts when the deficit was caused by a "collapse in tax revenues", and on the *BBC News* this tiny fragment:

> Will Hutton (Work Foundation): You can make decisions about whether you are going to tax capital and profits, whether you are going to tax the rich or whether you are going to distribute the pain more across the entire population.
>
> *BBC News at Ten, 23 March 2009*

Overall then, the message across the press and broadcasting was remarkably consistent. Austerity was the only solution, with alternatives such as pro-growth policies and or taxation targeted at companies or the better off almost invisible as public policy options.

Audience studies

Before commencing the focus group discussions, participants completed brief questionnaires on media use and their views on the deficit. These answers were then used as the starting point in discussions between the moderator and participants.

What caused the rise in the deficit?

Just under a fifth (10/56) of the respondents wrote that either they didn't know what had caused the rise in the deficit or provided answers which confused government debt with consumer or bank debt. Of the remainder just over one seventh (5/46) identified the role of the recession, or global recession (2/46). However, the dominant explanation which appeared in approximately four fifths of written responses (38/46) was that increased public spending was responsible. As one participant put it, the problem was "historical overspending as well, even before the crisis happened there has been overspending by government and increasing the debt and the problems trying to service that debt" (Low Income group, Glasgow). In another group a participant said:

> Over the last ten years national debt has been building, building into you know the amount owed by us as a nation has been growing it had to reach a tipping point.
>
> *Middle class group, Warwickshire*

TABLE 3.7 Elements of public spending identified as being responsible for the rise in public debt (individual written responses) ranked in order from the most frequently to the least frequently mentioned. Issues ranked equally were mentioned by exactly the same number of respondents

Rank	Issue
1	Banks/bank bailouts
2	Wars/military spending
3	Immigration/asylum seekers
4	Welfare/benefits claimants
5	MPs pay and expenses
6	Foreign aid
7=	Quangos
7=	More public sector workers
7=	Servicing historic debt
10=	Benefit fraud
10=	Olympics
10=	Health
10=	Education
10=	Policing

When the elements of public spending that were seen as responsible for the rise in the deficit were unpacked (see Table 3.7) it was clear that the media had a key role. However, it wasn't simply that respondents reproduced the explanations for the deficit that appeared at the time in media texts. Instead respondents pointed to issues with long-term media visibility but which often had little or no impact on the deficit. For instance, immigration was cited in nine out of the 16 focus groups, and it was particularly prominent as an explanation in groups of low-income or older participants, where it was often the first factor that was identified. In one group a participant spoke of immigrants "taking all the money and bleeding it dry" (Low Income group, Glasgow). In another group a participant spoke of how letting in more people meant that the "books are not going to balance":

> We can't afford to keep them right there's people paying tax for 40 year and then there's somebody comes in here with a full family and they're getting the benefits, the same benefits that someone's been here for fifty year and then at some point the books are not going to balance.
>
> *Low Income group, Glasgow*

A key reason for such beliefs was reports in the press on benefit fraud or welfare payments made to immigrants. As one participant put it:

> Look at that one a month ago in the paper she had ten passports for claiming for ten people. It was all illegal immigrants and she was claiming that they had kids and all the rest of it.
>
> *Low Income group, Glasgow*

It was also the case that benefit spending more widely was frequently seen as a major reason why the deficit had increased. One respondent argued that the "amount that goes on it is ridiculous" (low income group, Glasgow), whilst in another group participants complained about the rise of a "benefits culture":

Respondent 1: I think this country's got into a benefits culture.
Respondent 2: Yes definitely.
Moderator: And you see that as a big reason why the country owes so much money?
Respondent 2: Yes.
Respondent 1: Yeah.

Senior Citizen group, Surrey

Press influence could also be seen in linking of the deficit with other issues which have been a frequent focus of negative newspaper coverage such as quangos, foreign aid and the EU (Deacon and Monk, 2000; Anderson and Weymouth, 1999). One participant argued that the EU "costs millions, trillions even" (Middle Class group, Warwickshire) and in another group participants spoke of the EU as being a "black hole" and a "huge drain" on the country (Senior Citizen group, Surrey). In a similar vein, a number of respondents mentioned public sector pensions. One commented:

I think pensions, public sector pensions are taking a huge tranche out of income into the coffers if you like because we've now reached the baby boomers, my age group are now drawing huge tranches of money out of public funding either at local level or at national level.

Middle Class group, Coventry

Participants also reproduced arguments, common in the right-wing press, that the public sector was full of waste and 'non-jobs'. One complained about the number of equal opportunities officers and argued that "there must be thousands of people in local government who haven't really got a job" (Middle Class group, Warwickshire) The evidence from opinion polls suggests that such views were widespread. A Ipsos Mori poll (2009) found that 63% agreed with the statement that "there are many public services that are a waste of money and can be cut". Furthermore although that this perception was widespread it was more common amongst older voters (net agree 55+ 48% versus 29% for under 55s), those on low incomes (net agree ABC1 32% versus 41% for C2DEs[6]) and tabloid readers (net agree 46% versus 27% for broadsheet readers). Thus although the immediate media accounts identified earlier in the chapter were very significant in establishing the belief that 'overspending' was key, respondents drew on longer-term media narratives in identifying which aspects of spending were responsible.

How to reduce the deficit?

On the questionnaire participants were asked what proposals they heard for reducing the deficit. Just over a quarter of respondents (15/56) either hadn't heard of

TABLE 3.8 Measures for reducing public debt that respondents had heard about ranked in order from most to least frequent (individual written responses)

Rank	Solution
1	Public spending cuts (unspecified)
2	Tax rises (unspecified)
3	Freeze/reduce public sector wages
4	Reduce public sector employees
5	Reduce spending hospitals/schools
6	Reduce infrastructure spending
7=	Reduce benefits
7=	Scrap ID cards
7=	Scrap Trident
7=	Grow economy/get people back to work
7=	Introduction of 50% income tax rate
11=	Put up retirement age
11=	Cut quangos
11=	Reduce public sector pensions
11=	Increase VAT

any or confused public debt with corporate or household debt. Of the rest, most identified public spending cuts (23/41) or tax rises (15/41). Table 3.8 provides a list of all the proposals identified in written responses.

The measures recalled closely mapped both in occurrence and frequency what appeared in broadcasting and the press, demonstrating that the media set the agenda for possible solutions. However, this didn't necessarily mean that people accepted the legitimacy of these policies or were unable to go beyond them and suggest alternatives. Certainly in the focus groups (and opinion polls) there was widespread opposition to cuts to frontline services despite such arguments being strongly made in press accounts (Ipsos-Mori, 2009)

Nevertheless press reporting was significant in building support for cuts to other areas. For instance, a number of respondents echoed the argument prominent in newspaper accounts – that "gilt-edged" public sector pensions were being unfairly subsidised in comparison to those in the private sector and should be reduced:

> The only people who seem to be getting these gilt edged final salary schemes are civil servants. The whole private sector seems to going onto purchasing cheaper pension schemes so why should they sort of be different. I remember reading the amount of our council tax that goes to pensions, it's phenomenal.
> *Middle Class group, Warwickshire*

However, even here the concept of fairness could work in contradictory ways, with another participant arguing that that "public sector staff often get paid less so you've got to factor that in" whilst a third argued that people had joined the public sector partly because of the pension scheme and "you don't penalise in retrospect".

Questions of affordability were strongly linked with what was seen the scale of the debt and this reflected the threatening narratives that were common in the media. One participant who despite having voted Labour described them as a "worst government in the last 100 years or whatever" who had "led the country into a disaster owe money all over the damn place, got this national debt that's zooming up" (Middle Class group, Warwickshire).

Media accounts also influenced the belief – again reflected in large-scale polling – that waste in the public sector was so widespread that the deficit could be reduced primarily through efficiency savings (Ipsos-Mori, 2009). A common complaint was too many non-jobs or administrators: as one respondent put it, "you go into any hospital there are nearly as many administrators as there are doctors or nurses, they could away with them, they didn't have them years ago" (Senior Citizen group, Glasgow).

Another issue with high media visibility – immigration – was also frequently cited as a potential solution. Since immigration was seen as contributing to the rise in public debt, many people thought that by restricting it you could reduce the deficit.

Moderator: What should be done to reduce the deficit?
Respondent 1: They've got to stop all these immigrants coming in.
Moderator: Do you think that's a very big part of it?
Respondent 1: I think that's a lot to do with it.
Respondent 2: Yeah.
Respondent 1: Yes I do.
Moderator: If you had to put an idea of the proportion of it what sort of proportion would it be.
R2:   I think it would be quite high.
Moderator: Would it be a half, a quarter.
Respondent 2: I would say three quarters.

Senior Citizen group, Surrey

If the media were key in setting the agenda for what were seen as viable responses, would policies with little media visibility be unfamiliar to people? To test this participants were asked whether they had heard of alternative policies such a Land Value Tax or a Financial Transactions Tax. However, virtually nobody actually knew what these taxes were. When the moderatorexplained how the taxes worked, they were generally well received, though there was widespread scepticism that such policies could be introduced because a) politicians were seen as being in power to support the rich, b) the wealthy would use their power to block such legislation, or c) the wealthy would find ways to evade or avoid such taxes. Despite this, most participants thought that that the media – and public service broadcasting in particular – should feature alternative accounts and not just reproduce the perspectives of leading parties or politicians.

Conclusion

This chapter set out to establish how the media reported the debates over the public debt and deficit, and the impact that this coverage had on public belief and attitudes. The evidence presented here suggests that it is important to think of media influence in this area through both short-term effects and longer-term patterns of issue socialisation.

In terms of short-term impacts there is evidence that the crisis narratives that stressed the size and danger of the deficit convinced many members of our focus groups that the public finances were in serious trouble and action needed to be taken quickly. Furthermore, the framing of solutions to the problem of the deficit severely restricted the range of policy options that participants were aware of and led many to see cuts to public spending as unavoidable. However, this did not mean that those in our focus groups accepted all the arguments that were made in the media. There was a strong resistance to cuts in frontline services, whilst social values such as fairness sometimes influenced whether people thought specific cuts were acceptable. Nevertheless, the long-running press campaign alleging inefficiency in the public sector was successful in creating the impression that public spending could be cut without jeopardising services.[7]

This brings us to the second process of long-term media socialisation and how this interacted with very low levels of public understanding of the economy and the contours of government spending. This could clearly be seen in how participants understood the origins of the deficit, with most erroneously attributing it to increased public spending rather than the recession. Furthermore, participants didn't identify the ems of public spending which had seen significant growth, such as health and education. Instead, they pointed to areas such as immigration, waste, welfare, public sector pensions, quangos, foreign aid, the EU and MPs' expenses. This was due to the high visibility of these topics in the press over many years and the power of the repetition of emotionally charged messages which left many audience members feeling angry and resentful (Golding and Middleton, 1982; Anderson and Weymouth, 1999; Deacon and Monk, 2000; Lundström, 2011; Sage, 2012; Berry 2018). Nowhere was this starker than in relation to immigration and welfare spending. Respondents repeatedly brought up issues such as family allowance paid to immigrants (0.004% of total government spending) and benefit fraud by immigrants (a fraction of the estimated 0.8% of benefit spending lost to fraud) even though neither had any significant impact on the deficit (DWP, 2014; Eaton, 2016). Similarly many pointed to a welfare system that was seen as 'out of control' despite the fact that welfare spending fell as both a share of national income (13.1% to 11.1%) and public spending (33.0% to 27.1%) between 1997 and 2008, whilst the value of most out of work benefits were either static or declined in real terms (IFS, 2010; Rutherford, 2013).

The research therefore demonstrates that the widely held belief that public confusion over the origins of the deficit was primarily due to skilful Tory public relations and the failure of Labour to defend its economic record is inadequate (e.g. Gamble, 2015; Ussher, 2015). What is missing is the recognition that when the crisis hit, the public was already primed to see public spending as wasteful and excessive, whilst areas like immigration and welfare were viewed a major drain on the economy. It was only then a small jump to see these kinds of issues as being linked to the rise in the deficit and to see their reduction as being obvious solutions. Whilst a more robust attempt to counter false narratives may have had some success, there is a tendency to underestimate the durability of false beliefs created by long-term repeated exposure to media messages, especially when such beliefs appear intuitive and understanding of economic and fiscal fundamentals is extremely limited.

Notes

1 For a more complete account of the methods used to compile the newspaper sample see Berry (2016).
2 For a more complete account of the methods used to compile the television sample see Berry (2016).
3 For a more complete account of the methods used to compile the audience sample see Berry (2018)
4 Part of the variation between the relative frequency counts in broadcast and print media is because press reporting was coded for direct speech only whilst broadcast reporting coded both direct and reported speech. A decision was undertaken to code only direct speech in newspapers because of time constraints when working with a larger sample. Nevertheless, similar research on the banking crisis which captured only direct speech in both mediums still found that the presence of at least one source was significantly higher in broadcast than print journalism (Berry, 2018). This is probably a function of the need for broadcast journalists to avoid editorialising and protect against claims of partiality (Tuchman, 1972).
5 ONS refers to the Office for National Statistics.
6 For an explanation of socio-economic grading categories please see UK Geographics (2014).
7 For a discussion of press narratives on waste in public services see Berry (2018).

References

Aldrick, P. 2009. 'Robert Stheeman: The gatekeeper of UK debt'. *Daily Telegraph*. 27 April. Available at: www.telegraph.co.uk/finance/financetopics/profiles/5226378/Robert-Stheeman-the-gatekeeper-of-UK-debt.html [Accessed 13th June 2017].

Anderson, P. J., and Weymouth, T. 1999. *Insulting the public? The British press and the European Union*. London: Longman.

Ashcroft, M. 2010. *What future for Labour?* Available at: http://lordashcroft.com/pdf/25092010_ what_future_for_labour.pdf [Accessed 13th June 2017].

Berry, M. 2013. 'The Today programme and the banking crisis'. *Journalism*, 14(2), pp. 253–270.

Berry, M. 2016. 'The UK press and the deficit debate'. *Sociology*. 50(3), pp. 542–559.

Berry, M. 2018. *How economic news shapes public opinion*. London: Palgrave-Macmillan.

Broadcasters Audience Research Board (BARB) (2015) *Weekly top 30.* Available at: www.barb.co.uk/whats-new/weekly-top-30 [Accessed 13th June 2017].

Centreforum. 2009. *A balancing act*. Available at: www.centreforum.org/assets/pubs/a-balancing-act [Accessed 13th June 2017].

Chang, H. J. 2010. 'UK needs a selective industrial policy'. *Guardian*. 3 May. Available at: www.theguardian.com/commentisfree/2010/may/03/uk-selective-industrial-policy [Accessed 13th June 2017].

Clark, T., and Reed, H. 2013. 'If Britain is broke it has been for most of the last 300 years'. *Guardian*. 4 April. Available at: www.theguardian.com/commentisfree/2013/apr/04/britain-not-broke [Accessed 13th June 2017].

Conway, E. 2009. 'October 5. Joseph Stiglitz calls for a Tobin tax on all financial transactions'. *Telegraph*, 5 October. Available at: www.telegraph.co.uk/finance/financialcrisis/6262242/Joseph-Stiglitz-calls-for-Tobin-tax-on-all-financial-trading-transactions.html [Accessed 13th June 2017].

Conway, E. 2013. *Here's who the UK Government owes money to*. Available at: www.edmundconway.com/2013/10/heres-who-the-uk-government-owes-money-to/ [Accessed 13th June 2017].

Deacon, D., and Monk, W. 2000. 'Executive stressed: News reporting of quangos in Britain'. *The Harvard International Journal of Press/Politics*, 5(3), pp. 45–66.

Department for Work and Pensions (DWP). 2014. *Fraud and Error in the Benefit System 2013/14 Estimates*. Available at: www.gov.uk/government/uploads/system/uploads/attachment_data/file/371459/Statistical_Release.pdf [Accessed 13th June 2017].

Eaton, G. 2016. 'How much do benefits paid to EU migrants cost Britain?' *New Statesman*, 16 June. Available at: www.newstatesman.com/politics/welfare/2016/06/how-much-do-benefits-paid-eu-migrants-cost-britain [Accessed 13th June 2017].

Engelen, E., Eturk, I., Froud J., et al. 2011. *After the great complacence*. Oxford: Oxford University Press.

Eurostat. 2016. *General government gross debt – annual data*. Available at: http://ec.europa.eu/eurostat/tgm/table.do?tab=table&init=1&language=en&pcode=teina225&plugin=1 [Accessed 13th June 2017].

Gamble, A. 2015. 'The Economy'. *Parliamentary Affairs*, 68(1), pp. 154–167.

Glasgow Media Group. 1976. *Bad news*. London: Routledge & Kegan Paul.

Glasgow Media Group. 1980. *More bad news*. London: Routledge & Kegan Paul.

Glasgow Media Group. 1982. *Really bad news*. London: Routledge & Kegan Paul.

Glasgow Media Group. 1985. *War and peace news*. Oxford: Oxford University Press.

Golding, P., and Middleton, S. 1982. *Images of welfare*. Oxford: Blackwell.

Hunter, P. 2015. *Red Alert: Why Labour lost and what needs to change*. Smith Institute. Available at: https://smithinstitutethinktank.files.wordpress.com/2015/07/red-alert-why-labour-lost-and-what-needs-to-change.pdf [Accessed 13th June 2017].

Hutton, W. 2009. 'Hail the man who argues Britain should stop worrying about its debt'. *Guardian*, 5 July. Available at: www.theguardian.com/commentisfree/2009/jul/05/will-hutton-recession-britain-debt [Accessed 13th June 2017].

Institute for Fiscal Studies (IFS). 2010. *Public spending under labour*. Available at: www.ifs.org.uk/bns/bn92.pdf [Accessed 13th June 2017].

Institute for Fiscal Studies (IFS). 2012a. *Revenues including forecasts*. Available at: www.ifs.org.uk/ff/revenues.xls [Accessed 13th June 2017].

Institute for Fiscal Studies (IFS). 2012b. *2015 Spending Budget*. Available at: www.ifs.org.uk/uploads/publications/ff/lr_spending_budget15.xls [Accessed 13th June 2017].

Institute for Public Policy Research (IPPR). 2009. *Time for another people's budget*. Available at: www.ippr.org/files/images/media/files/publication/2011/05/peoples_budget_1687.pdf?noredirect=1[Accessed 13th June 2017].

Ipsos-Mori. 2009. *Public spending index – June 2009*. Available at: www.ipsos.com/sites/default/files/migrations/en-uk/files/Assets/Docs/poll-public-spending-charts-june-2009.pdf [Accessed 13th June 2017].

Kitzinger, J. 1994. 'The methodology of focus groups: The importance of interactions between research participants'. *Sociology of Health and Illness*, 16, pp. 103–121.

Keep, M (2018) *Government borrowing and debt: International comparisons*. House of Commons Briefing Paper Number 06054. Available at: http://researchbriefings.files.parliament.uk/documents/SN06054/SN06054.pdf [Accessed 13th June 2017].

Koo, R. C. 2011. 'The world in balance sheet recession: Causes, cure, and politics'. *Real World Economics Review*, 58, pp. 19–37.

Krugman, P. 2009a. *Deficit hysteria*. Available at: https://krugman.blogs.nytimes.com/2009/11/23/deficit-hysteria/ [Accessed 13th June 2017].

Krugman, P. 2009b. *Invisible bond vigilantes*. Available at: http://krugman.blogs.nytimes.com/2009/11/19/invisible-bond-vigilantes/ [Accessed 13th June 2017].

Lilico, A., O'Brien, N., and Atashzai, A. 2009. Controlling public spending: The scale of the challenge. *Policy Exchange*. Available at: https://policyexchange.org.uk/publication/controlling-public-spending-the-scale-of-the-challenge/ [Accessed 13th June 2017].

Lundström, R. 2011. 'Between the exceptional and the ordinary: A model for the comparative analysis of moral panics and moral regulation'. *Crime, Media, Culture*, 7(3), pp. 313–332.

Neild, R. 2010. 'The national debt in perspective'. *Newsletter of the royal economic society*. Available at: www.res.org.uk/view/article5jan12Correspondence.html [Accessed 13th June 2017].

Philo, G. 1995a. 'Political advertising and public belief'. *Media, Culture and Society*, 15, pp. 407–418.

Philo, G. 1995b. Television, politics and the rise of the new right. In: Philo, G. (ed.), *Glasgow media group reader, volume 2*. London: Longman, pp. 198–233.

Philo, G. 1999. *Message received*. London: Routledge.

Philo, G. 2010. 'Deficit Crisis: let's really be in it together'. *Guardian*, 15 August. Available at: www.theguardian.com/commentisfree/2010/aug/15/deficit-crisis-tax-the-rich [Accessed 13th June 2017].

Public and Commercial Services Union (PCSU). 2010. *There is an alternative to public spending cuts*. Available at: http://classonline.org.uk/docs/4015_there_is_an_alternative_Pamphlet1.pdf [Accessed 13th June 2017].

Reich, R. 2009. 'Why the deficit hysteria? I only wish we'd borrow more'. *Guardian*, 31 August. Available at: www.theguardian.com/commentisfree/2009/aug/31/us-uk-economy-deficit-debt [Accessed 13th June 2017].

Rutherford, T. 2013. 'Historical rates of social security benefits'. *House of commons library SN/SG 6762*. Available at: http://researchbriefings.files.parliament.uk/documents/SN06762/SN06762.pdf [Accessed 13th June 2017].

Sage, D. 2012. 'Fair conditions and fair consequences? Exploring New Labour, welfare contractualism and social attitudes'. *Social Policy and Society*. 11(3), pp. 359–373.

Sikka, P. 2009. 'There are alternatives to public spending cuts'. *Guardian*, 25 July. Available at: www.theguardian.com/commentisfree/2009/jul/25/public-spending-cuts [Accessed 13th June 2017].

Taylor, C., Farrugia, B., O'Connell, J., et. al. 2009. *How to Save £50 Billion*. Institute of Directors/Taxpayers' Alliance. Available at: https://d3n8a8pro7vhmx.cloudfront.net/taxpayersalliance/pages/211/attachments/original/1427715115/50bil.pdf?1427715115 [Accessed 13th June 2017].

Tuchman, G (1972) Objectivity as Strategic Ritual: An Examination of Newsmen's Notions of Objectivity. *American Journal of Sociology*, 77 (4), pp. 660–679.

UK Geographics (2014) Social Grade A, B, C1, C2, D, E. Available at: www.ukgeographics. co.uk/blog/social-grade-a-b-c1-c2-d-e [Accessed 8th January 2018]

Ussher, K. 2015. 'Labour did not cause the economic crisis – it must counter the myth that it did'. *Guardian*, 18 May. Available at: www.theguardian.com/commentisfree/2015/ may/18/labour-economic-crisis-tories [Accessed 13th June 2017].

Wahl-Jorgensen, K., Sambrook, R., Berry, M., et. al. 2013. *BBC breadth of opinion review: Content analysis*. Available at: http://downloads.bbc.co.uk/bbctrust/assets/files/pdf/our_ work/breadth_opinion/content_analysis.pdf [Accessed 13th June 2017].

4

THE ECONOMIC RECOVERY ON TV NEWS

Richard Thomas

Introduction

Like poverty, income inequality is a pejorative concept, reflecting the negativity of injustice, the "positive ethical value" of "equality" (Charles-Coll, 2011, p. 17) and sharing many of the same political, social, economic and institutional factors. In the UK, income inequality increased sharply during the 1980s, when Margaret Thatcher's government demonstrated a strategy of purposeful deregulation (Turnbull and Wass, 2010) and an ideological shift towards the supreme power of liberalised markets (McGuigan, 2005). More recently, it became a central focus in the UK General Election campaign of 2017, as the Labour Party contested Conservative Party policies that they claimed were elitist and unhelpful to the population at large.

Growth is the primary measure of economic performance (Picard, 2015). Accordingly, economic growth over 12 consecutive quarters until the end of 2015 (BBC, 2016) indicates that the UK is recovering from the global financial crisis. This appears to be good news for everyone; a growing economy, many might argue, means more prosperity. Such perceptions are strongly developed by the media. UK broadcasting combines public service and commercial logics, and within this over-arching system, the BBC for example, is a trusted source of news (Plunkett, 2016). This chapter argues that when discussing growth, broadcast news does not 'join the dots' between growth, how wealth is distributed and the wider social consequences.

Proving a causal relationship between growth and inequality is problematic. However, both have often occurred simultaneously. Dobson and Read (2015) describe the relationship between the two as "a macabre dance of reciprocal legitimation" where inequality is necessary for growth in order to provide incentives for social mobility, growth then providing "an ever bigger cake, from which some crumbs will surely find their way into the mouths of the less fortunate". If it is true that economic growth "is the single most powerful mechanism for generating long-term increases in income per capita" (Snowdon, 2006, p. 5), then to prevent these increases from concentrating only around high-income earners, some method of cascading wealth – the crumbs from the cake – is required. According to this 'trickle-down thesis', all citizens should benefit as economies grow. Growth is apparently the magic bullet – simultaneously an aspiration, a motivation and a solution.

This chapter develops the analysis of Lewis and Thomas (2015) who considered the presentation of economic growth within UK and US broadsheet newspapers in 2010 and 2011. In more than 90% of cases in their study, growth was presented as overwhelmingly good. Furthermore, its 'goodness' was generally unexplained, and when it was actually unpacked, the benefits of growth were usually expressed in terms of job creation and general well-being. Growth discourses embrace the language of dynamism, as, for example, the economy "moves forward" with "momentum", while low or no growth means that the economy is "stagnant" and the outlook "bleak" (Lewis and Thomas, 2015, p. 91).

Such overwhelmingly positive media presentation virtually ignores considerable evidence suggesting that growth, achieved by consumerism and fuelled by advertising, leads to ongoing environmental damage. Irrespective of the media prominence of environmental degradation,[1] such damage continues. Indeed, a Rubicon was crossed in 2015, when carbon dioxide emissions reached 400 parts per million (400 ppm). In response, one climate scientist warned that "climate change is a threat to life on Earth and we can no longer afford to be spectators" (NASA, 2013). Furthermore, former NASA climatologist James Hansen envisaged that "conflicts arising from forced migrations and economic collapse might make the planet ungovernable, threatening the fabric of civilization" (Hansen at al., 2015, p. 20119).

It seems clear that unimpeded growth gradually depletes the world's natural resources. "Bizarrely", note Lewis and Thomas (2015, p. 96), the one notable dissenting voice apparently battling against the tide of positivity about growth was Prince Charles. All other critical commentators were absent. Using examples from TV news reports on BBC1 and ITV1 in 2014, the focus of this chapter is to show how another series of 'dots' remain unconnected – those joining growth to income inequality and poverty, and the redistributive policies that would ease them.

This chapter analyses data generated by a large-scale content analysis looking at the coverage of inequality, and its associated elements on all available weeknight 10pm news bulletins on BBC and ITV during 2014. Only a few bulletins from each channel were unavailable on the electronic resource *Box of Broadcasts*, and the sample consisted of 245 bulletins on BBC, and 244 bulletins on ITV. All stories containing any trace of poverty, wealth and inequality were considered irrespective of whether these themes were central to the report or just mentioned in passing. In practice, this included stories ranging for example, from executive remuneration, to an increase in the use of foodbanks and the disparity in incomes between private equity executives and their cleaners. Both quantitatively through content analysis, and qualitatively through the critical discourse and multimodal analyses that follow it, economic growth emerges as a central theme both within and on the periphery of the reporting of inequality, poverty and wealth.

Increasing income inequality

Globalisation, it is claimed, increasingly benefits financial elites while everyone else are "losers" (Stiglitz, 2013, p. 80). For the many not directly benefiting from free-market systems, welfare is a critical and major source of income (Dorling, 2014). However, during austerity, welfare has been cut (Mason, 2016), and the criteria for eligibility has narrowed. Furthermore, weaker unions and personal pay arrangements superseding collective bargaining (Turnbull and Wass, 2010) are other factors widely understood to drive income inequality.

Most recently, income inequality has registered more prominently in the public consciousness. Corporate culture is "increasingly aggressive" (Giddens, 2004, p. 53) and characterised by greed (Dorling, 2014). Income inequality therefore, is often characterised by apparently limitless corporate salaries, such remuneration packages having risen considerably faster than average incomes (Turnbull and Wass, 2010). As a consequence, professional practices and personal behaviours – particularly within the financial sector – are more closely scrutinised, with particular attention often concentrated on the highest earners (see Thomas, 2016).

Capitalist populations have long since been stratified in terms of wealth, but why should the gap between extremes matter so much? The answer is that income inequality has economic, social and political implications that divide communities and impede democratic efficiency. Wilkinson and Pickett (2010), for example, conclude that higher rates of teenage pregnancy, crime, violence and mental illness; lower life expectancy; and a deficit of trust are more prevalent in the world's more unequal nations. Their research shows that such effects of income inequality are not merely confined to just those with the lowest incomes, but that these impacts are felt across whole societies. Of all the undesirable outcomes discussed by Wilkinson and Pickett (2010), Lynch et al. (2004), Torre and Myrskylä (2013) and others, the most compelling strand of research identifies the correlation between income inequality and pejorative health outcomes – 'the inequality-health hypothesis'. Notwithstanding any additional social or political outcomes, this alone is sufficient to deem income inequality as unwanted and damaging.

Yet income inequality continues to grow. As measured by the Gini coefficient,[2] UK income inequality rose in 2013/4 from 0.337 to 0.343 (Belfield et al., 2015, p. 33). Such growing inequality was subsequently described by one representative of the global banking sector as a "social time bomb" (Dorling, 2014, p. 116). Furthermore, in January 2014, the World Economic Forum (WEF) – incorporating powerful and influential policymaking elites – described income inequality as a major global risk, more serious, for example, than climate change and extreme weather systems (World Economic Forum, 2014). Consequently, 2014 was described as a "year of unprecedented inequality" (Williams, 2014) and either side of this nadir, Stiglitz (2013), Dorling (2014) and others have further popularised the issue to a wider audience. Indeed, Piketty's (2014) *Capital in the Twenty-First Century* was even an Amazon bestseller. As the rich/poor gap increases, instead of the binary comparison between the 'haves' and the 'have nots', comparing the 'have nots' with the "have yachts" (Hoggart, 2012) may now be more appropriate.

Despite concerns about inequality being widespread enough to drive the 'Occupy' protests in 2011, there is still doubt as to whether there is any serious political will to address income inequality. Indeed, there are concerns that it may not be an issue that policymakers even engage with. Even before 'Occupy' for example, senior banker Lord Griffiths suggested that we should "tolerate inequality as a way to achieve greater prosperity for all" (Hopkins, 2009). Moreover, in November 2013, then–London Mayor Boris Johnson claimed inequality was essential to generate "the spirit of envy" and trying to eradicate it was "futile" (Watt, 2013).

Growth on BBC and ITV: all good news

If there is indeed a current lack of political intent to address income inequality, then the media's role as inquisitors and challengers is even more important if the dangerous increase is to be arrested and reversed. According to the normative ideals of journalism, media should not only make sense of wider events, but by asking probing and incisive questions, should promote social justice. The UK's broadcasting system is governed by the principles of public service and as such, citizens can justifiably expect that seismic financial changes and wide-ranging social phenomena should be covered in useful, objective and informative ways. Citizens will develop their opinions about income inequality and economic growth according to the information they receive from the media. Then, the ways these issues are presented, framed and discussed are thought to generate the public opinion needed before politicians are forced to act.

Table 4.1 shows the type of language used by BBC1 and ITV1 to describe growth in news reports about poverty and inequality in 2014.

By using critical discourse analysis (CDA), which interprets language within wider socio-political backdrops (Taylor, 2004) and shows how power and ideology are perpetuated through language, it is clear that growth is habitually shown to be positive and dynamic, and its absence is pejorative and undesirable. Low or no growth means 'stagnation' and 'danger', while the opposite is framed in the upbeat language of 'recovery' and 'strength'.

In an example of how growth is presented as a universal antidote to inequality, Figure 4.1 shows part of a report by then–BBC Economics Editor Robert Peston from the WEF summit in Davos on 23/1/14. The report was unusual, in that it featured income inequality at the front and centre of its narrative.[3] Peston begins his commentary against footage of a helicopter delivering delegates to the summit, and later in the report, Peston invites viewers to "meet a new member of the Davos elite; the US Treasury Secretary", who responds to a question about the start of the world economy:

Setting the tone for what follows, Peston suggests that given the economic recovery, the world's problems do not seem "quite as deep or severe". Accordingly, growth is ascribed considerable healing power. The link between prosperity and growth is also made by US Treasury Secretary Jack Lew, who advocates pursuing

TABLE 4.1 Themes and descriptions within 'growth' stories in 2014

Date broadcast	Channel	Journalistic descriptions of growth
21/1/14	BBC1	"economy formerly . . . flat as a pancake"
		"recovery is accelerated"
		"kind of growth we enjoyed in the boom years"
		"gratifying . . . that we are growing again"
21/1/14	ITV1	"Britain among the fastest growing world economies"
28/1/14	BBC1	"strongest showing since the financial crisis"
		"growing faster than at any time since 2007"
		"the long stagnation is over"
19/3/14	BBC1	"robust / strong economic growth"
8/4/14	BBC1	"UK could become the fastest growing world economy"
		"Britain to top the premier league for growth"
29/4/14	BBC1	"the British economy is revving up"
		"the economy is motoring along"
		"UK predicted to be the fastest growing advanced economy this year"
29/4/14	ITV1	"economy has almost come full circle"
9/5/14	BBC1	"almost returned to levels not seen before its peak just before the recession in 2008"
		"economy on the move"
		"making up all the ground lost during the recession"
24/7/14	ITV1	UK "now expected to outperform every other country in the developed world this year"
		"the course is set fair"
24/7/14	BBC1	"UK growing faster than any other developed economy"
		"recovered to pre-recession levels"
14/8/14	BBC1	"Eurozone economy ground to a halt"
		"the recovery has stalled"
		"zero growth . . . is regarded as really disappointing"
24/10/14	BBC1	"expansion was slower than the previous period"
		"poor growth in the Eurozone"
		"economy motoring forward at a fair old clip"
24/10/14	ITV1	"Britain leads the pack"
		"UK is outpacing other developed economies"
		"Germany has started shrinking . . . France has stagnated"
17/11/14	ITV1	"world economy struggling to recover"
17/11/14	BBC1	"stalling growth in the Eurozone"
		"just when you think the economy is motoring again"
		"there has been plenty of good economic news – growth is up"
		"a slowdown in the Eurozone"
17/11/14	BBC1	"third largest economy said its GDP had shrunk. . ."
		"Eurozone . . . stopped shrinking . . . but it can't pick up speed"
24/11/14	BBC1	"a danger . . . that we are entering a prolonged period of low growth" (question)

FIGURE 4.1A   BBC1's report from Davos on 23/1/14

They come, from all over the world, to the top of magnificent Swiss mountain. The rich, the powerful – not to ski, but they say, to solve the world's problems. But in one sense, those problems don't seem quite as deep or severe as they have in recent years because there is a strengthening economic recovery, not only in Britain, but also in America, and much of the world.

FIGURE 4.1B   BBC1's report from Davos on 23/1/14

There's you know, a lot of signs that there's, there's growth … but there's still a lot of risks out there and you know, I've just spent some time in Europe, meeting with some of my counterparts. I very much think that it would be in Europe's interests for there to be policies that really drove investment and demand in countries that are surplus countries.

policies to drive investment and demand. Figure 4.2 shows another BBC1 report, from 29/4/14, further accentuating the importance of growth. Chief Economic Correspondent Hugh Pym begins his report about the economy with footage from a racetrack. The report then takes a general turn, as Pym compares the UK economy with other nations.

FIGURE 4.2A   BBC1's report about economic growth on 29/4/14

The British economy is revving up and world-leading industries like this are playing an important role. . . . Silverstone is at the heart of the so-called "Motorsport Valley" – 40,000 people are employed in hi-tech engineering business and the local area has the highest employment rate in the country.

FIGURE 4.2B   BBC1's report about economic growth on 29/4/14

The economy might be motoring along but getting back to where it was in 2008 before the recession is the key marker on the road towards a balanced and sustained recovery. The UK is getting there, but is still 0.6% below that pre-recession peak, in contrast, German has moved 3% beyond where it was in 2008, and the US economy is more than 6% above its previous peak.

Again, the metaphor of dynamic movement is used visually and verbally, as cars 'rev up' and 'motor forward'. Besides featuring this clear multimodal message about growth, this particular report is unusual in that presents a more confusing growth-centred narrative. On one hand, growth is "motoring along" and must continue to do so even faster to compete with Germany, for example. On the other hand, and in rare departure from the usual strongly pro-growth discourse, it is insufficient to ease the concerns of motor industry worker Nick Caceres, who as Hugh Pym explains in Figure 4.3, is still experiencing financial discomfort.

It seems that while the sector is thriving, Nick is hampered by inertia. Figure 4.4 shows excerpts from an ITV report about the economy on 28/1/14, where Political Editor Tom Bradby puts growth into a political context but also suggests – like Nick in the BBC report – that many are not feeling the benefits of growth.

Bradby's narrative that the recovery is concentrated at the wealthier end of the income continuum is unusual. Figure 4.5 concerns another BBC report, this time delivered by Washington Correspondent Nick Bryant on 29/1/14. The report describes President Obama's State of the Union speech, made only days after the WEF summit at Davos identified income inequality as a major risk. Bryant's over-riding narrative is that Obama's presidency was "gridlocked", and with his attempts to reform hampered the president was pledging to "by-pass the system". Figure 4.5 shows that the report featured the president's speech.

FIGURE 4.3 The continuation of BBC1's report about economic growth on 29/4/14

Nick, who is self-employed, has seen plenty of work come his way, thought he says keeping up with household bills isn't always easy.

NC – Renting is quite expensive and fuel is quite expensive . . . it's very slowly moving as far as I'm concerned.

FIGURE 4.4 ITV1's report about the economy on 28/1/14

The Tory playbook for the coming election was simple – nurse the economy back to health, make us all feel wealthier so we go out and vote for them. Simple. But nothing is ever easy and it seems that many of us fear that the recovery is ever only going to work for the wealthy. What isn't in doubt though is that long last, we are out of the economic woods.

FIGURE 4.5 BBC1's report on the State of the Union speech on 29/1/14

The cold hard fact is that even in the midst of recovery, too many Americans are working more than ever just to get by, let alone to get ahead.

The official transcript of Obama's speech[4] provides further context and, in particular, what the president says before the particular soundbite that was broadcast:

> Today, after four years of economic growth, corporate profits and stock prices have rarely been higher, and those at the top have never done better. But average wages have barely budged. Inequality has deepened. Upward mobility has stalled. The cold, hard fact is that even in the midst of recovery, too many Americans are working more than ever just to get by, let alone get ahead.

Silence, or the omission of particular discourses, is a notable concept within CDA (Huckin, 1997). In TV news, such discourses might be absent within social actor contributions, or removed by editing. Omission here is key, since the extended version of the president's comments about recovery shows, with considerably more compulsion, that Americans have not seen the benefits of recovery and that despite sustained growth, inequality has apparently increased. The motivations for such editing can only be speculated about, nonetheless, the report does not implicate the failure of growth as it might.

Though unusual within the wider sample of growth reporting, the message that many people do not feel growth's benefits is delivered both explicitly (for example, by Tom Bradby) and subtly (the Pym and Bryant examples). This adds to the argument that 'trickle down' economics does not work (Atkinson, 2014; Dorling, 2014; OECD, 2014). Since 2000, for example, "the poorest half of the world's population has received just 1% of the total increase in global wealth, while 50% of that has gone to the 1% of people on the top of the pile" (Childs, 2015). In sum, while it seems clear from TV news bulletins that policymakers have no choice other than to assertively pursue economic growth (Lugo-Ocando, 2014), Dobson and Read (2015) speak for many when asserting that "we must let go of this 'trickle-down' nonsense once and for all".

If the benefits of growth, therefore, do not trickle down, and if there is actually some will to ensure that all citizens can prosper, some mechanisms are needed to facilitate the downward flow (Whittaker, 2013; Blanchflower and Machin, 2014). Such redistribution can be through welfare/benefits or taxation, and these are not only advocated to ensure that recovery/growth benefits the wider population, but also because they ease income inequality (see inter alia, Jackson and Victor, 2014; OECD, 2014; Piketty, 2014). Crucially, even when TV news reports rarely depart from the relentless promotion of growth and concede that it may not be 'trickling down', it is even more rare for the discussion to extend as far as acknowledging that some redistributing policies and mechanisms might be required.

In fact, only one story within almost 500 bulletins makes such a link. The BBC report from 27/5/14 is narrated by Business Editor Kamal Ahmed, and concerns a speech by Mark Carney – the Governor of the Bank of England. Figure 4.6 shows that the report includes a clip from a speech by Prince Charles, which is then followed by an interview with International Monetary Fund Managing Director Christine Lagarde.

FIGURE 4.6A   BBC1's report about Mark Carney's speech on 27/5/14

At the end of the day, the primary purpose of capitalism should surely be to serve the wider long-term interests and concerns of humanity rather than the other way around.

FIGURE 4.6B   BBC1's report about Mark Carney's speech on 27/5/14

Clearly those fiscal rules that are conducive to less inequality include the likes of tax on real estate, appropriate but not excessive tax on inheritance, appropriate and properly redistributive tax on income – not excessive – but appropriately progressive.

The contribution from Prince Charles has a striking resonance with the analysis provided by Lewis and Thomas (2015). They report that in their newspaper sample, he alone was visible in challenging "the dominant consumer capitalist consensus" (Lewis and Thomas, 2015, p. 95). They note the irony that such criticism of the prevailing economic system was delivered by a member of the British Royal Family, highlighting that other key potential opponents – "economists, environmentalists, and social scientists" (Lewis and Thomas, 2015, p. 96) – are once again absent.

Equally important is the contribution from Lagarde. She proposes a programme of "tax on real estate, appropriate but not excessive tax on inheritance, appropriate and properly redistributive tax on income – not excessive – but appropriately progressive". This is the only report identified as mentioning any suggestion of a redistributive solution within the much broader analysis of news about income inequality.

Despite this example, there seems little to be otherwise optimistic about. In his report summary, Kamal Ahmed refers to Lagarde's forthcoming visit to Britain when, he explains, income inequality might be revisited. In newspaper coverage of her visit the following month, however, the singular thrust of reporting focused entirely on Lagarde's apology for underestimating the strength of the UK's economic growth instead of, as might have been hoped, a continued discussion about inequality. Further, the set piece interview with Andrew Marr on BBC1 broadcast on 8/6/14[5] does not mention income inequality at all, since it too, focuses entirely on the issue of underestimated growth. The inevitable conclusion is that while in the narrowest of contexts this report represents a small advancement in reporting income inequality, within the broader landscape the connections between the problem and those things that might solve it are not made. Growth – of itself and by itself – remains the standalone solution, irrespective of whether it 'trickles down' or not.

The neoliberal status quo: unchallenged

Analysis of these news reports reveals the ideological loadings underpinned by the principles of neoliberal economics. Neoliberalism favours individualism and competition (Tabb, 2003), restores hegemony to capitalism by removing state interference (Schmidt, 2000) and emphasises market dominance (Erjavec et al., 2008). Economies, it is claimed, will prosper when the state recedes since "a smaller state is believed to leave more space for private initiative and inspire confidence" (Schui, 2014, p. 2). Most significantly, neoliberalism is considered the system most qualified to navigate modern economies through recession (De Ville and Orbie, 2014).

Neoliberalism is most often associated with political Conservatism, but its dominion transcends traditional political divides. The Labour Party for example, is considered to have moved towards neoliberalism under Tony Blair (Schifferes and Knowles, 2015). Indeed, Walsh (2015) contends that irrespective of political affiliation, Chancellors have protected and promoted such dominant market philosophy. Neoliberalism's grip appears assured, and impervious to political shifts.

Despite such universal and cross party support, in the last decade, there have been sufficient grounds to seriously question economic neoliberalism. The near total economic collapse in Greece, for example, represents a notable event "in the long tradition of subordinating human welfare to financial power" (Monbiot, 2015a). In the UK, the neoliberal model pursued by UK governments throughout the financial crisis can be synthesised thus:

> The emphasis on spending cuts over tax rises as the means to cut the deficit and the very speed of change all add up to a reinforcing of neoliberalism which promises to generate adverse consequences for indicators of poverty and inequality.
>
> *Grimshaw and Rubery, 2012, p. 55*

If the wisdom of neoliberalism, the reach of the benefits of growth and the cost of inequality are ever to be challenged it seems, the time to do so is right now. Moreover, since TV is the most trusted news platform (McKendrick et al., 2008) and is vested with serving the public (who, in the case of the BBC, is also responsible for funding it), then it is reasonable to expect that these channels should play a significant role in doing so. The analysis here suggests that they do not fulfil such noble normative ideals.

Broadcasters can only report these issues, but Sikka (2015) goes further, and contends that those with the power to reverse such apparently socially damaging policies are delinquent because of their deference to neoliberalism. Even at the previously discussed WEF summits, agendas are often "far removed from the concerns of ordinary people", and that "despite the biggest banking crash, there has been little effective reform of the financial system as governments seem unwilling to upset the financial wheeler and dealers" (Sikka, 2015). Such claims seem justified in light of strident UK 'business-friendly' tax regimes which include the lowest rate of corporation tax in the G7 (Chakrabortty, 2015). Consequently, neoliberal policies are "inherently incompatible with democracy, as people will always rebel against the austerity and fiscal tyranny it prescribes" (Monbiot, 2015a).

In sum, despite it being "holed below the waterline" (Schifferes, 2011, p. 19), neoliberalism remains largely unchallenged; media shy away from blaming markets while governments are claimed to "overspend" and "interfere" (Davis, 2015, p. 40). More emphatically, despite neoliberalism's apparent vulnerability, journalists (including those on BBC and ITV) do not offer "credible alternatives for the high priests of casino capitalism who had served as authoritative news sources before the crisis" (Kleinnijenhuis et al., 2013, p. 287). Put succinctly, "at a moment when the systemic flaws of neoliberalism are exposed, its representation within the media and political mainstream as unassailable and inevitable seems increasingly assured" (Kay and Salter, 2014, p. 767).

Conclusion

This analysis of growth is conducted through the prism of poverty and inequality. Despite being obliged to adhere to public service ideals, besides hardly covering it at all, the UK's two primary TV news providers do not make the essential connection between the problem of income inequality, the role played by growth, and how it can 'trickle down' only when boosted by redistributive mechanisms. A problem is only a problem when it is recognised as such; thereafter, a problem might only be solved when policymakers feel public pressure. Without such influential news media commentary, the pursuit of traditional growth is unchallenged, redistribution is marginalised or more often completely ignored and, as a consequence, inequality prevails.

It seems appropriate, since metaphors are common within growth discourse, to use one in conclusion. Galbraith's conceptualisation of the failure of 'trickle down' concerned the "horse and sparrow". If the horse is fed enough oats, he suggests, "some will pass through onto the road to feed the sparrow" (Palley, 2012, p. 138). Instead, within our prevailing economic system, it seems the horse will continue to retain almost everything, and the way that these two large mainstream news providers present economic growth is unlikely to be interpreted as advocating any alternative.

Notes

1   Lewis (2015) and Monbiot (2015b) quote the author's research showing that in a large sample of BBC and ITV broadcast news from 2014, there was more coverage about the 2007 disappearance of British toddler Madeleine McCann than there was about the environment.
2   A Gini coefficient of 0 means everyone in a defined population have identical incomes. A rating of 1 means that one person receives all of the total available income.
3   As part of a wider content analysis of BBC and ITV late evening (10pm) bulletins, of the 5,414 news stories identified in 2014, only 28 contained traces of 'income inequality'. Of these, in only four stories was the issue central to the report.
4   The transcript is available at www.cbsnews.com/news/obamas-2014-state-of-the-union-address-full-text/
5   The full transcript of this interview is at http://news.bbc.co.uk/1/shared/bsp/hi/pdfs/0806201402.pdf

References

Atkinson, A. 2014. *Inequality: What can be done?* Cambridge, MA: Harvard University Press.
BBC. 2016. *UK economic growth confirmed at 0.5%.* [Online]. Available at: www.bbc.co.uk/news/business-35657308 [Accessed 6 March 2016].
Belfield, C., Cribb, J., Hood, A., and Joyce, R. 2015. *Living standards, poverty and inequality in the UK: 2015.* London: Institute for Fiscal Studies. [Online] Available at: www.ifs.org.uk/uploads/publications/comms/R107.pdf *p32/33* [Accessed 14 March 2016].
Blanchflower, D., and Machin, S. 2014. *Unless economic growth is more fairly distributed and productivity boosted, the typical UK worker can expect meagre real wage growth.* [Online]. Available at: http://blogs.lse.ac.uk/politicsandpolicy/falling-real-wages/ [Accessed on 7 March 2016].
Chakrabortty, A. 2015. *The £93bn handshake: businesses pocket huge subsidies and tax breaks.* [Online]. Available at: www.theguardian.com/politics/2015/jul/07/corporate-welfare-a-93bn-handshake [Accessed 13 March 2016].
Charles-Coll, J. 2011. 'Understanding income inequality: Concept, causes and Measurement'. *International Journal of Economics and Management Science*, 1(3), pp. 17–28.

Childs. A. 2015. *How the other 1% lives: wealth gap not the only way in which global elite is taking advantage.* [Online]. Available at: https://theconversation.com/how-the-other-1-lives-wealth-gap-not-the-only-way-in-which-global-elite-is-taking-advantage-53400 [Accessed 23rd February 2016].

Davis, A. 2015. Financial insider talk in the City of London. In: Murdock, G. and Gripsrud, J. (eds.), *Money talks: Media, markets, crisis.* Bristol: Intellect. pp. 31–43.

De Ville, F., and Orbie, J. 2014. 'The European Commission's neoliberal trade discourse since the crisis: Legitimizing continuity through subtle discursive change'. *British Journal of Politics and International Relations,* 16(1), pp. 149–167.

Dobson, A., and Read, R. 2015. *We must let go of this "trickle down" nonsense once and for all.* [Online]. Available at: www.theguardian.com/sustainable-business/2015/mar/23/growth-inequality-society-commons-commodification-happiness [Accessed on 7 March 2016].

Dorling, D. 2014. *Inequality and the 1%.* London: Verso.

Erjavec, K., Erjavec, E., and Juvancic, L. 2008. 'New wine in old Bottles: Critical discourse analysis of the current common EU agricultural policy reform agenda'. *Sociologia Ruralis,* 49(1), pp. 41–55.

Giddens, A. 2004. 'We can and should take action if the earnings of the rich set them apart at society'. *New Statesman.* 27th September 2013, pp. 50–53.

Grimshaw, D., and Rubery, J. 2012. Reinforcing neoliberalism: crisis and austerity in the UK. In: Lehndorff, S. (ed.), *A Triumph of failed ideas: European models of capitalism in the crisis.* Brussels: European Trade Union Institute. pp. 41–58.

Hansen, J. et al. 2015. Ice melt, sea level rise and superstorms: evidence at paleoclimate data, climate modeling, and modern observations that 2 C global warming is highly dangerous. *Atmospheric chemistry and physics.* [Online]. Available at: www.atmos-chem-phys-discuss.net/acp-2015-432/ [Accessed 16 March 2016].

Hoggart, S. 2012. *Nick Clegg plays the John Lewis card among the City's 'have-yachts'.* [Online]. Available at: www.theguardian.com/politics/2012/jan/16/nick-clegg-john-lewis-yachts [Accessed 15 October 2013].

Hopkins, K. 2009. *Public must learn to 'tolerate the inequality' of bonuses, says Goldman Sachs vice-chairman.* [Online]. Available at: www.theguardian.com/business/2009/oct/21/executive-pay-bonuses-goldmansachs [Accessed on 28 February 2016].

Huckin, T. 1997. Critical discourse analysis. In: Miller, T. (ed.), *Functional approaches to written text.* Washington, DC: US Department of State. pp. 78–92.

Jackson, T., and Victor, P. 2014. *Does slow growth increase inequality? Some reflections on Piketty's 'fundamental' laws of capitalism.* PASSAGE Working Paper 14/01. Guildford: University of Surrey. [Online]. Available at: www.prosperitas.org.uk/assets/does-slow-growth-increase-inequality – paper.pdf [Accessed 13th March 2016].

Jenkins, S. 1996. 'Recent trends in the UK income distribution'. *Oxford Review of Economic Policy,* 12(1), pp. 29–46.

Kay, J., and Salter, L. 2014. 'Framing the cuts: An analysis of the BBC's discursive framing of the ConDem cuts agenda'. *Journalism,* 15(6), pp. 754–772.

Kleinnijenhuis, J., Schultz, F., Oegema, D., and van Atteveldt, W. 2013. 'Financial news and market panics in the age of high-frequency sentiment trading algorithms'. *Journalism* 14(2), pp. 271–291.

Lewis, J. 2015. *Cycle of silence: The strange case of disappearing environmental issues.* [Online]. Available at: http://theconversation.com/cycle-of-silence-the-strange-case-of-disappearing-environmental-issues-36306 [Accessed on 7 March 2016].

Lewis, J., and Thomas, R. 2015. More of the same: News, economic growth and the recycling of conventional wisdom. In: Murdock, G. and Gripsrud. J. (eds.), *Money talks: Media, markets, crisis.* Bristol: Intellect. pp. 83–99.

Lugo-Ocando. J. 2014. *Blaming the Victim: How global journalism fails those in poverty*. 1st ed. London: Pluto Press.

Lynch, J., Smith, G., Harper, S., 'Hillemeier, M., and Ross, N. 2004. Is income inequality a determinant of population? Part 1. A systematic review'. *Milbank Quarterly*, 82(1), pp. 5–99.

Mason, R. 2016. *Disability benefit cuts could see 500,000 people lose £150 a week*. [Online]. Available at: www.theguardian.com/society/2016/mar/12/disability-benefit-cuts-could-see 500000-people-lose-150-a-week [Accessed 5 April 2016].

McGuigan, J. 2005. 'Neo-liberalism, culture and policy'. *International Journal of Cultural Policy* 11(3), pp. 229–241.

McKendrick, J., Sinclair, S., Irwin, A., O'Donnell, H., Scott, G., and Dobbie, L. 2008. *The media, poverty and public opinion in the UK*. New York: Joseph Rowntree.

Monbiot, G. 2015a. *Disinventing democracy*. [Online]. Available from: www.monbiot. com/2015/07/08/3796/ [Accessed on 28 February 2016].

Monbiot, G. 2015b. *Our impartial broadcasters have become mouthpieces of the elite*. [Online]. Available at: www.theguardian.com/commentisfree/2015/jan/20/broadcasters-mouth pieces-of-elite-balanced-news-journalists [Accessed on 28 February 2016].

NASA. 2013. *NASA scientists react to 400ppm carbon milestones*. [Online]. Available from: http://climate.nasa.gov/400ppmquotes/ [Accessed 13 March 2016].

Organisation for Economic Co-operation and Development (OECD). 2014. *Focus on Inequality and Growth December 2014*. [Online]. Available at: www.oecd.org/social/Focus-Inequality-and-Growth-2014.pdf [Accessed 13th March 2016].

Palley, T. 2012. *From financial crisis to stagnation: The destruction of shared prosperity and the role of economics*. New York: Cambridge University Press.

Picard, R. 2015. Understanding the crisis. In: Picard, R. (ed.), *The Euro crisis in the news: Journalistic coverage of the economic crisis and European institutions*. Oxford: Reuters Institute for the Study of Journalism, pp. 1–15.

Piketty, T. 2014. *Capital in the twenty-first century*. Cambridge, MA: The Belknap Press of Harvard University Press.

Plunkett, J. 2016. *BBC News most trusted source for more than half of people in the UK*. [Online]. Available at: www.theguardian.com/media/2016/mar/10/bbc-news-most-trusted-source-for-more-than-half-of-people-in-the-uk [Accessed 14 March 2016].

Schifferes, S. 2011. *The future of financial journalism in the age of austerity*. London: City University London. [Online]. Available at: www.city.ac.uk/__data/assets/pdf_file/0016/151063/The-Future-of-Financial-Journalism-in-the-Age-of-Austerity.pdf [Accessed 10 March 2015].

Schifferes, S., and Knowles, S. 2015. The British media and the "first crisis of globalization". In: Schifferes, V., and Roberts, R. (eds.), *The media and financial crises*. London; New York: Routledge. pp. 42–58.

Schmidt, S. 2000. 'Only an agenda setter? The European Commission's power over the Council of Ministers', *European Union Politics*, 1(1), pp. 37–61.

Schui, F. 2014. *Austerity: The great failure*. New Haven, CT: Yale University Press.

Sikka, P. 2015. *Davos delegates don't care about inequality or your debt*. [Online]. Available at: https://theconversation.com/davos-delegates-dont-care-about-inequality-or-your-debt-36511 [Accessed 13 March 2016].

Snowdon, B. 2006. 'The Enduring Elixir of Economic Growth'. *World Economics*, 7(1), pp. 73–130.

Stiglitz, E. 2013. *The price of inequality*. London: Penguin Books.

Tabb, W. 2003. 'Dubois vs. Neoliberalism'. *Monthly Review*, 55(6), pp. 33–40.

Taylor, S. 2004. 'Researching educational policy and change in 'new times': Using critical discourse analysis'. *Journal of Education Policy*, 19(4), pp. 433–451.

Thomas, R. 2016. 'I think it's absolutely exorbitant!' How UK television news reported the shareholder vote on executive remuneration at Barclays in 2012'. *Critical Discourse Studies*, 13(1), pp. 94–117.

Torre, R., and Myrskylä, M. 2013. 'Income inequality and population: a panel data analysis on 21 developed countries'. *Population Studies: A Journal of Demography*, 68(1), pp. 1–13.

Turnbull, P., and Wass, V. 2010. Earnings in equality and employment. In: Blyton, P., Heery, E., and Turnbull, P. (eds.), *Reassessing the employment relationship: Management, work and organisations*. Basingstoke: Palgrave Macmillan. pp. 273–298.

Walsh, C. 2015. Stating support or the city: Thirty years of budget talk. In: Murdock, V., and Gripsrud, J. (eds.), *Money talks: Media, markets, crisis*. Bristol: Intellect. pp. 67–78.

Watt, N. 2013. *Boris Johnson invokes Thatcher spirit with greed is good speech*. [Online]. Available at: www.theguardian.com/politics/2013/nov/27/boris-johnson-thatcher-greed-good [Accessed 13 October 2013].

Whittaker, M. 2013. *Squeezed Britain 2013*. [Online]. Available at: www.resolutionfoundation.org/publications/squeezed-britain-2013/ [Accessed 13 March 2016].

Wilkinson, R., and Pickett, K. 2010. *The spirit level: Why equality is better for everyone*. London: Penguin.

Williams, L. 2014. *I wish I was exaggerating, but it's true – 2014 has been a year of unprecedented inequality*. [Online] Available at: www.independent.co.uk/voices/comment/i-wish-i-was-exaggerating-but-its-true – 2014-has-been-a-year-of-unprecedented-inequality-9948 803.html [Accessed on 28 February 2016].

World Economic Forum. 2014. *Global risks 2014*. [Online]. Available at: http://www3.weforum.org/docs/WEF_GlobalRisks_Report_2014.pdf [Accessed 1 March 2013].

5

THE 'GEDDES AXE'

The press and Britain's first austerity drive

Richard Roberts

The anti-waste campaign: the Thanet by-election

It was the press barons of Britain who launched the campaign against waste and extravagant government spending.

"From first to last I told the electors there was but one issue – the financial position of the country and the need to put a stop to financial waste and extravagance" declared Esmond Harmsworth, the victor in a sensational by-election in November 1919. "I attribute my victory to the determination on the part of the people of Thanet to see that financial waste and extravagance are stopped".[1] "Mr Harmsworth First Anti-Waste M.P.", trumpeted the *Daily Mirror*, hailing his victory as "Thanet's Clear Verdict on Spendthrift Issues". Harmsworth was the son of press baron Lord Rothermere, owner of the *Daily Mirror* (circulation 1m); and a nephew of Lord Northcliffe, owner of the *Daily Mail,* the world's biggest selling newspaper (1.5m), and *The Times* (113,000), the establishment's paper of record (Jeffrey, 1987, p. 29)

The term 'anti-waste' made its debut in the press on 27 August 1919 as the signature of a letter to the editor of the *Daily Mail* attacking the alleged profligacy of a coalition minister – ironically, in light of his later role, Sir Eric Geddes. Then on 21 October it appeared simultaneously, and presumably not by accident, in articles in the *Daily Mirror, Daily Mail* and *The Times* reporting that Harmsworth had thrown his hat into the ring in the forthcoming Thanet by-election as an 'anti-waste' independent candidate. With the Harmsworth press stable backing him, the local Conservative Association hastened to adopt Harmsworth as their candidate. At twenty-one he was the youngest MP.

Lloyd George's post-war administration was a coalition between his Coalition Liberals and the Conservatives led by Andrew Bonar Law. In the General Election of December 1918 the coalition won a landslide victory with a combined total of

506 seats (379 Conservatives and 127 Coalition Liberals). The significant opposition parties numbered 57 Labour and 36 Independent Liberals, temporarily bereft of their leader, Herbert Asquith, who lost his seat. The lop-sided coalition was uneasy and ultimately unstable, with the level of government expenditure, taxation and government debt matters of mounting discontent among Conservatives in the House and the country.

The public finances – expenditure, taxation and debt

The First World War transformed Britain's public finances in a variety of ways that generated new problems and tensions. On the eve of war, central government expenditure was £198m (Table 5.1). Spending soared during the hostilities, peaking in fiscal year 1917–18 at £2.7bn – 14 times higher than pre-war (7-fold taking account of wartime inflation). With the end of fighting, central government expenditure declined as a result of mass demobilisation and falling military spending. But the peace dividend was offset by rising expenditure on post-war 'Reconstruction' – social provision, notably housing and education – and overseas peace-keeping. By 1921–22 spending had fallen to £1.1bn (including £340m of debt interest) but this was still six times higher than the pre-war level. Government spending pre-war was 8 per cent of Gross Domestic Product (GDP). By 1917–18, the last full year of fighting, the ratio was 55 per cent – a 6.5-fold rise on the pre-war level. In 1921–22, after four years of peace, it was still 27 per cent, 3.5 times the pre-war level and unprecedented in Britain in peacetime.

Before the war, government revenues and expenditures roughly balanced. Between 1915 and 1920, however, there was a large budgetary shortfall that peaked at £2bn in 1917–18; over these years the aggregate of deficits totalled £7.2bn. This was despite substantial increases in revenue from taxation, principally direct tax – 80 per cent of the total by 1918. Government revenue from income tax rose from £45m in 1913 to £394m in 1921, a 9-fold increase (5-fold inflation-adjusted). The standard rate of income tax increased 5-fold from 6 per cent in 1913 to 30 per cent in 1919, at which level it remained until the 1922 budget. High earners additionally paid super-tax, which by 1920 reached 30 per cent – meaning for them an overall income tax rate of 60 per cent (Morgan 1952, p. 94). Contemporary economist

TABLE 5.1 Central government expenditure, 1913–1922

Financial year	£bn	% of GDP
1913–14	0.2	8
1917–18	2.7	55
1918–19	2.6	50
1919–20	1.7	30
1920–21	1.2	26
1921–22	1.1	27

Source: Mitchell (1988)

Henry Higgs calculated that Britain's taxation per head of population had risen from £18 per annum in 1919, to £22 in 1920, and £24 in 1921; "we are", he protested, "the most heavily taxed community in the world" (Higgs, 1922, pp. 251–2).

The threshold for payment of income tax was lowered from £160 to £130 per year in 1915 (Daunton, 1996 p. 889). The reduction, in conjunction with wartime price and wage inflation of around 25 per cent a year, led to a 5-fold mushrooming in the number of earners eligible to pay income tax from 1.2 million in 1913 to 5.7 million in 1918 (2.2 million were relieved by allowances or rebates). The explosion in the ranks of income tax payers during the war meant that direct taxation affected all middle-class families and many working-class households; the direct tax burden and the scale and value-for-money of government expenditure became mass concerns and politically significant as never before with the advent in 1918 of universal male suffrage and votes for women aged 30 and older.

The budgetary shortfalls were bridged by massive borrowing at home and abroad. In 1913 Britain's national debt was £700m (31 per cent of GDP); in 1920 it was up 11-fold at £7.9bn. Massive borrowing and indebtedness were common features of Britain's three big wars, the French Wars, 1792–1815; the First World War, 1914–18; and the Second World War, 1939–45, that resulted in peaks of postwar debt to GDP ratios of, respectively, 260 per cent, 182 per cent and 238 per cent (Bank of England, 2017). Debt at these levels was crippling and unsustainable and austerity or 'economy', in one form or another, was a feature of post-war economic management (Crafts, 2012). After Waterloo the ratio was gradually brought down by budget surpluses to 25 per cent by 1913. Following the First World War government and business again saw budget surpluses as key to a return to fiscal sustainability, though now in the context of mass democracy and a vibrant popular press.

Waste and anti-waste

During the war it was the business of admirals and generals to win battles, not to economise. "'Hang the expense and get on with the war' was a phrase constantly in the mouths of civil and military authorities", observed Higgs, an authority on public finance (Higgs, 1922, p. 252). "Some of the general relief at the Armistice was due to the hope that we should at last see an end of reckless extravagance and get back to rational expenditure", he continued. 'Waste' in various forms was a prominent issue in wartime and afterwards.[2] During the war a government campaign addressed the issue of 'food waste' because of Britain's heavy reliance on imported foodstuffs; from spring 1917 waste of food was punishable by a £100 fine or six months' imprisonment.[3] With the lifting of wartime censorship, sensational stories about government waste during and after the war appeared in the press from spring 1919. In May *The Economist* expressed outrage at the "orgies of extravagance and waste that seem to have been the rule rather than the exception in most of the great spending departments".[4] Prompted by, as *The Times* put it, the "great public outcry against Government extravagance" the Prime Minister issued a letter to government departments demanding economy.[5]

The ups and downs of the *Daily Mirror's* concern about waste from the end of the war to the mid-1920s can be tracked by counting the number of pages on which the word 'waste' appeared in the newspaper each month (Table 5.2). In the first nine months of 1919 the count averaged 18 pages a month. But in October and November, the months of Esmond Harmsworth's by-election campaign, it was 60. The page count then fell to some 25 from December 1919 to November 1920. But in December 1920 and January 1921 it soared to 82 – the peak – and then averaged 55 through to July 1921. The count fell back to 28 a month in the latter half of 1921, and averaged 27 in 1922 and 20 in 1923; by 1925 mentions were sparse. The chronological incidence of the word 'waste' was similar in the *Daily Mail*, *The Times* and the *Manchester Guardian*. All in all, the word counts identify two peaks of press interest in 'waste': October–November 1919, at the time of the Thanet by-election; and December 1920–July 1921, between the Dover by-election and the appointment of an inquiry into national expenditure – the Geddes committee.

On 3 August 1919, Lord Rothermere issued a wake-up call regarding the nation''s "perilous financial situation" in the *Sunday Pictorial*, one of his press titles that he used as a personal mouthpiece. It was the first of twenty-five such broadsides over the following eighteen months. They were published as a book, *Solvency or Downfall? Squandermania and its Story* in June 1921; the dedication was to his son Esmond Harmsworth M.P. "My purpose," Rothermere explained, "was to arouse both the nation and the Government to a perception of the economic calamities which must ensue if our public expenditure is not brought into closer relation with our diminished resources" (Rothermere, 1921, pp. vii–x).

Charles Palmer another, 'anti-waste' independent, won the by-election at Wrekin, Shropshire, in January 1920.[6] "Vast crowds cheer anti-waste leader" reported the *Daily Mirror* on the arrival in Westminster of Herbert Asquith, victor in the March 1920 Paisley by-election.[7] "We have given up hoping that the Government of Wasters will mend its ways" protested a "Woman Voter" hailing the return of the Independent Liberals leader, Lloyd George's arch antagonist.[8] Responding to the anti-waste clamour, Lloyd George appointed a parliamentary select committee to review public spending and report "what, if any, economies . . . may be effected

TABLE 5.2 Occurrence of the word 'waste' in pages of the *Daily Mirror*, 1919–1923

Period	Average number of mentions per month
1919 Jan – 1919 Sep	18
1919 Oct – 1919 Nov	60
1919 Dec – 1920 Nov	25
1920 Dec – 1921 Jan	82
1921 Feb – 1921 Jul	55
1921 Aug – 1921 Dec	28
1922 Jan – 1911 Dec	27
1923 Jan – 1923 Dec	20

Source: *Daily Mirror*

therein."[9] This backfired – its report in June 1920 fuelled the "rising tide of anger in the country against the prodigious scale of Government expenditure".[10] The Federation of British Industries responded by proposing the establishment of a "Council of independent men selected for their wide financial or business experience" to review Britain''s taxable capacity and public expenditure – possibly the origin of the idea for the Geddes committee.[11]

Anti-waste league and by-elections

Colonel Sir Thomas Polson, an independent, scored a further by-election victory for anti-waste at Dover in January 1921. The Dover result persuaded Rothermere that the moment had come to establish an Anti-Waste League to assist independent anti-waste candidates to fight parliamentary by-elections.[12] Esmond became chairman, Ernest Outhwaite, Rothermere's personal assistant and secretary, and the League, adopted a "miniature axe for the button-hole" as its badge. "The League takes its stand on the contention that none of the existing parties have shown any clear consciousness of the grave financial plight into which the country is drifting", Rothermere wrote in the *Sunday Pictorial* in January 1921. "There is only one way of financial salvation, and that is the old British way, through the use of the vote. The purpose of the Anti-Waste League is to organise the vote".

"I rejoice to know that the Anti-Waste League is finding enthusiastic support among women", observed Rothermere. "I think it is quite possible that before very long the women members will be the mainstay of the League." The strong support of women for anti-waste had been noted at the Thanet and Dover by-elections. At Thanet it was estimated that 75 per cent exercised their new right to vote, substantially in support of Harmsworth and anti-waste. "Waste and extravagance affects every home and every housewife," commented the *Daily Mirror*. "The Anti-Waste League is the very first organisation to realise the overwhelming importance of the women''s vote, and to invite women to take a leading part in its work", stated Rothermere. "The young men won the War. The women must win the peace".

A revolt by Conservative backbenchers in February 1921 over Supplementary Estimates (additional non-budgeted spending) brought the coalition "unpleasantly near defeat" with its huge majority cut to just ten.[13] Soon after in March, Bonar Law resigned as Conservative leader because of ill-health. His place was taken by Austen Chamberlain, the Chancellor since January 1919. The new Chancellor, Sir Robert Horne, instilled a new resolve at the Treasury to address the public finances' wartime legacy: in May 1921 the spending departments were set the goal of reducing their expenditure from £603 million to £490 million in the forthcoming budget for 1922–23.[14]

The campaign against squandermania was in full flight in Summer 1921. In June an Anti-Waste League–backed candidate was victorious in a by-election at St George's, Westminster. "I won because the whole country demands economy", declared the victor. Shortly afterwards another anti-waste candidate won a by-election at Hertford. Lloyd George and Chamberlain, the Coalition leaders, were increasingly alarmed at anti-waste's electoral appeal (Morgan, 1979, p. 245). With the recession ever grimmer, the social reform programme, and specifically its key liberal figure, Christopher Addison, Minister of Health, had become political liabilities. Addison, the anti-waste campaigners' *bete noire*, was responsible for the administration's 'Homes for Heroes' public housing programme. This was repeatedly scaled back and in June Addison was demoted and his ministerial salary axed. His resignation personified the end of the government's social reform programme, reflecting the new reality that the Reconstruction programme had become both financially and politically unaffordable.

Among Lloyd George's guests at Chequers for the weekend of 2–3 July 1921 was Sir Eric Geddes, Minister of Transport. Geddes had been intending to return to the private sector but he acceded to an appeal from the Prime Minister to undertake a final service for him – the conduct of "an 'economy campaign' in government departments" (Riddell, 1933, p. 303; Stevenson, 1971, p. 225). "The fact is," commented Herbert Fisher, President of the Board of Education and the cabinet's other leading liberal and social reformer, in his diary, "the PM is dead tired & wants to throw a sop to anti-waste before the recess" (Fisher, 2006, p. 791). The sop was the Committee on National Expenditure (Geddes committee), whose establishment was principally a result of the economy campaign waged by and through the press.

The 'Geddes Axe'

A proposal for the establishment of a 'strong independent committee' to make recommendations for cuts in public expenditure was put to the cabinet by the Chancellor on 2 August. He mentioned the "meagre results" of previous appeals to the spending departments for economies and that there was "very little prospect of achieving this by the ordinary departmental methods".[15] Horne's proposal provoked "considerable discussion" in cabinet. The various objections boiled down to opposition to "irresponsible outside business men" trespassing on the affairs of "responsible ministers." Horne countered that the committee would be purely advisory and that no new doctrine was involved – the appointment of outside expert advisers was customary. Horne and Lloyd George got their way, but Winston Churchill, Colonial Secretary, dissented.

Geddes, a railway chief executive, was brought into government by Lloyd George in 1915 to sort out small-arms production (Grieves, 1989). After that he transformed military transportation on the Western Front and then Atlantic merchant shipping. To provide him with military authority he was made a Major-General and then a Vice-Admiral. Geddes's appointment to the War Cabinet in 1917 necessitated him becoming an MP. After the war he was given responsibility for demobilisation and then for the creation of a Ministry of Transport, restructuring Britain's railway system. He now headed a five-strong committee of businessmen to review public expenditure: the press dubbed the exercise the 'Geddes Axe'.

The Geddes committee's basic method was to compare pre-war expenditures in 1913–14 with 1921–22 (Burrows, 2009, pp. 205–11). Was the difference explained by new demands or was it waste? For each item of expenditure the minimum level of service or output required was identified. Then an estimate was made of the resources necessary to achieve that result, which was compared with actual expenditure. Benchmarking was used to provide yardsticks of best practice and to suggest opportunities for economy by outsourcing. The reports contained colourful examples of waste and mismanagement. Close attention was paid to the potential of new technologies to make savings. The much-increased state expenditure during and after the war on social measures was queried by the Committee. Its challenges reflected the traditional views of the members regarding the role of the state in social provision.

The Geddes committee delivered its findings in three 'interim' reports. The first report, submitted on 14 December 1921, covered the biggest spending departments – the 'fighting services' (army, navy and air force) and 'social services' (education, health, labour and pensions).[16] The second, 28 January 1922, dealt principally with police and prisons, trade support and agricultural support; and the third, 21 February 1922, government administration, including revenue departments, parliament, works and buildings, stationery office, foreign office and colonial office.[17]

In total the reports identified £86m of expenditure cuts (Table 5.3). In addition it was expected that the sitting Washington Conference on multilateral naval arms limitation would contribute a further £14m, achieving the Chancellor's £100m target. Military expenditure bore £60.5m of the total proposed cuts, with the navy contributing the lion's share, £34m; army, £20m; and air force, £5.5m, mostly through reductions in manpower and stores.

The other large proposed spending cut was on education – £18m. Central government expenditure on education had risen from £17m in 1913–14 to £54m in 1921–22 principally as a result of the 1918 Education Act that extended and enhanced provision, and soaring salary costs. The Geddes committee took the view that government expenditure on education (plus £43m from local taxation) was exceeding what the country could afford.[18] It advocated raising the primary school entry age from 5 to 6, larger class sizes, reductions in grants for secondary

TABLE 5.3 Geddes Report: proposed cuts and Cabinet-endorsed cuts

	Geddes Report–proposed cuts £m	Cabinet-endorsed cuts £m
Navy (incl. Washington Conference)	35	24
Army	20	14.5
Air force	5.5	3
Education	18	6.5
Other items	21.5	19
Total	100	67

Source: 'The Geddes Report', *Economist*, 18 February 1922.

and university education, and contributory pensions. It expressed astonishment at teachers' anomalous non-contributory pensions and the level of pay that had been fixed reflecting wartime inflation. In aggregate the Geddes reports proposed military and education cuts amounting to £78.5m; much smaller amounts from a large number of other departments summed to the further £21.5m.

Publication and the press

Press speculation about the Geddes committee's proposals was rife from mid-December 1921, with a growing clamour for publication. The delay in publication was largely due to consideration of the recommendations by three sub-committees of ministers that were charged with reporting on different aspects to the Cabinet. Many people had sight of the reports, and their contents leaked; as early as 12 December the *Manchester Guardian* reported a rumoured £20m of education cuts.[19] Speculation shifted from the content to the reasons for the delay in publication. Fisher, Education Minister, found his father-in-law "very suspicious about the non-publication of the Geddes Report. I endeavoured but unsuccessfully to assure him that there was no Machiavellian design" (Fisher, 2006, p. 899). *The Times* warned of a "plot to torpedo the Geddes Report".[20] "Strong public pressure" and the imminent resumption of parliament after the Christmas recess prompted the cabinet to sanction publication on Monday 6 February 1922.[21] "Axe intrigue fails" declared *The Times* reporting immediate publication of the reports "intact and unburdened with the comments of the Cabinet Committees".[22]

Publication of the first two reports on Friday 10 February generated great interest in the press and the public. HMSO sold out within hours and had to reprint several times; with sales topping 10,000 copies it was a best-seller.[23] *Punch* congratulated the government on its discovery of a hitherto untapped source of public revenue.[24] Higgs observed that the reports had a "wonderful reception . . . previous criticisms were forgotten and the Report and its authors were covered with great approval" (Higgs, 1922, p. 254) while *The Economist* noted that it "has been received with both wild approbation and qualified criticism, but in no quarter has it met with general condemnation".[25]

The Harmsworth titles welcomed the Geddes cuts. "There is an immense amount of meat on this Geddes joint and all is excellent", commented the *Daily Mail*, and called for "some sanity and economy in our education policy . . . The only unfavourable criticism we can make of an otherwise invaluable work is that they do not go far enough".[26] The *Daily Mirror* praised the "ability, penetration and courage of the compilers", while reminding readers that "fact by fact, figure by figure the Report echoes the recommendations made over and over again by Lord Rothermere in his articles in the *Daily Mirror* and the *Sunday Pictorial*".[27] Other Conservative-supporting papers praised the reports as "extraordinarily able, sincere and searching" (*Evening Standard*), "among the greatest State papers of modern times" (*Pall Mall Gazette*), "unique in our history" (*Daily Express*), "the more we look at the Geddes Report the better we like it" (*Evening News*), though the *Daily Telegraph* observed regarding education that "there are economies which in the long run prove the grossest of extravagances".[28] Liberal papers applauded economy but condemned the suggested education cuts: "we are out and out with them in the main . . . [but] the proposals regarding education must be rejected without compromise" (*Observer*), "the cuts in the three fighting services are, in the main, good . . . [but] . . . in the matter of education the Geddes Committee is at its worst" (*Manchester Guardian*). For Labour"s *Daily Herald* the "attack on excessive military and naval expenditure" was "admirable" but the social services cuts were "grotesquely foolish and wasteful", while the *Morning Post* at the other end of the political spectrum, the mouthpiece of the Tory "diehards", condemned "the sacrifice of the Fighting Services to the maintenance, upon a slightly reduced scale, of the new bureaucracy" and the £100m a year "wasted" on education.[29]

Admiralty hoists the "Jolly Roger"

The report's hurried publication occurred ahead of consideration of the sub-committee reports by the cabinet, which did not begin until 15 February. This provided an opportunity to influence the decision by mobilising opposition through the press. Along with the Report, newspapers received a "breezy" rebuttal by the Admiralty stating that the Committee's recommendations were "based on a serious misconception of the requirements of our naval organisation" and taking particular exception to criticisms of the navy's "lavish" manpower levels.[30] Rothermere's *Daily Mirror* accused the Admiralty of hoisting "a sort of 'Jolly Roger'".[31]

It was soon revealed that the author of the 'calculated indiscretion' was the junior Admiralty minister, Leo Amery, who was in charge since the senior minister was attending the Washington Conference.[32] At the 6 February cabinet, ministers had been given leave to publicly correct factual inaccuracies in the report.[33] Amery recalled that:

> I saw my opportunity . . . I hurried back to the Admiralty and saw Beatty [First Sea Lord], who agreed with me that we should lose not a moment in issuing our rejoinder simultaneously with the Report itself. Otherwise the whole Press would commit itself irretrievably to the theory of Admiralty wastefulness. By getting our blow in first we might get some active support from the outset, while even the least friendly papers might hesitate to condemn the Admiralty outright. . . .
>
> We sat down and, working at top speed for the next couple of hours, produced some 3,600 words of counterblast, couched, much of it, I confess, in some of my best controversial style. This reached the papers and Parliament together with the Report and was, I strongly suspect, read first by most of the journalists avid for a sensation.
>
> They had their sensation all right. What was more important, we got the effect we wanted. Some papers backed us straight away. None, even the

most violent 'anti-wasters', attempted to controvert our argument. Instead they launched out on my insubordination, as a Junior Minister, in venturing to torpedo the great Report. . . . Friendlier papers applauded the "Nelson touch". The Cabinet, as surprised as the public, began by being shocked, and even talking of my dismissal . . . Finally the humour of the situation, as well as the strength of my case, won the day.

Barnes & Nicolson, 1980

Lloyd George summoned Amery to Chequers and Chamberlain sent him a "very stuffy reprimand", but the Coalition leaders balked from dismissal for fear of exacerbating government disarray (Amery, 1953, p. 220).[34] Behind Amery, it was believed in the press, was Churchill who regarded the navy cuts "with obvious contempt and ranges himself with the Admiralty's protest".[35] Instead Chamberlain announced the publication of the Admiralty's broadside as a White Paper "for the House"'s information" being greeted by "palpably incredulous laughter".[36]

Education cuts campaign and 'the shopkeeper's calculus'

A public campaign against the rumoured education cuts had gotten underway well before the Admiralty's 'bombshell'.[37] Fisher discussed the possibility of reductions in teachers' salaries as an outcome of the Geddes review with the National Union of Teachers (NUT) on 15 November 1921 (Fisher, 2006, p. 849). By mid-December the correspondence columns of newspapers were full of protests against 'cuts' to education spending. Fisher, the architect of the 1918 Education Act and an ardent educationalist, received the Geddes Report on 21 December; "18 million cut in Education!" was his horrified diary entry (Fisher, 2006, p. 863). His officials estimated that retrenchment on the scale recommended would involve either the dismissal of 43,000 teachers or a "drastic" cut in salaries, or some combination thereof.[38] Fisher refused to accept the "sweeping and violent reductions" and determined that £6m of cuts was as far as he was prepared to go (Fisher, 2006, p. 863). If the cabinet decided on more he would resign.

The NUT Executive had already begun to mobilise; on 12 December it sent a circular to local associations asking them to pay their 1922 subscriptions early to provide a fighting fund. "The battle of the educational interests of the country against the rumoured recommendation of the Geddes Economy Committee was begun here today", *The Times* reported on 3 January 1922 from the annual conference of the National Union of Women Teachers in Manchester.[39] Welcoming delegates, Manchester's Director of Education "sounded the alarm" against the "keen insistent attack on education".

In early January the NUT Executive urged local associations to encourage the union's 115,000 members to participate in elections in support of "candidates in favour of the maintenance and support of Education irrespective of their party political views . . . the issue being between Education and obscurantism, advance and retrogression".[40] It issued a list of questions for parliamentary candidates. Local associations applauded the Executive's resistance.[41] Accounts of teachers' protest meetings proliferated in the liberal press. The *New Statesman* reported that teachers' organisations were raising special funds and setting aside money from their reserves "for the struggle" and that the Workers' Educational Association had inaugurated a national protest campaign.[42] The Prime Minister, just back from the Cannes Conference on reparations, and with much else on his plate, decided against cuts to teachers' salaries much to Fisher's relief, though he recorded in his diary on 24 January that he was "profoundly depressed" (Fisher, 2006, p. 894).

Lloyd George met teachers' leaders on 2 February and appealed for "a contribution to help the Nation" (Fisher, 2006, p. 902). But the NUT Executive was determined "to resist any education 'cuts'"; it launched its own 'National Campaign' of protest meetings, organised the provision of speakers for its local associations, and undertook the placement of 'special articles' in the press.[43] It also produced a "very large quantity of propaganda literature", notably a widely circulated pamphlet entitled *This Critical Year*.[44] Alderman Conway of Bradford, a member of the NUT Executive, was one of the most active speakers addressing 50 protest meetings; he told an audience at the London School of Economics that "if people will only agitate enough the Government will give way".[45] Ministers were inundated with representations from teachers' organisations, as well as a protest by 124 Oxford professors, fellows and heads of colleges (Fisher, 2006, p. 883).

There was much denunciation of the businessmen authors of the proposed education cuts among in high-brow weeklies. *Nineteenth Century and After* declared:

> The English philistine not merely suspects, he really dislikes, education. We should have had men to conduct this inquiry who would be able to discriminate between education and . . . cheese or butcher's meat. Instead of this we have had average English Philistines to whom education was just a commodity like everything else.[46]

Even the *Spectator*, a staunch critic of "the curse of high taxation and expenditure", called cuts in primary education "the falsest of false economies".[47] The *New Statesman* derided the Geddes Committee"'s economising as "the shopkeepers" calculus".[48]

Hard on the heels of publication of the Geddes Report came by-elections in two coalition-held constituencies. Fired by "high indignation" teachers "inundated" the challenger Labour candidates with offers of help. In London a meeting of 2,000 members of the National Association of Schoolmasters "decided to go to the by-election in Camberwell where there was one man with an axe and another with a shield".[49] "They were going to fight for the man with the shield no matter what his politics were".[50] "The government have declared war on the teachers" said the Labour agent, "and the teachers are going over the top in North Camberwell".[51] So too at Clayton, Manchester, where 'the publication of the Geddes Committee's report could not have fallen at a more advantageous time for Labour'.[52] Labour romped home in both seats; Charles Ammon, the winner in Camberwell, thanked "God and the Geddes Report" for his victory.[53]

Outcomes

The cabinet concluded its consideration of the Geddes Report the following week. Instead of £18m of education cuts it endorsed only £6.5m. "The full reduction would involve a breach of contract with the teaching profession in respect of their salaries," commented the Chancellor, "or the dismissal of tens of thousands of teachers, and the exclusion of children under six from the schools – a measure which would involve a storm of opposition in the large urban areas".[54] Moreover the impact of £6.5m was greatly tempered thanks to Fisher's precautionary budgeting and accounting (Fisher, 2006, p. 881). The Admiralty's broadside also paid off – the Geddes Committees' £35m of proposed navy cuts was reduced to £24m, with £14m coming from the Washington Conference. All-in-all, the cabinet endorsed cutbacks of £67m (Table 5.3) which were detailed to parliament on 1 March. Fisher noted that the Northcliffe press was "angry"; *The Times* described the outcome as "a great disappointment for taxpayers" (Fisher, 2006, p. 913). But liberal titles were delighted with the education result; the *Daily News* was "ecstatic" and the *Observer"s* headline was: "The Education Victory" (Fisher, 2006, p. 913).[55]

In the wake of the Chancellor's announcement the NUT received messages offering "heartfelt congratulations on the first result of the Executive's magnificent organised campaign".[56] But the General Secretary reminded colleagues that "cuts" were still intended in "two directions": larger classes, meaning the dismissal of teachers, and contributory pensions. The NUT's campaign against the Geddes Report and its authors continued for months, with its annual conference in mid-April, attended by 5,000 delegates and supporters, featuring widely reported outpourings of outrage.[57]

The press played key roles in the origins and development of the Geddes Axe economy drive. The appointment of the Geddes committee was largely the outcome of the anti-waste campaign waged by the Harmsworth titles from 1919, with calls for economy supported by much of the rest of the press. But an external review of government expenditures was the invention of the Prime Minister and Chancellor, not a demand of newspapers. The press was certainly in tune with the widespread public perception of government waste, and even opponents of education cuts in print and on platforms invariably paid homage to the need for economy – just not at the expense of children and teaching.

The press also played a significant part in shaping the scale and pattern of the government's acceptance of the Geddes committee's recommendations. The Admiralty used the press to deliver an instant rebuttal of the Geddes Report casting doubt on the calibre of its information and judgement in relation to the navy. The education protest meetings were widely reported and papers provided platforms for opponents to publicise their criticisms. The publicity helped to achieve the substantial reductions in the level of cuts imposed on these departments; other government departments saw much smaller proportionate reductions to their proposed cuts.

The Geddes Axe led to a £57m cut in departmental spending for 1922–23 (plus £10m in 1923–24), reducing projected spending from £538m to £481m – a 10 per cent reduction that otherwise would not have happened. The curtailment allowed tax reductions in the 1922 budget, including a cut in income tax from 30 to 25 per cent. Relative to GDP of £4.3bn the Geddes Axe cuts amounted to 1.5 per cent, a significant deflationary step but it proved to be more than outweighed by the tax cut stimulus and the general economic upturn. The fiscal out-turn for 1922–23 was an unanticipated surplus of £102m; it was applied to debt reduction. Contemporary economists assigned the Geddes economies a significant role in the rebalancing of Britain's public finances. Ursula Hicks, for instance, observed that it was "through the activity of the Geddes Committee. . . [that] the civil service was reduced to a peace-time footing, and . . . the budget was scaled down to reasonable proportions" (Hicks, 1938, p. 5).

As measured by by-election results, the Geddes Axe did the trick. In the subsequent six months there were 12 contests but coalition candidates suffered only two further defeats. Arguably the Geddes Report prolonged the life of the coalition (Mowat, 1968, p. 382), but it came to an end in October 1922 with a rebellion among Conservative back-benchers. The Conservatives emerged from the ensuing General Election as the largest party with an increased number of seats. Voters rewarded them for their association with economy and with tax cuts. Lloyd George's Coalition Liberals, on the other hand, lost more than half their seats being punished by liberal voters who associated them with the Geddes Axe–proposed economies in education and the end of the post-war social programme and defected to Labour.

The abundance and anger of the protest and press campaign against education cuts enduringly lodged the Geddes Axe in Britain's political and social folk-memory and in history textbooks as a dark chapter: "indiscriminate" and a "slaughter" (Taylor, 1965, pp. 183–4); "a by-word for callous meanness" (Pollard, 1969, p. 217); "a typical rich man's economy drive" (James, 1977, p. 159); and "economy cuts which brought an end to hopes of post-war social reform" (Marwick, 1965, p. 120). Half a century on it still had sufficient popular currency that when in 1975 four lads from Sheffield needed an evocative name for their Heavy Metal band they chose – Geddes Axe.

Notes

1 'Mr Harmsworth first Anti-Waste M.P', *Daily Mirror*, 29 November 1919.
2 J. Shield Nicolson, 'For and against a forced loan', *Scotsman*, 15 February 1917.
3 J. Shield Nicolson, 'Gluttony in war-time', *Scotsman*, 19 May 1917.
4 'Waste', *Economist*, 17 May 1919.
5 'Public anger at waste', *The Times*, 23 June 1920.
6 'Anti-Waste wins at Wrekin', *Daily Mail*, 21 February 1920.
7 'Vast crowds cheer anti-waste leader', *Daily Mirror*, 2 March 1920.
8 'Asquith anti-waste', *Daily Mirror*, 2 March 1920.

9 'Committee on National Expenditure', *The Times*, 20 March 1920, p. 11.

10 'Public anger at waste', *The Times*, 23 June 1920.

11 'A State Finance Council', *The Times*, 7 July 1920.

12 Lord Rothermere,'What the Anti-Waste League means', *Sunday Pictorial*, 30 January 1921.

13 'Unionist revolt', *The Times*, 26 February 1921.

14 'A business problem', *Economist*, 6 August 1921.

15 TNA. CAB 12/26/17. Cabinet Conclusions, 2 August 1921.

16 *First Interim Report of the Committee on National Expenditure* (HMSO, 1922) Cmd. 1581.

17 *Second Interim Report of the Committee on National Expenditure* (HMSO, 1922) Cmd. 1582; *Third Interim Report of the Committee on National Expenditure* (HMSO, 1922) Cmd. 1589.

18 'The Geddes Report', *Economist*, 18 February 1922.

19 'The Geddes Committee. £20m cut on education?' *Manchester Guardian*, 12 December 1921.

20 'Economy in danger', *The Times*, 6 February 1922.

21 TNA. CAB 23/29/8. Cabinet Conclusions, 6 February 1922.

22 'Axe intrigue fails', *The Times*, 8 February 1922.

23 'A "Best-Seller", *Evening News*, 11 February 1922; 'The most popular book of the season', *Manchester Guardian*, 13 February 1922.

24 'An untapped source of revenue', *Punch*, 1 March 1922.

25 'Economy – a Labour view', *Economist* 18 February 1922.

26 'The wasters on the warpath', *Daily Mail*, 11 February 1922.

27 'The Geddes Report', *Daily Mirror*, 11 February 1922.

28 'National economy', *Daily Telegraph*, 11 February 1922.

29 'The Geddes Report', *Daily Herald*, 11 February 1922; 'The Geddes Reports', *Morning Post*, 11 February 1922.

30 'Etiquette for the Admiralty', *Manchester Guardian*, 13 February 1922.

31 'Lord Beatty's Position', *Daily Mirror*, 13 February 1922.

32 'Cabinet and the Admiralty', *The Times*, 14 February 1922.

33 TNA. CAB 23/29/8. Cabinet Conclusions 6 February 1922.

34 'Economy Now', *The Times*, 13 February 1922;

35 'Events of the Week', *Nation & Athenaeum*, 18 February 1922.

36 'Departments and the report', *Manchester Guardian*, 14 February 1922.

37 'Admiralty's bombshell', *Daily Mail*, 11 February 1922.

38 TNA. ED 24/1304. Board of Education letter to Mr Chamberlain, 13 January 1922.

39 'Women teachers and Geddes "cuts"', *The Times*, 4 January 1922.

40 MRC. MSS.179/EXEC/1/4/1. N.U.T. Executive Committee Minutes, 7 January 1922.

41 'Double-edged axe', *Daily Herald*, 30 January 1922.

42 'Comment', *New Statesman*, 18 February 1922.

43 MRC. MSS.179/EXEC/1/4/1. N.U.T., Executive Committee Minutes of Special Meeting, 18 February 1922.

44 MRC. MSS.179/1/9/35. N.U.T. Fifty-Second Annual Report of the Executive 1922, p.li.

45 'Educationalists and the axe', *Manchester Guardian*, 17 March 1922.

46 'Committee of non-experts, *Nineteenth Century and After*, April 1922.

47 'The falsest of false economies', *Spectator*, 31 December 1921; 'The curse of high taxation and expenditure', *Spectator*, 29 April 1922.

48 'The shopkeepers' calculus', *New Statesman*, 18 February1922.

49 MRC. MSS.179/EXEC/1/4/1. N.U.T. Executive Committee Minutes, 7 January 1922.

50 'Not a penny off', *Manchester Guardian*, 13 February 1922.

51 'Teachers to help Labour in Camberwell', *Manchester Guardian*, 13 February 1922.

52 'Clayton and the axe', *Manchester Guardian*, 14 February 1922.

53 'Educationalists and the axe', *Manchester Guardian*, 17 March 1922.

54 TNA. CAB 23/29/14. Cabinet Conclusions, 24 February 1922.

55 'The education victory', *Observer*, 5 March 1922.

56 MRC. MSS.179/EXEC/1/4/1. N.U.T. Executive Committee Minutes, 4 March 1922.

57 'N.U.T. Conference', *The Times*, 18 April 1922.

Bibliography and references

The National Archives

Cabinet papers
Cabinet minutes
Treasury files

Newspapers

Nation and Athenaeum
Daily Mirror
Economist
Financial Times
Nineteenth Century and After
Statist
The Times

Published sources

Bank of England. 2017. *Three Centuries of Data*.

Barnes, J. and Nicolson, D. (eds.) 1980. *The Leo Amery Diaries: Volume I: 1869–1929*. London: Hutchinson. p. 219.

Beaverbrook, Lord. 1956. *Men and power 1917–1918*. London: Hutchinson.

Burrows, G. and Cobbin, P. 2009. 'Controlling government expenditure by external review: The 1921–2 "Geddes Axe"'. *Accounting History*, 14(3), pp. 199–220.

Butler, D. (ed.). 1978. *Coalitions in British politics*. London: Palgrave Macmillan.

Capie, F., and Collins, M. 1983. *The inter-war British economy: A statistical abstract*. Manchester: Manchester University Press.

Cline, P. K. 1974. Eric Geddes and the "Experiment" with Businessmen in Government, 1915–1922. In: Kenneth D. Brown (ed.), *Essays in anti-labour history*. London: Palgrave Macmillan. pp. 74–104.

Cowling, M. 1971. *The impact of labour, 1920–1924: The beginning of modern British politics*. Cambridge: Cambridge University Press.

Crafts, N. 2012. 'Reducing High Public Debt Ratios: Lessons from UK Experience'. University of Warwick Department of Economics Working Papers no.199, August.

Daunton, M. 1996. 'How to Pay for the War: State, Society and Taxation in Britain, 1917–24'. *English Historical Review*, 111, September, pp. 882–919.

Daunton, M. 2002. *Just taxes: The politics of taxation in Britain, 1914–1979*. Cambridge: Cambridge University Press.

Davenport-Hines, R. 1985. Alexander Henderson. *Dictionary of business biography*. London: Butterworth. pp. 153–158.

Dowie, J. A. 1975. '1919–20 is in Need of Attention'. *Economic History Review*, 28(3), pp. 429–450.

Eichengreen, B. 2004. The British economy between the wars. In: Floud, R., and Johnson, P. (eds.), *The Cambridge economic history of modern Britain: Volume II, economic maturity, 1860–1939*. Cambridge: Cambridge University Press. pp. 314–343.

Feinstein, C. H. 1972. *Statistical tables of national income, expenditure and output of the UK 1855–1965*. Cambridge: Cambridge University Press.

Fisher, H. A. L. 2006. *The coalition diaries and letters of H. A. L. Fisher, 1916–1922*, edited by F. Russell Bryant. Lewiston, NY: Edwin Mellen Press.

Grieves, K. 1989. *Sir Eric Geddes: Business and government in war and peace*. Manchester: Manchester University Press, pp. 101–107.

Hicks, U. K. 1938. *The finance of British government 1920–1936*. London: Oxford University Press.

Higgs, H. 1922. 'The Geddes Reports and the Budget'. *Economic Journal*, 32(126) June. pp. 251–264.

HMSO, 1922a, *First Interim Report of the Committee on National Expenditure* (London, London: HMSO, Cmd. 1581.

HMSO, 1922b, *Second Interim Report of the Committee on National Expenditure*, London: HMSO, Cmd. 1582.

HMSO, 1922c, *Third Interim Report of the Committee on National Expenditure*, London: HMSO, Cmd. 1589.

James, R. R. 1977. *The British revolution: British politics 1880–1939*, vol. 2. London: Hamish Hamilton.

Jeffery, T., and McClelland, K. 1987. A world fit to live in: The *Daily Mail* and the middle classes 1918–39. In: Curran, J., Smith, A., and Wingate, P. (eds.), *Impacts and influences: Essays on media power in the twentieth century*. London: Methuen. pp. 27–52.

Kinnear, M. 1979. *The fall of Lloyd George: The political crisis of 1922*. London: Palgrave Macmillan.

Lewis, W. Arthur. 1949. *Economic survey 1919–1939*. London: Allen and Unwin.

Mallet, Sir Bernard and Oswald George, C. 1933. *British Budgets 1921–22 to 1932–33* London: Palgrave Macmillan.

Marwick, A. 1965. *The Deluge: British Society and the First World War*, London: Bodley Head.

McDonald, A. 1989. 'The Geddes Committee and the formulation of public expenditure policy, 1921–1922'. *Historical Journal*, 32(3), pp. 643–674.

Mitchell, B. R. 1988. *British historical statistics*. Cambridge: Cambridge University Press.

Morgan, E. Victor. 1952. *Studies in British financial policy 1914–1925*. London: Palgrave Macmillan.

Morgan, K. O. 1979. *Consensus and disunity: The Lloyd George coalition government 1918–1922*. Oxford: Clarendon Press.

Parris, H. 1984. Sir guy granet. *Dictionary of business biography*. London: Butterworth. pp. 620–622.

Peden, G. 2000. *The Treasury and British public policy: 1906–1959*. Oxford: Oxford University Press.

Pollard, S. 1969. *The development of the British economy*. London: Edward Arnold.

Riddell, L. 1933. *Lord Riddell's intimate diary of the peace conference and after 1918–1923*. London: Victor Gollancz.

Smith, David B. 2006. *Living with Leviathan: Public spending, taxes and economic performance*. London: Institute of Economic Affairs.

Smith, David B. 2009. *How should Britain's government spending and tax burdens be measured? A historic perspective on the 2009 budget forecasts*. IEA Discussion Paper, 24, June.

Stevenson, F. 1971. *Lloyd George: A Diary by Frances Stevenson*, edited by A. J. P. Taylor. London: Hutchinson.

Stow, G. 1985. James Lyle Mackay. *Dictionary of business biography*. London: Butterworth. pp. 27–32.

Taylor, A. J. P. 1965. *English History 1914–1945* Oxford: Oxford University Press.

PART II
Continental perspectives

6

COVERING THE EURO CRISIS

Cleavages and convergences

Heinz-Werner Nienstedt

The Euro crisis

The Euro was introduced as a coronation and further driver of European unity. The expectation was that the Euro promoted convergence in economic and political structures and developments and supported growth and creation of wealth. Instead we see today some nations in the Euro zone with high and enduring unemployment especially of young people and social and political turmoil as a consequence of their economic crisis.

The illusions about the pure merits of the Euro vanished with the outbreak of the Euro crisis. Following the global financial crisis of 2008/2009 and the worldwide deep recession afterwards, the weakened financial markets were not willing to finance the public and private debt of some of the Euro countries any more, or at the least not at bearable interest rates. Greece, Italy, Ireland,[1] Portugal and Spain belonged to these countries and can, therefore, be addressed as 'crisis countries'. Their enormous debt levels were accumulated since the start of the Euro system[2] and were enabled by the low interest rates that these countries had to pay in contrast to the pre-Euro regime. In addition the costs in these countries had been inflated over time relative to the other Euro countries in an amount that weakened their competitive position and made their economic recovery even more difficult (see Sinn, 2014 for a comprehensive analysis of the issues raised in the previous paragraph).

Rescue programs to prevent bankruptcy of nations and banks were set into effect. These rescue programs had the character of a "credit cooperation" (Pisani-Ferry, 2011, p. 168ff) between the Euro nations. The consequence of such relations between lenders and payees' countries is "the danger of both dominance and resentment" (Fabrini, 2015, p. 150) and this danger eventuated.[3] The lenders were able to demand covenants and enforce austerity policies. As a consequence we see tensions between governments and the people of European nations to an extent not known for a long time in the history of the European Union. These tensions were propelled by different perceptions about the Euro crisis.

Perceptions of the Euro crisis between Europe's nations

In this research the pattern of different perceptions of the Euro crisis as presented by leading newspapers in a selection of European countries is traced and differences and similarities are analyzed. The analysis is based on the data of a broader study.

Scholars from 10 European countries, led by the Reuters Institute for the Study of Journalism, recently undertook an extensive content analysis of the four leading newspapers of each country (Picard, 2015). They covered two weeks around 11 major development periods of the Euro crisis between February 2010 and July 2012.[4] It is interesting to study this phase of the Euro crisis since the main political and economic mechanisms to cope with the Euro crisis were formed within this time span. The narratives of the public discourse and the political decisions taken in these times will have ongoing influence and its analysis may also help to interpret conflicts and cleavages of later phases of the crisis.

For this research six out of the 10 countries were selected: Greece, Italy and Spain, which were in the center of the turbulence; France and Germany as leading countries given their size and political power and their involvement in the process to fix the crisis; and the UK for a comparative analysis as it has been Europe's leading financial center during the Euro crisis and still is in the years after the Brexit poll. The perception concerning four questions which are central to understanding the attitudes of these countries towards the crisis will be analyzed: What are the fundamental roots of the crisis? Who should be responsible for solving the crisis? What should be the specific political and economic mechanisms to solve the crisis? And what should be the broader strategical and long-term responses to the crisis?

The research is based on the content of the four leading newspapers of the six countries. This is justified since one can assume that the reporting in the most important newspapers of a country influenced the reporting of many other newspapers and news media and initiated a co-orientating process among journalists (Breed, 1955; Noelle-Neumann and Mathes, 1987; Reinemann, 2003; Bach et al., 2013), forming and reflecting public opinion and the political agenda in their countries.

Previous research based on the same content analysis data already showed that "Countries still matter" (Mancini and Mazzoni, 2015). Salgado et al. (2015) provide evidence that national differences in the reporting of the Euro crisis are greater than those between the newspapers within each country and also greater than those between the conservative and liberal press (Salgado and Nienstedt, 2016; Nienstedt, 2017).

Research methods

Along the lines of Nienstedt et al. (2015) the analysis in this research is based on aggregated data for each country and over all 11 time periods which were covered, specifically the proportions with which certain views about the four issues have been covered by the press. Data for single nations indicate the total reporting of all four newspapers of that country. This aggregation level is relevant for two reasons: First, one can assume that the number of news items pointing in a specific direction plays a role in the perception of the public about this issue; second, the proportion of articles portraying specific views provides an indication of the national political discourse (for an explanation of so-called agenda building see, for example, Nisbet, 2008).

Similarities and differences between the reporting in the various countries are analyzed by applying a quantitative concept of diversity. To measure diversity Simpson's D (Simpson, 1949) is applied. The application of Simpson's diversity concept to content analysis was elaborated by Salgado et al. (2015) and Salgado and Nienstedt (2016) in the context of the analysis of the Euro crisis. The advantage of Simpson's diversity indices is that they allow a probabilistic interpretation (Lieberson, 1969; Agresti and Agresti, 1978; McDonald and Dimmick, 2003). In this research Simpson's D_w addresses country diversity. For example, it can measure the probability of finding different causes of the crisis in two randomly selected news stories from newspapers within a given country. Simpsons' D_b on the other hand, indicates diversity between the reporting of two countries.[5]

To better compare the size of diversity between several pairs of nations the concept of the diversity gain is applied. The gain is defined as the percentage increase of diversity between the nations (D_b) compared to the country diversity (D_w) of the less diverse nation.[6] This is a measure for the extent to which the reportings of the countries differ from each other.

Coverage of the four issues by the six countries

The four issues − roots of the crisis and responsibilities, specific mechanisms and broader responses to solve the crisis[7] − were covered broadly in the reporting of the six countries. They were detected 18.621 times in the 11.439 article data set.

Specific mechanisms to solve the crisis were covered most frequently, followed closely by responsibilities to solve. On the contrary, discussion of the roots of the crisis took place in only roughly half of the articles compared to those on specific mechanisms.

Most of the coding was for Germany (4 526), followed by Italy (4 008), Greece (3 607), France (2 592), Spain (2 097) and the UK (1 791) (see Table 6.1).

The *fundamental roots of the crisis* were discussed most frequently in Germany (816 articles) and Greece (639 articles). The audience in the other four countries was informed about roots of the crisis in 45% to 55% fewer articles than in Germany.

All countries deliver fairly high levels of diversity in the reporting about roots as measured by D_w and based on the seven categories of roots.[8] The most diversity in the coverage was found in Italy and Spain (79%), followed by Greece and the UK (74%), and Germany (73%). These results mean that the probability of finding different roots addressed in two randomly selected articles is more than 70% in each of the countries.[9]

TABLE 6.1 Number of articles by issue and countries

Issues	France	Germany	Greece	Italy	Spain	UK	Total
Roots	452	816	639	338	426	369	3 040
Responsibilities	772	1 198	1 190	1 422	663	326	5 571
Specific mechanism	720	1 426	1 123	1 284	571	626	5 750
Broader response	648	1 086	655	964	437	470	4 260
Total no. of codings	2 592	4 526	3 607	4 008	2 097	1 791	18 621

TABLE 6.2 Country diversity by issue

Issues	France	Germany	Greece	Italy	Spain	UK
Roots	73%	70%	74%	79%	79%	74%
Responsibilities	53%	73%	62%	66%	67%	64%
Specific mechanisms	59%	63%	75%	64%	73%	75%
Broader response	58%	62%	65%	72%	68%	64%

Note: $D_{w\ values}$

Responsibilities to solve the crisis were portrayed 5571 times in our total sample and made up 31% of the coding of the four issues (Table 6.1).

The diversity in which the reporting covered the issues showed variance. Diversity was highest in the German press (73%) and lowest in France (53%) (Table 6.2).

Specific mechanisms to counter the Euro crisis were addressed in 5 750 articles (Table 6.1). The diversity in which the specific mechanisms were covered was highest in Greece (72%) and lowest in France (58%; see Table 6.2).

The issue of *broader responses* (4 260 articles) was covered more diversely in the crisis countries, especially Italy (D_w 72%), than in Germany (62%) or in France (D_w 58%; see Table 6.2).

The categories which form the four issues and their relative distribution in the reporting of the six countries on which the analysis of diversity and the following comparison between countries is based are to be found in Tables 6.3, 6.4, 6.5 and 6.6.

Germany versus France

Major decisions about coping with the Euro crisis had been taken by summits of the Euro nations, usually with a unanimous vote. The lead was without doubt taken over by Germany, but no decision was put through without prior consent between Germany and France, in the "Merkozy" constellation, and soon also between Merkel and Hollande.

There had been unanimity between the leaders of the two nations that the Euro system should be preserved and Greece would be kept in the Euro zone. But often enough there were cleavages concerning the ways to achieve that. Such cleavages were reflected in the reporting of the press in the two countries. Figure 6.1 shows the pattern of differences between them as measured by the diversity gain.

Cross-national diversity gains between the reporting in the two countries are small to medium[10] concerning specific short-term mechanisms (5%) and the portrayal of the roots of the crisis (7%), but are quite high when it comes to responsibilities to solve (24%) it and the broader long-term responses (23%).

The diversity in the reporting of the *roots of the crisis* results from a stronger focus on national economic policies and private financial investors' misconduct in the German press and the structure of the Euro system in the French newspapers (see Table 6.3).

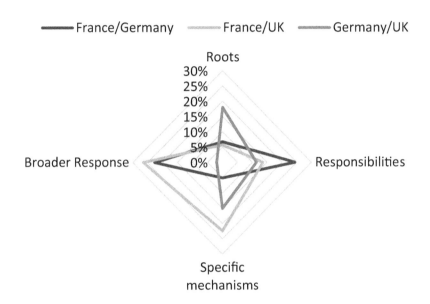

FIGURE 6.1 Diversity gains – northern countries

TABLE 6.3 Reporting on the fundamental roots of the Euro crisis

Category	France	Germany	Greece	Italy	Spain	UK	Total
National economic policies	33.2%	46.3%	40.2%	29.0%	27.2%	9.2%	34.0%
Structure of the Euro system	34.1%	13.2%	13.5%	21.9%	20.0%	39.8%	21.5%
Private financial actors' misconduct	16.8%	23.3%	3.6%	24.3%	20.0%	26.3%	18.2%
Political deficiencies	11.5%	8.6%	22.7%	13.0%	21.6%	12.7%	14.8%
General economic conditions	2.7%	5.1%	17.5%	3.0%	6.8%	3.0%	7.1%
Central banks' policies	0.9%	1.7%	1.1%	2.4%	0.5%	3.3%	1.5%
Other	0.9%	1.7%	1.4%	6.5%	4.0%	5.7%	2.9%
Number of articles	452	816	639	338	426	369	3040

Note: Percentage of all articles per country and total

Both countries focus on loans as specific mechanism to solve the crisis. The diversity in the reporting of *specific mechanisms* comes from the French newspapers' more intensive portrayal of the necessity of austerity measures and the reduction of budget deficits and a less frequent pointing to 'haircuts' than in German newspapers (see Table 6.5).

National structural reforms have been by far the number one *broader response* suggested in Germany. In France structural reforms had the lowest weight of all six countries. More EU power plays the dominant role in the French narrative about broader responses which does not play that role in Germany. This caused the huge diversity between the two countries concerning broader responses (see Table 6.6).

The French push for more centralized EU structures was also reflected in the category *responsibilities to solve* the crisis. Here France expressed a high priority for the EU institutions and the Euro zone countries as a whole to fix the problems of the crisis countries and to a much less extent the struggling countries themselves. This response and responsibility for the European institutions and the Euro zone countries as a whole was not addressed as often by the German press but the responsibility of the crisis countries themselves were mentioned double as much than in the French press, contributing to the extreme high diversity between the two countries (see Table 6.4).

TABLE 6.4 Reporting on the responsibility to solve the Euro crisis

Category	France	Germany	Greece	Italy	Spain	UK	Total
EU/Euro countries and institutions	66.1%	44.2%	48.6%	52.5%	47.5%	54.9%	51.3%
Struggling countries themselves	12.2%	20.0%	36.7%	20.1%	27.9%	8.9%	22.8%
Central banks	10.6%	10.2%	7.1%	13.9%	8.7%	17.2%	10.8%
Countries without debt problems	6.0%	11.9%	4.6%	4.9%	13.4%	2.5%	7.4%
Private debt holders	3.9%	6.7%	2.0%	3.0%	1.2%	0.6%	3.3%
Other	1.3%	7.0%	0.9%	5.6%	1.2%	16.0%	4.4%
Number of articles	772	1198	1190	1422	663	326	5571

Note: Percentage of all articles per country and total

TABLE 6.5 Reporting on specific mechanisms to counter the Euro crisis

Category	France	Germany	Greece	Italy	Spain	UK	Total
Loans from Euro countries and ECB	58.3%	56.1%	33.4%	54.4%	41.3%	34.8%	47.8%
Austerity measures	24.4%	16.3%	28.5%	16.7%	23.1%	20.0%	20.9%
Growth stimulus	9.4%	7.7%	18.1%	12.8%	14.2%	17.9%	12.8%
Haircut	3.6%	7.4%	13.6%	4.5%	8.8%	4.8%	7.4%
Other	4.2%	12.5%	6.4%	11.7%	12.6%	22.5%	11.2%
Number of articles	720	1.426	1.123	1.284	571	626	5750

Note: Percentage of all articles per country and total

TABLE 6.6 Reporting on the broader long-term responses to solve the Euro crisis

Category	France	Germany	Greece	Italy	Spain	UK	Total
National structural reforms	29.9%	56.0%	42.6%	39.4%	45.8%	53.8%	44.9%
More EU power	56.2%	18.2%	38.6%	20.5%	28.1%	14.7%	28.3%
Breaking up the Euro zone	10.2%	8.1%	13.4%	19.5%	11.7%	11.7%	12.6%
Other	3.7%	17.7%	5.3%	20.5%	14.4%	19.8%	14.2%
Number of articles	648	1086	655	964	437	470	4260

Note: Percentage of all articles per country and total

Thus it was predominantly the different views of the necessity of structural reforms as a strategic response to solve the problems of crisis countries and the demand for more power for central EU institutions which shaped a different portray of the Euro crisis in France and Germany.

UK versus France and Germany

The size of the area between the lines which link the cross national diversity gains of France and UK in Figure 6.1 shows that diversity between these two countries is high, in fact the highest between all the nations which we cover in this research. The area between the lines for the UK and Germany is smaller by comparison.

Concerning *roots* the diversity gain is higher for UK/Germany (18%) than for UK/France (6%), where it is only medium sized. National economic policies play a minor role in UK reporting, while they are higher in France and much higher in Germany. The structure of the Euro system is the dominant root of the crisis in the UK and the French press, but it has much less weight in Germany. The private financial investors' misconduct is stressed by the UK and Germany but much less by France (see Table 6.3).

There are high gains of diversity for the *responsibility to solve* the crisis between the UK and the two continental nations (UK/France 14%, UK/Germany 11%) especially because central banks play a much higher role in the UK reporting (see Table 6.4).

For *specific mechanisms* the gains are even higher (UK/France 22%, UK/Germany 15%). This is because loans do not play such a dominant role in the UK press, but growth stimuli are promoted to a higher extent (see Table 6.5).

Concerning *broader responses,* the UK and the German press paint a nearly similar picture of what has to be done (gain = 2%). For the UK and France the opposite is the case with a gain of 26%. The same differences, which were pointed out between the German and the French press above apply here (see Table 6.6).

Looking at the reporting in the UK, which was included in the sample for comparative purposes as an outsider of the Euro system and as Europe's financial center, we see major differences with the two biggest continental Euro nations. The UK focusses on the deficiencies of the structure of the Euro system as well as private investors' misconduct as a cause of the crisis, has more trust in the central bank as an

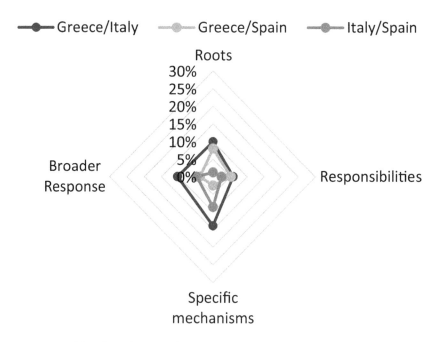

FIGURE 6.2   Diversity gains – southern countries

institution to solve the crisis and advises more emphatically to implement growth stimuli as an immediate reaction. Although the UK has a different view of the roots of the crisis than Germany, both countries have nearly same views on the broader long-term responses to solve the crisis but different ones from France.

Greece, Italy and Spain

In their analysis of *roots* as well as *responsibilities,* Italy and Spain paint nearly the same picture, indicated by the gain of only 1% and 2%. But the portrayal of roots in Italy and Spain both differ from that of Greece, with a gain of 10% and 8%, respectively because they focus less on national economic policies, more on the structure of the Euro system, and much more on private investors' misconduct (see Tables 6.3 and 6.4).

Spain and Greece report quite similarly on *specific mechanisms* (with a gain of 3%). In contrast, we find more diverse portrayals on these mechanisms between Italy and Greece (14%) as well as Spain (9%) in this category. Where Italy focusses on loans from the European Union and neither on austerity nor on growth stimuli, Greece and Spain focus more on fiscal policies, austerity measures, and growth stimuli than Italy does (see Table 6.5).

The diversity gain of the reporting between Italy and Greece (10%) concerning *broader responses*, and to a lesser extent between Italy and Spain (5%), and Spain and Greece (4%), results from Italy's lack of focus on national structural reforms and more EU power, but more focus on breaking up the Euro zone (see Table 6.6).

There is overall much less diversity of coverage between the southern countries than diversity between the northern countries. Only Greece and Italy show gains of 10% and more.

North and south

A comparison of Figures 6.1 to 6.5 gives the impression of smaller gains of diversity between countries of the north and south than between the countries of the north. We focus on the most expressive gains here.

Germany and Italy's reporting on *specific mechanisms* is highly consonant (1%). Italy and Germany both promote loans, from the perspective of a receiver and of a lender. But they differ on *broader responses* (12%) because of Italy's low focus on national structural reforms and higher focus on breaking up the Euro zone (see Tables 6.5 and 6.6).

Germany's and Spain's diversity is greatest on *roots* (11%), given Spain's lower attention to national economic policies, and high attention to political deficiencies, as well as on *specific mechanisms* (10%) where Germany again focusses on loans and Spain stronger on austerity as well as on growth stimuli (see Tables 6.3 and 6.5).

The greatest differences are between Germany and Greece. Here differences concerning responsibilities to solve the crisis and the specific mechanisms to do so stand out. *Specific mechanisms* which should be set into effect are portrayed in Greece quite differently from Germany (16%). Greece focusses on austerity measures, growth stimulus and 'haircuts', where Germany focuses predominantly on loans. The reporting on *broader responses* is somewhat more consonant (9%). While Greece calls for more EU power and less structural reform, it also focusses much

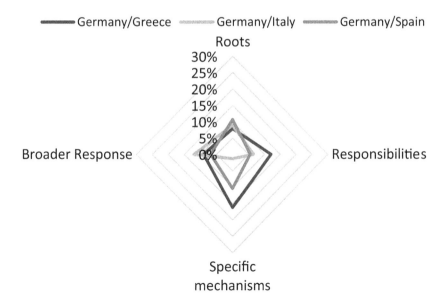

FIGURE 6.3   Diversity gains – Germany (southern countries)

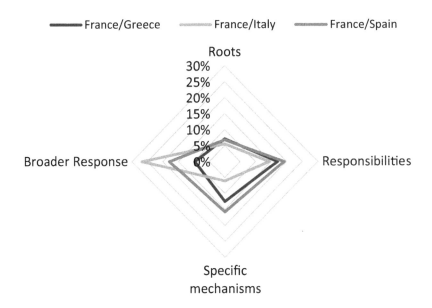

FIGURE 6.4 Diversity gains – France (compared to southern countries)

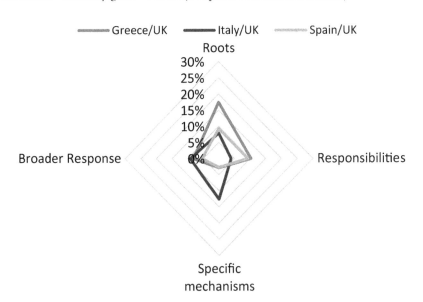

FIGURE 6.5 Diversity gains – UK (compared to southern countries)

more on the *responsibility* of the struggling countries themselves than Germany (see Tables 6.4, 6.5 and 6.6).

Diversity between France and the southern countries is most evident for three of the categories: broader responses, responsibility to solve and specific mechanisms. For *broader responses* this results mainly from the strong French focus on more EU power and even lower focus on national structural reforms than Italy (27%), Spain

(18%) and Greece (10%). France's widely reported recommendation for the EU/ Euro countries instead of countries themselves to be *responsible to solve the crisis* drives the high gain of diversity between France and Spain (19%), Greece (17%) and Italy (14%). Concerning *specific mechanisms* French reporting differs most when compared to Spain (16%) and Greece (13%) because of its stronger focus on loans and smaller on growth stimulus and 'haircuts' (see Tables 6.4, 6.5 and 6.6).

The UK and Spain have diversity gains all below 10% and specifically low ones for short-term mechanisms (3%) and broader responses (5%). The UK and Italy differ mostly concerning *specific mechanisms* (13%) caused by Italy's stronger push for loans and the UK's push for growth stimulus. Similar to its diversity with Germany, the UK reporting on *roots* differs highly from that of Greece (18%) with great differences on nearly each of the *roots*.

There is no homogenous north–south pattern of diversity in the portrayal of the Euro crisis but specific differences which are a consequence of the national patterns concerning the various issues in the north as well as in the south. Overall greater differences are found between the reporting of the crisis countries with France than with Germany and the UK. They all have more focus on their own responsibility to solve the crisis and for national structural reforms, and less focus on more EU power than can be found in French reporting.

Summary and discussion

The analysis of diversity gains between the six countries revealed interesting cleavages between the reporting of nations about the Euro crisis. The research uncovers dissonance between the big northern countries (France, Germany and the UK) that is much more significant than that which exists between the southern countries (Spain, Italy and Greece).[11] The cleavages and consonances between France and Germany – as far as they indeed reflect the political agenda of the two countries – are of specific interest, since both nations play a central role in the political process of crisis management. To start with a consonant point: neither country considers breaking up the Euro zone as a broader response to the crisis to be noteworthy. When in 2015 the former German finance minister, Wolfgang Schäuble, indicated the possibility of expelling Greece from the Euro, the consequence was been a storm of outrage in the European as well as in German media.

The main dissonance between these countries is about the importance of national structural reforms in the crisis countries – and maybe in France as a potential one. Another difference is the importance of European initiatives to solve the crisis and more EU power (France) versus the stronger focus on the responsibility of the countries themselves (Germany). The French initiatives to compromise with Greece before the settlement of the third rescue program in 2015, the French tolerant view on the inspection of the Greece fulfillment of covenants as a prerequisite to release further money in the following period and the reported greater sympathy for debt relief, can be interpreted against the background of different views on broader responses. The differences concerning structural reforms also shed light on the public opinion in France on how to cope with its own growth and unemployment problems after the financial crisis. It will be interesting to learn whether President Emmanuel Macron, backed by his majority in the French parliament, will turn this attitude around and put his announced reforms into effect. His push for more Europe on the other hand is supported by the French reporting already found in this study.

The UK press has another view on the roots of the crisis, especially compared to Germany, putting more blame on the structure of the Euro system, political deficiencies and private financial actors' misconduct. It shares the German view towards the necessity of structural reforms but differs from France in this respect. Concerning specific mechanisms it differs from the two continental nations in that it strongly recommends growth stimuli. It also regards, more than France and Germany, the European Central Bank (ECB) as responsible for solving the crisis. Today's predominant support of the ECB's quantitative ease policy by the UK press and the statements of the city's financial community has its parallel in the reporting of the time studied here.

There is less difference in the portrayal of the Euro crisis between the southern countries. Greater diversity can be found between Italy on the one side and Greece and Spain on the other concerning specific mechanisms as well as broader responses. Italy differs from both in assigning less responsibility to solve the crisis to the struggling countries themselves. It has a stronger focus on loans from the Euro countries as the desirable mechanism, which it indeed received from the ECB to bridge its debt problems. On the other side Greece and Spain focused much more on austerity as well as growth stimuli. Italy gives a significantly lower voice to structural reforms than the two other countries do. This reflects the uneven amount of structural reforms which happened in Italy compared to Greece and Spain since the outbreak of the crisis. In addition, when compared to all other countries, Italy most vehemently leans toward breaking up the Euro zone.

Interestingly enough, this research does not find a homogenous pattern of diversity between the northern and the southern countries in the portrayal of the Euro crisis. Instead there are specific differences between single northern and single southern countries which result from the national patterns of the reporting concerning the various issues within the northern and southern group of countries. Cumulatively, significant cleavages between the reporting of the northern countries and remarkable ones between the southern countries are detected by this study. As far as these differences reflect the public opinion and the political agenda of the respective nations, they reveal the potential to further the European conflicts about the solution of the ongoing Euro crisis.

One can assume that the narratives of the public discourse in the times after the outbreak of the Euro crisis which is studied here will have ongoing influence, but political events after this period may lead to changes. After the Brexit decision, the UK no longer has direct influence on European policies – and France undergoes dramatic political disruptions with the rise of Macron and his "En Marche" movement. Expressive cleavages have been found between the German and the

French positions towards the solution of the Euro crisis. It will be interesting to observe whether there will be more convergence of the political agenda as well as of the public opinion and its reflection in the press between the two countries in the Macron era: more EU power, which is promoted by Macron, supporting the French position which was already found in this study, and more structural reforms that support the German focus to fix the crisis, which Macron has announced.

Notes

1 Ireland seems to have mostly recovered from the crisis, "While other crisis countries suffered from a double dip recession or even depression, Irish industrial production recovered more quickly from the crisis than even Germany or the United States" (Sinn, 2014, p. 128). In the last years, since 2014, Ireland showed the highest real GDP growth rates of all EU countries according to Eurostat data, Database, Economy and Finance.
2 Main convergence of the monetary systems started after the December 1995 Madrid Summit, where the timetable for the introduction of the Euro was fixed and it became clear which countries would participate. This summit can therefore be identified as the start of the Euro System for the purpose of economic analyses (see Sinn, 2014, pp. 42–43).
3 Today the quantitative ease policy of the European Central Bank makes it possible to prevent bankruptcies of nations and banks and a new explosion of interest spreads for those countries which are still deep in debt. This type of transfer policy to the crisis countries is more disguised and thus does not cause similar tensions between nations.
4 For details of the project, the selected newspapers, the codebook and outcomes of the research see Picard (2015).
5 Given the contingency table, Dw is calculated by "summing the squared proportions and subtracting the sum from 1.0" (McDonald and Dimmick, 2003, p. 66). Db is calculated as "the simple average of the between-groups diversity indices for the m pairs of marginal distributions of the m variables" (Agresti and Agresti, 1978, pp. 226). We express these measures as percentages here.
6 In previous research (e.g. Salgado et al., 2015) we applied the gain by comparing D_b to the average D_w of two nations. Although this approach is justified in some cases, the comparison to the nation with the lower D_w gives a better impression of the transnational gain for the readers of one nation's press.
7 The codings of these issues, which are included in Tables 6.3, 6.4, 6.5 and 6.6 are explained in more detail in Nienstedt et al. (2015, p. 42ff)
8 See Table 6.3 for the seven categories of roots.
9 This does not mean, however, that the various economic aspects of these roots have been analyzed in a highly differentiated way. This is revealed if one looks deeper into the coverage of single items which were later aggregated to the seven categories of roots. Twenty-one of forty items were not covered at all or constituted a maximum of 1 % in the articles concerning roots.
10 We deem diversity gains up to 5% to be small, between 6% and 10% medium and greater than 10% as high. This is clearly arbitrarily, but results in a good description of differences in this case.
11 This result was also found in a similar analysis by Salgado et al. (2015).

References

Agresti, A., and Agresti, B. 1978. 'Statistical analysis of qualitative variation', Sociological Methodology (9), pp. 204–237.

Bach, T., Weber, M., and Quiring, O. 2013. 'News frames, inter-media frame transfer and the financial crisis'. *Zeszyty Prasoznawcze*, 1(213), pp. 90–110.

Breed, W. 1955. 'Social control in the newsroom: A functional analysis'. *Social Forces*, 33(4), pp. 326–335.

Fabrini, S. 2015. *Which European Union? Europe after the Euro Crisis.* Cambridge: Cambridge University Press.

Lieberson, S. 1969. 'Measuring population diversity'. *American Sociological Review*, 34(6), pp. 850–862.

Mancini, P., and Mazzoni, M. 2015. Countries still matter. In: Picard, R., (ed.), *The Euro crisis and the media: Journalistic coverage of economic crisis and European institutions.* London: L. B. Tauris & Co. pp. 177–194.

McDonald, D., and Dimmick, J. 2003. 'The Conceptualization and Measurement of Diversity'. *Communication Research*, 30, pp. 60–79.

Nienstedt, H-W. 2017. 'Corrections to Salgado, S., Nienstedt, H-W. 2016. Euro Crisis and Plurality: Does the political Orientation of Newspapers Determine the Selection and Spin of Information?' *European Journal of Communication*, 31(4), pp. 462–478, www.researchgate.net/profile/Heinz-Werner_Nienstedt/contributions.

Nienstedt, H-W., Kepplinger, H-M., and Quiring, O. 2015. What went wrong and why? Roots, responsibilities and solutions of the Euro crisis in European newspapers. In: Picard, R. (ed.), *The Euro crisis and the media: Journalistic coverage of economic crisis and European institutions.* London: I. B. Tauris & Co. pp. 19–45.

Nisbet, M. C. 2008. Agenda building. In: Donsbach, W. (ed.), *The international encyclopedia of communication.* Oxford: John Wiley & Sons. pp. 140–145.

Noelle-Neumann, E., and Mathes, R. 1987. 'The 'Event as Event' and the 'Event as News': The significance of 'Consonance' for media effects research'. *European Journal of Communication*, 2, pp. 391–414.

Picard, R., (ed.). 2015. *The Euro crisis and the media: Journalistic coverage of economic crisis and European institutions.* London: I. B. Tauris & Co.

Picard, R. 2015. Understanding the crisis. In: Picard, R. (ed.), *The Euro crisis and the media: Journalistic coverage of economic crisis and European institutions.* London: I. B. Tauris & Co. pp. 1–18.

Pisani-Ferry, J. 2011. *The Euro crisis and its aftermath.* Oxford: Oxford University Press.

Reinemann, C. 2003. *Medienmacher als Mediennutzer: Kommunikations und Einflussstrukturen im politischen Journalismus der Gegenwart.* Böhlau: Köln.

Salgado, S., and Nienstedt, H-W. 2016. 'Euro crisis and plurality: Does the political orientation of newspapers determine the selection and spin of information?. *European Journal of Communication*, 31(4), pp. 462–478.

Salgado, S., Nienstedt, H-W., and Schneider, L. 2015. Consensus or discussion. An Analysis of Plurality and Consonance in Coverage. In: Picard, R. (ed.), *The Euro crisis and the media: Journalistic coverage of economic crisis and European institutions.* London: I. B. Tauris & Co. pp. 103–124.

Simpson, E.H. 1949. Measurement of diversity. *Nature,* 163(4), pp. 313–327. Sinn, W. 2014. *Euro trap, on bursting bubbles, budgets and beliefs.* Oxford: Oxford University Press.

7

AUSTERITY POLICIES IN THE EUROPEAN PRESS

A divided Europe?

Ángel Arrese

Austerity has been the dominant frame in the discussions of the appropriate public policies to respond to the European sovereign debt crisis. Both at a European and a national level, there is an impression both in public opinion and the academic literature that this frame has been translated to the media coverage of the crisis in a very standardised and uniform way, irrespective of the ideological, economical, geographical, or other media-related factors that could justify different views and opinions about economic policies. In the particular case of the press coverage, an elitist and technical analysis of the Euro crisis seems to have been the trigger for a common and dominant approach that favoured 'austerity solutions'. This chapter aims to analyse if this impression is correct or if, on the contrary, there are other factors that must be considered when analysing the different salience of austerity discourses in the European press.

To carry out this analysis, first, the coverage of austerity measures and issues will be contextualised into a framework of a more general analysis of the media coverage of the crisis of 2008. In this regard, the chapter will analyse the special complexity of this crisis, which would justify coverage adapted to and conditioned by the nature of different media outlets, such as their audiences, their countries of origin, and their editorial orientation. Second, the research on the coverage of austerity issues will be reviewed, with special attention to those studies based on news content analysis. Finally, the empirical analysis will deal with the press coverage of austerity in 10 European countries, focusing on 11 key news events related to the European sovereign debt crisis between February 2010 and July 2012. The chapter will study whether austerity measures, as short- and long-term responses to the crisis, were covered in a uniform way, testing, among others, variables such as the ideological orientation of newspapers, type of publication (business and general), country of origin, and economic conditions (countries with or without sovereign debt problems, for example).

The general hypothesis is that, even considering the general prevalence of the view that austerity was the main solution to the crisis, as a 'no alternative' policy, significant differences in the coverage of this issue depending on the geographical, political, and journalistic differences between the newspapers in our sample are to be expected.

The crisis as a complex public issue

The financial and economic crisis that started in the United States and Europe in 2008 is an important subject of study in order to further analyse the economic discourse in the media. There have been many studies that have addressed some of the dimensions of this media coverage of the crisis, applying both domestic and comparative analysis. One of the recurring ideas is that in the years before the crisis, news organizations were more or less unable to warn of existing risks in the financial industry, about housing bubbles, etc. (Schiffrin, 2011; Arrese and Vara, 2012; Usher, 2012; Mercille, 2013; Starkman, 2014; Kalogeropoulos et al., 2015; van Dalen et al., 2015). Already in the middle of the economic crisis, the media was often criticised for its simplistic, acritical, or alarmist view of the economic and financial problems (Tulloch, 2009; Arlt and Storz, 2010; Fahy et al., 2010; Uchitelle, 2011; Titley, 2012; Quiring and Weber, 2012; Mercille, 2013).

However, there are many new issues to examine, and one of them is the role of different types of media when analysing certain aspects of the crisis. This comparison between different media outlets can be done at a European level, in order to develop a better understanding of the influence of the media in shaping certain states of opinion, in Europe as a whole and country by country. Two questions can be asked: Is the crisis reported in a significantly different way to specialised audiences than to the general public? Are there clear differences in the coverage in different countries, or in groups of countries – more or less affected by the crisis – or in light of the ideological orientation of the media outlet?

There are at least three characteristics of this crisis which make it particularly suitable to answering these questions. These features are as follows:

Novelty and complexity. As explained by Reinhardt and Rogoff (2009), although this crisis shares many features with other financial crises throughout history, the truth is that it has largely been perceived as different. It was an unforeseen crisis – which has affected the real and financial economy, especially in richer countries – and how to interpret the crisis has generated a great deal of debate. It is understandable that in these novel and sometimes perplexing circumstances, and with so many doubts about how the economic problems can be solved, an intense and multifaceted debate developed.

International and national. There is no doubt that the 2008 crisis had an international character – some would argue a global character – which explains the fundamental role played by international organizations and institutions, such as the International Monetary Fund (IMF), World Bank, Organisation for Economic Co-operation and Development (OECD), rating agencies, etc.). However, at the same time, the considerably different impacts that this crisis has had on each country in the world – for example, in the European Union and the United States, or between different Eurozone countries – is quite striking. Therefore, the interaction between global or European explanations of the crisis, and the specific interpretations in each country – sometimes with very different approaches – is of special interest from the point of view of a comparative cross-national analysis.

Technical and popular. Paradoxically, perhaps the most complex economic situation of the last century has been the one that has generated the greatest interest from the general public and the media. The media themselves have been a key factor in the crisis, to the extent that the news reports helped shape more or less favourable opinions regarding certain economic policies, and created a climate of trust or distrust among citizens, between some countries with respect to others, etc. (Arrese and Vara, 2014). Perhaps more than ever, the old tensions between journalism and economics, between the rigor of expert analysis and the necessary simplifications required with respect to information about the current economic and financial events, have emerged once again.

These three characteristics of the crisis are applicable to the Euro crisis, and more particularly to the debate on austerity versus growth in the definition of economic policies to fight against it. On the one hand, the crisis has very clear technical dimensions associated with its economic and financial nature (reporting on public finances, bailouts, single currency, banking, etc.). On the other hand, many events stand out for their political significance, as the Euro crisis has evolved in response to European summits, changes of governments, national political disputes, etc. Finally, the crisis has created great interest among almost all citizens, as the different public and economic policy decisions have had enormous personal and social impacts (wage cuts, unemployment, strikes, business bankruptcies, etc.). Austerity debates have played an important role in this polyhedral discussion on the economic, political, and social dimensions of the crisis.

Austerity in the European media

Martin Wolf, chief economics commentator at the *Financial Times*, explains in his book *The Shifts and the Shocks* (2014) how the European financial and economic crisis has had two very clear phases: a first period of expansive policies from 2008 and 2010, and a second period of contractive measures from 2010 onwards. As summarised by Hall (2012), the revaluation of Greek budget deficits in 2010 turned a liquidity squeeze in the European financial system into a sovereign debt crisis, and the IMF and European Union bailed out Greece in return for deep budgetary austerity and promises of economic reform. The attention of the markets turned to Ireland, after its government unwisely guaranteed the bonds of its grossly overextended banks, and it too was forced to accept European loans in exchange for fiscal austerity. Portugal was forced into a similar deal in 2011, and new governments in Spain and Italy adopted austerity programs under pressure from the bond markets and the European Central Bank (ECB), followed by a bailout of the Spanish banks in 2012. According to Wolf (2014) "in the middle of 2010 the leaders shifted away from their strong counter-cyclical action towards austerity" (p. 90). Since then, austerity has been promoted as the hegemonic crisis discourse in Europe and elsewhere, a discourse amplified by the media, and built on the argument that there is no viable alternative to that economic policy (Blyth, 2013; Schaefer and Streeck, 2013; Karyotis and Gerodimos, 2015).

Economic policies based on austerity principles have many dimensions. Blyth describes austerity as: "[A] form of voluntary deflation in which the economy adjusts through the reduction of wages, prices, and public spending to restore competitiveness, which is (supposedly) best achieved by cutting the state's Budget, debts and deficits" (Blyth, 2013, p. 2).

In fact, austerity can also be understood as one of the two competitive frames which have been used to conceptualize and articulate the Eurozone crisis. Such frames largely pit those who explain the crisis in terms of excessive private sector debt, insufficient regulation of the global financial markets, and the need for expansionary state intervention to rescue countries in distress, against those who understand the crisis, instead, in terms of excessive public sector debt in peripheral countries, the failure of states to reign in their finances, and the need for budgetary austerity and structural reform for countries in trouble. As Schmidt points out, "while the latter are generally termed 'neo-liberals' or 'ordo-liberals' (read neo-liberals with rules, a primarily German approach to economics) the former are often called 'neo-Keynesians', although 'non-neo-liberals' might be a more accurate term" (Schmidt, 2014, p. 191).

From 2010 onwards, the neoliberal frame – pursued by European economic and political elites, in spite of a growing resistance by many European citizens and popular movements – was not only the dominant frame in European governments and institutions, but also in the mainstream media. Different studies have analysed how austerity measures have been represented in the media as a fairly unilateral and hegemonic crisis discourse, through ideological mechanisms of language and discourse (Vaara, 2014; Kelsey et al., 2016; Szabo, 2016). There have also been recent investigations of the uncritical coverage of austerity, and of the persuasive strategies which have characterised the news about the implementation of concrete austerity policies such as budget deficit cuts or fiscal consolidation measures (Mercille, 2014; Boyce and Salter, 2014; Fairclough, 2015; Berry, 2016a, 2016b; Harkins and Lugo-Ocando, 2016).

The dominant austerity narratives are also interpreted as part of a more general prevalence of neoliberal discourse in the media. Mylonas (2015), in his analysis of *Der Spiegel*, uses the coverage of austerity to criticize,

> the neoliberal hegemony of the EU's crisis politics and foregrounds the role of mainstream media, including progressivistic or objectivistic ones such as *Spiegel*, in the reproduction of neoliberal ideas that expand far beyond the crisis, to produce the institutions, social relations, beliefs and subjectivities for a post-crisis configuration of capitalism.
>
> *p. 248*

Of course, in the specific case of the Eurozone, the extension of the austerity frame as a 'no alternative' solution to the crisis has been connected to the dominant German ordoliberal thinking, as the key European 'agenda setter' (Young, 2014). As pointed out by Ojala and Harjuniemi (2016, p. 13), the German agenda, focusing on the imposition of new fiscal rules and austerity, and the need for competitiveness-enhancing structural reforms, has been a prevalent feature of the public debate across the Eurozone. As much of this agenda follows popularised ordoliberal conceptions about the causes of the crisis, emphasizing the problems of public debt, lack of fiscal discipline, and loss of competitiveness, the mainstream European press has actively contributed to the transnational mediation of 'the German ideology'.

All of the studies mentioned earlier say that the logic of austerity policies is the only and the best solution for the crisis that captured the media frame almost by storm. As commented by Compton (2014), when the crisis broke the financial implosion threw media into a disarray, reflecting the confusion of the supposedly authoritative primary definers of hegemonic 'common sense', but "very soon, despite the continuing material effects of the crash in unemployment, foreclosures and insecurity, this moment of ideological turmoil subsided. Another 'common sense' congealed, one that neutralised the radical implications of the disaster. Its watchword: 'age of austerity'" (p. 1.202). In their analysis of the press coverage of the sovereign debt crisis across Europe, Salgado et al. (2015) reinforce Compton's comments, concluding that their data analysis shows that alternatives to austerity were not intensively discussed, especially in the first phase of crisis, in 2010, when most of the decisions on how to tackle the crisis were made.

However, in order to provide a better account of the role of the media in spreading austerity thinking within the context of the European economic crisis, additional research should be conducted. For instance, Mercille (2014) has asked for research concerning, first, the differences between individual countries and also between groups of countries (southern and northern Europe countries); and second, the analysis of other elements of austerity programs – not only fiscal consolidation – such as labour reforms and the privatization of public assets (p. 296). A third interesting dimension is the contrast in how austerity measures are framed in different types of media, characterised by diverse editorial/ideological orientations, content focus, and audiences.

This chapter tries to give an answer to some of the above questions by exploring the coverage of the European sovereign debt crisis in 10 European countries and 40 newspapers, taking as a reference an analysis of the prevalence in the news of specific short-term and long-term solutions to the crisis, solutions which can be framed through the austerity versus growth debate.

Empirical research

Methodology

The analysis for this article is based on a study of 13,718 news stories about the Euro crisis published in newspapers from 10 countries of the European Union

(Finland, Belgium, France, Germany, Greece, Italy, Netherlands, Poland, Spain, and the UK) (for detailed research project explanations, see Picard [2015]).

The selection of cases was made in an effort to draw comparisons between countries that in the period researched had very different and contrasting economic circumstances: countries with serious problems of sovereign debt (Italy, Greece, and Spain), and countries without them (the rest). For each country, the printed editions of four types of daily national newspapers – the leading brand in each category – were analysed: three types of general newspapers (a conservative daily, a liberal daily, and a popular newspaper) and an economic newspaper. In the event that a country had no representative of a popular newspaper – as in the case of Spain, Italy, and France – the choice was made to include a third quality paper, one more centrist than the dailies (conservative and liberal) already selected.

Full-text articles were retrieved by national researchers from two databases: Factiva and LexisNexis. The criteria for searching the news articles that were to be included in the sample was all the articles that had the words 'euro' and 'crisis' in any part of the text: the headline, the lead, or the body. All of them had to have been published around eleven key events or developments that had been selected by the multinational research team as being representative of the evolution of the Euro crisis between 2010 and 2012, when the austerity logic emerged as the dominant narrative (Wolf, 2014). More precisely, dailies were analysed for seven days prior to and seven days after each of those events. Articles from each country were analysed by national researchers and by encoders trained in content analysis, who worked with a coding sheet of nearly 50 variables. The coding was carried out between January and March of 2013.

As for statistical methodology, in this article categorical variables have been compared between groups (types of daily newspapers) with Chi-square tests for independence and Phi (φ) values for measuring the level of association between variables. Being well aware of the limitations of Chi-square tests when used with big sample sizes – as in this case – one must be cautious not to reach uncertain conclusions derived from the data. To partly avoid this problem, a very conservative two-tailed alpha of .001 was used to determine the level of statistical significance.

Dependent variables

Coverage of austerity issues was measured by the answers to the content analysis questions centred on the short- and long-term responses to the crisis. Each article was coded according to both the short-term policy response it promoted and the more long-term reforms it presented as a way out of the crisis. The short-term policies question was: "What does the article indicate should be the main (short-term) response to the crisis?" The question had eight possible answers: the coder had to select one of them, and only if the article clearly dealt with it. The short-term responses were:

1   Loans from other countries without supervision (troika, ESM, ESFS)
2   Loans from other countries with supervision

3   ECB loans and bond purchases
4   Abatement of existing loan provisions (extension, reduced rates, haircut)
5   Reduction of budget deficits (tax increases, austerity measures)
6   Fiscal stimulus
7   Growth policies
8   None of them.

Using the same selection criteria – one response if the article clearly dealt with the issue – the coverage of long-term policies was drawn from the question: 'What does the article indicate should be the main (long-term) response to the crisis?' The answers were:

1   More European Union power over national budgets
2   Nations with weak economies dropping the Euro
3   Nations with strong economies dropping the Euro
4   National structural reforms in countries with problems (labour markets, education, tax structures)
5   Breaking up the Eurozone altogether
6   None of them.

A secondary level of analysis, especially with respect to the comparison between countries, was based on the aggregation of responses under the labels 'austerity policies' and 'growth policies'. Ojala and Harjuniemi (2016), who used the same data but for a different purpose, distinguish between 'ordoliberal', 'Keynesian', and ambivalent treatment recommendations (p. 9). This research follows basically that division. However, with respect to the austerity and growth dichotomy, the measures that Ojala and Harjuniemi consider ambivalent ('Loans from other countries without supervision', and 'More European Union power over national budgets') can easily be reassigned to one of the two frames used in this chapter: the first to the growth frame, and the second to the austerity frame.

Independent variables

Three independent variables related to the newspapers were used to test our research questions: type of newspaper, nationality, and the economic conditions of the country of origin (countries with sovereign debt problems or without them). As for the classification of newspapers, a distinction was made between business and general papers (quality and tabloids), and between centre-left, centrist and centre-right newspapers (see, for the rationale of this classification, Picard, 2015, p. 270–271). Regarding nationality, it was used as grouping variable for the 10 countries under analysis (Finland, Belgium, France, Germany, Greece, Italy, Netherlands, Poland, Spain, and the UK). Finally, a two-group variable was defined representing countries with severe sovereign debt problems (Greece, Italy, and Spain) and countries without them (the rest of them). This distinction makes reference to the Eurozone conflict area, which is structured around a powerful European core of 'strong' countries (especially Germany and France), on the one side, and a European periphery of 'weak' relatively indebted countries (Greece, Portugal, Spain, Ireland and Italy), which have had harsh austerity measures imposed upon them, on the other (Statham and Trenz, 2015, p. 13).

Results

Table 7.1 shows an overview of the quite different levels of media attention, by country, to news focused on the short- and long-term responses to the crisis. A first look at the data shows that there are three groups of countries: a first group where the newspapers had an intense interest in these issues (Greece, Italy, Germany, Netherlands, and Belgium), with around two thirds of articles (69,2%) discussing short-term measures and almost half of them (49,7%) long-term policies; a second group of countries with a much lower level of coverage, with only around one third of articles focused on those subjects (France, Poland, and UK; 32,2% and 28,3%, respectively), and two countries, Finland and Spain, with more balanced proportions. Overall, in the whole sample, 54.1% of the articles included mentions of short-term measures and 39.8% of long-term policies.

This first result is important because it indicates that the press coverage of economic measures and policies, and, as a consequence, the public debate on austerity and growth programs, has been very uneven across Europe, at least during the study period between 2010 and 2012.

When taking into account just the articles that analyse concrete responses to the crisis (leaving out the "None of them" category), and without forgetting the different extent of the overall weight of coverage between countries, Table 7.2 shows the results with respect to the coverage of the short-term responses, depending on the independent variables used in this study.

As expected, there is a clear pattern of predominance of two types of measures linked to austerity ("Loans from other countries with supervision" and "Reduction of budget deficits"), but the economic policy mix that emerges from the analysis of the press coverage varies significantly depending on both the editorial orientation (X2 [12, N = 3.859] = 76.26, p < .001, φ = .141) and the economic conditions in the country of origin (X2 [6, N = 6.557] = 147.50, p < .001, φ = .150) of the newspapers. The data indicate that the conservative press and the papers in countries without serious sovereign debt problems pay more attention to proposals based on austerity thinking than to measures following a growth rationale. These differences in coverage do not exist, however, when analysing the contrast between the economic press and the general interest press. In this case, the differences that are shown in Table 7.2 are not statistically significant (X2 [6, N = 6.557] = 22.19, p = .001), although they are at the limit of significance (p < .001) adopted for this study. It is interesting to note that, in fact, according to the data, it appears that the economic press discusses expansionary policies a bit more frequently than the general press.

TABLE 7.1 Articles which mention short- and long-term responses to the crisis

	Belgium	Finland	France	Germany	Greece	Italy	Nether.	Poland	Spain	UK	Total
Short-term responses	529	503	720	1.426	1.123	1.284	446	196	571	626	**7.424**
%	66.7%	57.4%	31.6%	62.5%	82.7%	67.8%	66.5%	32.1%	53.8%	33.0%	**54.1%**
None	264	373	1.558	854	235	610	225	414	491	1.270	**6.294**
%	33.3%	42.6%	68.4%	37.5%	17.3%	32.2%	33.5%	67.9%	46.2%	67.0%	**45.9%**
Long-term responses	376	260	648	1.086	655	964	367	193	437	470	**5.456**
%	47.4%	29.7%	28.4%	47.6%	48.2%	50.9%	54.7%	31.6%	41.1%	24.8%	**39.8%**
None	417	616	1.630	1.194	703	930	304	417	625	1.426	**8.262**
%	52.6%	70.3%	71.6%	52.4%	51.8%	49.1%	45.3%	68.4%	58.9%	75.2%	**60.2%**
Total	**793**	**876**	**2.278**	**2.280**	**1.358**	**1.894**	**671**	**610**	**1.062**	**1.896**	**13.718**

TABLE 7.2 Short-term responses to the crisis

	Loans from other countries without supervision		Loans from other countries with supervision		ECB loans and bond purchases		Abatement of existing loan provision		Reduction of budget deficits		Fiscal stimulus		Growth policies	
Type of newspaper	**N° Articles**	**%**	**N° Articles**	**%**	**N° Articles**	**%**	**N° Articles**	**%**	**N° Articles**	**%**	**N° Articles**	**%**	**N° Articles**	**%**
Business	352	17.5	385	19.1	375	18.6	175	8.7	467	23.2	72	3.6	188	9.3
General interest	709	15.6	1.064	23.4	749	16.5	351	7.7	1.099	24.2	181	4.0	390	8.6
Editorial orientation														
Conservative	195	13.8	363	25.7	243	17.2	101	7.1	373	26.4	44	3.1	94	6.7
Liberal	302	16.7	415	23.0	288	15.9	141	7.8	410	22.7	66	3.7	184	10.2
Center	156	24.4	108	16.9	121	18.9	33	5.2	142	22.2	11	1.7	69	10.8
Group of countries of origin														
With debt problems	353	13.2	519	19.3	437	16.3	261	9.7	666	24.8	171	6.4	277	10.3
Without debt problems	708	18.3	930	24.0	687	17.7	265	6.8	900	23.2	82	2.1	301	7.8

The same pattern was shown in the coverage of long-term responses to the crisis. As can be seen in Table 7.3, an economic policy clearly aligned with the frame of austerity ("National structural reforms in countries with problems") was the focus in around 50% of the articles dealing with this subject. But again, the map of the specific set of proposals differs in a statistically significant way between publications with different editorial orientations (X2 [8, N = 2,895] = 30.81, p < .001, φ = .103) and between those published in countries with very different economic circumstances (X2 [4, N = 4.679] = 69.10, p < .001, φ = .122). However, the differences are not significant when comparing the coverage carried out by business and general newspapers (X2 [4, N = 4.679] = 2.13, p =.710).

Similar results in statistical terms are obtained when analysing the coverage of measures grouped into two categories: austerity measures and growth measures. When considering the grouping of short-term responses to the crisis in this way, the results for the three variables investigated are the following: editorial orientation (X2 [2, N = 3.859] = 31.52, p < .001, φ = .090), group of countries of origin (X2 [1, N = 6.557] = 14.13, p < .001, φ = .046), and type of newspaper (business vs. general) (X2 [1, N = 6.557] = 6.04, p = .014). Once again, the difference between general and specialised press coverage is not statistically significant.

This more general and dual distinction between austerity and growth measures is also useful for showing how the nationality of publications (country as a grouping variable) is associated with significant differences in coverage (X2 [9, N = 6.557] = 224.86, p < .001, φ = .185), despite the basic trend of giving more space to austerity policies. Table 7.4 gives the data for the distribution, by country, of news focused on the two types of measures.

As can be seen from the data in Table 7.4, in general terms the number of articles devoted to austerity measures (63.1%) are almost double to those focused on growth measures (36.9%). Three countries (Greece, Poland, and Spain) follow the average pattern. For its part, Germany, UK, and Belgium stand out by the higher prevalence of the austerity frame (77.6%, 69.9%, and 67.9%, respectively), and France, Finland, and Italy by a higher-than-average attention to growth policies (46.4%. 45.8%, and 42.2%, respectively). Only in one country – the Netherlands – was the attention paid by newspapers to growth measures (53.6% of all articles) greater than the attention paid to austerity measures (46.4% of articles). In fact, as shown in Table 7.4, the country variable is the most significant factor among those investigated in this chapter.

To sum up, the results of the statistical analysis allow us to conclude that the press coverage of austerity and growth policies as responses to the sovereign debt crisis has not been uniform across Europe. Although there is more coverage supporting austerity overall, as has already been analysed in other studies, both the editorial orientation and the country of origin of newspapers are associated with significant divergences in the economic policy mix which they present. Although the size of the statistical associations between variables are in general weak (in the range of small effects φ values between .1 and .2), the results revealed enough consistency (a regular pattern in the case of short- and long-term measures) and statistical significance (with a conservative p value < .001) so as to take them into consideration, at

TABLE 7.3 Long-term responses to the crisis

	More EU power over national budgets		Nations with weak economies dropping the Euro		Nations with strong economies dropping the Euro		National structural reforms in nations with problems		Breaking up the Eurozone altogether	
	N° Articles	%	N° Articles	%	N° Articles	%	N° Articles	%	N° Articles	%
Type of newspaper										
Business	496	34.9	137	9.6	20	1.4	745	52.4	24	1.7
General Interest	1176	36.1	339	10.4	52	1.6	1638	50.3	52	1.6
Editorial orientation										
Conservative	403	36.3	107	9.6	17	1.5	564	50.8	19	1.7
Liberal	436	33.9	139	10.8	18	1.4	674	52.4	19	1.5
Center	228	45.7	44	8.8	14	2.8	203	40.7	10	2.0
Group of countries of origin										
With debt problems	574	32.6	248	14.1	36	2.0	859	48.8	43	2.4
Without debt problems	1098	37.6	228	7.8	36	1.2	1524	52.2	33	1.1

TABLE 7.4 Coverage of austerity and growth policies by country

	Belgium	Finland	France	Germany	Greece	Italy	Nether.	Poland	Spain	UK	Total
Growth policies	152	201	320	280	395	478	192	65	189	146	2.418
%	32.1%	45.8%	46.4%	22.4%	37.6%	42.2%	53.6%	36.1%	37.9%	30.1%	36.9%
Austerity policies	321	238	370	968	656	656	166	115	310	339	4.139
%	67.9%	54.2%	53.6%	77.6%	62.4%	57.8%	46.4%	63.9%	62.1%	69.9%	63.1%
Total	473	439	690	1.248	1.051	1.134	358	180	499	485	6.557
%	100.0%	100.0%	100.0%	100.0%	100.0%	100.0%	100.0%	100.0%	100.0%	100.0%	100.0%

least from a theoretical, more so than applied, point of view. This also applies to the most interesting result of this chapter, namely the strong uniformity in the coverage of austerity and growth measures among the business and the general interest press.

Conclusion

The analysis of the economic discourse of the media on austerity adds a new dimension to the debate about the extent to which the media coverage of economic issues tends to produce uniform thinking, interpretations dominated by technical arguments, and institutional and elitist explanations of current events.

On the one hand, this analysis confirms that the austerity discourse has dominated the European press coverage on the short- and long-term solutions to the sovereign debt crisis. However, the study also shows that the concrete mix of economic policies, and the balance between austerity and growth frames, differs significantly among countries, groups of countries with different economic circumstances, and newspapers with different editorial orientations. This finding confirms the hypothesis that, even accepting a general prevalence of the austerity frame as the main guide for responding to the crisis, as a 'no alternative' policy, significant differences in the media's (newspapers') coverage of this issue depending on the geographical, political, and journalistic differences between press outlets are to be expected.

On the other hand, an unexpectedly strong uniformity was found in the coverage of short- and long-term solutions to the crisis among the business and the general press. This finding could reinforce the results of other studies on the media coverage of the Euro crisis, which have demonstrated that the media has not been able to distance itself from the specialised frameworks of analysis used by experts and economic agents (Arrese and Vara, 2015). They define the European institutional debate and are very active in setting its limits. This idea has been supported by several studies, such as Fahy et al. (2010), Titley (2012), and Mercille (2014) on the Euro crisis coverage by Irish general newspapers, and Mylonas (2012) on the representation of the Greek crisis in the German popular daily *Bild*. All of these studies have pointed out that the discussion about the crisis has been dominated by the logic of elite-to-elite communication, which highlights the views of political, business, and financial institutions, at the expense of 'man-on-the-street' perspectives.

The homogeneous coverage of austerity and growth measures carried out by the general and specialised press, around a public issue with so many effects and consequences for every European citizen, shows how difficult it is for the media to stand aside from expert and institutional discourses or to forge new frames for analysing economic events outside the prevalent consensus, usually guided by the principles of a free market economy. The case analysed in this chapter could also be used as an example of the extension of elite-to-elite communication logic and practices to the journalistic coverage of complex issues which are important for the whole society, and which should be better dealt with through a more generic, elite-to-masses communication logic (Davis, 2000, 2003, 2005; Strömbäck, 2008; Kunelis and Reunanen, 2012; Thompson, 2013).

References

Arlt, H.-J., and Storz, W. 2010. *Wirtschaftsjournalismus in der Krise*. Frankfurt/Main: Otto Brenner Stiftung.

Arrese, Á., and Vara, A. 2012. 'Canarios en la mina? La prensa y los riesgos de la "burbuja inmobiliaria" en España'. Comunicación y riesgo. III Congreso Internacional de la Asociación Española de Investigación en Comunicación, AE-IC, Tarragona, 20 December.

Arrese, A., and Vara, A. 2015. Divergent perspectives? Financial newspapers and the general interest press. In: Picard, R. (ed.), *The Euro crisis in the media: Journalistic coverage of economic crisis and European institutions*. London: I. B Tauris & The Reuters Institute for the Study of Journalism, University of Oxford. pp. 149–176.

Arrese, Á., and Vara, A. 2014. 'Alarma y alarmismo: medios de comunicación y crisis económica'. *Estudios sobre el Mensaje Periodístico*, 20(2), pp. 933–951.

Berry, M. 2016a. 'The UK press and the deficit debate'. *Sociology*, 50(3), pp. 542–559.

Berry, M. 2016b. 'No alternative to austerity: how BBC broadcast news reported the deficit debate'. *Media, Culture & Society*, 38(6), pp. 844–863.

Blyth, M. 2013. *Austerity: The history of a dangerous idea*. New York: Oxford University Press.

Boyce, J., and Salter, L. 2014. 'Framing the cuts: An analysis of the BBC's discursive framing of the ConDem cuts agenda'. *Journalism*, 15(6), pp. 754–772.

Compton, J. 2014. 'Prolegomenon to a theory of slump media'. *Media, Culture & Society*, 36(8), pp. 1196–1206.

Davis, A. 2000. 'Public relations, business news, and the reproduction of corporate elite power'. *Journalism*, 1(3), pp. 282–304.

Davis, A. 2003. 'Whither mass media and power? Evidence for a critical elite theory alternative'. *Media, Culture and Society*, 25(5), pp. 669–690.

Davis, A. 2005. 'Media effects and the active elite audience. A study of communication in the London Stock Exchange'. *European Journal of Communication*, 20(3), pp. 303–326.

Fahy, D., O'Brien, M., and Poti, V. 2010. 'Combative critics or captured collaborators? Irish financial journalism and the end of the Celtic tiger.' *Irish Communications Review*, 12, pp. 5–21.

Fairclough, I. 2015. 'Evaluating policy as argument: the public debate over the first UK austerity budget.' *Critical Discourse Studies*, 13(1), pp. 57–77.

Hall, P. A. 2012. 'The economics and politics of the Euro Crisis'. *German Politics*, 21(4), pp. 355–371.

Harkins, S., and Lugo-Ocando, J. 2016. 'How Malthusian ideology crept into the newsroom: British tabloids and the coverage of the 'underclass''. *Critical Discourse Studies*, 13(1), pp. 78–93.

Kalogeropoulos, A., Svensson, H. M., van Dalen, A., de Vreese, C., and Albaek, E. 2015. 'Are watchdogs doing their business? Media coverage of economic news'. *Journalism*, 16 (8), 993–1009.

Karyotis, G., and Gerodimos, R. (eds.). 2015. *The politics of extreme Austerity: Greece in the Eurozone crisis*. London: Palgrave Macmillan.

Kelsey, D., Mueller, F., Whittle, A., and KhosraviNik, M. 2016. 'Financial crisis and austerity: interdisciplinary concerns in critical discourse studies'. *Critical Discourse Studies*, 13(1), pp. 1–19.

Kunelis, R., and Reunanen, E. 2012. 'Media in political power: A Parsonian view on the differentiated mediatization of Finnish Decision Makers'. *The International Journal of Press/Politics*, 17(1), pp. 56–75.

Mercille, J. 2013. 'The role of the media in sustaining Ireland's housing bubble'. *New Political Economy*, 19(2), pp. 282–301.

Mercille, J. 2014. 'The role of media in fiscal consolidation programmes: The case of Ireland'. *Cambridge Journal of Economics*, 3 (2), pp. 281–300.

Mylonas, Y. 2012. 'Media and the economic crisis of the EU: The 'Culturalization' of a systemic crisis and Bild-Zeitung's Framing of Greece'. *Triple C*, 10(2), pp. 646–671.

Mylonas, Y. 2015. 'Austerity discourses in 'Der Spiegel' Journal, 2009–2014'. *Triple C*, 13 (1), pp. 248–269.

Ojala, M., and Harjuniemi T. 2016. 'Mediating the German ideology: Ordoliberal framing in European Press coverage of the Eurozone crisis'. *Journal of Contemporary European Studies*, 24(3), pp. 414–430.

Picard, R. (ed.). 2015. *The Euro crisis in the media: Journalistic coverage of economic crisis and European institutions*. London: I. B Tauris & The Reuters Institute for the Study of Journalism, University of Oxford.

Quiring, O., and Weber, M. 2012. 'Between usefulness and legitimacy: Media coverage of governmental intervention during the financial Crisis and selected effects'. *The International Journal of Press/Politics*, 17(3), pp. 294–315.

Reinhardt, C., and Rogoff, K. S. 2009. *This time is different: Eight centuries of financial folly*. Princeton: Princeton University Press.

Salgado, S., Nienstedt, H.-W., and Schneider, L. 2015. Consensus or discussion? An analysis of plurality and consonance in coverage. In: Picard, R. (ed.), *The Euro crisis in the media: Journalistic coverage of economic crisis and European institutions*. London: I. B Tauris & The Reuters Institute for the Study of Journalism, University of Oxford. pp. 103–124.

Schaefer, A., and Streeck, W. (eds.). 2013. *Politics in the age of austerity*. Cambridge: Polity.

Schiffrin, A. (ed.). 2011. *Bad news. How America's business press missed the story of the century*. New York: The New Press.

Schmidt, V. A. 2014. 'Speaking to the markets or to the people? A discursive Institutionalist analysis of the EU's Sovereign Debt Crisis'. *The British Journal of Politics and Institutional Relations*, 16, pp. 188–209.

Starkman, D. 2014. *The watchdog that didn't bark: The financial crisis and the disappearance of investigative journalism*. New York: Columbia University Press.

Statham, P., and Trenz, H.-J. 2015. 'Understanding the mechanisms of the EU politicization: Lessons from the Eurozone crisis'. *Comparative European Politics*, 13, pp. 287–306.

Strömbäck, J. 2008. 'Four phases of mediatization: An analysis of the mediatization of politics'. *International Journal of Press/Politics*, 13(3), pp. 228–246.

Szabo, A. 2016. 'Organizing the (sociomaterial) economy: Ritual, agency, and economic models'. *Critical Discourse Studies*, 13(1), pp. 118–136.

Thompson, P. A. 2013. 'Invested interests? Reflexivity, representation, and reporting in financial markets'. *Journalism*, 14(2), pp. 208–227.

Titley, G. 2012. 'Budgetjam! A communications intervention in the political-economic crisis in Ireland'. *Journalism*, 14(2), pp. 292–306.

Tulloch, J. 2009. 'From amnesia to apocalypse: Reflections on journalism and the credit crunch'. *Ethical Space: The International Journal of Communication Ethics*, 6(3/4), pp. 99–109.

Uchitelle, L. 2011. 'The uses and misuses of economics in daily journalism'. *History of Political Economy*, 43(2), pp. 363–368.

Usher, N. 2012. 'Ignored, uninterested, and the blame game: How the New York Times, Marketplace and The street distanced themselves from preventing the 2007–2008 financial crisis'. *Journalism*, 14(2), pp. 190–207.

Vaara, E. 2014. 'Struggles over legitimacy in the Eurozone crisis: Discursive legitimation strategies and their ideological underpinnings'. *Discourse & Society*, 25(4), pp. 500–518.

van Dalen, A., de Vreese, C., and Albæk, E. 2015. 'Economic news through the magnifying glass'. *Journalism Studies*, DOI: 10.1080/1461670X.2015.1089183

Wolf, M. 2014. *The shifts and the shocks: What we've learned-and have still to learn-from the financial crisis*. New York: Penguin Press.

Young B. 2014. 'German Ordoliberalism as agenda setter for the Euro crisis: Myth trumps reality'. *Journal of Contemporary European Studies*, 22(3), pp. 276–287.

8

SAFEGUARDING THE STATUS QUO

The press and the emergence of a new left
in Greece and Spain

Maria Kyriakidou and Iñaki Garcia-Blanco

Introduction

SYRIZA and Podemos, the two Southern European parties, have emerged as
two major anti-austerity voices within the context of the Euro crisis, bringing
left politics to the fore of the European public sphere. SYRIZA and Podemos
have obtained significant electoral successes over the last few years, after having
embraced the claims of the 2011 Indignados protests in Spain and Greece. This success was fuelled by civic resentment towards political corruption and the austerity
politics imposed by Eurozone officials and national governments in an attempt to
tackle the economic crisis. Their anti-austerity and anti-establishment politics are
signaled by some to be at the root of a transformation of the political left in Europe
and beyond (Jones, 2016; Cassidy, 2016). This chapter examines how the ascendance
of SYRIZA and Podemos was portrayed in the mainstream press in Greece and
Spain, respectively.

SYRIZA, a party formed through a coalition of Greek left-wing and radical-left
parties in 2004, was the winner in the Greek General Elections in January 2015 and
has been in power through a coalition government since. This brought the two-
party system (PASOK and New Democracy) that had alternated in government
since 1977 to an end. Meanwhile, Podemos was founded in early 2014 in Spain and
has obtained remarkable results in the European Parliament elections in 2014, as
well as in the regional, municipal,[1] and General Elections held in 2015, constituting
the third-most-voted party at the national level (after the People's Party and the
Socialist Party, alternating in government since 1982). In both countries, these elections marked a historical low for the established two-party systems.

Being the most significant political parties challenging austerity policies within
Europe, Podemos and SYRIZA do not only contest hegemonic definitions of the
crisis: they also pose a challenge to well-established national political landscapes

and by extension to the mainstream media discourses that have reproduced and legitimised them. Classic and contemporary works in media research illustrate how the mainstream media privilege the discourses of elites and adopt their framing of issues (Gitlin, 1980; Glasgow Media Group, 1980; Wahl-Jorgensen et al., 2013). This has been especially the case in the construction of the Euro crisis (Mylonas, 2014; Doudaki, 2015; Berry, 2016). Through a textual analysis, we explore how the Greek and Spanish domestic press covered these parties during the electoral campaigns that confirmed SYRIZA and Podemos as significant political actors. Although the analysis does not follow pre-existing categories, it is informed by Laclau and Mouffe's approach to discourse theory (2001) and Fairclough's Critical Discourse Analysis, inasmuch as we take the reports analyzed to be the "outcome of power relations and power struggle" (Fairclough, 1989, p. 2). The choice of newspapers for the study was based on the papers' ideological allegiances and circulation numbers. For Greece, these choices were *Kathimerini* (conservative, centre-right), *Ta Nea* (centre-left, middle-class readership), and *Naftemporiki* (daily financial newspaper). For Spain, the respective choices were the centre-right *El Mundo*, the centre-left *El País*, and the conservative *ABC*. Our sample consists of all articles containing the words 'SYRIZA' (in the Greek sample) or 'Podemos' (in the Spanish sample) during the week preceding each of the key dates (18–24 May 2014 for both countries, 18–24 January 2015 for Greece and 17–23 May 2015 for Spain).

We start from the assumption that a crucial dimension of the media's power is the power to create the contexts of political life – and legitimise its actors – since media discourses constantly provide us with interpretations of politics which normalise some definitions while discrediting others (Cammaerts and Carpentier, 2007). In particular, we are interested in the discursive mechanisms employed by the national press to portray these parties as legitimate political actors and as (un)able to deal with the crisis. We also explore whether the newspapers' construction of these parties and their anti-austerity politics are filtered through dominant neoliberal narratives of domestic politics and crisis management. We do not take these media discourses to be closed and fixed systems of meaning. Our research, in fact, shows that there were differences, both among the different newspapers and between the two countries. However, there were also common practices through which meanings and interpretations of these two parties of the left were constructed. It is these commonalities that we focus on here.

Political context, the crisis (and how to solve it), and the media

The current economic crisis has dominated European politics since it started in 2008. After a two-year period pursuing economic stimulus policies a move towards austerity politics gained force following the Greek debt crisis in 2010. Either embraced by national governments (such as in the British case), or imposed by supranational organisations upon bailed-out countries (such as in the case of Spain and Greece), austerity became the standard political solution to bring state finances back in order.

Although readily applied by political leaders, strict austerity policies have asphyxiated the economies and social landscapes of Southern European countries, deepening problems of poverty and unemployment, and hitting the already disadvantaged. After one bailout, and five years of austerity policies, unemployment continues to be above the 20% mark in Spain and the share of population at risk of poverty or social exclusion above 25% (European Commission, 2016). The situation is worse in Greece, where unemployment rates reached 24.4% in January 2016 (Eurostat, 2016) and about 36% of the population is at risk of poverty or social exclusion (Eurostat, 2015).

Despite the obvious failures of austerity policies, financial experts, politicians, and supranational organisations have adhered to the doctrine of austerity almost en bloc. This doctrine dominated mainstream media discourses (Berry, 2016), in spite of the fact that critical economists (cf. Wren-Lewis, 2015) and civil society organisations such as trade unions (Picard, 2015) advocated for alternative remedies. Media coverage deflected from the structural and political problems within the Eurozone that were at the root of the crisis. Through privileging government leaders, bankers, or economists as primary news sources, and downplaying the stakes and interests of citizens and civil society organisations, the mainstream media constructed the crisis as an exclusively financial or economic issue (Picard, 2015). At the same time, they legitimised austerity policies imposed by the Eurozone leaders and thus empowered the construction of the hegemonic neoliberal rhetoric (Mylonas, 2014; Doudaki, 2015).

These modalities of covering the crisis and (anti-)austerity politics need to be viewed within a broader context of neoliberal discourses supported and reproduced by the media. Austerity policies themselves, and the related privatisation and deregulation of the economy imposed by creditors, are an illustration of how "the power bloc of the debt economy has seized on the latest financial crisis as the perfect occasion to extend and deepen the logic of neoliberal politics" (Lazzarato, 2012, p. 29), a logic which is supported and enabled by mainstream media.

The emergence of SYRIZA and Podemos as prominent political players brought anti-austerity politics to the centre stage, challenging the views held by established political parties, commentators, and the media. Taking into account the hitherto stability of the two-party system and the high degree of political parallelism in both countries (Hallin and Mancini, 2004), some reservations towards these new parties could be expected in the newspaper coverage. The following section will explore the ways in which these reservations materialised in the media.

The political left and the threat of populism

The origins of SYRIZA and Podemos differ significantly. Podemos was founded in early 2014, as a rushed attempt to create a new anti-austerity option for the European Parliament elections. Founded in 2004, SYRIZA had already overtaken PASOK in the legislative elections in 2012 (from being the fifth party in 2009). In 2014, opinion polls indicated that SYRIZA could win the elections, breaking the duopoly of New Democracy and PASOK for the first time in 50 years. Newspaper coverage in the two countries reflected the different nature of the parties.

The strong, stable bipartisanship that had defined Spanish politics since the country's transition to democracy led to meager coverage for Podemos in the European election campaign (only 17 stories mentioned Podemos in our sample. Out of these stories, only one focused exclusively on Podemos). Eight stories forecasted Podemos to get one (maximum two) seats, relatively far from the five seats it finally obtained. There was no coverage of the party's suggested policies, apart from the two electoral commitments from its candidates: their refusal to fly in business class if elected to Parliament, and their pledge to limit the salary of any elected members of the European Parliament (MEP) from this party to 1,930 Euros/month (instead of the 8,000 Euros/month that MEPs get). Although scant, coverage of Podemos in 2014 already shared traits with SYRIZA's media portrayal, a feature that would intensify in our sample from the elections in 2015.

Throughout our entire sample, the two parties were constructed as political risks and, by extension, voting for them as an unwise choice. Greek newspapers presented SYRIZA as a threat to the political stability reportedly achieved by the coalition government of New Democracy, PASOK, and DIMAR. In both pre-election periods, 'stability' became a nodal point in the discussion of Greek politics, organising competing narratives on the country's future. Employed along with terms such as 'bailout program', 'sustainable path', and 'taken reforms', political stability acquired an economic meaning and came to signify the austerity measures imposed by Greece's creditors and adopted by the coalition government.

What is more, the construction of political stability as a path equivalent to austerity reforms is almost exclusively based on the use of institutional sources and financial experts. Introducing a short interview with Finnish PM, Alex Stubb, *Kathimerini* writes:

> Although Mr Stubb is not openly referring to SYRIZA, his message is clear. Greece must fulfill the whole program and its sustainable path without cancelling former reforms.
>
> *Varvitsioti, 2015*

Constructing the fulfillment of the bailout program as the only way forward for the country leaves no space for alternative interpretations. At the same time, the framing of Stubb's interview constructs SYRIZA as 'clearly' a divergence from this 'sustainable path' and therefore a threat to stability. *Ta Nea* also warns that trying a new government under such conditions:

> is not something neutral, we are not talking here about a bottle of wine, but the country's direction after the coming elections. And given the medley of views within SYRIZA, this direction is not at all clear.
>
> *Mitsos, 2014*

In this process, the 'market' is constructed as an entity independent of human agency and therefore politically neutral. Market sources are, by extension, constructed as objective commentators. The Greek press often provided insights into how 'foreign firms' view the 'political developments' in Greece. For Credit Agricole, the French banking group, *Kathimerini* argues:

> The main threat is that anti-European parties will get a considerable number of votes, which will probably reverse part of the progress that has been achieved through economic reforms . . . the biggest threat is in Greece . . . if SYRIZA wins with a big majority.
>
> *Kathimerini, 2014*

SYRIZA is therefore equated not only to the "biggest threat" for "progress" but also implicitly described as an "anti-European" party.

Similarly, Podemos' politics and policies are repeatedly defined as "impracticable", as "left populism is incompatible with market social economy" (Moscoso, 2015). Such claims invariably reinforce the idea that there is no alternative to the (austerity) economic policies currently in place, and that any attempt to formulate an alternative is either undesirable, or deemed to failure. Coverage in Spain also warned about the risks that a victory of Podemos candidates in the municipal and regional elections could bring upon international trade:

> If the surge of populism in Spain is confirmed, stability will be affected. This will reduce the trust of international investors, and will have unpredictable consequences.
>
> *Alcázar, 2015*

Juxtaposed to the master signifier of stability, SYRIZA (and its politics) is presented as a political risk and destabilising factor. The construction of the party as a political liability takes place through the organisation of a chain of equivalence, whereby SYRIZA"s left-wing politics are discussed along with "emotional fantasies", "inexperience", "indignation", "extremism", "anti-Europeanism", and "populism". The construction of SYRIZA as a populist threat to political and economic stability was further articulated through a process of personalisation, whereby Alexis Tsipras, the leader of the party, was discussed in parallel to Andreas Papandreou (PASOK), whose virtually fifteen-year reign in the eighties has been linked to excessive expenditures, overgrowth of the public sector, and other policies considered partially responsible for the country's current crisis. Such a comparison undermined SYRIZA policies as lacking in novelty and radicalism, and implicitly constructed them as further risking the Greek economy.

The coverage of SYRIZA as an extreme political formation also constructed the party as the left equivalent of the far-right Golden Dawn. This theory of the two extremes, or the "horseshoe theory" (Faye, 2004), dominated public discourse in Greece throughout SYRIZA's evolution as a leading party (Anastasakis, 2013). Ideologically, this assumption undermined the party's anti-austerity arguments as populist rhetoric and framed them as a political threat, thus serving the interests of the coalition government. At the same time, it articulated a discursive equivalence between SYRIZA and Golden Dawn, which apart from undermining left politics also wrongly drew parallels between the inclusionary left-wing populism of the left and the far-right's racist, nationalist, and exclusionary rhetoric (Stavrakakis and Katsambekis, 2014).

In the absence of an extreme-right party in Spanish political institutions, Podemos was often linked with SYRIZA, an association that even journalists defined as "recurrent" (Sánchez-Vallejo, 2015). The "populist" label, however, was also used to link both parties to right-wing formations: "Common sense (rather than fear) will win the battle against the populism of parties like Podemos, UKIP or SYRIZA" (González, 2015). Most importantly, though, Podemos was often framed as the equivalent of socialism, particularly (but not only) as advocated by Hugo Chávez in Venezuela. References to Podemos' 'totalitarian', 'Bolivarian', 'communist', or 'radical' nature could be found across the three newspapers. The association with Chávez was not entirely gratuitous: Podemos' founders had an academic interest in Latin America, had carried out research commissioned by the Venezuelan government in the past, and embraced what the leader of Podemos defined as Latin American "theoretical tools" to interpret Spanish reality (Iglesias, 2015, p. 14). Podemos, however, never advocated for the instauration of a Bolivarian regime in Spain, and embraced social democracy as a political model instead. Similarly to SYRIZA's case in Greece, the party's novelty was discredited and presented as a mere replication of socialist or Bolivarian regimes, implicitly or explicitly constructing Podemos as devoid of political awareness and proposals. In this vein, commentators resorted to simplistic, reductionist, and derogatory characterisations of left-wing politics instead of discussing Podemos' policy proposals.

Populism – or demagoguery – and its allusion to Venezuelan politics, was key in this discursive construction that ultimately presented Podemos as a threat not only to established politics, but even to democracy itself. An article in *El País* read:

> In Latin America, demagogues reach power, and take over the people's will, instituting tyranny. This happened in Venezuela, whose government inspired (and on occasion funded) Podemos' leaders. One would imagine that Venezuela's obvious tragedy would be enough for sound voters to be dissuaded from importing this political model. But soundness is not a virtue that is democratically distributed.
>
> *Krauze, 2015*

If SYRIZA was covered as a threat to the Greek economic stability, Podemos was constructed as a risk to the democratic system in Spain (Calleja and Mira, 2015; Jabois, 2015). There were voices associating Podemos with the Republican side in the Spanish Civil War too. In this vein, Sostres (2015), an extremely controversial right-wing commentator, warned in *El Mundo*:

> If we managed to save our lives, it would be the first time that the extreme left is in power and does not kill us all. Podemos is nostalgic of a horrifying bloodbath. . . . Most of those who will not vote on Sunday will be hunted for in their houses on Monday. This is an imminent danger: firing squads are only a step-up from 'escraches'.[2]

Such hyperbole, drawing links of equivalence between Podemos' populism and so-called left-wing authoritarian regimes, to the Republican faction in the Spanish Civil War, or to political systems with questionable democratic standards (such as Venezuela) constructs Podemos as an extremist, revolutionary party which would pose a threat to Spanish democracy. An extreme case formulation opposes Podemos' 'impracticable policies' and the threat the party poses to democracy on one side of this constructed spectrum, against the 'stability' and the democratic credentials of mainstream political parties. This construction does not only undermine Podemos' credibility as a legitimate political actor: it also contributes to justify the soundness of mainstream parties' policies (including austerity policies).

The press in both countries uses populism as a central signifier of political threat and a discursive mechanism for the delegitimisation of the left. Such anti-populist discourses, Stavrakakis and Katsambekis (2014) argue, have proliferated during the crisis and ultimately aim at the discursive policing and political marginalisation of emerging anti-austerity voices.

Affective politics and the win of SYRIZA

Anti-populist rhetoric and the construction of SYRIZA's anti-austerity politics as a threat to political and economic stability were prominent during the period before the General Elections of January 2015 in Greece. At the same time, however, and given the fact that there were indications of a SYRIZA win, there was a slight change in the coverage of the party, or rather an addition of a further dimension in its discursive delegitimisation. This had to do with the drawing of a dichotomy between *affective politics*, as reportedly expressed by SYRIZA and its voters, and *real politics*, represented by the political status quo. To the latter, SYRIZA was juxtaposed once again as inexperienced and lacking awareness. Stability in this period remains a nodal point against which the narratives of the forthcoming election are organised, but now this stability seems to be threatened not only by populism, but mostly by its emotional appeal.

In this context, there are two competing chains of equivalence constructed through the press coverage. On the one hand, SYRIZA is constructed as "the tiny radical left party made of the utopian dream of lecture theatres, which suffered electoral bloating" (Georgakopoulos, 2015). The political propositions of the party are discussed in emotional terms, as "lyrical promises", "utopias", manipulations of the "despair of the voters" and their "hope". Illustrative of this discursive trope is the following description of the party's pre-election campaign spot:

> SYRIZA's campaign draws from the value-tanks of the left, has empathy, passion, music that moves you. . . . But how useful is the power of hope when it has no control over the reality it aspires to change? The discourse of SYRIZA blooms in ambiguity, blank points and inconsistencies.
>
> *Pagoulatos, 2015*

On the other hand, "inevitable reality" is expressed by the coalition government, and discussed along "commitments" towards the European partners, "Europe", "necessary reforms". "Politics" and "reality" are juxtaposed to "the value-tanks of the left", "empathy" and "passion". Interestingly, the predicted win of SYRIZA is mostly framed as a loss of the coalition government, caused by "tactical" or "strategic mistakes". SYRIZA's win, in this context, is constructed as the result of the manipulation of emotions rather than a "strategic" or "tactical" win. The party is still constructed as a risk, but in that period

> The risk is that it's about a party of 3.5% leveraged to the hilt because of popular ire and populism.
>
> *Mitropoulos, 2015*

The construction of affect and emotions as apolitical undermines the politics of SYRIZA and the left as a legitimate political proposal to the economic solutions to the Euro crisis imposed by the Troika and implemented by the Greek coalition government. At the same time, however, it also undermines the everyday experience of citizens as a legitimate basis for politics. On the contrary, voters are constructed as emotionally driven and politically naive, at best, or ignorant, at worst.

Podemos and political inconsistency

For Podemos, the period between the European elections of 2014 and the local elections of 2015 also seemed to have enriched the discursive techniques of undermining the legitimacy of the party as a political alternative. The framing of the party as a populist threat continued and was most prominent in the conservatives *ABC* and *El Mundo*, which still identified Podemos' political project as "authoritarian. An anti-capitalist project that goes against the basis of the system" (Camacho, 2015).

This discursive repertoire aside, there was a further practice of neutralising the party's politics through press coverage. Although Podemos did not officially participate in the municipal elections of 2015, the party had already gained momentum and become more vocal in Spanish politics. This seemed to signal a move from its framing as being a threat – although this framing was not completely abandoned – to the neutralising of the political voice of the party through a double process.

On the one hand, the newspapers constructed Podemos as a moderate party, which had abandoned its radicalism and novel ideas:

> Podemos' manifesto has switched to the centre, abandoning their more radical ideas, such as the sovereign debt default, or the basic universal allowance.
>
> *Manetto, 2015*

> Podemos has been switching towards the centre in recent weeks, hoping to appeal to a wider sector of the electorate.
>
> *El Mundo, 2015b*

> Podemos has turned into one of the parties that it aimed to destroy.
>
> *Pérez-Maura, 2015*

Described as centrist in its politics, the party is no longer undermined because it stands in opposition to the stability provided by the existing status quo, but precisely because it becomes part of the status quo. By creating equivalence between Podemos' political propositions and mainstream parties, the novelty of the party and the distinctiveness of its anti-austerity politics are neutralised.

This is further supported through the presentation of the other parties as equally changed. In an article in *El País*, the reporters describe how the legacy of the Indignados movement has trickled down to all parties in the Spanish political spectrum:

> After four years of the emergence of 15-M movement [Indignados], its political impact is still clear. Its legacy is reflected in the surge of Podemos, but also in the policy proposals in the manifestos of mainstream parties: the democratisation of politics, the fight against corruption, and the participation of citizens in political institutions are central issues in nowadays' political debates, and have been incorporated into the manifestos of all parties.
>
> *García de Blas and Gálvez, 2015*

Podemos is a party directly born from the Indignados movement, a relationship that has been highlighted both in the press and by the party itself. This relationship has attributed to the party an inclusive character, expressing the voice of the citizens. The suggestion that all parties had been equally transformed by the Indignados contributes to the neutralisation of Podemos' voice, since it undermines its distinctiveness by muting its transformative anti-austerity agenda. At the same time, it further legitimises mainstream parties as attentive to the demands of the citizens participating in the protest movement and transforming themselves accordingly.

On the other hand, the framing of the party as a threat did not subside. Indeed, *El Mundo* warned that the apparent moderation of Podemos was only a political manoeuvre, as

> they will not betray their radical origins, and are still infatuated with Latin American populism. Their economic ideas are based on a disproportionate increase in public spending that would necessarily bring our country back to the disastrous context that led to the current economic crisis.
>
> *El Mundo, 2015a*

Conclusion

In this chapter, we employed textual analysis to explore the pre-election press coverage of the two most prominent anti-austerity parties in Europe. The chapter has illustrated the role of the mainstream press in the discursive processes through which these new left parties and their anti-austerity positions are delegitimised as valid political alternatives in Greece and Spain accordingly.

Despite the variations in the coverage of the two parties, two main discursive tropes were identified, namely their construction as political threats to political and economic stability, and the delegitimisation or neutralisation of their policies. This coverage drew upon an anti-populist discourse that constructed parallels between the two parties and what was described as catastrophic populism, namely PASOK in the case of SYRIZA, and Latin American populism in Spain. At the same time, the parties' policy proposals were systematically ignored and their rhetoric was presented as purely emotional, vague, utopian, unrealistic, or impracticable.

We do not argue that the field of representations of the two parties is restricted to these newspapers, as there are of course alternative narratives provided both in other mainstream and especially alternative media. Given the privileged status, however, of these media, exploring their coverage offers insights into the ways hegemonic ideas about the left are reproduced under conditions of financial crisis. Framing SYRIZA and Podemos as extreme populist or radical parties constructs, by extension, anti-austerity arguments as equally extreme political positions. This further legitimises imposed austerity policies and reifies neoliberal definitions and narratives of the crisis. Consequently, this presentation of anti-austerity parties implicitly supports the traditional political actors effectively safeguarding the status quo. Such discursive struggles are, nevertheless, open-ended and in constant flux – and always ongoing.

Notes

1 Technically, local lists including candidates affiliated with Podemos.
2 'Escraches' are a form of protest consisting of standing outside the private houses of political representatives. In recent years this has been used by activists fighting against draconian mortgage clauses.

References

Alcázar, M. 2015. 'Las municipales se ganan por la mínima'. *ABC*, 21 May.

Anastasakis, O. 2013. *The far right in Greece and the theory of the two extremes*. 13 May. Available at www.opendemocracy.net/othon-anastasakis/far-right-in-greece-and-theory-of-two-extremes-0 [Accessed 29 October 2015]

Berry, M. 2016. 'No alternative to austerity: how BBC broadcast news reported the deficit debate'. *Media, Culture & Society*, 38(6), pp. 844–863.

Calleja, M., and Mira, M. N. 2015. 'Aznar reivindica el ADN del PP frente a ocurrencias y populismos'. *ABC*, 18 May.

Camacho, I. 2015, 'Pueden'. *ABC*, 17 May.

Cammaerts, B., and Carpentier, N. (eds.). 2007. Reclaiming the media: Communication rights and expanding democratic media roles. In: *Reclaiming the media: Communication rights and democratic media roles*. Bristol: Intellect. pp. xi-xviii.

Cassidy, J. 2016. *Bernie Sanders and the new populism*. Available at: www.newyorker.com/news/john-cassidy/bernie-sanders-and-the-new-populism on [Accessed 5 February 2016]

Doudaki, V. 2015. 'Legitimation Mechanisms in the Bailout Discourse'. *Javnost – The Public*, 22(1), pp. 1–17.

El Mundo. 2015a. 'Iglesias pule un discurso inviable'. *El Mundo*, 17 May.

El Mundo. 2015b. 'La campaña del 24-M, laboratorio de una nueva forma de hacer política'. *El Mundo*, 23 May.

European Commission. 2016. *Country Report Spain 2016*. Available at http://ec.europa.eu/europe2020/pdf/csr2016/cr2016_spain_en.pdf [Accessed 3 April 2016,]

Eurostat. 2015. *People at risk of poverty or social exclusion*. Available at http://ec.europa.eu/eurostat/statistics-explained/index.php/People_at_risk_of_poverty_or_social_exclusion[Accessed 3 April 2016]

Eurostat. 2016. *Euro area unemployment down to 10.2%*. Available at http://ec.europa.eu/eurostat/documents/2995521/7244015/3-29042016-AP-EN.pdf/735afc8c-bb8e-4698-8129-860e1ce273df[Accessed 29 April 2016]

Fairclough, N. 1989. *Language and Power*. Pearson Education.

Faye, J.-P. 2004. *Langages totalitaires*. Paris: Hermann.

García de Blas, E., and Gálvez, J. J. 2015 'Las demandas del 15-M marcan ahora la agenda política'. *El País*. 16 May.

Georgakopoulos, T. 2015. 'Elliniki gremokratia [Greek edge-ocracy]'. *Kathimerini*. 23 January

Gitlin, T. 1980. *The whole world is watching: Mass media in the making & the unmaking of the New Left*. Berkeley, CA: University of California Press.

Glasgow Media Group. 1980. *More bad news*. London: Routledge and Kegan Paul.

González, M. 2015. 'El PP y el centro'. *El País*, 18 May.

Hallin, D. C., and Mancini, P. 2004. *Comparing media systems: Three models of media and politics*. Cambridge: Cambridge University Press.

Iglesias, P. 2015. 'Understanding Podemos'. *New Left Review*, 93, pp. 7–22.

Jabois, M. 2015. 'Disparar a un fantasma'. *El País*. 20 May.

Jones, O. 2016. 'First Corbyn, now Sanders: How young voters' despair is fuelling movements on the left'. *The Guardian*, 11 May.

Kathimerini. 2014. 'Credit Agricole: Kindinos gia tis Euroagores o SYRIZA [Credit Agricole: Syriza is a risk for euromarkets]'. *Kathimerini*. 20 May.

Krauze, E. 2015. 'Arqueología del populismo'. *El País*. 21 May.

Laclau, E., and Mouffe, C. 2001. *Hegemony and socialist strategy: Towards a radical democratic politics*. London: Verso.

Lazzarato, M. 2012. *The making of the indebted man: Essay on the neoliberal condition*. Los Angeles, CA: MIT Press.

Manetto, F. 2015. El día 25 mucha gente verá que no hay ningún apocalipsis. *El País*, 21 May.

Mitropoulos, D. 2015. I epomeni mera [The next day]. *Ta Nea*, 23 January.

Mitsos, M. 2014. O neos ine, aplos, neos [The new one is merely new]. *Ta Nea*, 23 May.

Moscoso, J. 2015, Crecimiento (pero no de la productividad).*El Mundo*, 22 May.

Mylonas, Y. 2014. 'Crisis, Austerity and Opposition in Mainstream Media Discourses of Greece'. *Critical Discourse Studies*, 11(3), pp. 305–321.

Pagoulatos, G. 2015. Mprosta stin kalpi [In front of the ballot box]. *Kathimerini*, 18 January.

Pérez-Maura, R. 2015. Esas encuestas. . . . *ABC*, 19 May.

Picard, R. G. (ed.). 2015. *The Euro crisis in the media: Journalistic coverage of economic crisis and European institutions*. London: I. B. Tauris.

Sánchez-Vallejo, M.J. 2015. Un referéndum es la solución de los más cobardes. *El País*, 19 May.

Sostres, S. 2015. Los ganchos. *El Mundo*, 21 May.

Stavrakakis, Y., and Katsambekis, G. 2014. 'Left-wing populism in the European periphery: The case of SYRIZA'. *Journal of Political Ideologies*, 19(2), pp. 119–142.

Varvitsioti, E. 2015. Alex Stubb:'Mi apodekti mia diagrafi tou xreous' [Alex Stubb:"Writing off debt is unacceptable."] *Kathimerini*, 15 January.

Wahl-Jorgensen, K., Sambrook, R., Berry, M., Moore, K., Bennett, L., Cable, J., Garcia-Blanco, I., Kidd, J., Dencik, L., and Hintz, A. 2013. *BBC Breadth of Opinion Review: Content Analysis*. Available at http://downloads.bbc.co.uk/bbctrust/assets/files/pdf/our_work/breadth_opinion/content_analysis.pdf [Accessed 15 October 2016]

Wren-Lewis, S. 2015. 'The austerity con'. *London Review of Books*, 37(4), pp. 9–11.

9

RACE AND CLASS IN GERMAN MEDIA REPRESENTATIONS OF THE 'GREEK CRISIS'

Yiannis Mylonas

Introduction: a critical understanding of the Eurozone crisis and its public construction

> *"Fass mich nicht an, du dreckiger Grieche", ("Don't touch me, you filthy Greek")*

Those were the words of the former German Transportation minister Peter Ramsauer, uttered both in German and in English to a Greek reporter, after an unintentional physical contact.[1] This racist assault occurred on 30/06/2016, while a German delegation was visiting the Greek Prime Minister. Rather than seeing this racist event as an isolated one, I argue that it is a crude expression of an enduring, Orientalist construction of Greece, connected to the colonial legacies of the West (García, 2013; Carastathis, 2014; Fekete, 2017). Since 2009, the Occidentalist 'common-sense' conceptualization of Greece as a 'non-modern' entity, was politically instrumentalized to publicly produce a culturalistic-moralistic understanding of the so-called Greek crisis as a crisis that bears cultural origins and is 'self-inflicted'. This Orientalist discourse served to publicly legitimize austerity regimes and privatizations in Greece (Fairclough and Fairclough, 2012; Arrese and Vara-Miguel, 2015; Doudaki, 2015; Van Vossole, 2016), following a policy aiming to secure the Euro-currency – and the interests of core Eurozone countries, particularly Germany – in the midst of a global economic crisis (Streeck, 2016).

Apart from the racial construction of the Greeks as European Others, critical scholars should also notice the class dimension of this process. Class in the hegemonic discursive framing of the current capitalist crisis requires further theorization. Various scholars (Jacobsson and Ekström, 2016; Harkins and Lugo-Ocando, 2016) have critically foregrounded the reproduction of demeaning stereotypes of working class and poverty in the media, formed under a middle/upper class gaze (Skeggs, 2003; Jones, 2016; Bennett, 2013). This chapter will thus present the main findings of a study of the German mainstream press' representations of the so-called Greek crisis, analyzed through the lens of class and race.

The attention to the German mass media is due to the pivotal role of the conservative German government (in power since 2005) in imposing a draconian austerity at the EU's periphery, disregarding its human, social, political and economic costs for the majority of the population there (and also austerity's utter failure to reach its self-proclaimed goals, such as economic growth), as well as in setting the ordoliberal policy framework that currently drives the EU, and the normalization of the political right in the EU (Berezin, 2013). On a further level, the focus on Germany is also meant to challenge popular views seeing Germany as the 'Eurozone's saviour'[2], or, as the world's pillar of liberalism (Balhorn, 2016), particularly after Trump's election in the US. Instead, I perceive such views as outcomes of a successful national branding process, necessary, not only to achieve socio-political hegemony, but also to increase economic competitiveness (Davies, 2014).

To put in brief, German ordoliberalism – one of neoliberalism's two main variants (Foucault, 2008, p. 216) – advocates 'market freedom' safeguarded by a regulatory state protecting and promoting competition. For ordoliberalism, "the market is not defined by exchange but by competition" (Dardot and Laval, 2013, p. 83). Competition thus forms the basis of the ordoliberal politico-economic order constituted on "the principles of monetary stability, open markets, private property, freedom of contracts and responsible economic agents" (Dardot and Laval, 2013, p. 84). Dardot and Laval (2013, p. 195) argue that the EU is constructed on ordoliberal ideas, stressing the development of a common market (other than the development of a constitutional federation that Habermas (2012) envisioned) through reforms targeting a) the flexibilization of wages; b) the restructuring of welfare by prioritizing individual saving; c) the promotion of entrepreneurialism; and d) 'the defence of the civilization ideal against nihilism', with 'nihilism' referring to socialism.

The Eurozone itself was "designed to inject a new, neoliberal form of money into the national economies that would enforce the development of an institutional context appropriate to its own needs" (Streeck, 2016, p. 172). Indeed, the Euro is a currency made according to the requirements of the export-based, hard-currency EU countries, emphasizing the need for fiscal stability, "wary of both inflation and debt" (Streeck, 2016, p. 173). In this context Germany "de facto governs the European Monetary Union (EMU) as a German economic empire" (Streeck, 2016, p. 131). The crisis management imposed by the so-called donor countries through bailout loans that sustain the Eurozone's stability undermines citizens' rights and democratic sovereignty, making the EU's core countries behave like imperialists (Streeck, 2016, p. 180; Fekete, 2017, p. 4). In the times of augmented national debt, due to a variety of reasons connected to the neoliberal restructuring and financial deregulation that occurred in the late 20th century, Streeck (2016, p. 122) understands the EU as a "consolidation state" comprised of "market conforming democracies" – quoting Merkel – (Streeck, 2016, p. 186), with its main purpose to provide confidence to financial markets and investors, through policies that will guarantee the effective payment of national debts and, in turn, sustain the competitiveness of the Euro-currency.

Race and class in the hegemonic discourses of the 'Greek crisis'

Political economy theorists like Harvey (2014) or Chomsky (Goodman, 2015) demonstrated that the austerity regimes implemented across the EU, particularly in the South as 'no alternative' remedies for the capitalist crisis, are class-orientated policies. They are related to what Harvey described as "accumulation through dispossession" (Harvey, 2014, p. 60), or wealth redistribution from the bottom to the top, or, what others perceive as "destructive creation" (Büscher and Fletcher, 2017, p. 659), developing through the violent imposition of neoliberal reforms for the reproduction of capitalist accumulation.

As Fairclough and Fairclough (2012, p. 7) showed, the capitalist crisis that begun in the US in 2008 was publicly explained in moralistic terms, rather than in systemic ones. This way, the crisis was seen as something having to do with the excessive behaviour of immoral professionals and individuals (e.g. specific greedy bankers in the US), or with problematic individual and social behaviours and cultures. With regards to Europe, Greece – the Eurozone crisis epicentre – was addressed in both a moralistic and a culturalistic framework (Stavrakakis, 2013). This way, Greece was seen as non-European and unmodern, and the Greek people as corrupt, idle and unworthy of their antique legacy.

The conceptual framework of Orientalism is useful to critically address the ways that Greece was constructed as Europe's Other. Although Greece was never exactly a Western colony, it was imagined by Western colonial powers as the Occident's symbolic centre (Carastathis, 2014, p. 2). The emergence of the new Greek state was marked by constant interventions from Western imperial powers. Simultaneously, the identity of modern Greece came to be defined by the West in comparison to Greece's classical heritage, however that was fantasized by Western imperialism (Hamilakis, 2016, p. 238). Bozatzis (2016, p. 49) explains that Greece's Orientalization today is situated within the broader neoliberal assemblage of governance, "mobilized to justify austerity" (Kompatsiaris, 2017, p. 361). In today's context, Orientalism is understood as a flexible, historically developing, discriminatory discursive framework, eligible to include anything departing from the politico-economic and cultural cannons and imperatives of the European center/core states.

> the new European orientalism is a derivative or correlate of a phenomenon covered by such concepts as globalization, the expansion of multinational capital, flexible capitalism, transgressions, migrations, transnationalism or the media-covered global village. With these changes the meaning of orientalism acquires entirely new dimensions . . . in a sense that covers not only Saidian distinction into orient and occident, but also into capitalism and socialism, civility and primitivism, and class distinction into elites and plebs.
>
> *Buchowski, 2006, pp. 465–466*

In its different facets, racism has always been a constitutive part of bourgeois societies' disciplinary technologies that reproduce power relations and social hierarchies.

Racism is further connected to what Isabelle Lorey (2015) describes as the development of governance through "precarisation". Precarization involves the rise of an individualist type of subjectivity that is risk-taking, competitive, entrepreneurial and hostile towards taxation and various forms of institutional solidarity, seeing human suffering in subjective terms (as something that individuals are responsible for). Those failing to adapt are vilified as parasitic 'losers', through a Malthusian repertoire that individualizes pauperization, disempowerment and exclusion (Harkins and Lugo-Ocando, 2016, p. 79). The Orientalist framing of the 'Greek crisis' is thus associated with the reproduction and intensification of established bourgeois values associated to the primacy of private property and hard work. Indeed, as Wendling (2012, p. 178) demonstrates, "the demoralization, infantilization and alienation of the working class, as practiced by its domination by capital, serve the productive interests of capitalism as a whole". Hence, race and class constructions are intimately connected.

The German mainstream media and the Eurozone crisis

The findings of previously published research (Mylonas, 2012, 2015, 2018) are re-examined here under the lens of class and race. The chapter presents key findings of the Greek crisis coverage by both 'serious' (*Der Spiegel*) and 'light' (*Bild*) German media, as it appeared in the German public sphere between late 2009 and early 2015. Both *Bild* and *Der Spiegel* were studied through the same critical premises, although different qualitative analytical methods are followed, notably, frame analysis for *Bild* and discourse theory analysis for *Der Spiegel*. The study of *Bild* concerned its coverage of the crisis between late 2009 (regarding the official announcement of the Greek crisis, with Greece's inability to borrow funds at a low interest rate), until July 2012 (after the Greek national elections). For *Der Spiegel*, the study focused on its equivalent crisis coverage between late 2009 and early 2015 (right before the January 2015 Greek national elections). For the study of *Bild*, I used its online search engine at www.bild.de under the search phrase 'Griechen Pleite' (Bankrupt Greeks) – a categorical title frequently used in *Bild*'s articles on Greece. The search produced 486 related articles. Regarding *Der Spiegel*, I focused on both its German (www.spiegel.de) and its English-speaking (www.spiegel.de/international/) versions online. I used the key phrase 'Finanzkrize-in-Griechenland' in the site's search engine, which produced 440 related articles. The analysis focused in specific articles published in important moments with regards to the crisis (such as national elections, the passing of austerity measures in Greece and the approval of bailout loans by the German parliament, among others).

Analysis: exceptionalism as a key discursive framework legitimizing austerity

The concept of 'exception' (Agamben, 2005) is useful to understand the ways that emergency crisis policies (like the kind of austerity imposed in Greece) are established and publicly legitimized. The Eurozone crisis is an exceptional situation of threat that requires emergency measures to be resolved, with Greece forming an exceptional case in the EU and the Eurozone. The exceptionalist 'Greek crisis' narrative thus legitimizes a) the claim that the 'Greek crisis' is not systemic (but 'self-inflicted'), b) the emergency pretext of the austerity policy-framework. The discursive constructions of race and class analyzed below operate under this framework of exceptionalism.

The culturalist/racist moment

In the case of *Bild*, an 'infotaining' popular tabloid (Germany's most popular publication), largely consumed by the German lower and middle classes, one notices a spectacular construction of the exceptionalized Greek, related to Occidentalist banalities and stereotypes further developed by popular culture and the leisure industry (e.g. tourism):

> (11/06/2010) Daily fresh shock-news from Athens: Panic on the Titanic? You must be joking! The Greeks celebrate! It is the biggest bankruptcy party in Athens!
> (27/10/2010) Sell your islands, you bankrupt Greeks! And sell the Acropolis too! The Greeks are now making a serious attempt to save their country from bankruptcy, without being dependent on EU aid!
> (19/05/2011) Merkel escalates pressure: Greeks should take less holidays. Pressure on Europe's debt sinners: Chancellor Angela Merkel wants the people in the indebted states to work longer and to have less vacation.

Through falsehoods (see endnote 2), such frames 'prove' and reproduce a point that is (supposedly) already 'known' to the general German public: that Greece is exotic, idle, irrational, poor, corrupt and backwards, unlike Germany. Simultaneously, these frames also celebrate Merkel's government's stance against Greece, as a moral force punishing 'debt sinners'. Greek society is reified by *Bild* into a homogenous whole, irrespectively of internal social class or other differences. Constructed by the tourist gaze, the exotic and fetishized image of Greece mirrors the idle practices of the (Northern) petty bourgeois tourist, disconnected from the lived realities that the majority of Greeks face. The tourist experience is projected as the native population's actual state of being. Therefore, for *Bild*, 'the Greeks' appear to be living like tourists in their own country. To do that, they avoid work by depending on the EU, which is funded by the hard-working taxpayers of the North, notably the Germans.

In the case of *Der Spiegel*, one notices a more austere reproduction of cultural stereotypes, often in the form of a 'pop-science' approach, based on the views of 'experts'. For example, in an article published in a *Der Spiegel* "Cultural History" section entitled "What separates Greece from Europe" (18/5/2012), a certain Dietmar Pieper argues that

> The chain of dark centuries with foreign powers ruling the Greeks has left deep scars. . . . The former greatness exists only in museums. Politics and economics are oligarchical in modern Greece; power is almost inherited by dynasties like those of Papandreou or Karamanlis; personal relationships are often more important than election results or formal rules. Everything is pretty Byzantine. . . . The Oriental Schism of 1054. . . has torn a deep trench in Europe. Such ancient antagonisms do not disappear without a trace.

Culture is here explained through a historical determinist narrative: as the Germans (and other Europeans) were ruled by 'their own' hegemons, they developed 'normally', unlike the Greeks. Accordingly, the Greek polity and the Greek economy are exceptional for European standards, because kinship defines the politics and economic practices of Greece. One may think of, not only the Clinton or the Bush families in the US, but also, the major German capitalist oligopolies such as those of Thyssen-Krupp, Siemens, Henkel or Hugo Boss among others, and their politico-economic influence in Germany and elsewhere over the last one hundred years, including their thriving under the Nazi reign. For instance, Fuchs (2016, p. 129) notes that at least 2,500 German companies used forced labor during the Nazi reign, many of which still operate today. To be sure, liberal authors such as the afformentioned Dietmar Pieper, do not engage with questions of politico-economic inequality in today's globalized capitalism, its crisis and its local dynamics – for, if they did, a different image would emerge, showing the ties of the German oligopolistic capital to the Greek elites, including high corruption scandals, with Siemens being an indicative case (Mavraka and Papatheodorou, 2012). Instead, selected historical moments are instrumentalized to assert the liberal myths of progress and Western secularism. Out of all possible dates, 1054 is meant to disclose the fundamental religious difference between Orthodox Greece and Catholic/Protestant Europe, with religion being a central topos for today's cultural racist repertoire (Salem and Thompson, 2016). If the German media were to be fair, they could produce a more nuanced picture by addressing Germany's own problematic aspects related to the non-democratic, colonialist, imperialist and Nazi legacies: after all, 1933 or 1945 – landmark dates for contemporary Germany (and consequently, also Europe) – are closer to the present than 1054. Such a case would demonstrate the contradictions of the culturalist crisis framing and its weaknesses; as Gumpert (2017, p. 31) argues "what finally underlies Europe's resentment of Greece is . . . the fear that Greece is either not enough or too much like Europe". The particular Der Spiegel author could also refer to the period of 1941–1944, which concerns the murderous and destructive occupation of Greece by Nazi Germany. The ferocity of the German occupation of Greece during the Second World War, is comparable only to the German occupation of Soviet Union territories, Yugoslavia, and Poland, where their populations were also treated as inferior by the Wermacht and the German occupying forces, and the countries plundered and ravaged by scorched earth strategies. This would also inform today's German public on its ancestors' atrocities in Greece, which are hardly known in today's Germany (Mazower, 2001; Fleischer, 2008). The nationalist and also bourgeois ideology thus emerges in such banal understandings of history:

> Reason itself has become the mere instrument of the all-inclusive economic apparatus. It serves as a general tool, useful for the manufacture of all other tools, firmly directed toward its end, as fateful as the precisely calculated movement of material production, whose result for mankind is beyond all calculation.
>
> *Adorno and Horkheimer, 1989, p. 30*

Whatever the intention of individual journalists, the uncritical presentation of Germany's ordoliberal policy framework, presented as realistic, responsible, just and even 'altruistic' (by supposedly 'helping' Greece), performs an ideological function, which effectively serves a national branding process, helping to legitimize Germany's geopolitical might and to boost its economic competitiveness. As William Davies (2014, p. 134) argues in his discussion of the position of nationalism in global neoliberalism,

> a political community is treated as a quasi-firm to be managed and measured in a strategic fashion, in the hope of out-competing rival communities. National characteristics and political will become resources, to be evaluated and strategically employed, using techniques drawn from management and business schools.

The class moment

The class aspect in the media studied concerns a) the construction of the "loser", the deceitful and undeserving one, who cannot compete or cannot adjust to the "reality" of late capitalism, and b) the expression of spite against an "underclass" of scoundrels that (supposedly) threatens "our" well-being (Skeggs, 2003, p. 85). Both points are underlined by a prevailing "bourgeois gaze" (Bourdieu, 2010) that is cast upon the subject-in-crisis, examining, shaming, ridiculing and evaluating it.

The first point has to do with the individualist ideology of neoliberalism, related to the "turning of oneself into a marketable and competitive product" (Skeggs, 2003, p. 73). This ideology advanced alongside the defeats of working-class struggles, after the politico-economic restructuring that followed the global economic crisis of the early 1970s (Skeggs, 2003, p. 47). Skeggs (2003, p. 99) demonstrates that there is a long history of representing the lower/working classes through the idea of excess, as being wasteful, tasteless, self-damaging, deceitful, and irrational. The lower/working classes are generally constructed as regressive and moronic by the middle/upper classes (Skeggs, 2003, p. 111). Opposed to such excesses, the middle/upper classes are liberal, rational, self-constrained, mannered, austere and motivated. Bearing politico-economic and socio-cultural capital, the upper classes have adequate access to social institutions and the media to set their own agendas and ways of seeing (Van Dijk, 1991, p. 49). This way, it is the upper class that produces the identity of the working class and its problems in the mainstream public sphere.

Der Spiegel follows a more politically correct and objectivist approach, appearing to take distance from the excessive, spectacular constructions of *Bild*. *Der Spiegel* presupposes a different audience, more connected to the middle/upper classes, of educated, 'liberal' German citizens, as opposed to *Bild* that focuses on the lower and middle working-class 'patriotic' Germany. The bourgeois gaze here surfaces through the neoliberal presuppositions of the crisis reproduced by *Der Spiegel*. On the one hand, resistance is futile because, according to the neoliberal mantra, austerity is without an alternative, and on the other, the 'Greek crisis' is self-caused, due to the unmodern and corrupt character of Greece. In *Der Spiegel* one also notices a distance from the vulgar constructions of *Bild* that potentially expose the 'low taste' of the masses. The objectivist and constrained, competitive bourgeois subject emerges through an objective and often ironic gaze cast towards the Greek people, particularly towards those resisting austerity:

> (24/06/2011) Greek crisis: in the stronghold of self-pity.
> The Greeks fight against state bankruptcy, and their financial degradation, and many are foaming with rage. They make external enemies responsible for the crisis: the EU, the Monetary Fund, but above all, the Germans. Why?
> (15/07/2013) Demos in Greece: civil servants protest against mass layoffs
> The rubbish is piling up in many places. In Athens, chaos was caused by police and other government employees parading with car and motorbikes . . . In the evening, state officials wanted to protest against the planned redundancies before Parliament . . . Tourism is however expected to be largely spared: Ferries, and also hotels, banks, taxis and shops should not be on strike.
> (13/06/2012) Greece's leftist-star Tsipras: The man who makes Europe anxious
> In theory, Tsipras may have allies, but his solutions may hardly apply. His populist trick is that he promises a way out of the crisis through the same recipes which led the country in its misery.
> (26/05/2014) Greek left-wing politician Tsipras: The Euro-horror
> His furious performances – combined with a good dose of patriotism – are appealing to many Greeks in the confusing times of crisis.

Counter-austerity resistances and politics are represented as either hopeless – by providing an image of chaos and misery brought by protests, instead of one of struggle and potential – or as mere reactions of confused, angry people lacking knowledge and incentives. As the system is not to be criticized, and the Greek crisis is self-inflicted by 'all', and as austerity reforms are not to be contested because there is no alternative to them, the Greek government needs to implement austerity and the (guilty) people need to accept and support it instead of 'blaming others' for what themselves caused. A post-political position is expressed, where technocracy (as far as governance is concerned) and conformity (as far as citizens are concerned) are to resolve social problems 'objectively'. Such a position, however, masks wealth and other inequalities and advances the interests of the bourgeoisie – for, austerity is a class assault, aiming to restructure the position of the working class to capital's post-crisis requirements, and to reproduce the capitalist politico-economic order. Within that, the entrepreneurial, mobile, risk-taking, flexible, individualistic subject is central for the modelling of society by the enterprise (Dardot and Laval, 2013, p. 259). This implies the lack of a mainstream systemic analysis of the general state of insecurity caused by the political interventions pursuing this agenda, and the blaming of individuals and groups of people (usually the poorer) for systemic problems, like the construction of pauperization as a "culture of dependency" (Skeggs, 2003, p. 87).

Bild's take on the Greek anti-austerity resistances is much more openly hostile: "Mass uprising strikes: did the Greeks lose their dreamland? A mass uprising occurs against the shock-saving program of the government that is threatening to destroy the Greeks' reality image. Are they striking their destroyed country?" (12/03/2010). An 'irrational opposition' rhetorical topos in this excerpt is grounding the argument that discredits anti-austerity resistances. A right-wing tabloid, *Bild* demonstrates its reactionary institutional position against protests and social movements, while addressing the German working class – its main readership – in victimized, nationalist terms, fuelling resentment against 'the Greeks'. Victimization occurs by presenting Germany as a 'helper' that pays Greece with the German hardworking taxpayers' money, and Greece as an ungrateful and irresponsible scrounger: "Greek press' hate-speech against our Chancellor. You get money from us. A lot of money! And what do the bankrupt Greeks do: they swear against our chancellor. There are even Stasi-Nazi comparisons!" (04/05/2010). The Greek crisis is mediated as a national conflict between Greece and Germany, with Germany being on the defensive. This way, internationalist class affinities are blocked, while the nationally defined working class is called to celebrate the advance of German capitalist interests, as 'national interests'. This celebration occurs through depictions of banal nationalism, for instance:

> our petrol stations have cash registers, taxi drivers give receipts and farmers don't swindle EU subsidies with millions of non-existent olive trees. Germany also has high debts but we can settle them. That's because we get up early and work all day.

Nationalist conformity is also evident through the support shown to Merkel's government (e.g. "The Good Godmother of Europe" [27/10/2011]) while pursuing austerity in Greece.

The second point mentioned in this section, regarding the spiteful representations of Greece, derives from the general structural insecurity provoked by neoliberal demands for competition, mobility and the demise of welfare institutions, in

Europe and elsewhere. A key construction of national uniformity here is that of the 'hardworking German taxpayer', advanced by both media studied, though in a different tone:

> (*Bild*, 21/04/2010) Germany is to pay € 18 billion! Greece is for the German taxpayer a financial nightmare! 18 billion euros from Germany to the bankrupt Greeks.
>
> (*Bild*, 07/05/2010) The Greeks make our bread more expensive! The Greeks weaken the euro. We can feel this: the prices are rising. Even bread is more expensive. The recovery is in danger!
>
> (*Der Spiegel*, 10/02/2012) What would a Greek bankruptcy cost to every German Citizen? The Eurozone's finance ministers are not satisfied with the Athenian reforms' plan, while the always-open debate on national bankruptcy continues. How much would a Greek bankruptcy cost each individual German?
>
> (*Der Spiegel*, 26/11/2012) Meeting of Finance Ministers: Europe's citizens have to pay for Greece. The IMF and the ECB demand a radical haircut for Greece. But who is to bear the costs? Most creditors are already protected against potential losses – in the end, the citizens of the Eurozone will pay.

It is in the German taxpayer's name that drastic austerity is imposed on Greece. Due to his/her hard work, the German and European taxpayer is entitled to demand austerity from Greece, so as to secure his/her money return. The (bourgeois) value of "hard work" (Wendling, 2012, p. 22) produces the identity and the rights of the working class, while legitimizing austerity on the lazy Other. The framing of Greeks as 'lazy' also legitimizes their exception from political, social and human rights, striped by austerity in the name of the hard working German and European taxpayer. Hall (2011) argued that the idea of the "hardworking taxpayer" is central in the foundational discourses of neoliberal policies. In the neoliberal context, the taxpayer's identity, however, is the flip side of the 'consumer', another central trait of the neoliberal subject. The taxpayer pays and is therefore entitled to specific claims and services, just like the consumer. The taxpayer is invited to actively participate in the demand for austerity in Greece, by policing the developing of austerity in Greece through the crisis' publicity offered by mainstream media, and by understanding the matter in the dry, totalitarian language of neoliberal technocrats that masks the violence of austerity and the inanity that such knowledge advances. Simultaneously, the taxpayer is the opposite of the 'welfare scrounger', a parasite living off hard-working people's toil. This regressive articulation of the taxpayer transforms social rights into exclusive services, while dividing working-class groups on both national and international levels. Of course, the taxpayer is rarely (if ever) solicited on the use of his/her taxes, nor is s/he adequately informed on how the public funds are managed. The bailing out of bankrupt banks after the 2008 credit crunch worldwide (Harvey, 2014, p. 132), makes a good case for that, transforming the Greek national debt owed to private banks to a debt owned by nation states – through the taxpayers' funds.

Conclusions: plundering, double standards, racism; only Greece is to 'honour its debts'

> The Greek demand for the payment of war reparations from Germany is fully justified, since Greece was the only non-Slavic occupied country by Nazi Germany, which (after Poland, Yugoslavia and the Soviet Union) had the greatest loss of human lives and suffered the greatest material damages, says the Austrian historian and professor of Modern History at the University of Athens, Hagen Fleischer, in an interview with the Austrian newspaper *Der Standard*. Enumerating these losses, he notes that, beyond the 60,000 Greek Jews who were murdered, tens of thousands of other Greeks were also executed; furthermore, at least 100,000 died of hunger; one in three Greeks suffered from epidemic diseases after the German withdrawal; many were left homeless after the destruction of 100,000 houses; the whole economy and the country's infrastructure was destroyed during the German occupation, and *Greece has never recovered since then*. . . . In the Cold War context and under the US pressure, the question of reparations was practically "choked" to make Germany a front against the eastern countries.
>
> (*To Vima*, 2012)

The Greek-crisis discourses appearing in both *Bild* and *Der Spiegel* studied bear more similarities than differences. A middle/upper-class habitus is implied in the frames studied in this chapter, to publicly produce the ideal Occidental/European/bourgeois self, while shaming and denouncing the failed Other in both racial (as non-European enough) and in class terms (as poor, irrational and infantilized). This ideal self comprises the biopolitical dimension of austerity reforms, connected to the development of the *homo-economicus* subjectivity (Foucault, 2008, p. 268).

German nationalism lies at the antipode of the demeaning constructions of Greece, with Greece representing everything that Germany is not. German nationalism appears in both a regressive working-class framework, and most crucially, in a liberal, Europeanist and technocratic – yet victimized – guise, developing in a context of global economic competition. As Harvey (2005, p. 85) argues, "the neoliberal state needs nationalism of a certain sort to survive". Indeed, nationalism is meant to boost competitiveness through an effective national branding that produces the identity of the non-adoptable, unreliable, threatening Other.

Capitalist culture produces flattening narratives of the world to facilitate the expansion and reproduction of the capitalist accumulation process. Alternatives are constantly being excluded from the mainstream public sphere as socio-politically irrelevant (Buck-Morss, 2002, p. 256). Therefore, I use Fleischer's excerpt to close this chapter, so as to further disrupt the neoliberal-capitalist-Occidentalist grand narrative analyzed here, by emphasizing the memory of lasting traumatic legacies, while taking into account locality and class. Refuting the hegemonic crisis narratives involves what Noys (2010, p. 156) describes as the development of a negative position towards "the existent set of positivities". In our context, this concerns the rejection of a market-centered understanding of the world that is advance by neoliberalism, and the challenging and abandoning of the prevailing understanding of the EU as something generally positive, progressive or democratic. A negative stance, "ruthlessly criticizing the existing order" (Marx, 1844), foregrounds the EU's bourgeois and Occidentalist foundations, its centrality in sustaining and advancing neoliberalism in the world, its power asymmetries and center-periphery divisions, along with its post-democratic, neoliberal and neocolonial (e.g. Karnitschnig, 2017) developments in times of crisis, pointing towards an internationalist and working class orientated vision for an alternative (to Occidentalism and capitalism) future.

Notes

1 More information on this incident can be found here: https://en.wikipedia.org/wiki/Peter_Ramsauer#Alleged_Racist_Attack
2 A simple fact check can challenge this claim, by demonstrating the falsehoods that the Eurozone crisis narrative was built upon, as well as the Orwellian language of 'help' and 'solidarity' launched by neoliberal Europe. The available Organisation for Economic Co-operation and Development (2017) data on the annual work hours worldwide show that the people of the South work more than the people of the global and European North, while also paid much less and entitled to considerably less welfare benefits, than they do in the North. As for the so-called bailout funds paid by the Eurozone member states to Greece, they transformed a national debt owed to private creditors (such as international banks) to a debt owed to national budgets, so as to sustain the Euro's 'stability' by not 'stressing' the international banking system. Only a minimum of these loans is going to support the shrinking-due-to-austerity Greek budget (Mouzakis and Malkoutzis, 2015).

References

Adorno, T., and Horkheimer, M. 1989. *The dialectic of the enlightenment*. New York: Continuum.

Agamben, G. 2005. *State of exception*. Chicago: Chicago University Press.

Arrese, Á., and Vara-Miguel, A. 2015. 'A comparative study of metaphors in press reporting of the Euro crisis'. *Discourse & Society*, 27(2), pp. 133–155.

Balhorn, L. 2016. 'Merkeling to the right'. Available at: www.jacobinmag.com/2016/12/merkel-burqa-ban-refugees-cdu-germany/ [accessed 6 February 2017].

Bennett, J. 2013. 'Moralizing class: A discourse analysis of the mainstream political response to Occupy and the August 2011 British riots'. *Discourse & Society* 4(1), pp. 27–45.

Berezin, M. 2013. The normalization of the right in post-security Europe. In: Schäfer, A., and Wolfgang Streeck, W. (eds.), *Politics in the age of Austerity*. Cambridge: Polity Press. pp. 239–261.

Bild. 2010a. 'Aufstand gegen Spar-Programm: Streiken die Griechen ihr Traumland kaputt?' Available at: www.bild.de/politik/wirtschaft/massen-aufstand-gefaehrdet-die-wirtschaft-11781908.bild.html [Accessed 9th October 2017].

Bild. 2010b. 'Euro im Absturz: Griechen machen unser Brot teurer!' Available at: www.bild.de/politik/wirtschaft/schwacher-euro-aufschwung-kaputt-12412158.bild.html [Accessed 9th October 2017].

Bild. 2010c. 'Griechenlandkrise: Deutschland soll 18 Milliarden Euro zahlen!' Available at: www.bild.de/politik/wirtschaft/deutschland-soll-18-milliarden-euro-zahlen-12279284.bild.html [Accessed 9th October 2017].

Bild. 2010d. 'Hass-Tiraden gegen unsere Kanzlerin: Deutschen-feindliche Stimmung macht sich breit. Sogar Rehagel fällt in Ungnade'. Available at: www.bild.de/politik/2010/gegen-unsere-kanzlerin-12424326.bild.html [Accessed 9th October 2017].

Bild. 2010e. 'Jeden Tag neue Schock-Nachrichten aus Athen. Panik auf der Titanic? Von wegen! Die Griechen feiern!' Available at: www.bild.de/politik/wirtschaft/die-griechen-feiern-und-feiern-12373912.bild.html [Accessed 9th October 2017].

Bild. 2011a. 'Die gute Patin Europas: Merkel machte ein Angebot, das keiner ablehnen konnte'. Available at: www.bild.de/geld/wirtschaft/angela-merkel/macht-angebot-das-keiner-ablehnen-konnte-20688644.bild.html [Accessed 9th October 2017].

Bild. 2011b. 'Merkel Erhöht Druck auf Europas Schuldenstaaten: Griechen Sollen Weniger Urlaub Machen'. Available at: www.bild.de/politik/inland/griechenland-krise/griechen-sollen-weniger-urlaub-machen-17973738.bild.html [Accessed 9th October 2017].

Bourdieu, P. 2010. *Distinction*. Abington: Routledge.

Bozatzis, N. 2016. 'Cultural othering, banal occidentalism and the discursive construction of the "Greek crisis" in global media: a case study'. *Suomen Anthropologi*, 41(2), pp. 47–71.

Buchowski, M. 2006. 'The specter of Orientalism in Europe: From exotic Other to stigmatized brother'. *Anthropological Quarterly*, 79(3), pp. 463–482.

Buck-Morss, S. 2002. *Dreamworld and Catastrophe: The passing of mass utopia in East and West*. Cambridge: The MIT Press.

Büscher, B., and Fletcher, R. 2017. 'Destructive creation: Capital accumulation and the structural violence of tourism'. *Journal of Sustainable Tourism*, 25(5), pp. 651–667.

Carastathis, A. 2014. 'Is Hellenism an Orientalism? Reflections on the boundaries of "Europe" in an age of austerity'. *Critical Race and Whiteness Studies*, 10(1), pp. 1–17.

Dardot, P., and Laval, C. 2013. *The new way of the world: on the neoliberal society*. London: Verso.

Davies, W. 2014. *The limits of neoliberalism, authority, sovereignty and the logic of competition*. London: Sage.

Doudaki, V. 2015. 'Legitimation mechanisms in the bailout discourse'. *Javnost*, 22(1), pp. 1–17.

Fairclough, N., and Fairclough, I. 2012. *Political discourse analysis*. London: Routledge.

Fekete, L. 2017. 'Flying the flag for neoliberalism'. *Race and Class*, 58(3), pp. 3–22.

Fleischer, H. 2008. *Memory wars: The Second World War in contemporary public history*. Athens: Nefeli.

Foucault, M. 2008. *The birth of biopolitics: Lectures at college de France, 1978–1979*. London: Palgrave Macmillan.

García, Á. M. 2013. Haunted communities: The Greek vampire or the uncanny at the core of nation construction. In: Stasiewicz-Bieńkowska, A., and Graham, K. (eds.), *Monstrous Manifestations: Realities and imaginings of the monster*. Inter-Disciplinary Press, pp. 53–64.

Goodman, E. 2015. *Noam Chomsky: austerity is just class war*. Available at: www.alternet.org/economy/noam-chomsky-austerity-just-class-war [Accessed 24th November 2016].

Guardian. 2010. *Get up earlier, Germans tell Greeks*. Available at: www.guardian.co.uk/business/2010/mar/05/bild-open-letter-greece-papandreou?intcmp=ilcnettxt3487H [Accessed 13th June 2017].

Gumpert, M. 2017. 'Beware of Greeks bearing gifts: Metaphors as viruses in discourses on the Greek crisis'. *Journal of Greek Media & Culture*, 3(1), pp. 31–51.

Habermas, J. 2012. *The crisis of the European union: A response*. Cambridge: Polity.

Hall, S. 2011. 'The neoliberal revolution'. *Cultural Studies*, 25(6), pp. 705–728.

Hall, S., Critcher, C., Jefferson, T., Clarke, J., and Roberts, B. 1978. *Policing the crisis: Mugging, the state, law and order*. London: Palgrave Macmillan Press.

Hamilakis, Y. 2016. 'Some debts can never be repaid: the archaeo-politics of the crisis'. *Journal of Modern Greek Studies*, 34(2), 27–64.

Harkins, S. and Jairo Lugo-Ocando, J. 2016. 'How Malthusian ideology crept into the newsroom: British tabloids and the coverage of the underclass'. *Critical Discourse Studies*, 13(1), pp. 78–93.

Harvey, D. 2005. *A brief history of neoliberalism*. Oxford: Oxford University Press.

Harvey, D. 2014. *Seventeen contradictions and the end of capitalism*. Oxford: Oxford University Press.

Jacobsson, D., and Ekström, M. 2016. 'Dismantling discourses: Compassion, coping and consumption in journalistic representations of the working class'. *Critical Discourse Studies*, 13(4), pp. 379–396.

Jones, O. 2016. *Chavs: The demonization of the working class*. London: Verso.

Karnitschnig, M. 2017. *Why Greece is Germany's "defacto colony"*. Available at: www.politico. eu/article/why-greece-is-germanys-de-facto-colony/ [Accessed 16th June 2017].

Kompatsiaris, P. 2017. 'Whitewashing the nation: racist jokes and the construction of the African "other" in Greek popular cinema'. *Social Identities*, 23(3), pp. 360–375.

Lorey, I. 2015. *States of insecurity*. London: Verso.

Marx, K. 1844. *Letter from Marx to Arnold Ruge*. Available at: www.marxists.org/archive/ marx/works/1843/letters/43_09-alt.htm [Accessed 16th June 2017].

Mavraka, L., and Papatheodorou, V. 2012. *Forgiving siemens: Unraveling a Tangled tale of German corruption in Greece*. Available at: www.corpwatch.org/article.php?id=15740 [Accessed 23rd May 2017].

Mazower, M. 2001. *Inside Hitler's Greece: The experience of occupation, 1941–44*. New Heaven and London: Yale University Press.

Mouzakis, Y., and Malkoutzis, N. 2015. *You've heard the Greek crisis myths, now here are some truths*. Available at: www.macropolis.gr/?i=portal.en.the-agora.2268 [Accessed 23rd May 2017].

Mylonas, Y. 2012. 'Media and the economic crisis of the EU: The "culturalization" of a systemic crisis and Bild-Zeitung's framing of Greece'. *TripleC*, 10(2), pp. 646–671.

Mylonas, Y. 2015. 'Austerity discourses in "Der Spiegel" Journal, 2009–2014'. *TripleC*, 13(1), pp. 248–269.

Mylonas, Y. 2018. 'Constructions of the opposition to "structural adjustment reforms" in the German mass-media'. *Journal of Political Ideologies* [In press].

Noys, B. 2010. *The persistence of the negative: A critique of contemporary continental theory*. Edinburgh: Edinburgh University Press.

Organisation for Economic Co-operation and Development (OECD). 2017. *Average annual hours actually worked per worker*. Available at: https://stats.oecd.org/Index. aspx?DataSetCode=ANHRS [Accessed 23rd May 2017].

Salem, S., and Thompson, V. 2016. 'Old racisms, new masks: on the continuing discontinuities of racism and the erasure of race in European contexts'. *Nineteen Sixty Nine: An Ethnic Studies Journal*, 3(1). Available from: http://escholarship.org/uc/item/98p8q169 [Accessed 23rd May 2017].

Skeggs, B. 2003. *Class, self, culture*. London: Routledge.

Spiegel. 2011. *Griechenland-Krise: In der Trutzburg des Selbstmitleids*. Available at: www.spiegel. de/politik/ausland/griechenland-krise-in-der-trutzburg-des-selbstmitleids-a-770038. html [Accessed 9th October 2017].

Spiegel. 2012a. *Griechischer Linken-Politiker Tsipras: Der Euro-Schreck*. Available at: www. spiegel.de/politik/ausland/griechenlands-tsipras-liegt-mit-radikaler-linken-in-umfrage-vorn-a-833874.html [Accessed 9th October 2017].

Spiegel. 2012b. *Griechenlands Linken-Star Tsipras: Der Mann, der Europa Angst macht*. Available at: www.spiegel.de/politik/ausland/griechenland-vor-der-wahl-radikaler-linker-tsipras-hat-gute-chancen-a-838538.html [Accessed 9th October 2017].

Spiegel. 2012c. *Staatsbankrott: Was eine Griechen-Pleite jeden Bundesbürger kosten würde*. Available at: www.spiegel.de/wirtschaft/soziales/staatsbankrott-was-cine-griechen-pleite-jeden-bundesbuerger-kosten-wuerde-a-814477.html [Accessed 9th October 2017].

Spiegel. 2012d. *Treffen der Finanzminister: Europas Bürger müssen für Griechenland zahlen.* Available at: www.spiegel.de/wirtschaft/soziales/griechenland-ein-schuldenschnitt-wuerde-die-steuerzahler-treffen-a-869400.html [Accessed 9th October 2017].

Spiegel. 2012e. *Was Griechenland von Europa Trennt.* Available at: www.spiegel.de/politik/ausland/was-griechenland-und-europa-historisch-trennt-a-832657.html [Accessed 9th October 2017].

Spiegel. 2013. *Demos in Griechenland: Staatsdiener protestieren gegen Massenentlassungen.* Available at: www.spiegel.de/wirtschaft/soziales/in-griechenland-protestieren-staatdiener-gegen-entlassungen-a-911234.html [Accessed 9th October 2017].

Stavrakakis, Y. 2013. 'Dispatches from the Greek lab: metaphors, strategies and debt in the European crisis'. *Psychoanalysis, Culture & Society*, 18, pp. 313–324.

Streeck, W. 2016. *How will capitalism end?* London: Verso.

To Vima. 2012. *Haagen Fleischer: Greece is entitled to war reparations.* Available at: www.tovima.gr/society/article/?aid=475511#.UFnLilpl0OI [Accessed 7th November 2016].

Van Dijk, T. 1991. *Racism and the press.* London: Routledge.

Van Vossole, J. 2016. 'Framing PIGS: patterns of racism and neocolonialism in the Euro crisis'. *Patterns of Prejudice*, 50(1), pp. 1–20.

Wendling, A. E. 2012. *The ruling ideas: Bourgeois political concepts.* Lanham: Lexington Books.

PART III

Journalistic practice and the crisis

10

WHOSE ECONOMY, WHOSE NEWS?

Aeron Davis

Introduction

This chapter offers a historical overview of how economic, business and financial news reporting has changed in the UK since the 1970s. It traces the shifts in both general news production and economic news, arguing that economic news content has become increasingly narrow. As changes have occurred in the traditional business model of news production, and the range of news sources shifted, so 'economic news' itself has become less pluralist and more ideologically limited. Consequently, economic news has edged ever further away from discussing 'the real economy', as experienced by most people. Instead, it has come to be defined in extremely restrictive, elite and financialized terms. Ultimately, this not only contributed to the financial crash of 2007–08 and the economic slump that followed, but it has also ensured that very little changed in economic public debate and policy-making since. This state of affairs has left states and ordinary citizens bearing the costs, which, in turn, has contributed to the Brexit vote and a wider public rejection of political and economic elites. The piece focuses specifically on the recent historical experience of the UK, but the argument and findings have clear resonances with the US and other nations with mature economies, established media and rising levels of inequality.

The chapter is in four sections. The first briefly discusses the key factors that have traditionally influenced news production – factors which have tended to produce economic news content that is more centred on elite rather than public interests. The second section will trace some of the key changes in UK economic news from the 1970s to the 2007–08 financial crisis, a period in which economic news became increasingly narrow and focused on the interests of transnational corporate CEOs and international financiers. The third section explains how this has produced economic news that cheers on investment fashions and bubbles; disseminates a pro-market, anti-state discourse; and defines the 'economy' in abstract, elite terms. The last section explains how each of these trends has produced a real gap between how economic elites conceive of and publicly talk about 'the economy', and how ordinary people experience it. It is this gap which partly explains why such large swathes of the UK and US population stopped believing in economic 'experts' and their political elite establishments and also why so many members of those establishments failed to understand why.

Before continuing, a qualifying statement is necessary. The term 'economic news' is often used in this chapter (as elsewhere) as shorthand for a range of types of economically oriented news, including financial, companies and markets, personal finance, industrial relations, macroeconomic policy, government budget analysis, etc. Clearly, these are not all the same thing, having differing sources, frames and audiences. So, too, economic elite news sources can be competitive as well as enter into clear conflicts of opinion (Davis, 2002), as evidenced during the Brexit campaign. The arguments made therefore, reflect generalised patterns and mainstream economic elite views and news content.

The mismatch of elite and public interests in economic news production

To discuss the changing shape of economic, business and financial news, we need to start with an understanding of how news is produced generally and, also, an explanation of the key differences between economic and other news formats.

Journalism of all varieties has always come out of an uneasy compromise between public and elite interests. On the one hand, it is produced for a general audience, guided by public interest concerns and professional news values. On the other, it is also affected by owner and other powerful interests, and the need for financial viability. This combination of factors then influence the practices of production, from the way news agendas develop and stories are selected, to how information is sourced and outputs are framed. Over time, and across different news sectors, this combination of factors varies, producing news outputs which serve wider publics to a greater or lesser extent. As I will argue here, economic, business and financial news traditionally has been written more for elite than public interests.

In classic media sociology accounts of news production, journalists aim to produce outputs that are impartial, fact-centred and related to public interest concerns but, at the same time, struggle to overcome various practical constraints (Tunstall, 1971; Gans, 1979; Schudson, 2006). Reporters constantly have to overcome a number of time, resource and knowledge barriers, as well as the demands of owners, to remain financially viable. To navigate through these problems, journalists have adopted a series of structures and practices, organisational and professional norms that aim at routinely producing content that appears balanced and objective content in cost-effective ways. So news corporations organise news gathering around tight editorial hierarchies, news beats, perceived 'news values', codes of ethics and practices that, hopefully, then generate a mix of differing opinions and 'expert' evidence. Ultimately, news production can never fully realise its professional, 'ideal' remit of serving the public while also remaining profitable – but its practices, codes and cultures at least orient it in that direction.

In contrast, critical scholars have argued that a number of factors tend to lead to a 'mobilisation of bias' in the news production process which regularly steers content towards elite rather than public interests (Herman and Chomsky, 1988; Philo, 1995; Miller and Dinan, 2008). These detail several control mechanisms through which media owners, big advertisers and governments attempt to exert influence over reporters, eroding journalist autonomy, objectivity and balance.

Stepping aside from these overt, conscious means of elite control, it can also be argued that the very practices, cultures and discourses of professional news production can, less consciously, be causes of greater elite orientation and bias. For example, advertisers can shape news to cater more to particular audiences simply by choosing who to advertise too and where (see Curran, 1978). News gathering increasingly gravitates towards organisations and sources which are able to regularly supply newsworthy 'information subsidies' (Sigal, 1973; Fishman, 1980; Gandy, 1982). In fact, the more a news operation is struggling financially, the greater its dependency on the kinds of PR material supplied by such sources. Journalists tend to interview powerful elite figures in large, authoritative institutions, rather than ordinary citizens or smaller, weaker organisations. In so doing, they reinforce power imbalances, awarding elites greater visibility, legitimacy and 'primary definer' status (Hall et al., 1978; Lance Bennett, 1990). Consequently, on a day-to-day basis, public interest may be all-too-narrowly defined, not by the wider public, but by those elites and organisations already in dominant positions of power.

Each of these issues are particularly relevant to the reporting of economic, business and financial news. First, this news area does not attract large, public audiences. As Tunstall (1996) found, only a few percent of readers, even in the broadsheet press, choose to read this section of news. Despite this, such sections make up roughly a third of editorial content. This continues because it brings in high levels of advertising aimed at small, elite audiences with greater purchasing power (Newman, 1984; Davis, 2002). Consequently, content is produced more with these wealthier audiences in mind.

Second, certain parts of the business and financial sector fit the requirements of news producers, so offering the same kind of "bureaucratic affinity" (Fishman, 1980) that government does. Capital cities contain relatively confined financial districts as well as housing the main offices of big multi-national corporations. Large corporations, as well as financial analysts offer a regular supply of industry information, financial data and business stories. Thus, they have become regular suppliers of information subsidies for economic news, just as government institutions have for political news (Davis, 2002).

Third, journalists seek out top CEOs, large investors, and City economists and analysts as their main sources of economic news and information. They are seen as both 'expert' and influential players here. In so doing, economic news makes such figures 'primary definers' when it comes to discussing wider economic matters

(Philo, 1995; Bennett et al., 2004; Durham, 2007). The only sources with comparable primary definer status are in government central banks and treasury departments. Thus, the UK Chancellor of the Exchequer and Governor of the Bank of
England, the US Treasury Secretary and Head of the Federal Reserve are all frequent suppliers of direct quotes and supporting economic data.

Fourth, reporter–business source relations, which often entail a "tug of war"
(Gans, 1979) with conflicting objectives, heavily favour sources, more so than in
most other reporting areas. Businesses do not need the same kind of public coverage that politicians and parties do. Corporations communicate with their key investors and political audiences through other channels (Mitchell, 1997). They sell their
goods to larger consumer groups through advertising and sponsorship. They make
great efforts to avoid large, negative stories but they do not need regular coverage
in mainstream media. This all makes journalist access more limited and restricted.

Fifth, many aspects of business and financial news are highly complex, requiring advanced economic and accounting knowledge. They are also fast moving and
information dense. This leaves even experienced journalists struggling to understand and keep up, and they are more dependent on explanation and insider interpretation (see Davis, 2002; Doyle, 2006; Thompson, 2017).

In effect, all these factors mean that most financial and business reporting gravitates more towards reporting economic elite rather than public interests. Such elites
provide a generous and regular supply of advertising as well as PR and other information subsidies. They are the main sources reported and the most common consumers of such news. The journalist–source power balance heavily favours sources.
Consequently, journalists are highly dependent on the goodwill of economic elites
in their roles as sources, advertisers, consumers, interpreters and gatekeepers.

The changing shape of economic news production from the 1970s to the financial crisis

In earlier centuries, economic news and information originated to serve wealthier individuals and business interests seeking to invest in expanding industries and
international markets. However, for much of the 20th century, as news organisations became more professional and expanded their audiences, so copy also came to
include a wider range of public issues and debates. Topics from industrial relations
and regional industry developments, to discussions of macroeconomic policy and
commentary on government finances, broadened content.

As this section now argues, the very means and practices by which news became
more professional and cost-efficient have also driven news, once again, to become
more oriented towards a relatively small economic elite. The tendencies described
earlier in this chapter have compounded this shift, resulting in content becoming increasingly narrow in scope. This has resulted in a more reductive and less
pluralistic account of what constitutes 'the economy', filtering out many more
public-interest elements, with a greater focus on the economic concerns of finance
ministers, transnational corporations and international financiers. This in turn, has

encouraged the generation of a series of dominant economic discourses that favour such economic elites.

One clear driving force of the post-war expansion of business and financial news was related to wider public interests in matters economic, linked to post-war economic affluence (Newman, 1984; Parsons, 1989; Tunstall, 1996). Levels of home and share ownership, consumption and savings all rose across the wider population, thus driving a greater appetite for economic news as well as personal finance advice in relation to pensions, mortgages, savings, and so on. This in turn generated greater advertising. According to Curran (1978), by far the largest increase in advertising and advertising-related features, in the period 1946–76, took place in the business and financial sections of newspapers. Such developments were boosted by the policies of the Thatcher administration in the 1980s with home ownership, personal equity plans (PEPs), individual savings accounts (ISAs) and privatization of the nationalized industries rolled out. Financial advertising tripled in the period 1975–83 (Newman, 1984).

A second key area of economic reporting was big industry as well as the activities of trade unions and union leaders. Post-war UK economic policy revolved around the large nationalised industries, and the tripartite consensus of the state, Confederation of British Industry (CBI) and Trades Union Congress (TUC). Unions were far larger and more powerful, and the financial sector rather smaller and weaker. Although unions had come be reported very critically in the national media by the 1970s, they gained regular coverage from a sizeable group of industrial-relations correspondents (Manning, 1999). Studies of the period (Annan Report, 1977; McQuail, 1977) revealed that union sources were cited more than business managers and government officials put together. Hall et al. (1978) even identified them as being amongst the nation's "primary definers".

Third, economic and business news reported a range of opinions, from government, industry and academia, as well as the City. For Parsons (1989) and Hutton (1996), from the late 19th century until the 1980s, the business press had been a crucial space in which conflicting economic ideas and policies were debated. In Parson's (1989) historical account of the financial press, Keynes, Galbraith, Samuelson and Friedman, all made their impact on policy-makers through their frequent, public interventions in the financial media. The adoption of monetarism and Thatcher–Reagan era neoliberal economic policies, was fought out as much in the business press as it was in university economics departments and policy circles.

A fourth factor worth mentioning is the differences of opinion that existed across different economic elite groups in the post-war period. The primary definers of government were dominated by a Keynesian consensus that included assumptions about the state playing a significant role in national economic management through the powerful Departments of Trade and Industry (DTI). The City of London had a much more free-market perspective and, along with the treasury, was more critical about state policy here and critical of the large nationalised industries (see Davis and Walsh, 2016). This meant that economic news was an area of "legitimate controversy" (Hallin, 1994) that spilled across political and other news sections.

The post-war expansion of pluralist economic news shifted from the 1970s onwards. This followed the political and economic turn towards neoliberalism and neoclassical economics in the UK, US and elsewhere (Harvey, 2007; Mirowski and Plehwe, 2009). This shift directed a set of economic policies, including: supply-side measures such as lower taxes and less regulation, monetarist policy levers over fiscal ones, programmes of privatization and state withdrawal from industry, the mar-ketization of state functions, weakening employee rights and trade unions, reduced welfare state support, market deregulation, open trading borders, low inflation and price stability.

Less obviously, at least until the 2007–08 financial crisis, the UK, the US and other nations were becoming more financialized (Epstein, 2005; Krippner, 2011). From the 1970s, financial institutions grew significantly, coming to manage larger amounts of capital, provide a greater percentage of corporate profits, and make a greater contribution to national Gross Domestic Product (GDP) growth. For example, in the UK case, until the 1970s, UK bank assets had been equal to roughly half the value of UK GDP for a century. By the mid-2000s, they had risen to five times the value of GDP (Haldane, 2010). So, to, markets in stocks and shares, bonds, currencies and exotic financial products all expanded hugely in value and, at the same time, so did government, corporate and personal debt levels. Consequently, the financial sector increased its influence over corporations, individuals and states (see accounts in Krippner, 2011; Davis and Walsh, 2016). It was not just unions and the welfare state that came to be scaled back in this period, it was also traditional, often regionally based industries and small and medium sized businesses (SMEs). Large corporations become increasingly geared towards producing 'shareholder value' over limited time horizons. Small shareholders, who held a majority of shares in the 1960s, became irrelevant as large international institutions stepped in. By 2012, individuals held 10% of shares, and big foreign investors 53.2% (ONS, 2012).

Such developments came to be reflected in the content of economic, business and financial news in the UK. Large-scale debates about industrial and macro-economic policy ended in the 1980s (Parsons, 1989; Hutton, 1996). Nationalised industries were sold off, 'industrial policy' as it existed was abandoned, and the DTI was pummelled into shape by a resurgent treasury. Chancellors now talked much more about finance, banking, share ownership and international investment (see Davis and Walsh, 2016). As union power declined and strike activity dropped several-fold, union reporting was scaled back and industrial correspondents became a thing of the past (Manning, 1999; Davis, 2002).

But parallel changes within the general news media sector also encouraged change and a narrowing of the field of economic reporting. Over the same period, news media in the UK, US and elsewhere experienced a steady decline in consum-ers as competition grew (Franklin, 1997, Davies, 2008). Journalists had to produce more copy with fewer resources, filling up to three times as much news space as they did in 1985 (Davies, 2008). From the 1980s, this gap came to be neatly filled by the impressive expansion of corporate public relations (see Davis, 2002). The PR consultancy sector rose by a factor of 31 (or 11-fold in real terms) between 1979 and 1998 (Miller and Dinan, 2000, p. 10). By the 21st century, the extent of journalist dependency on PR was being revealed in UK and US studies (Lewis et al., 2008; McChesney and Pickard, 2011).

An important point to note is that financial PR led the expansion of the sector in these years (Davis, 2002) as the focus on 'shareholder value' and financial regulation hugely inflated company information flows to investors and the London Stock Market. Financial deregulation spurred much higher levels of City trading and merger and acquisition activity. By various accounts, financial news, which came to dominate economic news content, became more PR-dependent than any other sector (Davis, 2002). A 1994 PRCA survey found that the *Financial Times* (*FT*) used considerably more public relations material than any other national paper, with 26% of its output being PR-generated – 62% in the companies and markets section.

Ultimately, from the 1970s onwards, UK economic news became narrower and more focused on relatively small networks of economic elites, employed in the City, large corporations and the treasury, and later, included the Bank of England. Economists working elsewhere, from academia to unions, became marginalised. Larger debates about macroeconomic policy, reporting on union activities and labour relations, and coverage of regional economic issues declined or were pushed into other news sections. The primary definers of economic news, from government to the City, came to a broad agreement on economic policy and the state's minimal role here, thus pushing economic news more into the "sphere of consensus" (Hallin, 1994).

At the same time, economic news came to be increasingly dependent on corporate PR information subsidies, and to revolve more around the communicative exchanges of big finance and large corporations. This has become extremely clear in any news content analysis in this area where City sources and top CEOs dominate, occasionally punctuated by the pronouncements of chancellors and central bankers. Thus, Davis (2002) found, when analysing a widely reported 1990s corporate take-over that affected hundreds of thousands of employees and millions of customers, that only 2.8% of sources cited came from outside the business and financial sector. Knowles et al. (2017) produced a longitudinal, tri-nation study of papers in the UK, US and Australia, looking at three periods from the late 1980s to the latter part of the financial crash in 2008. The study not only recorded the clear dominance of business elite sources, but also found that the disparity between this group and others grew over time.

Narrow production produces narrow and blinkered economic news content

As economic news has become increasingly captured by and oriented towards international, financial economic elites, so there have been clear consequences for content. First, such news, rather than reporting on ordinary, mundane companies, regions and employment conditions, has become an uncritical cheerleader for new companies and investment fashions. In the 1990s, several accounts record how economic reporting widely promoted the narratives and trading practices that drove the high-tech or dot.com boom, creating a huge bubble and then crash in 2000 (Cassidy, 2002; Davis, 2007). Stories of 'the new era economy', the 'end of the traditional business cycle' and the 'great moderation' were common in coverage, as was the encouragement to buy stock in every new high-tech company, regardless of the lack of any assets or profits. Ultimately, in the collapse that begin in 2000, both the US and UK stock markets lost over half their value. Many high-tech companies, wildly promoted at the time, then became worthless.

The lead up to the 2007–08 financial crisis showed that few lessons had been learned in the interim. The poorly regulated banking sector got completely out of control, creating huge liabilities and instabilities across the global financial system (see accounts in Krugman, 2008; Cable, 2009; Elliott and Atkinson, 2009). Banks became hugely overleveraged while also trading in opaque products worth hundreds of billions that they did not really understand. The derivatives market rose in value over a decade, from $15 trillion to be valued at $600 trillion, or ten times total world output (Cable, 2009, p. 34). Property and stock market bubbles became hugely over-inflated. Throughout this period, a small minority of economic journalists found the time and resources to ask more difficult questions – but these alternative 'doomsayers' were marginalised and easily drowned out by the general wave of traditional, uncritical business coverage (Schiffrin, 2011; Starkman, 2014) in the UK (Schifferes, 2011; Manning, 2013), which was far more likely to promote each new bull market sector.

Second, economic, business and financial news came to promote and push a series of ideas and discourses critical of states, while also being pro big finance, free trade and globalization. Such is the strength of these ideas that they have merged into a dominant ideology that came to be circulated and shared by economic and political elites of both left (Labour, Democrat) and right (Conservative, Republican) (Hutton, 1996; Doyle, 2006; Kantola, 2006, Davis, 2007). Any proposals for more regulation, higher taxes, stronger consumer or trade union rights came to be treated as both extreme and prehistoric. In contrast, globalisation and international free trade was uncritically accepted.

Such discourse regularly supported the interests of international (often Western-based) financial institutions and investors over national governments and democratic processes. Durham's analysis of the *FT's* coverage (2007) of the Thai currency crisis in 1997, produced "a consistent ideological position" that elevated International Monetary Fund explanations and demands over those of the Thai Government. The Bennett et al. (2004) study of the reporting of the World Economic Forum at Davos found that the dominant reporting frames strongly promoted the interests and policy positions of such financial elites over those of citizens and activists. Similarly, Kantola's (2006) analysis of *FT* content reveals that its coverage of some 32 elections between 2000 and 2005 repeatedly backed candidates which supported pro-market reforms, and was critical of democracies, publics and leaders which did not.

Third, economic news came to reproduce an economic elite discourse of what the 'UK economy' is, based on the perspectives of financial, corporate, central bank and treasury sources; a discourse that, in many ways was divorced from that experienced by most of the public. This focuses on a series of headline macroeconomic indicators, each of which can be positively spun by governments or used to make international (usually financial) investment decisions. Every day UK news operations quote changes to the FTSE 100 index as an indicative snapshot of the UK economy – but many FTSE 100 companies are based in other countries and do their dealing in other currencies. Their rise and fall often relates more to speculative activities that bear little relation to the actual health of the economy. Changes to the larger FTSE 350 or other indices of smaller and medium-sized, predominantly nationally centred businesses, are rarely quoted.

The most quoted defining measure of the UK economy (as with many economies) is GDP growth. This aggregate measure is problematic in that it does not record large inequalities and differences across the economy. More importantly, it is usually presented as GDP rather than GDP per capita. So, economies such as the UK can be recorded as growing, even though a large proportion of that growth results from population rises, often linked to immigration. Another commonly quoted figure is the inflation rate – something key to monetary policy, interest rate setting and pay rise negotiations. But the Consumer Price Index (CPI) used excludes housing costs and mortgage interest payments, as well as many financial services, and certainly not the trillions in value of exotic financial products being created and circulated. So, inflation may be officially low, but as housing costs usually rise well above inflation and wage rises, personal income can easily be dropping in real terms. Another figure is levels of unemployment, recently often presented in terms of either employment or unemployment benefit claimant counts. These figures all say little about the rise of low paid, temporary, part-time and zero-hours employment, all of which have increased.

Conclusions: post-crash economic news and the roads to Brexit and Trump

In the immediate aftermath of the financial crisis, economic elite consensus temporarily broke down and that was reflected in news coverage. Neoclassical economics, central to government policy for decades, neither predicted nor explained what had happened. Fury at the banking sector was relayed across news sections, in broadsheets and tabloids, politically left and right. Doubts about capitalism and the global financial system were frequently voiced. Brown's Labour government responded by nationalising or part nationalising banks and Keynesian stimulus packages (QE or quantitative easing, tax cuts, low interest rates) – so did the US and many other governments, thus temporarily overturning decades of economic policy. For a period, economic elite dissensus and confusion was reported (2008–2010). Financial system problems, bad behaviour and years of deregulation were blamed. Responses revolved around stabilising the banking system and the economy generally (see Berry, 2016; Basu, 2016, Chapter 2 in this volume). Re-regulation, increasing higher rate taxes and alternative Keynesian stimuli were discussed. Keynesian and other economists, such as Joseph Stiglitz and Paul Krugman, got rather more coverage.

However, in 2010, the Conservative-led Coalition government came in and began to dominate the news agenda. They offered a line that recreated a sphere of economic elite consensus (Hallin, 1994) across government, the financial sector and big business. A round of enquiries and new regulations resulted in the financial sector being declared safe once again (see Engelen et al., 2011). Instead of the financial system it was government profligacy and mismanagement that were to blame. So too, once the immediate financial crisis receded and the banking system was (seemingly) stabilised, the anti-state, pro-market and international investor line prevailed again. Following a period of banker bailouts and new rounds of financial regulation, the media moved to a default position supporting state economic withdrawal, fiscal prudence and debt management. Budget cuts and austerity economics over other alternatives became the norm again (Schiffrin, 2011; Berry, 2016, Basu, Chapter 2 in this volume) – a discourse that became even more dominant when the Conservatives gained full control in 2015.

At the same time, conventional news began to hit a tipping point, with huge revenue drops and online competition everywhere. Indeed, the slow decline of news consumption has become very extreme during the last decade as a combination of the internet and recession has entirely destabilised the business model of the sector (McChesney and Pickard, 2011; Davis, 2017). Pew (2012) calculated that the US newspaper industry had shrunk 43% and lost 28% of journalist jobs since 2000 (see also Schiffrin, 2011). In 2011, US newspapers gained $207 million in online advertising but lost $2.1 billion in print advertising. This has left news operations desperately cutting back on editorial staff and news-gathering budgets while increasing their reliance on a whole range of 'information subsidies': news wire services, public relations material, recycled and plagiarised copy, and so on. Economic news has been no exception here. Thus, just when the financial sector was reasserting itself, and economic elites moved to a renewed consensus position, so established news organisations were left with fewer resources with which to investigate and challenge the austerity consensus. So too, dependency on company PR material and the reporting of speculative investment fashions have proved too enticing.

In recent years, chancellors, bankers and top CEOs have moved beyond 'economic crisis' talk, to suggest stability and/or slow recovery, trumpeting every indicator from rises in GDP and the FTSE 100 to declining unemployment and reduced borrowing. However, for many people, the economic reality is very different. Average wage income has stagnated since the crisis, and it had been stagnating in certain regions and sectors a lot longer (Tetlow, 2016). Such calculations, although adjusting for inflation, have not included rising rental costs or house prices, which have risen an average of 6.9% a year since 1980. The headline figures on employment, which show this growing for several years, does not include the growth of insecure employment that had risen to three million, or one in ten of the workforce, by the start of 2017 (Klair, 2017). In fact, the UK is the only leading economy to record both GDP growth and a fall in real wages between 2007 and 2015 (see Wren-Lewis, 2017). The headline figures on GDP also fail to register the huge regional imbalances in the national economy. London and the South East have grown considerably faster since the financial crisis than the rest of the country, with some areas growing barely at all. London Gross Value Added (GVA) per head in London is now 72% higher on average than the rest of the nation and more than double that of six of the other 11 regions recorded (Harari, 2016).

The year 2016 was when these huge differences in economic perception and experience became suddenly clear during the Brexit referendum in June. In Britain, London, Scotland, Northern Ireland, parts of the South East and a few thriving cities voted to remain in the EU. Those more likely to vote to leave were generally in the poorer deindustrialised regions, were less educated, and in poorer and more precarious employment (BBC, 2016). The dire warnings of what would happen to the economy if the UK left seemed largely irrelevant to those who, contrary to personal experience, were used to being told the economy was doing better. So too, it was a similar story for the US presidential election, with those who were less educated and poorer, as well as those in the poorer, deindustrialised regions of the country, voting for Trump (Pew, 2016). Traditional working-class Labour and Democratic voters had lost faith in their parties. While their party leaders had been embracing mainstream economic thinking and media commentary, so they had appeared to lose touch with how this partial, mediated vision of 'the economy' was not the one experienced by ordinary citizens.

References

Annan Report. 1977. *Report of the committee on the future of broadcasting*, London: HMSO.

Basu, L. 2016. 'Rewriting the crisis: the media coverage over time', Paper at *Austerity and the Media Conference*, City University, London.

BBC. 2016. 'EU Referendum: The result in maps and charts'. *BBC*, 24 June.

Bennett, W. L. 1990. 'Towards a theory of press-state relations in the United States'. *Journal of Communication*, 40(2), pp. 103–125.

Bennett, W. L., Pickard, V., Lozzi, D., Shroder, C., Lagos, T., and Lasswell, C. 2004. 'Managing the public sphere: Journalistic construction of the great globalization debate'. *Journal of Communication*, 54(3), pp. 37–55.

Berry, M. 2016. 'The UK press and the deficit debate', *Sociology*, 50(3), pp. 542–559.

Cable, V. 2009. *The storm: The world economic crisis and what it means*. London: Atlantic Books.

Cassidy, J. 2002. *Dot.Con: The greatest story ever told*. London: Penguin/Allen Lane.

Curran, J. 1978. Advertising and the press. In: Curran, J. (ed.), *The British press: A Manifesto*, London: Macmillan, pp. 229–267.

Davies, N. 2008. *Flat Earth news*. London: Chatto and Windus.

Davis, A. 2002. *Public relations democracy: Public relations, politics and the mass media in Britain*, Manchester: Manchester University Press.

Davis, A. 2007. *The mediation of power: A Critical Introduction*, London: Routledge.

Davis, A. (ed.). 2017. *The death of public knowledge?* Goldsmiths-MIT Press.

Davis, A., and Walsh, C. 2016. 'The role of the state in the financialisation of the UK economy'. *Political Studies*, 64(3), pp. 666–682.

Doyle, G. 2006. 'Financial news journalism: A post-Enron analysis of approaches towards economic and financial news production in the UK'. *Journalism: Theory, Practice and Criticism*, 7(4), pp. 433–452.

Durham, F. 2007. 'Framing the state in globalization: The Financial Times' coverage of the 1997 Thai currency crisis'. *Critical Studies in Media Communication*, 24(1), pp. 57–76.

Elliott, L., and Atkinson, D. 2009. *The Gods that failed: How the financial elite have gambled away our futures*. London: Vintage.

Engelen, E., Ertürk, I., Froud, J., Johal, S., Leaver, A., Moran, M., Nilsson, A., and Williams, K., 2011. *After the great complacence: Financial crisis and the politics of reform*. Oxford: Oxford University Press.

Epstein, G. (ed.), 2005. *Financialization and the world economy*. Cheltenham: Edward Elgar.

Fishman. 1980. *Manufacturing news*. Austin: University of Texas.

Franklin, B. 1997. *Newszak and news media*. London: Arnold.

Gandy, O. 1982. *Beyond agenda setting: Information subsidies and public policy*. Norwood, NJ: Ablex Publishing Corporation.

Gans, H. J. 1979. *Deciding what's news: A study of CBS evening news, NBC nightly news, Newsweek and Time*. New York: Pantheon.

Haldane, A. 2010. *The Contribution of the Financial Sector: Miracle or Mirage?* Speech at the Future of Finance Conference, LSE, 14 July.

Hall, S., Critcher, C., Jefferson, T., Clarke, J., and Roberts, B. 1978. *Policing the crisis – mugging, the state, and law and order*. London: Palgrave Macmillan.

Hallin, D. 1994. *We keep America on top of the world: Television journalism and the public sphere*. London: Routledge.

Harari, D. 2016. *Regional and local economic growth statistics*. House of Commons Briefing Paper 05795, London: HMSO.

Harvey, D. 2007. *A brief history of neoliberalism*. Oxford: Oxford University Press.

Herman, E., and Chomsky, N. 1988. *Manufacturing consent: The political economy of the mass media*. New York: Pantheon Books.

Hutton, W. 1996. *The state we're in*. London: Vintage.

Kantola, A. 2006. On the dark Side of democracy: The global imaginary of financial journalism. In: Cammaerts, B., and Carpentier, N. (eds.), *Reclaiming the media: Communication, rights and democratic media roles*. Bristol: Intellect.

Klair, A. 2017. *Insecure work is up by a quarter since 2011*. TUC Briefing Note, London: TUC, 2 July.

Knowles, S., Phillips, G., and Lidberg, J. 2017. 'Reporting the Global Financial Crisis: A longitudinal tri-nation study of mainstream financial journalism'. *Journalism Studies*, 18(3), pp. 322–340.

Krippner, G. R. 2011. *Capitalizing on crisis: The political origins of the rise of finance*. Cambridge: Harvard University Press.

Krugman, P. 2008. *The return of depression economics and the crisis of 2008*. London: Penguin Books.

Lewis, J., Williams, A., and Franklin, B. 2008. 'A compromised Fourth Estate? UK news journalism, public relations and news sources'. *Journalism Studies*, 9(1), pp. 1–20.

Manning, P. 1999. 'Categories of knowledge and information flows: Reasons for the decline of the British Labour and Industrial Correspondents Group', *Media, Culture and Society*, 21(3), pp. 313–336.

Manning, P. 2013. 'Financial journalism, news sources and the banking crisis'. *Journalism*, 14(2), pp. 173–189.

McChesney, R., and Pickard, R. (eds.). 2011. *Will the last reporter please turn out the lights: The collapse of journalism and what can be done to fix it*. New York: New Press.

McQuail, D. 1977. *Analysis of newspaper content, report for the Royal Commission on the press.* London: HMSO.

Miller, D., and Dinan, W. 2000. 'The rise of the PR industry in Britain, 1979–98'. *European Journal of Communication*, 15(1), pp. 5–35.

Miller, D., and Dinan, W. 2008. *A century of spin: How public relations became the cutting edge of corporate power.* London: Pluto Press.

Mirowski, P., and Plehwe, D. (eds.). 2009. *The road to Mont Pelerin: The making of the neoliberal thought collective.* Cambridge, MA: Harvard University Press.

Mitchell, N. 1997. *The conspicuous corporation – Business, publicity, and representative democracy.* Ann Arbor, MI: University of Michigan Press.

Newman, K. 1984. *Financial marketing and communications.* London: Holt, Rinehart and Winston.

Parsons, W. 1989. *The power of the financial press: Journalism and economic opinion in Britain and America.* London: Edward Elgar.

Pew. 2012. *The state of the news media reports.* Washington DC: Pew/The Project for Excellence in Journalism.

Pew. 2016. *Behind Trump's victory.* Washington DC: Pew/The Project for Excellence in Journalism, 9 November.

Philo, G. 1995. *Glasgow media group reader, Vol. 2: Industry, economy, war and politics.* London: Routledge.

Schifferes, S. 2011. The financial crisis and the UK media. In: Schiffrin, A. (ed.), *Bad news: How America's business press missed the story of the century.* New York: The New Press. pp. 148–178.

Schiffrin, A. 2011. The US Press and the financial crisis. In: Schiffrin, A. (ed.), *Bad news: How America's business press missed the story of the century.* New York: The New Press. pp. 1–21.

Schudson, M. 2006. *Why democracies need an unlovable press.* Cambridge: Polity.

Sigal, L. V. 1973. *Reporters and officials – The organisation and politics of newsmaking.* Lexington, MA: Lexington Books.

Starkman, D. 2014. *The watchdog that didn't bark: The financial crisis and the disappearance of investigative journalism.* New York: Columbia University Press.

Tetlow, G. 2016. 'Is income inequality increasing in the UK?' in *Financial Times*, *Financial Times*, 11 December.

Thompson, P. 2017. Putting the lies into Libor: The mediation of a financial scandal. In: Davis, A. (ed.), *The death of public knowledge?* Goldsmiths-MIT Press.

Tunstall, J. 1971. *Journalists at work.* London: Sage.

Tunstall, J. 1996. *Newspaper power: The national press in Britain.* Oxford: Oxford University Press.

Wren-Lewis, S. 2017. 'Why it's your bloody GDP, not ours', 6 March, *Online blog.* Available at: https://mainlymacro.blogspot.co.uk/ [Accessed 8 March 2017]

11

'MEDIAMACRO'

Why the news media ignores economic experts

Simon Wren-Lewis

This chapter is about the disconnect between how the media presents key economic issues and how they are viewed by academic economists. I will focus on the broadcast media, because it is to this part of the media that most people look to find unbiased analysis. Large sections of the print media are highly partisan, and their economic reporting will inevitably reflect that bias. The *Financial Times* and *Economist* generally provide analysis which draws on academic views and research (although with perhaps a bias towards some perspectives rather than others), but their readership is comparatively small. Readers often recognise this political bias in their newspaper, and look to the broadcast media for an unbiased perspective.

I started thinking about the gap between the broadcast media and academic economics seriously with the advent of austerity. There are some who believe (Pettifor, 2017) that austerity was backed by most mainstream economists, or at least most senior members of the discipline. We do not have much evidence on what academic economists as a whole thought about austerity, but we do have some pieces of imperfect evidence, and these point to the opposite conclusion. Let me take each of these pieces of evidence in turn.

A good deal of attention has been paid to the letter from 20 economists, some very eminent, in February 2010 – during the run-up to the General Election – that was widely interpreted as offering support for the Conservative shadow Chancellor George Osborne's proposals for greater austerity. Actually the letter was a little more nuanced than that. It said:

> In order to minimise this risk and support a sustainable recovery, the next government should set out a detailed plan to reduce the structural budget deficit more quickly than set out in the 2009 pre-budget report. The exact timing of measures should be sensitive to developments in the economy,

particularly the fragility of the recovery. However, in order to be credible, the government"s goal should be to eliminate the structural current budget deficit over the course of a parliament, and there is a compelling case, all else being equal, for the first measures beginning to take effect in the 2010–11 fiscal year.

Besley et al., 2010

The phrase about exact timing and the fragility of the economy are important. When the 20 economists were asked two years later whether they still held that opinion, around half were prepared to admit that they had to some extent changed their mind (*New Statesman*, 2012). I remember corresponding with one. He explained that when he signed the original letter he thought the recovery from the Great Recession was well entrenched, and was sufficiently strong not to be adversely affected by greater fiscal consolidation. Had he known what he knew now, he would not have signed. Ken Rogoff, who also signed the original letter, did not approve of the sharp cutback in public investment that did so much damage in the first two years of austerity.

While this letter from 20 economists is well known, it is also relevant that just four days later more than 60 economists, led by Lord Skidelsky, signed two letters to the *Financial Times* arguing that the 20 were wrong (*Guardian*, 2010). Although some of these signatories could be described as heterodox economists, there are plenty of eminent mainstream economists among them (*Financial Times*, 2010). There must have been plenty of others who, like me, would have signed if they had gotten the letter in time. Neither letter formally endorsed plans from any party, but focused on the macroeconomics.

Part of the motivation from the minority of macroeconomists who supported austerity in 2010 were concerns about the emerging Eurozone crisis, when markets stopped buying the debt of first Greece and later other member governments on the periphery of the Eurozone. At first there was uncertainty among many macroeconomists about what was going on, and according to an International Monetary Fund (IMF) internal evaluation (*IMF*, 2014) this uncertainty helped move the IMF's position from supporting fiscal stimulus in 2009 to supporting austerity in 2010.

However by late 2011 and early 2012 it was becoming clear what the underlying cause of the Eurozone crisis was. Paul De Grauwe (e.g. De Grauwe, 2011) argued that the European Central Bank (ECB) was failing to undertake an essential part of being a central bank, which was to be a lender of last resort to governments. Later in 2012 he was proved correct. In September 2012 the ECB changed its policy by introducing a programme to purchase sovereign government debt for all Eurozone countries affected by the crisis, not just Greece, and the Eurozone crisis came to an end. As a result, the same IMF internal evaluation says the move to general austerity in 2010 was incorrect. (It is important to distinguish between the IMF's economists and their political masters. These internal evaluations have the advantage of being written by economists independently of their political overseers.)

By 2015 a survey of selected UK (mainly academic) macroeconomists had only 15% agreeing with the statement that austerity had helped GDP (Centre for Macroeconomics, 2015). In the US the regular IGM forum survey of leading academic economists had also shown that a clear majority believed the Obama stimulus had helped reduce unemployment, and by 2015 only 2% thought otherwise. Although all this evidence is far from ideal (a point I will return to later), it is consistent with the view that austerity was never backed by a majority of academic economists, and that this majority against austerity grew over time.

We can also look at the models academics and central banks use. The dominant model for analysing the business cycle is the New Keynesian model, and central bank models are elaborations of it. This model shows clearly and unequivocally that spending cuts reduce output when interest rates are at their lower bound. As a result, nearly all the model-based analysis of austerity I have seen published shows austerity reduced GDP. There has been no concerted attempt to overturn the dominant role of this model, which would be surprising if most economists favoured austerity. Instead, a lot academic work has involved extending the model's scope to include a financial sector, for obvious reasons.

A final piece of evidence for the UK is the analysis of the independent Office for Budget Responsibility. Its forecast evaluation report (Office for Budget Responsibility, 2014) calculated that austerity reduced GDP growth by about 1% in financial year 2010/11, and by about 1% again in the following financial year. It is difficult to imagine the economy bouncing back from this hit to demand and output before 2013. I calculated that on the extremely optimistic view that the economy did recover from all this fiscal tightening by 2013 austerity had cost every UK household resources worth £4,000 (Wren-Lewis, 2015).

Many people still believe that we had to have austerity in 2010 because otherwise the markets would have stopped buying UK government debt. Why are most academic economists not swayed by this argument? The first point is that there is no evidence I know of that the markets were about to do this, and of course we know that interest rates on government debt fell after 2010, suggesting ample demand for government debt. But more importantly, because the Bank of England acts as a lender of last resort for the UK government, and was actually buying large quantities of debt through its QE programme, the UK government can never be forced to default by the markets. As I have already noted, the Eurozone crisis was a strictly Eurozone affair, with no implication for countries such as the UK with their own central banks.

One of the mysteries of this period is why, given these basic facts, the UK government pursued the austerity policy with such vigour. From an economic point of view it would have been much more sensible and less costly to delay austerity until interest rates were no longer at their lower bound (Wren-Lewis, 2016). My concern here is why the views of the majority of economists who understood this were hardly ever heard in the media. I think an important clue is provided by the myth of Labour profligacy.

The myth of Labour profligacy

One of the most incredible poll findings before the 2015 election was that a large number of voters blamed the Labour government for austerity. It is incredible not because it is difficult to understand why they did this: The Conservatives kept repeating that they were having to clear up the mess that Labour had left. In other words Labour had been profligate when in office, and austerity had been forced on Chancellor George Osborne because there was no alternative but to reduce the deficit as quickly as possible. What is incredible is that this story is obviously untrue, and it is easy to show it is untrue.

Looking at Figure 11.1, which presents the UK public sector deficit over time, with an arrow pointing to the start of the financial crisis, is revealing.

The deficit was perhaps slightly higher than would have been optimal in 2007, but nothing that could justifiably be called profligacy. (With debt of around 40% of GDP, as it was at the time, the deficit should be between 1.5% and 2% of GDP to keep the debt-to-GDP ratio stable.) What is absolutely clear from this chart is that the cause of the high level of debt in 2009 was the Great Recession. Deficits normally rise in a recession for well-understood reasons, as the chart shows happened in the early 1990s, and the recession that followed the financial crisis was the largest seen since the 1930s.

Is there some reason this data is misleading? I had examined this issue extensively in my article on Labour's fiscal policy record (Wren-Lewis, 2013), and the short answer is no. The idea that the Labour government had been profligate is a complete myth.

So why was this myth believed by so many people? The answer is that it was never seriously challenged, by either the Labour Party or the media. The reasons for Labour's silence remain a bit of a mystery. The media's response makes sense only if you recognise that political journalists do not have the knowledge or expertise to

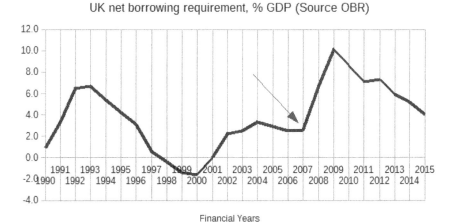

FIGURE 11.1 UK net borrowing requirement, % GDP

make such a challenge, and so if the opposing party does not make the challenge for them, they will let statements like 'clearing up the mess' pass.

Economic journalists should know better, but they are rare in the broadcast media, and rarely interview major politicians. If they are critical of the government they also risk incurring the wrath of ministers. Such complaints can cause them significant grief. Take the case of Stephanie Flanders when she worked for the BBC as economics editor (reported in Wren-Lewis, 2013b). Appearing on the *Radio 4 Today Programme,* she made the pertinent and entirely correct observation that rapid employment growth combined with weak output growth was problematic, because it meant productivity was not growing. For this important and indisputable observation she drew criticism and a formal complaint from a Conservative Cabinet Minister, Ian Duncan Smith, who accused her of "peeing all over British workers".

There is one further reason why, on macroeconomic issues in particular, economic journalists are out of touch with academic economics, which I explore in the next section. (Guardian 19 August 2012).

'Mediamacro': macroeconomics in the media

Not only did the myth of Labour profligacy go unchallenged in the media, but also did the idea that austerity was essential. Indeed the media seemed to actively promote this idea. By 2014 I had started using the term 'mediamacro' to describe how macroeconomics was presented on the media. Mediamacro seemed to have no relation to the macroeconomics every academic taught first-year undergraduates, and indeed sometimes it was directly opposed. The textbooks advise allowing the deficit to rise in a recession because this is a good thing (we even call it 'the automatic stabiliser'), but mediamacro says deficits are bad.

It is important not to dismiss mediamacro as simply political bias in favour of the Conservative Party. It is more general than that. Take for example the time that Jon Snow, the presenter of Channel 4 news, who is no right-wing hack, played gotcha politics with Labour leader Ed Miliband over not mentioning the deficit (see Wren-Lewis, 2014b). After his Labour Party conference speech in September 2014 – where the big news in the right wing press was that Ed Miliband had forgotten the paragraph on how important the deficit is – Jon Snow asked Miliband what the greatest issue facing the next British government was. Mr Miliband responded that it is getting the country to work for most working people rather than be stuck with a more unequal country. It was an interesting answer, particularly now in the light of Brexit, but Snow did not follow it up. It was a trick question. Jon Snow pressed him saying that he had forgotten to mention the deficit twice, and asked how he could you not mention paying off this appalling-surely the most important issue of all. It is the essence of our economic crisis. (Channel 4 News, 2014).

Mediamacro is a combination of macroeconomics as seen by the Swabian housewife and the City economist. The analogy used constantly by Prime Minister David Cameron and George Osborne, that the UK had 'maxed out its credit card', makes no sense in terms of textbook macroeconomics, but it works on political journalists as much as it does for ordinary voters. It reflects the fact that journalists in general hardly ever access academic economists for their expertise in areas where academics have knowledge that others lack.

The economists that journalists do generally talk to are City economists. City economists are employed by financial institutions mainly to impress clients and to put the firm 'on the map' by appearing in the media. They are selected mainly for their ability to tell convincing stories about the economy that the firm's clients will find acceptable, and not for their economic expertise. This ability, together with their ready availability, makes them attractive to the media. In particular the main task that the media uses economists for is to tell what some academics call 'up and down stories'.

By 'up and down stories' I mean the provision of one- or two-line simple explanations about why markets have moved, usually over a short time span (typically one day). I use the word 'stories' advisably. No one actually knows why financial markets move on a particular day. To do so would require asking everyone who bought and sold in the market that day why they did so, and no one does that. If you are lucky, the City economist might have asked the traders in their firm why the market moved, but that is a sample of one amongst thousands. The stories City economists tell are often plausible, by which I mean that they make sense in terms of economic theory, but they remain stories.

It is interesting that no one tells you they are stories as they are presented. Instead the stories are always told as if they were known facts. I have never heard an 'up and down economist' say that of course no one knows why the market has just moved, or even say 'my guess is'. This is an interesting example of where the broadcast media acquiesces in deceiving viewers about how certain economic explanations are.

Why are City economists not a good source for journalists writing about economic policy? First, they are just not that knowledgeable about economic policy, or even about how markets will respond to aspects of policy. Academics are selected for their ability to understand their field, while City economists are selected to appear convincing in telling stories to clients. A City economist will therefore need to know much more about recent data movements over a wide range of countries than most academics could manage, but the quid pro quo of that is that an academic will generally have a much deeper knowledge of how economy policy works. There are, of course, important exceptions to this generalisation – partly because very occasionally academics move to the City.

Second, City economists tend to be politically biased in a right-wing direction, and this does influence their views on policy. I have an acid test for political bias, related to austerity. In the UK in 2013 there was finally a recovery of sorts in the UK, after three years of very low rates of growth. The *Financial Times* asked a panel of economists whether this recovery vindicated austerity. Whatever your views on austerity, the answer to this question has to be no. The austerity undertaken by Osborne was front loaded (concentrated in the early years of the coalition government), and any Keynesian model would suggest that the impact on economic *growth* was therefore bound to be temporary. A revival of growth could not therefore vindicate austerity.

Thus growth in 2013 was completely consistent with claims that austerity had been very damaging, by delaying the recovery until then. Among the *Financial Times* panel, 10 out of the 12 academics replied that the recovery did not vindicate austerity (Wren-Lewis, 2014). That was the correct answer, which any good student would have given if asked this question in an exam. In contrast, around half of the larger group of City economists surveyed said it did vindicate austerity. The only way to explain why so many City economists would give an obviously incorrect answer is political bias. (Even the *Financial Times,* which can normally be relied on to get the economics right, declared after the recovery that Osborne had been proved right.) For this reason City economists, together with economists from the right-wing think tanks – the Institute for Economic Affairs and the Adam Smith Institute – are often favoured by Conservative politicians and ministers.

One final point is that City economists have a vested interest in talking up the uncertainty of markets, as long as the media and politicians continue to believe (incorrectly) that they have some kind of unique insight into how they behave. As a result, they tended to play up the chances of the market not buying UK government debt during the recession.

Academic economists, in contrast to City economists, tend to be pretty hopeless at up and down economics. First, they are difficult to get hold of, partly because they receive no academic kudos from media appearances. Second, they will almost certainly respond to questions about market moves with explanations that involve statements of ignorance and plenty of 'on the other hand' clauses. But on questions of economic policy and welfare, rather than day-to-day movements, they have the advantage of being more knowledgeable and in the most part are relatively unbiased. An academic economist who gives biased accounts of academic knowledge will suffer in terms of their academic reputation. This is one reason why academics tend to be high on the list of people whom the public trusts.

The absence of the voice of academic economists became particularly apparent in the 2015 General Election. It was generally agreed by political journalists that the economy was the Conservatives' strong card, indeed perhaps their only strong card. This appeared to be based on a number of misconceptions about recent macroeconomic history. I have already talked about the myth of Labour profligacy, which went largely unchallenged in the media. To this we can add the following points:

1   The strength of the recovery. This was celebrated by Coalition politicians, but in reality growth in GDP per head from 2013 was close to its long-run trend. A true recovery would involve GDP growing faster than trend. Furthermore we had to wait until 2013 for even this modest growth. As a result, it was the slowest recovery in living memory.

2   The strong growth in employment was also celebrated, even though it implied extremely low productivity growth. As I have already noted, a BBC economics

editor attracted a formal complaint from a Conservative minister when she pointed this out.

3   Low productivity growth helped produce the longest decline in real earnings ever recorded.

A number of academic economists made these points during the election campaign, as well as pointing out the myth of Labour profligacy and the foolishness of austerity. They had no noticeable impact on political journalists, who continued to adhere to the tenets of mediamacro. I think it is no exaggeration to say that mediamacro was crucial in winning the 2015 General Election for the Conservatives. To paraphrase a headline from the Sun after Neil Kinnock's 1992 election defeat, in 2015 'it's mediamacro wot won it'.

The Impact on Brexit

The failure of the media to present academic knowledge became most apparent in the debate before the EU referendum which took place in June 2016. A major reason not to leave the EU was that membership in the Single Market was very beneficial to the UK. This was the case that the government chose to focus on. It is an area where academic economists, particular those who specialise in international trade, are the only real experts in the room. They should have been centre stage during the debate, but they were hardly ever seen.

As it happens, amongst these experts the essential elements of the government's case was uncontroversial. Leaving the EU, particularly if it meant leaving the Single Market, would have large costs for every citizen in the UK, and the only question was how large. A survey showed that an unprecedented 90+% of members of the Royal Economic Society thought Brexit would be bad for the economy. This fact was almost completely absent from media coverage, which instead chose to focus on a 'he said, she said' debate among politicians.

A majority that large is as close to unanimous as economists will ever get. As a result, their views on Brexit should have been treated by the broadcast media as knowledge, and the media should have helped these economists explain what this knowledge was based on. Instead it was treated as just an opinion, to always be balanced by an opinion from the other side. As a result, the BBC and the rest of the broadcast media devalued the knowledge economists had, and grossly misinformed their viewers.

I strongly endorse the views of Professor John Van Reenen, who was Director of LSE's Centre for Economic Performance and produced probably the most comprehensive and authoritative study of the economic impact of Brexit, who was very critical of the BBC's role. (Van Reenen, 2016):

> Most of the British press has been unrelentingly Eurosceptic and anti-immigrant for decades. This built to a crescendo during the Brexit campaign with

the most popular dailies like the Sun, Mail and Express little more than the propaganda arm of the Leave campaign.

The main alternative source of information for ordinary people was the BBC, which was particularly awful throughout the referendum debate. It supinely reported the breath-taking lies of the Leave campaign in particularly over the "£350 million a week EU budget contribution". Rather than confront Leave campaigners and call the claim untruthful, BBC broadcasters would say things like "now this is a contested figure, but let's move on". This created the impression that there was just some disagreement between the sides, whereas it was clearly a lie. It's like saying "One side says that world is flat, but this is contested by Remain who say it is round. We'll let you decide." The public broadcaster failed a basic duty of care to the British people. There was a need to tell people the truth for probably the most important vote any of us will have in our lifetimes. And the BBC failed.

The BBC also failed to reflect the consensus view of the economics profession on the harm of Brexit. A huge survey of British economists showed that for every one respondent who thought there would be economic benefits from Brexit over the next five years, there were 22 who thought we would be worse off. Yet time and again, there would always be some maverick Leave economist given equal airtime to anyone articulating the standard arguments.

There are good reasons for thinking that, as with the 2015 election, the failure of journalists to treat what academic economists had to say in an appropriate manner could have had a decisive influence on the result. The first obvious point is that the majority in favour of leaving the EU was not large. Second, polls before and *after* the vote suggest both that a large proportion of Leave voters did not expect to be worse off as a result of leaving, and would not be happy with a final deal that left them worse off (Guardian, 2016). There are two explanations for this, given the advice from economists. Perhaps people understood what economists were saying, but decided not to believe it. Alternatively, they thought that economists were divided on whether Brexit would be good or bad. Given the way the debate was framed by the media, the latter explanation must be the most likely cause.

There is a third reason why the broadcast media might be responsible for the Brexit result. One of the key reasons for the Leave victory was a desire to reduce immigration. A key motive for wanting to reduce immigration was a belief held by a great many that immigration reduced their access to public services, and the NHS in particular. The particular Ipsos/Mori poll shown in Figure 11.2, Attitudes to EU immigration, suggests this is the main reason why people think that immigration is bad for them.

In reality, nearly all economists agree that immigration improves the public finances, and therefore makes additional resources available to the NHS that more than compensate from actual usage by immigrants. The Office for Budget Responsibility has repeatedly made this point, and its latest projections show a deterioration in the public finances because it expects lower immigration following Brexit.

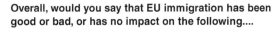

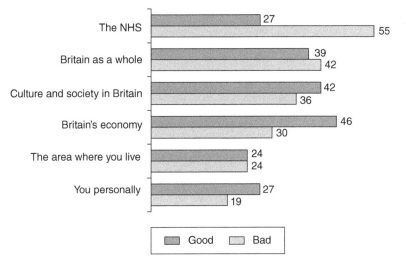

Base: 1,257 GB adults, aged 18+, interviewed by telephone, FW 11-14 June 2016

FIGURE 11.2   Attitudes to EU immigration.

The reason is straightforward: immigrants tend to be younger than the population as a whole. That this public misperception about immigration can persist reflects a failure of the broadcast media to inform.

Is there hope for change?

It seems that the default mode of broadcasters is to treat any view on an issue that is politically contested as just another opinion, generally (always before an election) to be balanced by an opposing opinion. We have seen this with climate change. As groups began to emerge that contest climate change, the media began to give these climate change deniers equal time to climate scientists. In this particular case pressure from leading scientific institutions helped the BBC change its policy (BBC Trust, 2014), and it now tends to treat man-made climate change as an accepted fact. However we do not know (and I hope we will never find out) whether this policy would survive if one of the major political parties adopted climate change denial.

   One of the arguments frequently put forward is that the economic understanding of most people is quite low, and therefore journalists find it is difficult to get economics across to the public (BBC Trust, 2012). It is so much easier, therefore, to pretend in the context of austerity that the government is like a household because the public can relate to this analogy – but imagine the same point being made about climate change. It is difficult to get across the idea that one cold winter in the UK is quite compatible with a rising temperature trend, so let's instead say that a cold winter does cast doubt on climate change. No reputable scientific journalist would do this, so why is it an excuse for poor economics reporting?

In practice I think the opposite is often true. In the EU referendum debate the economic case against leaving relied on 'gravity equations'. The economics behind the key aspects of gravity equations is very easy to explain: it is easier to trade with your near neighbours, so trade agreements elsewhere cannot compensate for making trade with the EU more difficult. Yet this was hardly ever done by the broadcast media, which meant that assertions by the Leave campaign that 'defied gravity' went unchallenged.

The resistance to adopting the same model as climate change to economics when economists are united on any issue seems to run very deep among broadcasters. I think there are a number of reasons for this:

1   Many broadcasters are deeply suspicious about economics. Part of that comes from their preoccupation with unconditional macroeconomic forecasts. Yet no one would seriously say that because doctors cannot forecast exactly when you will die if you smoke we should ignore what they say about smoking decreasing your expected lifespan. But routinely during the Brexit campaign that argument was made for economists' views on the long term cost of Brexit. A macro forecast about what growth will be in 2017 is unconditional in the sense that it could go wrong for an almost infinite number of reasons, just as could a forecast about how long you will live. A view that Brexit will reduce long-run prosperity is a conditional forecast, like a forecast that smoking will reduce your life. It is much less likely to be wrong.

2   A related argument is that macroeconomics has become discredited because of the financial crisis. It is undoubtedly true that the financial crisis showed up some inadequacies in mainstream macro. But you can equally argue that increased macroeconomic understanding among policymakers stopped the recession that followed the financial crisis becoming as bad at the Depression of the 1930s. Furthermore, the long-term impact of Brexit mostly involved the economics of international trade, which had nothing to do with the financial crisis.

3   Political broadcasters feel threatened by economics. A large amount of the discussion of economics in the media involves political journalists, only a few of whom have any economic expertise. That does not mean that every political journalist should have economic expertise – although those who do are noticeably better as a result – but rather that political journalists should be backed up by research which does source economic expertise from academics.

4   Journalistic culture prizes headlines over providing information. It likes the entertainment value of debate. You get scoops from spending a lot of time with politicians rather than talking to academics. Whether all this really produces better television is debatable, but it is part of the culture. In the 1970s Peter Jay and John Birt diagnosed similar problems to the ones I have addressed, and proposed that broadcasters should adopt a mission to explain. Their proposal

lost out to the adversarial model focused largely on debates among Westminster politicians, a model that not only neutralises knowledge but also gives airtime to extreme positions.

5   The pernicious influence of the right-wing press constantly puts the BBC on the defensive and provides the 'talking points' for the day's news. As Robert Peston has said,[1] *BBC News* is "completely obsessed" by the agenda set by newspapers and follows the lead of the *Daily Mail* and *Daily Telegraph* too much.

6   So much of politics involves economics. If the media started treating issues on which there was an academic consensus as expertise rather than as opinion to be contested, they would have politicians on their back far more often than they do now.

The consequence is that when it comes to issues where political views conflict with those of nearly all economists, the media abandons its duty to inform because keeping on the right side of politicians is more important. That there are so many reasons why journalists ignore academic economists indicates that the situation will be hard to change. But as I have also shown with the example of climate change, altering this situation is not impossible.

I think a prerequisite for such a change is for economists to organise as a collective, and to start to put pressure on the broadcast media that goes beyond writing angry letters. The obvious group to do that is the Royal Economic Society (RES), of which most UK academic economists are members. The RES needs to regularly survey all its members on key policy issues. In areas where a strong majority exists, it should then act as a pressure group, actively promoting this point of view. This will be far more effective and efficient than trying to improve the PR skills of individual economists. A society should not have to rely on the PR skills of its scientists to get academic knowledge into the public arena. The fact that the media ignores academic economics can change only as the result of concerted pressure by economists acting as a collective.

Note

1   *Guardian* 6 June 2014.

References

BBC Trust. 2012. 'BBC Trust Seminar on Impartiality and Economic Reporting', BBC Trust.

BBC Trust. 2014. 'Trust Conclusions on the Executive Report on Science Impartiality Review Actions', BBC Trust.

Beasley, Tim, et al. 2010. Letter to the *Sunday Times*. Available at www.lancaster.ac.uk/staff/ecagrs/atotl.pdf [Accessed 10 February]

Centre for Macroeconomics, Cambridge University, 2015. CFM Survey 28th March, 'The Importance of Elections for UK Economic Activity' http://cfmsurvey.org/surveys/importance-elections-uk-economic-activity

Channel 4 News, (2014), 'Is Ed Miliband Ready to Become Prime Minister?', interview with Jon Snow for Channel 4 News, 24 September. Available at https://www.channel4.com/news/ed-miliband-labour-politics-jon-snow-interview [Accessed 14 February 2018]

De Grauwe, Paul, 2011. 'Only a more active ECB can solve the Euro crisis'. *CEPS Papers* 5963, Centre for European Policy Studies.

Financial Times, 2010. 'Letter from Lord Skidelsky and others'. Available at www.lancaster.ac.uk/staff/ecagrs/atotl.pdf [Accessed 18 February 2017].

Guardian. 2010. 'Top Economists Hit Back at Tories over Spending Cuts', by Heather Stewart and Patrick Wintour. Available at www.theguardian.com/politics/2010/feb/18/spending-cuts-economists-deficit [Accessed 18 February 2017]

Guardian. 2016. *Poll Suggests Public Will not accept a Brexit that leaves them worse off*, 10 December, Available at www.theguardian.com/politics/2016/dec/10/poll-public-will-not-accept-brexit-worse-off-tim-farron-ukip-lib-dem-yougov

International Monetary Fund (IMF). 2014. *IMF Response to the Financial and Economic Crisis*, Independent Evaluation Office.

New Statesman, 2012. 'Exclusive: Osborne's Supporters Turn on Him'. 15 August, Available at www.newstatesman.com/blogs/politics/2012/08/exclusive-osbornes-supporters-turn-him

Office for Budget Responsibility. 2014. Forecast Evaluation Report, Chart 2.9.

Pettifor, A. 2017. 'Brexit and its Consequences', *Globalisations*, 14(1), pp. 127–132.

Van Reenen, J. 2016. *The aftermath of the Brexit vote – the verdict from a derided expert, LSE British Politics and Policy blog*. 2 August, Available at http://blogs.lse.ac.uk/brexit/2016/08/04/why-we-lost-the-referendum-a-derided-expert-writes/

Wren-Lewis, S. 2013. 'Aggregate fiscal policy under the Labour government, 1997–2010'. *Oxford Review of Economic Policy*, 29(1), pp. 25–46.

Wren-Lewis, S. 2013b. 'Behaving like Luddites, Mainly Macro blog'. 14 July.

Wren-Lewis, S. 2014. 'On city economists and the FT survey, Mainly macro blog'. 2 January.

Wren-Lewis, S. 2014b. 'More mediamacro, Mainly Macro blog'. 27 September.

Wren-Lewis, S. 2015. 'The Austerity Con'. *London Review of Books*, 37(4) 19t February, pp. 9–11.

Wren-Lewis, S. 2016. 'A General Theory of Austerity'. Blavatnik Working Paper No. 2016/014.

12

FINANCIAL JOURNALISTS, THE FINANCIAL CRISIS AND THE 'CRISIS' IN JOURNALISM

Sophie Knowles

> The message which comes screaming through all of this is the importance of those journalists who are willing to swim against the tide, those who will be pessimists in a sea of optimism, who are prepared to ask the tough questions and who will deliver the hard answers. That takes courage, bravery, knowledge and skill.
>
> (Anton Harber, 2009)

Introduction

The Global Financial Crisis (GFC) which began in 2008, and which continues to impact on the political and economic spheres across much of the developed world, has brought critical attention to some key institutions, including the media. Studies on the role played by the media before and during the GFC have pointed to financial reporting that is narrowly framed, being based on the information that market insiders provide, and shaped by what market investors want to know. This form of financial journalism, which leaves out the general public and focuses attention on free financial market activity, has also been described as "neoliberal newspeak": neoliberal ideology that is so entrenched in the media that it has become part of everyday news routines and news production (Chakravartty and Schiller, 2010, p. 677).

Neoliberalism – proselytising the free market, deregulation, and privatisation – has become visible in the support in the press for a continuation of austerity policies that have seen a cutback in the welfare state and public spending across much of Europe (Kelsey et al., 2016; Schifferes and Knowles, 2014). The GFC, which saw the bursting of a super asset bubble (Soros, 2008) and a crisis in capitalism, was an opportunity for critique and overhaul of the system. Instead, the critique was short-lived and, rather than instigating reform in the system, the crisis has resulted in the consolidation of the policies and practices associated with neoliberalism (Blyth, 2013; Lewis, 2010). This includes the media industry, as neoliberal policies have underpinned the changes that have been taking place in media systems, such as large transnational media mergers, the reduction of journalism staff globally, and an intensification of labour (Knoche, 2016; McChesney, 2015).

Concurrently, journalism has been suffering from a crisis of its own. Perpetuated by neoliberal policies, commercialisation, and the GFC, this crisis relates to the news industry as it tries to figure out its place in an online and digital world without its traditional funding stream from advertising. The word 'crisis' is also being used to describe the relationship between journalism and the public, as there has been a steady decline in public trust in news (Franklin, 2014; Schifferes, 2014), and new spaces have opened up for citizen, social, and collaborative media.

This chapter explores the influence the intensification of neoliberal policies has had on financial reporting over the past three decades, according to journalists themselves. Journalists arguably produce the narratives and discourse that create the perpetuating loop of information that shapes political and economic reality, depending on what they cover, who they speak with, and how they frame their articles. Interviews with journalists are, therefore, used here to examine the dynamic of the workplace and the organisational norms that influence them in their work on a day-to-day basis. The chapter asks what influences or factors, if any, have contributed to a neoliberal news logic, and to what degree, if any, have commercial challenges in the industry impacted on news quality?

While a number of academic studies have analysed financial news content, the position and role of financial journalists has been less closely examined (see for example the surveys done by Henningham, 1997; Schultz, 1993 in Australia and more recently the interview-based and ethnographic studies by Doyle, 2006; Tambini, 2010 in the UK; and Usher, 2013, 2017 in the US). The analysis in this chapter is derived from interviews with fifteen experienced mainstream practitioners from three developed and democratic countries – the US, UK, and Australia – about the following trends across the past three decades: pressures to report along optimistic lines, routine sources used for information, a newsroom culture predicated on capitalism and neoliberalism, and market pressures on mainstream financial news.

The newsroom and everyday reporting practices and cultures

Financial journalism has been growing alongside capitalism, constructing and mediating the world of finance and the economy since the seventeenth century (Parsons, 1989). As a genre it is intrinsically tied to the institutions it reports on and the capitalist system that it operates within. It has received similar criticism time and time again for being too optimistic and lacking in skepticism during boom phases, and too reactionary and too inflammatory in the reporting of downturns (Carswell, 1938; Taylor, 2014). While reporting optimistically and with little skepticism may buoy markets, it is shortsighted and does not benefit investors, shareholders, or the public, as evidenced by the sheer scale of the GFC, rising unemployment, and taxpayer-funded bailouts.

Interviews with financial journalists in previous studies have presented a mixed picture of how journalists see their role, with some who think they should play a watchdog role for the public, and others – usually those working for a specialist news outlet – who do not see this as an essential duty (Tambini, 2010; Usher, 2013). During the GFC journalists themselves wrote about the topic, some with a sense of mea culpa, and some on a more defensive note (Brummer, 2009; Schechter, 2009). Gillian Tett, deputy editor of the *Financial Times*, and one of the few to forewarn others about the dangers and risks that were building up in the debt and derivatives markets, has written that in the decade before the credit bubble burst in 2007, the financial media paid remarkably little attention to growth in debt and derivatives (Tett, 2009, p. 9). She describes a "Titanic-sized iceberg" that hid all of the debt and derivatives that were growing dangerously and under-reported below water, while all focus and attention served the growth-driven – profit-driven – capitalist model. Tett explains that journalists and their editors think debt is dull and some are suffering from cognitive capture. Pointing to Bourdieu's field theory, she explains that what really matters in terms of controlling a cognitive map is not what *is* publicly discussed, but what is *not* discussed.

To explore the degree to which there were pressures within the newsroom to report along optimistic lines during this and past global financial crises – the 1990 recession, the dot com boom of 1998, and the GFC of 2008 – journalists operating in the UK, US, and Australia were asked whether there is pressure to report optimistically and in a similar way to other media outlets. Generally speaking, the journalists do not think there is pressure as such, but that financial events have been reported on in a similar and positive way during the past three financial crises because of two main reasons: human psychology during a period of market euphoria, and not wanting to stand out in the newsroom as a Cassandra. Only one of the journalists (the UK's Robert Peston) mentioned the fact that good reporting is contingent on accuracy, and stories that are not verifiable are difficult to report – especially on TV.

Peston, former BBC economics editor, responsible for breaking the Northern Rock story, and now political editor at ITV, explains the difficulty he experienced pitching a story about an asset bubble that had not yet happened and that had very little visual material for use on TV:

> There was a famous day when I had a conversation with the head of news. I said we're heading for a crash and he said, well when will it be? I said I don't know, because the thing about bubbles is you can never be certain when they will burst, and he said okay well the story will hold then. That sort of is a problem with these sorts of stories, TV in particular want an event. I wasn't sure whether it would be 2007 or 2008 and it makes it quite hard to cover.

Also in the UK, Larry Elliott, the long-serving economics editor at the *Guardian*, thinks it was difficult to "stand out against the pack" during both the dot com bubble and the GFC: "It's quite difficult to write stories saying this is all going to go to custard in a big way when everything seems to be going really swimmingly."

This sentiment is echoed by journalists in Australia and the US who refer to the difficulty of going against the grain when something is fashionable and popular. In Australia, Alan Kohler, founder of *Business Spectator*, thinks "This comes down to the herd mentality, not of the newspapers, but of the public." Also in Australia, Colleen Ryan, previously editor of the *Australian Financial Review*, says "there's a pressure to get it right and have a good story. I think journalists get swept up in the market optimism just as market players do."

Ryan also points unprompted to commercial pressures that she thinks have changed the "views of the owners and managers" and made them "reactive", as they are less likely to support lengthy investigations. Glenda Korporaal, executive editor for business in the *Australian* newspaper, expresses the same viewpoint that media owners have "less stomach" for the potential legal battles that investigations can bring. This view is echoed by Peter Goodman, European economics correspondent for the *New York Times*:

> More than ideology or business model decisions, the thing that's most defining is that there aren't enough people working financial beats to enable you to let people fail. Back in the monopoly days they could put people on a project that eventually turned in to nothing.

The journalists expressed similar viewpoints, namely that any pressures that exist to report with optimism are psychological. Pressures come mainly from the investing public that want to hear good news about the markets and the economy. Moreover, it is difficult to pitch a 'what if' story that is difficult to verify and illustrate. For these reasons, it is difficult to go against the grain and be a doomsayer. This, according to some, is being exacerbated on a practical level by the fact that there are fewer reporters, less time and less appetite for potentially litigious investigations.

Sources of information

While both the literature and the journalists indicate a newsroom culture that favours market growth, another important part of the news production process involves the selection of sources used for information (Philo, 2007, p. 182). A number of studies into financial journalism have shown elites tend to shape coverage most frequently and thereby have an influence on the angle of a story. This has been the case historically in the US, Australia, and the UK, but it is a trend that has become more evident in recent years and particularly during the GFC (Berry, 2013; Knowles et al., 2017; Lewis et al. 2008; Manning, 2013). This results in a narrow frame of reality, which limits critique and disables a discussion of alternatives.

To understand this trend, journalists were asked why executive business sources (such as CEOs, managers etc.) are used so often while other sources such as academics and members of the public are used so rarely.

There is consensus that business sources are faster to respond with market-relevant information than other sources such as academics. Here the private sector is far superior to the slow and bloated public sector. Academics are viewed not only as slow to respond, but also as too abstract in their thinking, and generally ignorant of the speed and nature of the news production process. It is also clear that members of the public, academics, NGOs etc. are not part of the news shaping process – but provide a context about the impact of a story once it has broken.

Ian King, formerly financial editor at the *Times* in the UK and now a presenter on Sky, says "In our field they [executives, CEOs etc.] tend to know more than most people. A lot of academics don't tend to have real-world experience. Members of the public can often be ignorant and ill-informed." Goodman, in the US, provides a blunt assessment about academics as potential sources:

> They are less likely to wander around with blackberries and respond in real time to a reporter on deadline. They can be impatient talking to people who don't have the same expertise or grasp that they have. It's very rare to find a credentialed, insightful academic, who is willing to take the time with a neophyte financial journalist or even someone who is up-to-speed.

Only two journalists – who have left the news industry for academia (Chris Roush, founder of the Carolina Business News Initiative, and Dean Starkman, previously a reporter for the *Wall Street Journal*) – brought up the idea that alternative sources would provide alternative perspectives. The interviews with the practitioners also revealed a difference in the sources used by economics and financial journalists – with those writing on economics pointing to econocrats and others as sources of information, as opposed to financial analysts and investors. It is interesting also to note the two economic editors (Larry Elliott, *Guardian*, and Ross Gittins, *Sydney Morning Herald*) see their role as writing for a more general public, not the markets, and they do not see their work as necessarily belonging within the financial section.

The end result of this propensity to select executive sources above all else is that only people in power shape the story. A number of the journalists pointed to powerful politicians who dictated the news agenda, particularly as neoliberalism was being peddled in the 1980s. While practicalities like speed and prominence play a significant role in the selection of sources, it was politics and ideology that framed the story. Interestingly, Peston points to a shift in power from unions to politicians in the 1980s:

> It's no great mystery that under the Reagan/Thatcher political reforms, the power of trade unions was reduced and the power of the private sector was increased, and in those circumstances I guess the quotes from the people who are making the decisions, are more powerful than they [the trade unions] were.

Financial news and neoliberalism

Since 2007/8 neoliberalism has continued to be the dominant political ideology – it has been reinvigorated by austerity policies that have been favoured across much of Europe and largely supported by the press (Blyth, 2013; Hall, 2011; Schifferes and Knowles, 2014). Indeed financial journalism's role as a conduit for a form of capitalism that prioritizes the interests of business has been especially evident in the past few decades. The media's carriage of neoliberal policy as a norm has been confirmed by a number of studies that have found supportive, or uncritical, reporting of neoliberalism and narratives such as the efficient market hypothesis in the US, UK, and Australia (Bourdieu and Wacquant, 2001; Davis, 2011), and in developing countries like India (Dutta and Sen, 2014, p. 209).

To provide some practical reflection on the way neoliberal policymaking has been covered in the newsroom from the 1980s onward, journalists were asked if they ever felt pressure to accept neoliberalism as an economic and financial norm.

The journalists referred mostly to policy around deregulation and explained that during the 1980s and 90s a lot of the changes in the economy were being reported through the prism of politics and what was happening at the time. Peston brings in key politicians who drove the coverage, especially the UK under Tony Blair and the US under Clinton and explains that, as a journalist, "even if you yourself are hostile to those ideas, or sceptical of those ideas, you'll adapt your views because you know that's what's expected of you."

Hamish McRae, economics commentator and executive editor of the *Independent* online, agrees that journalists are tasked with reporting events as they happen:

> When privatisation was sweeping the world to a greater or lesser extent it was an intellectual topic that swept through the world. You were obliged to write about what was happening – the same now with de-regulation the same now with re-regulation.

The *Guardian* is an exception, according to its economics editor, Elliott, with the paper covering issues such as green economics and Keynesianism. Referring to the impact 'neoliberal policy-making' on his personal practice, he says:

> I think there are papers that go along with neoliberal mainstream – which is that the world economy was on its knees in the 1970s and needed a strong dose of neoliberal medicine, which it received under Thatcher and Reagan, deregulation, privatization. . . . I fundamentally reject that story and have made it clear that I do throughout my journalistic life.

In Australia, Paul Cleary from the *Australian* also explains that coverage which "embraced these neoliberal values and ideas" was being driven by strong and charismatic individuals like Paul Keating. Ross Gittins, economics editor of the *Sydney*

Morning Herald, and Australian financial journalist Colleen Ryan agree that journalists addressed the topic of deregulation with little scepticism. Ryan thinks journalists today need to operate with more scepticism because "we're getting back to some of the business hero coverage [of the 70s and 80s], which is a real worry."

In the US journalists echoed the premise that journalists report on what is happening, as their primary function as journalists. For instance, Eduardo Porter at the *New York Times* expressed the view that "Any intellectual endeavour in writing newspaper articles are embedded in a context and a political and economic system of which you accept certain things and you critique others."

The question on neoliberal policymaking elicited more differences in opinion amongst the journalists interviewed than questions around groupthink and sources used for information. A number of the journalists agree that deregulation and privatisation went too far in the 1980/90s, and that journalists could have been more sceptical. A majority think politics played the biggest role in dominating the coverage and that journalism cannot divorce itself from what is happening and what needs to be covered.

Overall, while this picture is mixed, it does raise a further question of whether financial journalists will ever report on alternative lines of enquiry or schools of thought outside of the status quo and neoliberal system they either fit within or report objectively on. Certainly, it does not seem likely that the press will be the place where we find either "communicative action" or third-order (institutional) change (Habermas, 1989; Schmidt, 2008).

The 'crisis' in journalism

The 'crisis' of modern journalism in the wake of globalisation, digitalisation, and the rise of social media is only being exacerbated by the neoliberal commercial model which places profits and returns to shareholders above all else and in place of public interest. As newsrooms are slashed (in May 2017 Australian journalists went on strike as Fairfax announced around a third of journalists would lose their jobs in yet another round of budget cutting) there has been a decline in corporate investigations (Carson, 2017; Starkman, 2014). Journalists interviewed for this study were asked how commercial pressures are affecting the day-to-day practice of financial journalism, and whether they have noticed any impact on the quality of financial reporting.

While only two (one in Australia and another in the US) actually used the term 'crisis' unprompted, there is consensus that they are increasingly under-resourced and time poor. Eduardo Porter at the *New York Times*, Hamish McRae, executive editor of the Independent online, and Andrew Palmer at the *Economist* stand apart here by revealing that time pressures on a weekly specialist publication or as a columnist are less of a problem. Palmer says "the rhythm [at the *Economist*] enables us to think a bit more to give people a new perspective on things, or alert them to potential threats and opportunities."

Consequently, the tendencies already noted in financial journalism as a genre (acceptance of neoliberal policy, reporting that follows market trends, and a limited range of elite sources) are exacerbated in the context of current mainstream report-ing. This is having a very real impact on the quality of financial news, as there is less time to find stories and cultivate contacts, which leads to superficial rough copy, less investigation into misdeeds, and greater reliance on PR material. Only one of the journalists mentions reductions of staff in the newsroom as good for news quality.

In the UK, Larry Elliott describes the change at the *Guardian* as journalists have moved on from having the time to reflect upon a story to a process that involves "banging something out":

> When I joined the *Guardian* in 1988, you'd come in in the morning, maybe go to a press conference, go to lunch, read a report, then four or five o'clock you might actually write something for the next day's paper. Now, you get in at 9 in the morning, and the first thing you do is bang something out.

The journalists also point to the very real phenomenon of "churnalism" (Davies, 2009) and a decline in proactive investigative journalism. In Australia, Ryan refers to a reduction in "what you call long-form journalism in the business sector" as "a big change in the last 20 years." In the US, Paul Goodman describes, "Every day is a crisis; filing a twenty-inch story right now, with no time to get educated on the overall merits of a system. We can't see clearly to the horizons."

Only one journalist highlighted what he thought to be some of the more posi-tive aspects of commercial pressures. Ian King describes that at the *Times* it "made life harder" but also that it cleared the way for better reporters: "I have a third fewer people than I had three years ago. If I look at my department, we've had enormous changes; we've got rid of a lot of dead wood – people that were underperforming."

Journalists were also asked about two related issues that recur in the literature: the lack of training in this area and the traction the public relations industry has had in the news media. While some do not think training is necessary and consider a sceptical attitude as the main characteristic of a financial journalist, the majority do not have formal training themselves. This is despite the fact that, as the GFC evidenced, the financial system is increasing in complexity. Kohler, in Australia, laments: "Financial journalists aren't numerate enough, they don't know how to operate spreadsheets, and they don't know how to read balance sheets sufficiently." A lack of training is confirmed by King, in the UK, who admits, "I've never been given a day of training in my life in terms of reading a balance sheet and so forth." In practice, this means sources of information are less likely to be held to account and important stories may go undetected.

Moreover, as the news industry is in a state of flux and pressures are falling on journalists to produce more in difficult circumstances, the public relations industry is on the rise. While PR is not a new player, it has been gaining traction over the past two to three decades – a trend that is being felt by the journalists who describe a situation where PR has the upper hand in terms of the time and resources to devote to shaping a story. To journalists who are time-and resource-poor, pre-pack-aged PR material is increasingly 'seductive.'

In Australia, Kohler thinks "PR is making the day to day practice of financial journalism very difficult. It makes it easy, but it's seductively easy, in the sense that you're publishing stories in the interests of the people you are writing about." In the US, Starkman compares the growth of corporations and the resources they have to pour into their PR machine with the news industry. For example, "in the mid-1990s, the New York Times Company and Morgan Stanley were about the same size financially. . . . Today, Morgan Stanley is thirty times bigger than the New York Times Company." Also in the US, Goodman points to PR practitioners who have "become very good at taking advantage of a relative lack of skill amongst the ranks of the new reporters."

While there is a general agreement among experienced practitioners that stories are increasingly reactive and rushed, they pointed to the new social and digital space online as providing new opportunities and challenges for journalists and for the public alike. Elliott describes the digital changes at the *Guardian* and comments pages which mean a more iterative process. Peston refers to Twitter as providing a wealth of sources and stories for journalists. Meanwhile, King thinks it is difficult for newspapers to compete with entities like the BBC, and a number of the journalists referred to continuously producing material for an online site. McRae thinks it provides more opportunities for PR companies to post online and upset the balance in news. In the US, Goodman agrees and thinks "the Web has helped alleviate some of the following of the herd" while Australia's Korporaal views the internet as a "beast" that always needs to be fed.

With more noise online, and the same corporate voices, we are yet to see whether this new space will make up for what is clearly being lost in terms of quality analysis and investigations (Anstead and Chadwick, 2017; Fenton, 2011; McChesney, 2015).

Conclusion

The journalist interviews undertaken for this study provide something of a clue about how and why neoliberalism has been absorbed by and influenced mainstream financial reporting globally. Responses from journalists indicate that the criticisms received during the GFC – i.e. lack of warning and a limited range of sources used for information, and neoliberal logic and reasoning – are the product of an incremental build-up of a newsroom culture that favours growth-related stories and elite sources for information. This culture, which takes the neoliberal system as a given and is now firmly part of the status quo, has arguably provided the pretext for the support in the press for the age of austerity (it has also been found elsewhere, see Usher, 2017).

While the journalists individually expressed a desire to report on potential dangers in the system, most agreed that this dominant culture and way of thinking is very difficult to get away from. It meant that a financial development as widespread and serious as deregulation was framed by politicians and written about with too little criticism. This was true regardless of which country the journalist worked within. The impact on reporting is that there is less critique of the overarching political and economic systems and what is presented is consequently a narrowing view of the financial world – one which does not always factor in (sometimes dangerous) financial developments and a discussion of alternatives to the current system.

The impact of neoliberalism on the shaping of economic and financial news discourses, and its ramifications for the non-shareholding and non-investing public, should, therefore, be a matter for concern and for further analysis. The need is particularly acute given the impact of neoliberalism on the media business itself, with drastic cutbacks in staff and resources that further impede appropriate scrutiny. We need more analysis of both mainstream and alternative forms of financial news online, as media continues to proliferate and shape the way society understands financial matters.

Also, we cannot distinguish between the phenomena that are affecting financial journalists and those affecting journalists generally as part of what has become known as the 'crisis' of journalism. These interviews have wider implications for a world that is being redefined by increasingly populist rhetoric in a changing political and economic landscape. Brexit, the rise of Trump, and other forms of nationalism have been accompanied by debates around fake news, alternative facts, and echo chambers online. It is more important than ever to ensure that the general public understands the role of economics in their lives and can therefore form political judgments based on sound facts and reason. The journalists made some suggestions to ensure quality reporting on finance and economy. Most of the responses to this question hinged on the provision of additional resources in the industry: to train, to recruit, to investigate, and to provide more time. Given the current commercial environment, this is unlikely without support from the public purse.

To reverse this trend managers and editors are needed who believe in public service ideals, encourage investigation of 'what if' stories, and champion high standards of values and ethics. However, it is also important that the public have an appetite for this type of news and a basic understanding of how and why economic and financial topics affect their everyday lives. This might mean building financial and media literacy into the school curriculum and teaching the public about the importance of keeping abreast of financial and economic developments. To be able to deconstruct and better understand how a neoliberal discourse has developed, it is important to consider a full cycle from news production to reception and circulation (Philo, 2007).

Also, the discussion around using academics as sources made something else painfully clear: there is a clear antipathy towards the use of academics as specialist sources. They can potentially play a vital role to ensure balanced and alternative perspectives are included in reportage, as well as the in-depth analysis and critique journalists now struggle to find the time for. More interviews with financial journalists, and their editors and managers, might help to clarify the source of the problem and its potential solution, for example through media training and in building understanding of how the media works.

Finally, these interviews indicate that financial journalists are in a precarious position: they are tasked with producing more with less while reporting on a system to which they are intrinsically tied that arguably undermines the core journalistic values of objectivity and public service. While we need more than ever journalists with the desire to educate and enlighten and contribute to a better informed society, it seems the stakes are against them.

References

Anstead, N., and Chadwick, A., 2017. 'A primary definer online: the construction and propagation of a think tank's authority on social media'. *Media, Culture & Society*. ISSN 0163–4437

Berry, M., 2013. 'The Today Programme and the banking crisis'. *Journalism* 14(2), pp. 253–270.

Blyth, M. 2013. *Austerity: the history of a dangerous idea*. New York: Oxford University Press.

Bourdieu, P., and Wacquant, L., 2001. 'New liberal speak: notes on the new planetary vulgate'. *Radical Philosophy*, Jan/Feb, 105, pp. 2–5.

Brummer, A. 2009. Far from scaring people, the press were providing readers with reliable information. In: Mair, J., and Keeble, L. (eds.), *Playing Footsie with the FTSE? The great crash of 2008*. Suffolk: Abramic Academic. pp. 38–41.

Carson, A. 2017. 'The political economy of the print media and the decline of corporate investigative journalism in Australia'. *Australian Journal of Political Science*, 49(4), pp. 726–742.

Carswell, H., 1938. 'Business news and reader interest'. *Journalism Quarterly*, 15, pp. 191–195.

Chakravartty, P., and Schiller, D., 2010. 'Neoliberal newspeak and digital capitalism in crisis'. *International Journal of Communication*, 4, pp. 670–692.

Davies, N. 2009. *Flat Earth news*. London: Vintage.

Davis, A. 2011. Mediation, financialization, and the Global Financial Crisis. In: Winseck, D., and Yong, V. (eds.), *The political economies of media: The transformation of the global media*. London: Bloomsbury Publishing. pp. 241–254.

Doyle, G., 2006. 'Financial news journalism: A post-Enron analysis of approaches towards economic and financial news production'. *Journalism*, 7(4), pp. 433–452.

Dutta, M., and Sen, S., 2014. 'Coverage of the financial crisis in English language print media in India ideologies of neoliberalism'. *Journal of Creative Communications* 9(3), pp. 199–213.

Fenton, N., 2011. 'Deregulation or democracy? New media, news, neoliberalism and the public interest'. *Continuum*, 25(1), pp. 63–72.

Franklin, B., 2014. 'The future of journalism'. *Journalism Practice*, 8(5), pp. 469–487.

Habermas, J. 1989. *The structural transformation of the public sphere*. Cambridge, MA: MIT Press.

Hall, S., 2011. 'The neo-liberal revolution'. *Cultural Studies*, 25(6), pp. 705–728, DOI: 10.1080/09502386.2011.619886

Harber, A., 2009. 'When a watchdog doesn't bark'. *Rhodes Journalism Review*, 29 September.

Henningham, J., 1997. 'Characteristics and attitudes of Australia's finance Journalists'. *Economic Analysis and Policy*, 27(1), pp. 45–58.

Kelsey, D., Mueller, F., Whittle, A., and KhosraviNik, M., 2016. 'Financial crisis and austerity: interdisciplinary concerns in critical discourse studies', *Critical Discourse Studies*, 13(1), pp. 1–19.

Knoche, M., 2016. 'The media industry's structural transformation in capitalism and the role of the state: Media economics in the age of digital communications', *Triple C*, 14(1).

Knowles, S., Phillips, G., and Lidberg, J., 2017. 'Reporting the Global Financial Crisis: A longitudinal tri-nation study into mainstream financial journalism'. *Journalism Studies*, 18(3), pp. 322–340.

Lewis, J., 2010. 'Normal viewing will be resumed shortly: News, recession and the politics of growth.' *Popular Communication*, 8(3), pp. 161–165.

Lewis, J., Williams, A., and Franklin, B., 2008. 'A compromised fourth estate? UK news journalism, public relations and news sources.' *Journalism Studies*, 9(1), pp. 1–20. Manning, P., 2013. 'Financial journalism, news sources and the banking crisis'. *Journalism*, 14(2), pp. 173–189.

McChesney, R. 2015. *Rich media, poor democracy, communication politics in dubious times*. New York: The New Press.

Parsons, W. 1989. *The power of the financial press: Journalism and economic opinion in Britain and America*. New Brunswick: Rutgers University.

Philo, G., 2007. 'Can discourse analysis successfully explain the content of media and journalistic practice?' *Journalism Studies*, 8(2), pp. 175–196. DOI: 10.1080/14616700601148804

Schechter, D., 2009. 'Credit Crisis: How did we miss it?' *British Journalism Review*, 20(19), pp. 19–26.

Schifferes, S. 2014. Why the public doesn't trust the business press. In: Schifferes, S., and Roberts, R. (eds.), *The media and financial crises: Comparative and historical perspectives*. London: Routledge. pp. 153–168.

Schifferes, S., and Knowles, S. 2014. The British media and the 'first crisis of globalization'. In: Schifferes, S. and Roberts, R. (eds.), *The media and financial crises: Comparative and historical perspectives*. London: Routledge. pp. 42–58.

Schmidt, V., 2008. 'Discursive institutionalism: the explanatory power of ideas and discourse'. *Annual Review of Political Science*, 11, pp. 303–26.

Schultz, J., 1993. 'Reporting Business – A Changing Feast. In: J. Schultz *Reporting Business'*. Working Paper. Sydney: Australian Centre for Independent Journalism. p. 1–8.

Soros, G. 2008. *The crash of 2008 and what it means: The new paradigm for financial markets*. New York: Public Affairs.

Starkman, D. 2014. *The watchdog that didn't bark: The financial crisis and the disappearance of investigative journalism*. New York: Columbia University Press.

Tambini, D., 2010. 'What are financial journalists for?' *Journalism Studies*, 11(2), pp. 158–174.

Taylor, J. 2014. Financial crises and the birth of the financial press 1825–1872. In: Schifferes, S. and Roberts, V. (eds.), *The media and financial crises: comparative and historical perspectives*. London: Routledge. pp. 42–58.

Tett, G., 2009. 'Icebergs and Ideologies'. *Anthropology News*. October.

Usher, N., 2017. 'Making business news: A production analysis of the New York Times, Public'. *International Journal of Communication*, 11, pp. 363–382.

Usher, N., 2013. 'Ignored, uninterested, and the blame game: How the New York Times, marketplace, and the street distanced themselves from preventing the 2007–2009 financial crisis'. *Journalism*, 14(2), pp. 190–207.

A note on method

The interviews were purposive, targeting journalists who had worked for at least two decades. The questions were prompted by results from a content analysis (see Knowles et al., 2017) and a review of literature on the topic and conducted between 2012 and 2017. The author acknowledges that it is not possible to generalise from the responses of 15 journalists. Most currently write, or have written for mainstream publications, while a few are specialist journalists. Journalists interviewed are:

Robert Peston (ITV); Larry Elliott (*Guardian*); Andrew Palmer (*Economist*); Hamish McRae (*Independent*); Alan Kohler (*Business Spectator*); Colleen Ryan (previously *Australian Financial Review*); Glenada Korpooral (*Australian*); Paul Cleary (*Australian*); Eduardo Porter (*New York Times*); Greg David (previously *Crain's*); Paul Goodman (*New York Times*); Dean Starkman (previously *Wall Street Journal*).

13

REFORM IN RETREAT

The media, the banks and the attack on Dodd-Frank

Adam Cox

Introduction

A running theme in post-financial crisis academic literature has been the resilience of a regulatory policy paradigm that emphasises the importance of unfettered financial markets rather than state-directed rules and restrictions. By policy paradigm, I rely here on Hall's definition as one being "a framework of standards and ideas that specifies not only the goals of policy and the kind of instruments that can be used to attain them, but also the very nature of the problems they are meant to be addressing" (Hall, 1993, p. 279). The policy paradigm that had come to dominate decision-making for at least a quarter-century leading up to the 2008 crisis has been described – often by critics – as 'market fundamentalism' and has been bound up in a loosely defined ideological stance broadly labelled as 'neoliberalism'.[1] Springing up from the economic ideas of Hayek and his followers, market fundamentalism held that deregulation was the answer to a wide array of public problems.

Yet in the immediate aftermath of the 2008 financial crisis, it was that very deregulatory zeal that many academics, commentators, policymakers and politicians blamed for the turmoil. A consensus seemed to have emerged that some form of reregulation was needed. Had large institutions truly become 'too big to fail', and could anything be done about it? Should derivatives (so complex, opaque and sinister) be monitored more closely? Could the systemic incentives that encouraged risk-taking be addressed? Large swathes of the populations in the United States and Europe were suffering from crisis-induced hardship, prompting policymakers and their political bosses to try to work through these thorny questions in the knowledge that voters expected action. For a brief period – perhaps a year and a half – the prevailing view in governments on both sides of the Atlantic was guided by the idea that the state had a role to play in rebuilding and improving the financial system. Then, just as quickly, this notion appeared to lose its power and the tenets of a free market–oriented paradigm were reasserted in public discourse.

This chapter will explore the media's treatment of these competing regulatory paradigms – market fundamentalism versus state interventionism – by considering news coverage of a US law enacted in 2010 known as the Dodd-Frank Act. Intended to address problems highlighted by the crisis and prevent such events in future, this sprawling piece of legislation called for more stringent oversight of markets and greater consumer protection. "The Act is widely described as the most ambitious and far-reaching overhaul of financial regulation since the 1930s" (Acharya et al., 2010, p. 1).

Democratic Senator Christopher Dodd, one of the bill's sponsors, himself compared the act with landmark reforms of the 1930s such as Glass-Steagall, a law that had placed strict limits on banking activity. Both pieces of legislation were responses to crises that had threatened to derail the financial systems of their day. Both came in the wake of mass unemployment and widespread public anger with the financial industry following years of anything-goes behaviour. Glass-Steagall required commercial banks and investment banks to be kept separate; Dodd-Frank included a provision to prohibit investment banks from proprietary trading. In each case, the idea was to prevent the country's banking system from being put at risk from reckless speculative trading.

There were, of course, significant differences too. Dodd, within weeks of the law's signing, noted that Glass-Steagall had been just 37 pages long, whereas the bill that he and Representative Barney Frank produced ran to 848 pages. Markets were simply far more complex and interconnected than what Senator Carter Glass and Representative Henry B. Steagall had faced (Dodd, 2010). But the two acts would come to differ in a more telling respect than page totals. It took 66 years before Glass-Steagall was undone, despite strenuous lobbying efforts by banks and numerous legislative bills to repeal the act (Crawford, 2011). It would be little more than six years before formal notice would be given that an incoming Trump administration planned to dismantle much of Dodd-Frank. Soon after taking office, Trump signed an executive order for a review of the law so that it aligned with a set of 'core principles' of his administration, such as the need to empower individuals to make independent financial decisions and to enable US companies to be competitive internationally (White House Office of the Press Secretary, 2017). This was followthrough on an often-repeated campaign promise to gut Dodd-Frank.

Prior to the crisis, there was little literature concerning financial policy and how it has been covered by the media. Financial regulation traditionally has had low salience with the public, resulting in subdued levels of both news supply and demand. Nonetheless, the crisis of 2008 was a once-in-a-generation event, affecting so many people so profoundly that, for a time, a matter as technical as Wall Street trading rules became headline news.[2] Furthermore, as an effort to address some of the causes of the largest financial crisis since the Great Depression, Dodd-Frank and the politics surrounding it can be viewed in paradigmatic terms. In other words, by systematically examining coverage of Dodd-Frank, we may be able to explore how media behaved at a paradigmatic level. Did media support or undermine policymakers' efforts to introduce more state oversight? Questions about media and policy paradigms speak to journalists' role in a broader agenda-building process, in which media represents one of several groups of actors, including the state, the financial industry, independent elites and advocacy groups. We are asked to think about not only whom media might influence, but also who influences media.

This line of inquiry builds on the burgeoning literature concerning journalism and the crisis. Much of the initial research focused on suggestions about the media's failure to fulfil a watchdog role (see Fraser, 2009; Guerrera, 2009; Harber, 2009; Schechter, 2009; Tambini, 2010; Schiffrin, 2011; Schifferes and Roberts, 2015). Where were the journalists when banks were taking on so much excessive risk? As Britain's Queen Elizabeth asked during a briefing she was given on the crisis, "Why did nobody notice it?" (Pierce, 2008) Had the press become too dependent on, or too trusting of, the bankers and state officials they were meant to cover? Did reporters have the knowledge and professionalism to probe sources properly? These were valid and important questions. But from a paradigmatic perspective, a slghtly different question arises. It begins with the premise that the media had little chance of seeing the crisis coming because it could have been wearing paradigmatic blinkers. As Hall says, much of a policy paradigm's influence comes because "so much of it is taken for granted and unamenable to scrutiny as a whole". (Hall, 1993, p. 277) He was writing about policymakers but the same could be said of journalists. Did the media even have the capacity to, in the Queen's terms, "notice it"? That possibility also asks us to consider the media's paradigmatic leanings *after* the crisis as much as to dwell on what happened in the run-up.

Dodd-Frank and the crisis of market fundamentalism

As Dodd-Frank was debated in Congress, some academics and financial industry figures speculated as to whether a paradigm shift might be underway. Embraced politically during the Reagan–Thatcher era, market fundamentalism had offered its adherents an alternative to the supposedly ham-fisted arbitrariness of the state. A response to the extended post-war period of Keynesian interventionism, the adoption of the paradigm was accompanied by long periods of economic growth. Eventually market fundamentalism was no longer just the purview of the political right, which had long championed free markets. Tony Blair had found success through his "third way" vision and a strategist for Bill Clinton had coined the phrase "The economy, stupid". Both became emblematic of what worked in 1990s politics: embrace the markets and win. Indeed, it was Clinton who signed the repeal of Glass-Steagall. So widely accepted was the paradigm by that point that the repeal made few ripples in the media. Editors simply weren't interested in the idea of an outdated law finally dying a death. Just 10 US newspapers carried accounts of the act's repeal and mostly with little fanfare, a Nexis database search showed.[3]

The scale and ferocity of the 2008 crisis then brought the supposed merits of a market-oriented policy paradigm into question. Former Federal Reserve Chairman Alan Greenspan, a hero for free-marketeers, famously acknowledged that the market's capacity for self-regulation had failed. "Those of us who have looked to

the self-interest of lending institutions to protect shareholders' equity, myself especially, are in a state of shocked disbelief," Greenspan told a Congressional panel
(U.S. House Hearing, 2008). Prior to 2008, he had been worshiped not only by
markets but also by the press. He had made the cover of *TIME* magazine on multiple occasions. Bob Woodward wrote a book about him called *Maestro*. To confirm
an impression I had from my time as an editor at Reuters, I contacted James Saft,
the news agency's global editor in charge of economic and financial market news
during Greenspan's last years at the Fed. Saft recalled journalists at the news agency
who seemed reluctant to include critical angles in their stories about Greenspan. If
the 'Maestro' was in a state of shocked disbelief, what were the rest of us to think?
Writing in *The New Yorker* just a few months after the Dodd-Frank bill was proposed, Pulitzer Prize winner James B. Stewart summed up the moment after the
crisis-triggering collapse of US bank Lehman Brothers in paradigmatic terms: "In
an intellectual debate that has been going on since the Depression, Lehman's failure
may mark a victory of John Maynard Keynes over Adam Smith – the government
interventionists over laissez-faire capitalists" (Stewart, 2009).[4] As the crisis was a
moment of reckoning for Greenspan and other policymakers, could it also have
been for the journalists who covered it?

Yet by late 2016, it seemed clear that any supposed 'victory' of an interventionist paradigm may have been brief or non-existent. On 10 November 2016,
two days after Trump's election victory, his transition team followed through on
a campaign pledge by announcing the intention to dismantle Dodd-Frank (Geewax, 2016). Two weeks after his inauguration, Trump signed the executive order
that called for the Treasury to consult with government agencies and report back
on whatever changes to laws, regulations or other documents had taken place or
would be needed to promote the new administration's core principles. The order
came after a well-publicised meeting with Wall Street executives, an ironic coda to
a similarly publicised meeting Barack Obama had held with Wall Street CEOs in
December 2009 as he was laying the groundwork for Dodd-Frank. This was all part
of a wider deregulatory effort Trump had initiated affecting all aspects of government, one that required that for every new regulation introduced, two had to be
eliminated.

Even before Trump had announced his candidacy, some researchers were suggesting a market-oriented paradigm might have managed to survive despite the
2008 crisis. Their views rested on critical early decisions by the US and British
governments, arguing that interventionist moves by the state were focused more
on shoring up the private sector rather than transforming the public-private sector relationship (Hodson and Mabbett, 2009; Glinavos, 2010). Nonetheless, Dodd-
Frank did amount to a significant step in the direction of interventionism. What's
more, the idea of the paradigm's survival in one respect goes against a tenant of
Kuhn's theory of paradigm shift (1970). Kuhn found that a prerequisite for paradigm shift was the discovery of an anomaly that could not be explained by an
existing paradigm. In such a case, either the paradigm would need to be adjusted to
accommodate the anomaly or a new paradigm would be needed that could explain

it. The 2008 crisis, as Greenspan and millions of others discovered, represented an anomaly that could not easily be easily explained by market fundamentalism.

If one subscribes to Kuhn's theory, there are two main scenarios that can account for what may have occurred in the post-crisis period – or may still be occurring. In one scenario, it is too soon to say whether market fundamentalism has definitely survived because paradigm shift plays out over a long timeframe. As seen in the 1930s and 1940s with the adoption of Keynesianism, and again in the 1970s and 1980s, paradigm shift can be a multi-year or even multi-decade process. In this account, those who suggest an interventionist-oriented paradigm may still prevail could argue that not all of Trump's initiatives will survive Congressional and public scrutiny or could be reversed by subsequent administrations. Another scenario is that politicians, policymakers and the public simply came to ignore the anomaly that the crisis represented, displaying collective amnesia for the sake of retaining a paradigm which they believed, despite the hardship endured, remained superior to any rival approach.

This second scenario required a media narrative that could counter the early post-crisis discourse which Stewart described, when Washington was looking to re-regulate and when even die-hard free-marketeers knew that arguing for the primacy of markets was a losing proposition. Such a narrative could focus on the *causes* of the crisis, suggesting that it had little to do with a lack of deregulation; or it could focus on the *consequences* of a 'big government' solution. Regulation, by this account, is seen as an impediment to growth rather than a public good. The idea was most famously encapsulated by Reagan when he said government was not the solution to the problem but rather: "Government is the problem" (Reagan, 1981).

Kuhn offers another concept that is helpful when considering media behaviour. He sees the process of paradigm shift as gradual. It occurs not from a 'Eureka!' moment but from the slow process of adherents of one paradigm gradually becoming convinced that a new paradigm offers a better model. This is essentially a social process involving all of the relevant actors in a given arena. Hall's work offers an example of that process as he charts Britain's move away from Keynesian economics towards monetarism in the 1970s and 1980s; he notes how influential journalists such as William Rees-Mogg and Samuel Brittan and politicians such as Thatcher persuaded others of the advantages of monetarism, leading to a shift in policymaking. In an agenda-building environment, actors will seek to influence other actors and may in turn be influenced by them. From a media perspective, the question then becomes: how does one identify and understand influence?

Determining media influence within a low-salience subject appears problematic. How could one show whether the regulatory community has been influenced by media coverage of a given issue? However, identifying ways in which the media itself may be influenced – or at least may reflect other actors' agendas – may be more feasible. That is the subject of the research I will present in the next part of this chapter.

Media and paradigmatic alignment: framing the regulation debate

To understand how media might lean towards one paradigm or another, I reviewed a sample of articles about Dodd-Frank at a granular level, considering the frames used on a sentence-by-sentence basis. Journalists make choices with each sentence they write, whether it concerns the sources they quote, the issues they focus on, the language and concepts employed, or a variety of other issues. I was interested to see whether patterns could be determined based on those choices.

Entman's (1993) categories of media frames – problems, causes, solutions and moral judgments – provide a starting point for the types of frames which journalists and other actors use when discussing policy. Framing theory is particularly useful as a way to consider how policy paradigms are contested since actors will frequently frame arguments and observations that fall within the categories Entman lists. For my research, I used two additional categories based on analysis by De Vreese, Peter and Semetko. Citing various US studies, they suggest that "news about politics and the economy is often framed in terms of conflict or in terms of the economic consequences of events, issues, and policies" (De Vreese, Peter and Semetko, 2001 p. 109).

A sample of news articles thus could be analysed based on the types of frames most often used and which actors used them. Still, that only takes one so far. To understand whether media exhibit paradigmatic bias, frames would need to be examined based on their alignment with the tenets of market fundamentalism or interventionism. To give an example of how alignment could be determined, a *Washington Post* article on 9 June 2009, as the Obama administration was formulating its regulatory plans, quoted a consumer advocacy campaigner calling for a single agency with a mission to protect consumers. The author noted how financial firms were concerned that this would limit the types of loans they could make and what they could charge, writing: "That, in turn, would curb profits. Industry officials say such a commission would not have enough information about financial firms to make sound decisions about whether to limit the sale of financial products" (Goldfarb, 2009). The journalist has included a *consequence* frame about a move to restrict banking activity. In this case, the consequence of an interventionist idea is negative (reduced profits). It is a position consistent with market fundamentalism as the paradigm holds that state-led initiatives will typically produce less favourable outcomes than the 'invisible hand' of the market. In contrast, an example of an interventionist-aligned frame can be seen in a *Washington Post* article on 11 February 2010. The article, which also concerned consumer protection, reported remarks by Iowa Attorney General Tom Miller in support of the new consumer agency. The article quotes Miller saying, "Senators have to ask themselves: 'Whose side am I on? Am I on the side of the public, or am I on the side of big banks?'" (Dennis, 2010). Here the official framed the choice in moral terms. His rhetorical question suggests the agency would be with the people, not the banks. Such a moral judgment frame is aligned with an interventionist paradigm which holds that allowing markets to dictate is inherently unfair as ordinary people may get trampled. Determining patterns of paradigm alignment thus may be not only based on what frames are being used but also on which actors are doing the framing.

The findings that follow are based on a subset of preliminary data, using nearly 100 articles in the *Washington Post* from June 2009 to March 2012. The *Washington Post* was chosen because it has a national readership, is followed closely in governmental circles and has a focus on policy. Articles were selected based on a search that featured the terms 'financial crisis', 'regulation', and either 'Dodd' or 'Frank'.[5] The unit of analysis – the individual sentence – could contain multiple frames. In total, 927 frames were identified in the many hundreds of sentences that made up these stories, although more than a third of the frames were not clearly aligned with either paradigm. Frames were categorised by type (problems, solutions, et cetera) and source (journalists, politicians, regulators, the financial industry or others).

As can be seen in Figure 13.1, just after the bill was introduced and during the run-up to its passage, coverage was high, resulting in higher numbers of frames. During summer periods, when Congress was in recess, coverage died down. Most frames were aligned with an interventionist paradigm, often for the simple reason that writing about Dodd-Frank meant writing about state efforts to create new regulation. More than a third of the frames (366) concerned solutions, of which all but 60 were interventionist-aligned. Problem frames were also prevalent (110 frames),

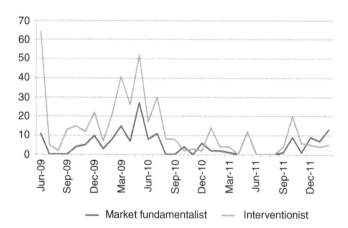

— Market fundamentalist   — Interventionist

FIGURE 13.1 Neoliberal versus interventionist news frames in Dodd-Frank coverage, *Washington Post*, June 2009–March 2012

Key: This chart shows the numbers of news frames (vertical axis) that were clearly aligned with either a market fundamentalist or interventionist paradigm from the introduction of the Dodd-Frank bill (June 2009) through to its passage (July 2010) to the start of the 2012 General Election campaign (early 2012). A total of 928 frames were identified in 97 news articles. There were more than twice as many frames categorised as interventionist than market fundamentalist. As time passed, the differences narrowed.

as journalists noted the hardship and economic damage wrought by the crisis. But cause frames were less common (87 frames); this suggests a hesitancy by reporters to assign definitive blame for what caused the crisis.[6] One unsurprising finding: when figures from the financial industry featured in the coverage, they were overwhelmingly opposed to increased regulation, with 89% of the aligned frames they offered being classified as market fundamentalist.

A deeper dive into the data offers a more nuanced reading. Over time, market fundamentalist frames began to track interventionist frames more closely, even as overall coverage about regulation was waning. Up until the law's signing, interventionist frames vastly outnumbered those aligned with market fundamentalism. Afterwards, the gap narrowed, with frames that offered free market–oriented concepts and arguments nearly drawing level (see Figure 13.2). Notably, in the early months of campaigning for the 2012 General Election, market fundamentalist frames began to exceed interventionist frames.

But the most telling finding can be seen by looking at frames focused on policy consequences. Consequence frames were the second most common type in the sample, with 157 of such frames excluding op-ed content. When the bill was unveiled and first debated, frames focused on the expected consequences of proposals (or any lack of government action) tended to be interventionist. As political and financial industry opposition mounted, consequence frames came to be dominated by free market ideals. A refrain about the job-choking effects of too much regulation took hold and grew louder just before Dodd-Frank was passed. Typical frames invoked images of government as a massive bureaucracy that would stifle innovation, prevent capital from flowing, limit personal choice, add to government

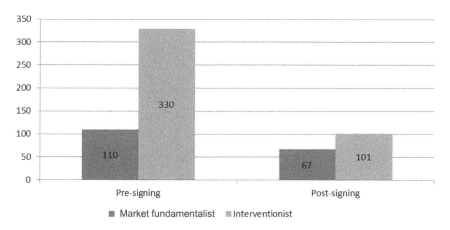

FIGURE 13.2 Market fundamentalist and interventionist framing before and after Dodd-Frank was signed

Key: During the period from Dodd-Frank's unveiling in June 2009 to its signing in July 2010, most coverage was framed in interventionist terms, by a three-to-one margin. After the signing, as coverage dwindled, neoliberal frames began to catch up with interventionist frames.

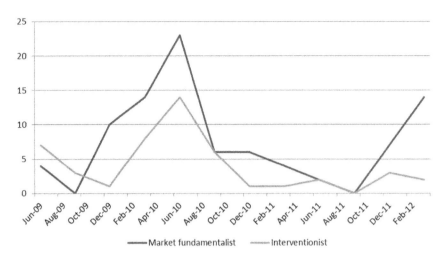

FIGURE 13.3 Frames based on policy consequences in Dodd-Frank coverage, *Washington Post,* June 2009–March 2012

Key: This chart shows a subset of the overall data, considering the numbers of news frames (vertical axis) that were based on policy consequences. A total of 157 frames were identified, with 92 aligned with a market fundamentalist paradigm, 42 classified as interventionist and 23 as unaligned.

spending, boost personal tax bills, reduce competitiveness and generally deliver a blow to the economy.

As the bill neared approval, and in the run-up to mid-term elections, politicians opposed to Dodd-Frank attracted increased news coverage and they grew bolder about presenting pro-market ideas (see Figure 13.3). This theme continued in the period leading into the 2012 General Elections and was readily taken up again in the 2016 campaign. In a word, the speed with which free-marketeers were able to grab hold of the narrative so soon after the crisis was remarkable.

Framing regulation in the Trump era

Politicians live and die by their success in framing issues. Trump in his campaign appeared to have a natural impulse to frame; he spoke liberally in terms of the problems besetting Americans, the causes of those problems, his solutions and the consequences from either following his lead (beneficial) or not (disastrous). In terms of regulation, his frames pushed a distinctly neoliberal agenda. Announcing his executive order on Dodd-Frank, he spoke of the law as a "very negative force" (Puzzanghera et al., 2017) that had led to banks restricting their lending. During his campaign and afterwards, he was effectively reframing the regulation discourse; what had once been framed as potential consequences had now become actual problems.

In covering Trump's executive order on Dodd-Frank, many newspapers and news services focused on his comments about how the law had become a problem. The *Washington Post* reported on 4 February 2017 Trump saying his administration expected to cut "a lot" out of Dodd Frank: "Because frankly, I have so many people, friends of mine, that had nice businesses, they just can't borrow money . . . because the banks just won't let them borrow because of the rules and regulations in Dodd-Frank" (Merle and Mufson, 2017).

Versions of the same quote appeared in reports by the *New York Times*, the *Los Angeles Times* and the Associated Press, as well as numerous newspapers around the country. Newspapers such as the *Daily Reporter* in Milwaukee and the *Journal Record* in Oklahoma City filed reports quoting local home building and financing figures echoing Trump's view that Dodd-Frank had restricted activity (see Brus, 2017; Zank, 2017). The *Los Angeles Times* quotes a business lobby executive speaking of "the dysfunctional regulation of the past" (Puzzanghera et al., 2017). The Associated Press characterised the measure as rules that were "rushed into law" and described the act as "devilishly complex" (Colvin and Gordon, 2017).

Trump had channelled Reagan in characterising government as the problem. Media, in covering his actions, relayed this frame. Absent from Trump's narrative: cause frames as to what led to the regulation. Here the media were more prepared to use cause frames. Dozens of news articles reporting on the executive order referred to the 2008 crisis as the reason for Dodd-Frank's existence. Also notable were consequence frames that were interventionist in nature. Many reports featured remarks from Senator Elizabeth Warren, a prominent critic of Wall Street, or comments from advocacy groups, all offering frames about the negative consequences from any dismantling of Dodd-Frank.

More systematic analysis of the coverage of Trump-era regulatory policy will be needed to determine whether there were patterns in favour of market fundamentalism or interventionism. But one development from Trump's Dodd-Frank move that was evident is that the salience of regulatory news received a boost. The breadth of coverage about Dodd-Frank following Trump's order even exceeded that of when Dodd-Frank was introduced. A search of 'Dodd-Frank' over one week from the day it was signed showed only 41 articles in US newspapers. Compare that to the results of a Nexis search of US newspaper coverage, which showed 142 articles contained the terms 'Trump' and 'Dodd-Frank' in the week following the executive order.

This relative paucity of coverage of the 2010 signing is striking given that some of the harshest effects of the global crisis were being felt at the time. Perhaps it is understandable given the traditional low-salience nature of regulatory news.[7] But what explains the greater intensity of coverage of the executive order? Some may be put down to a 'Trump effect'.[8] By that account, the plan to dismantle Dodd-Frank was news not because of the regulation itself; it was news because editors knew readers were interested in Trump. This also explains why something as little known as Dodd-Frank generated strong social media activity.[9]

The power of modern agenda building

Some frames owe their power to matters of the moment as issues command public attention. Other frames may be thought of as evergreen because they tap into deeper cultural myths and belief systems. Reagan's anti-government framing, emblematic of the market fundamentalist paradigm, falls into this latter category. Arguably this may account not only for Trump's apparent success in redeploying the frame but also for the readiness of many politicians and financial industry figures to promote it so soon after the crisis. Yet from a Kuhnian perspective, the ability of free-market-eers to advance their frames remains counter-intuitive: they offered little to explain the anomaly that the crisis represented, a point highlighted by the dearth of market fundamentalist cause frames in the sample. Perhaps this merely points to a more sophisticated framing strategy on the part of those attached to the paradigm. They avoided discussion of the *past* and instead focused on the *future*: consequence frames.

All of this leaves open the question as to why such a strategy may have worked with the media. Does the complex and unfamiliar nature of financial regulation make journalists more susceptible to the frames of their sources? That possibility is central to the "crash blindness" theory (Fraser, 2009). Yet *Washington Post* report-ers followed Dodd-Frank over many months and had the benefit of hindsight in terms of the crisis itself. They also frequently displayed an acute awareness of efforts by their sources to frame issues; they wrote about the millions of dollars spent by lobby organisations. An 11 February 2010 article notes how one political consultant offered Dodd-Frank opponents a guide of "words to use": Terms such as "bloated bureaucracy," "big bank bailout bill," "wasteful Washington spending" and "unin-tended consequences" were suggested, the article said (Dennis, 2010). The advice is tantamount to a primer in framing.

The simplest explanation may lie in the power of consistent messaging and con-certed agenda-building efforts. The ascendency of market fundamentalism itself can be seen as a result of agenda building. When Hayek and his followers founded the Mont Pèlerin Society, they understood the need for effective messaging as they set about on a long-term project to challenge Keynesianism. Paradigmatic agenda building since then has merely speeded up and become more sophisticated in the age of electronic media and big data. Threatened by the prospect of paradigm shift, free-marketeers knew it was crucial to stay on message. Interventionists, perhaps believing the crisis had already made their point for them, may not have been so disciplined. In such an environment, it is not difficult to see why market fundamentalist frames found traction.

Notes

1 Market fundamentalism has been used by economists such as Krugman and Stiglitz as a pejorative term; similarly, neoliberalism has acquired a pejorative tone (see, for exam-ple, activist journalist George Monbiot). This is not to say that the negative connota-tions attached to the terms are universally endorsed. Schwartz (2013) writes in praise of neoliberalism as he seeks to put its ideals in the context of a long tradition of political economy liberalism. For my purposes, I wish to use the two terms purely in a descriptive way, without value judgment, if such a thing is possible.

2 Pagliari (2013) collected data showing US media coverage of financial regulation spiked to more than 0.4 percentage point of all measured articles in 2009–2010 from below 0.1 point in 2007 and below 0.05 point for much of the 1994–2007 period. Data for the UK

showed a similar pattern. Some 8.0 million articles in the US and 7.9 million in the UK were analysed.

3   This was based on a Nexis search for the week of 12–19 November 1999, using terms "Glass-Steagall" or "financial regulation" or "Gramm-Leach-Biley" (the name of the legislation Clinton signed). The *New York Times* was among those newspapers, but notably the *Washington Post* did not cover the news.

4   Laissez-faire economics and neoliberalism are not synonymous. Hayek and numerous others who are seen as the forerunners of neoliberal thinking saw a role for regulation so long as it was designed to bolster the integrity of markets. The classic example of this is anti-monopoly regulation.

5   The research forms part of a yet-to-be-submitted doctoral thesis. The case study includes articles from the *New York Times* and the *Washington Post*, although here I have only used data from one publication.

6   Cause frames were primarily interventionist, with only eight out of 87 identified being classified as market fundamentalist, 59 as interventionist and 20 unaligned.

7   In particular, the complexity of financial regulatory policies and their frequently indirect impact over stakeholders outside of finance limits the general public's capacity and incentives to pay attention to financial regulatory developments and to invest time and resources to understand where their interests lie.

Pagliari, 2013, p. 7

8   Since Trump's candidacy began, there have been numerous examples of ratings or readership increases based on news about Trump. One of the most famous illustrations of the trend came from the CEO of US broadcaster CBS, when he said of Trump's candidacy: "It may not be good for America, but it's damn good for CBS" (Bond, 2016).

9   Data from NewsWhip (www.newswhip.com), a media research tool, showed one *Wall Street Journal* article on the plan to undo Dodd-Frank generated more than 50,000 shares or retweets. An article in which Senator Bernie Sanders called Trump a "fraud" because of the executive order was shared or retweeted more than 90,000 times.

References

Acharya, V., Cooley, T., Richardson, M., and Walter, I. (2010) *Regulating wall street: The Dodd-Frank act and the new architecture of global finance*. Hoboken, NJ: John Wiley & Sons.

Bond, P. (19 February 2016) Leslie Moonves on Donald Trump: "It May Not Be Good for America, but It's Damn Good for CBS". The Hollywood Reporter. Available at www.hollywoodreporter.com/news/leslie-moonves-donald-trump-may-871464, [Accessed 12 June 2017]

Colvin, J., and Gordon, M. 2017. Trump launches his attack on banks' financial restraints. *Associated Press*. 3 February.

Crawford, C. 2011. 'The repeal of the Glass-Steagall act and the current financial crisis'. *Journal of Business and Economic Research*, 9(1), pp. 128–130.

de Vreese, C. H., Peter, J., and Semetko, H. 2001. Framing politics at the launch of the Euro: a cross-national comparative study of frames in the news. *Political Communications*, 18 pp. 107–122.

Dennis, B. 2010. Campaign builds for consumer protection agency; Advocates counter banks' push against stand-alone unit. *Washington Post*. 11 February.

Dodd, C. 2010. Implementing the Dodd-Frank Wall Street Reform and Consumer Protection Act, transcript. U.S. Government Printing Office. 30 September. Available at www.gpo.gov/fdsys/pkg/CHRG-111shrg64796/html/CHRG-111shrg64796.htm [Accessed 3 May 2017]

Entman, R. 1993. 'Framing: Towards clarification of a fractured paradigm'. *Journal of Communications*, 43(4), pp. 51–58.

Fraser, M. 2009. 'Five reasons for crash blindness'. *British Journalism Review*, 20(4), pp. 78–83.

Geewax, M. 2016. Trump Team Promises to 'Dismantle' Dodd-Frank Bank Regulations. *NPR*. 10 November. Available at www.npr.org/sections/thetwo-way/2016/11/10/501610842/trump-team-promises-to-dismantle-dodd-frank-bank-regulations%29 [Accessed 3 May 2017]

Glinavos, I. 2010. 'Regulation and the Role of Law in Economic Crisis'. *European Business Law Review*, 4, pp. 539–557.

Guerrera, F. 2009. 'Why generalists were not equipped to cover the complexities of the crisis'. *The International Journal of Communication Ethics*, 6(3/4), pp. 44–49.

Hall, P. A. 1993. 'Policy paradigms, social learning and the state'. *Comparative Politics*, 23 pp. 275–296.

Harber, A. 2009. 'When a watch dog doesn't bark'. *Rhodes Journalism Review*, 29, pp. 20–21.

Hodson, D., and Mabbett, D. 2009. 'UK economic policy and the Global Financial Crisis: Paradigm lost?' *Journal of Common Market Studies*, 47(5), pp. 1041–1061.

Kuhn, T. S. 1970. *The structure of scientific revolutions*. Chicago: The University of Chicago Press.

Merle, R., and Mufson, S. 2017. Trump signs order to begin rolling back Wall Street regulations. *Washington Post*. 3 February.

Newswhip 2017. 'Results from search for data concerning Trump executive order'. subscription service Available at www.newswhip.com [Accessed 4 March 2017]

Pagliari, S. 2013. 'Public salience and international financial regulation'. PHD Thesis. University of Waterloo. Available at https://uwspace.uwaterloo.ca/bitstream/handle/10012/7344/Pagliari_Stefano.pdf?sequence=1&isAllowed=y [Accessed 3 May 2017]

Pierce, A. 2008. The Queen asks why no one saw the credit crunch coming. *The Telegraph*. 5 November Available at www.telegraph.co.uk/news/uknews/theroyalfamily/3386353/The-Queen-asks-why-no-one-saw-the-credit-crunch-coming.html [Accessed 3 May 2017]

Puzzanghera, J., Memoli, M. A., and Koren, J. R. 2017. Trump orders review of Dodd-Frank financial regulations, suspends retirement advisor rule. *Los Angeles Times*. 3 February.

Reagan, R., 1981. Inaugural Address. *The American Presidency Project*. 20 January www.presidency.ucsb.edu/ws/?pid=43130, [Accessed 3 May 2017]

Saft, J. 2017. *Email to Adam Cox*. 18 February.

Schechter, D. 2009. 'Credit crisis: How did we miss it?' *British Journalism Review*, 20(1), pp. 19–26.

Schifferes, S., and Roberts, R. 2015. *The media and financial crisis*. New York: Routledge.

Schiffrin, A. 2011. *Bad news: How America's business press missed the story of the century*. New York, NY: New Press.

Schwartz, P. 2013. In Praise of Neo-liberalism, Library of Economics and Liberty. 5 August Available at www.econlib.org/library/Columns/y2013/Schwartzneoliberalism.html [Accessed 12 June 2017]

Stewart, J. 2009. Eight Days. *The New Yorker*. 21 September. Available at www.newyorker.com/magazine/2009/09/21/eight-days[Accessed 3 May 2017]

Tambini, D. 2010. 'What are financial journalists for?' *Journalism Studies*, 11(2), pp. 158–174.

U.S. House. 2008. *The Financial Crisis and the Role of Federal Regulators, Hearing*. 23 October, Washington: Government Printing Office. Available at www.gpo.gov/fdsys/pkg/CHRG-110hhrg55764/html/CHRG-110hhrg55764.htm [Accessed 3 May 2017]

White House Office of the Press Secretary. 2017. *Presidential Executive Order on Core Principles for Regulating the United States Financial System*. 3 February. Available at www.whitehouse.gov/the-press-office/2017/02/03/presidential-executive-order-core-principles-regulating-united-states [Accessed 3 May 2017]

PART IV

Social media, social movements and the crisis

14
SOCIAL MEDIA AND THE CAPITALIST CRISIS

Christian Fuchs

Introduction

In this work, I focus on discussing selected aspects of the relationship between social media and the capitalist crisis. Detailed critical analyses of political, economic and ideological aspects of social media can be found in associated publications (Fuchs et al., 2012; Fuchs, 2014a, 2014b, 2014c, 2015, 2016a, 2016b, 2016c, 2017; Fuchs and Sandoval, 2014; Trottier and Fuchs, 2014; Fisher and Fuchs, 2015; Fuchs and Mosco, 2016). I first give an introduction to Marxist crisis theory and summarise my analysis of the crisis, then discuss aspects of targeted advertising, the ideology of Twitter revolutions, and anti-socialist ideology on Twitter. The basic point that I make in the chapter is that capitalist development is an important factor that has conditioned the emergence of social media, social media's economy and ideology on social media.

Foundations of crisis theory

The profit rate is a key category of Marxist political economy (Marx, 1867, chapter 17; for a discussion see Fuchs, 2016b, chapter 17).

The rate of profit is the relationship of profit and investment or of the monetary expression of surplus-value and the value of the means of production (constant and variable capital). The profit rate expresses to which degree capitalism is grown or shrinking, it is a measure of accumulation and crisis.

$$ROP = \frac{s}{c + v}$$

s . . . surplus-value/profit, c . . . constant capital, v. . . . variable capital
If we divide the numerator and the denominator by v, then we get:

$$ROP = \frac{\frac{s}{v}}{\frac{c}{v} + 1}$$

This formula shows that the rate of profit depends a) on the rate of surplus value s/v that Marx also calls the rate of exploitation because it described the relationship of unpaid and paid labour; and b) the organic composition of capital c/v that represents the relationship of dead and living labour, constant and variable capital, the value of machinery/resources and labour power. The organic composition is a measure of an economy's technological intensity. The rate of profit is directly proportional to the rate of surplus-value and indirectly proportional to the organic composition of capital.

New technology has the potential to both increase the rate of surplus-value and the organic composition of capital. The effects of new technology on the rate of profit depend on the relationship between the rate of surplus-value and the organic composition. If the organic composition increases more than the rate of surplus-value, then a fall of the rate of profit emerges. Vice versa, if the rate of surplus-value increases more than the organic composition, then the rate of profit increases. An important factor in this respect is class struggle that influences the absolute value of variable capital V. In any case, the formula for the rate of profit shows that technification has contradictory potentials: it can increase the investment costs, productivity and the exploitation of labour.

The increase of the organic composition as structural tendency of capital stands in contradiction to class struggles. The outcomes of this contradiction cannot be predicted in advance, but depend on historical circumstances. If the organic composition increases and there are no or unsuccessful workers' struggles so that the wage sum decreases, then the rate of profit can increase. If however workers' struggles are successful and they resist layoffs and achieve wage increases, the profit rate is more likely to fall.

Capitalist crisis

Figures 14.1 and 14.2 show the development of the rate of profit, the organic composition, and the rate of surplus-value in the USA and the EU15 countries.

The rate of surplus-value (i.e. the degree of exploitation) decreased in the 1960s and was relatively low in the 1970s in both the USA and the EU15. This is an indication that working-class struggles were relatively successful in this time period and resulted in relative wage increases. In the early 1980s – the time of the rise of neoliberal politics such as Reagonomics and Thatcherism – the degree of exploitation started a long-term increase caused by wage repression.

The time period 1960–2015 is one in which the computer has arisen, shaped and transformed capitalist economies. As a result, both in the USA and the EU15 countries the organic composition has in this period covering 55 years increased from around 20% to almost 30%, which confirms Marx's analysis that there is a

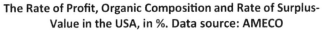

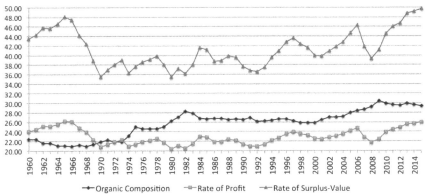

FIGURE 14.1   Economic development in the USA

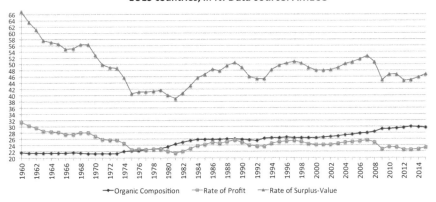

FIGURE 14.2   Economic development in the EU15 countries

tendency of the organic composition to rise that results from the technification and scientification of production. The rate of profit in both the USA and the EU dropped as a result of increasing wages and the working-class struggles in the 1960s until the middle of the 1970s, the time of a large global economic crisis.

The wage share is the share of the total wages in the gross domestic product (GDP), whereas the capital share is the share of capital (profits and constant capital) in the GDP. These two shares are indicators of the power of labour and capital. Figures 14.3 and 14.4 show the development of these two variables in the USA and the EU.

From the early 1960s until the mid-1970s, the wage share increased in both the USA and the EU, which signified an increasing power of the working class and relatively successful class struggles during this period that compelled capital to

FIGURE 14.3 The wage share in the USA and the EU

FIGURE 14.4 The capital share in the USA and the EU

increase wages. In the mid-1970s a period of wage repression started in both the EU and the USA, which result in significant drops in the wage share. At the same time, the share of capital in the total economy increased.

Since the mid-1970s, two contradictory tendencies have shaped capitalism: a) computerisation's increase of the organic composition that resulted in increasing constant capital costs; and b) top-down capitalist class struggle that decreased the wage share. As a result, the profit rate remained relatively constant and never returned to the levels of the 1960s. Capital was therefore searching for other ways for making profits, which resulted in an increased financialisation of capitalism. Significant shares of profits were invested in finance because capital is driven by the need to accumulate ever more profits and financial speculation promised high returns. The volatility of the economy steadily increased.

The share of the finance industry in the total value added has in many countries significantly increased. A general increase can be observed that has been especially strong in the USA, where the share has doubled from 1970 until 2005, when it made up 8.1% of the US economy's total value added (data source: OECD iLibrary, STAN, financial industry = ISIC Rev. 3: C65–C67). There has been an increasing financialisation of capitalism.

The rise of neoliberalism resulted in relative stagnation and wage losses, whereas profits rapidly increased. Neoliberalism therefore is a class struggle project of the ruling class aiming at increasing profits by decreasing wages with the help of strategies such as deregulation of labour laws, precarious labour conditions, welfare and public expenditure cuts, tax cuts for the rich and companies, the privatisation of public goods, the global offshoring and outsourcing of labour, etc. Many working families had to take out loans, consumer credits and mortgages in order to be able to pay for their everyday life requirements. At the same time, capital investment into high-risk financial instruments boomed because the growing profits needed to be reinvested. These high-risk financial instruments included Asset Backed Securities (ABS), Mortgage Backed Securities (MBS), Collateralised Debt Obligations (CDOs) and Credit Default Swaps (CDSs). The financial market promised high financial gains, but the profits in the non-financial economy could in the long run not fulfil these growth expectations, which created a mismatch between financial values and the profits of corporations, and the expectations of shareholders and the reality of capitalist accumulation. The results were financial bubbles that burst in the 2008 crisis.

The data show that the capitalist economy has since the middle of the 1970s been shaped by the capitalist class's neoliberal struggle against the working class, increasing inequality between capital and labour, an increase of household debts, a decrease of capital taxation, a rising financialisation of the economy and as a consequence an increased crisis volatility. The contradictions between capital and labour, fictitious value and actual profit, and the production and consumption/investment of capital were heightened by the development dynamics of neoliberal capitalism and finally resulted in a new world economic crisis and a crisis of capitalist society.

The next three sections aim to show that capitalism and its crisis are important factors that have shaped social media. One aspect is that capitalism's crisis has favoured the expansion of targeted online advertising.

Targeted advertising and the crisis

Tables 14.1 and 14.2 show the development of global advertising revenues. Whereas the share of broadcast advertising (radio and television) has in the years from 2009 until 2013 slightly declined from 43.6% to 42.0%, the decline was more drastic in the print industry, where the share went from 32.4% to 25.2%. At the same time, the share of Internet advertising increased from 15.7% to 24.8%. These statistical data give grounds to the assumption that advertisers find online advertising more secure than other forms of advertising because it can be targeted and personalised, and it is based on consumer and user surveillance. The new capitalist crisis may

TABLE 14.1 The development of global advertising revenues, in £ billion.

	2009	2010	2011	2012	2013
Television	84.5	93.9	98.0	102.8	105.2
Internet	37.5	44.7	54.6	63.8	75.0
Newspapers	55.0	54.8	54.3	53.0	52.2
Magazines	22.6	23.4	24.0	23.9	23.9
Outdoor	18.6	20.0	21.0	21.6	22.6
Radio	20.0	20.4	20.9	21.3	21.8
Cinema	1.3	1.4	1.5	1.6	1.7

Data source: Ofcom (2014, p. 22)

have accelerated this shift from traditional advertising to online advertising because corporations are then especially afraid of bankrupcy and taking losses. The crisis of journalism and the print news media stands in the context of the commercialisation of the media and the changes in advertising. In the UK, 37.1% of advertising revenue was spent in the online industry, 28.3% in broadcasting, 18.7% in the print industry, 9.5% on direct mail advertising, 5.3% on outdoor ads and 1.0% in the movie industry (Ofcom, 2015, p. 375).

In 2014, Google had a 31.10% share of global digital ad revenue, Facebook 7.75%, Baidu 4.68%, Alibaba 4.66%, Microsoft 2.72%, Yahoo! 2.36%, IAC 1.00%, Twitter 0.84%, Tencent 0.83%, AOL 0.81%, Amazon 0.70%, Pandora 0.50%, LinkedIn 0.49%, SINA 0.38%, Yelp 0.24% and Millennial Media 0.08%.[1] Such data indicate that Google, Facebook and Baidu are the key beneficiaries of Internet advertising's growth. One should not be mistaken: Google, Facebook and Baidu are not communications companies. They do not sell digital content or access to online platforms. They are some of the world's largest advertising companies. They sell user data as a commodity to advertisers, who in return can present targeted ads to users: In 2014, 89% of Google's revenues came from advertising (data source: SEC Filings Google, Form 10-K 2014). In the case of Facebook this figure was 92% in 2014 (data source: SEC Filings Facebook, Form 10-K 2014) and for Baidu it was in the same year 98.9% online marketing services (data source: SEC Filings Baidu, Form 20-F 2014).

Google and Facebook are very profitable companies (see Figures 14.5 and 14.6). They not only monopolise online search and online social networking, but are also key players in the business of targeted advertising. In 2016, Google was the world's 27th largest transnational company and Facebook the 188th largest (Forbes 2000, 2016).

Twitter and Weibo are the world's two leading microblog services. Twitter has been struggling financially. It became a stock-traded public company in November 2013, although its annual net losses were US$645.32 million in 2013 (Twitter SEC filings, form 10-K 2013). Weibo – a subsidiary of Sina – made losses of US$116.74 million in 2011, US$102.47 million in 2012, US$38.12 million in 2013 and US$62.7 million in 2014 (Weibo SEC filings, form F-1 registration statement).

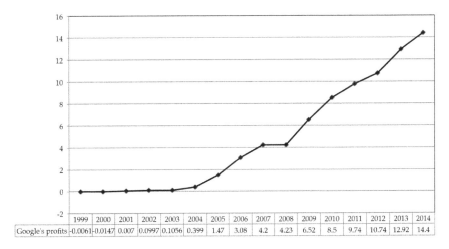

FIGURE 14.5 The development of Google's profits, in billion US\$. Data source: SEC filings, from 10-k, various years.

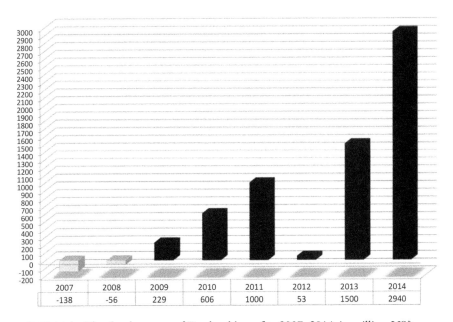

FIGURE 14.6 The development of Facebook's profits, 2007–2014, in million US\$

Just like Twitter in 2013, Weibo became a stock-marketed listed corporation in April 2014 when it made its Initial Public Offering (IPO) on the NASDAQ stock exchange. And also like Twitter it made this move although it had significant losses in the previous years and continued to make a total loss of US\$62.6 million in financial year 2014. Weibo and Twitter's share values have been fluctuating. In December 2014, eight months after its IPO, Weibo's share value dropped below its

TABLE 14.2 The development of global advertising revenues, in % of total ad revenue

	2009	2010	2011	2012	2013
Television	35.3%	36.3%	35.7%	35.7%	34.8%
Internet	15.7%	17.3%	19.9%	22.2%	24.8%
Newspapers	23.0%	21.2%	19.8%	18.4%	17.3%
Magazines	9.4%	9.0%	8.7%	8.3%	7.9%
Outdoor	7.8%	7.7%	7.7%	7.5%	7.5%
Radio	8.4%	7.9%	7.6%	7.4%	7.2%
Cinema	0.5%	0.5%	0.5%	0.6%	0.6%

Data source: Ofcom (2014, p. 22)

initial value of US$17. The same happened to Twitter's share value in August 2015, when it dropped below the initial value of US$26. Both shares have been fluctuating and volatile, and did not see large increases until late 2015.

Twitter and Weibo are not communications companies, but predominantly large advertising agencies. Targeted advertising is their main revenue source: 85% of Twitter's revenues came from advertising in 2012 and 89% in 2013 (Twitter SEC filings, form 10-K: annual report for 2013), and 78.8% of Weibo's 2013 revenues were derived from advertising and marketing, 12.2% from games and 5.9% from VIP membership services (Weibo SEC filings, form F-1, registration statement). In 2014, Weibo generated 79% of its revenue from advertising and marketing (ibid.). The rest of the revenue was made from online games and data licencing (ibid.).

Weibo and Twitter are high-risk financial companies because they have been listed on the stock market without making profits. So whereas their share values are positive, their net income is negative, which constitutes a divergence between profits and share values. Both companies hope that their large numbers of users attract advertisers and financial investors. They assume that they will make large profits in the future and that this hope will keep investors confident.

The risks these companies face is twofold: a) They face a highly competitive online advertising market, in which Google and Facebook dominate in the West and Baidu is a big player in China; and b) microblog communication has an immensely high speed and a short attention span. It is difficult to place targeted ads on them and make users click on these ads. It is not easy to make profits with targeted advertising because the average click-through rate is around 0.1% (Comscore, 2012): users only click on every 1,000th online ad presented to them – and even then it is not sure if such clicks on targeted ads tend to result in purchases.

Twitter and Weibo's political economy is an indication that the social media economy is highly financialised and that investments in it are insecure. Financial crises can start if finance bubbles burst because there is a large divergence between actual profits and stock market valuation, and investors lose confidence. The dot. com crisis in 2000 was an earlier expression of the high financialisation of the Internet economy, in which actual profits could not keep up with the promises of high stock market values. A new round of financialisation in the Internet industry has enabled the rise of social media while the ongoing world economic crisis showed us how crisis-prone financial markets are. Targeted advertising is a high-risk business.

The future of the social media economy in China and the West is uncertain. Both in China and the West we find a highly financialised capitalist industry that depends on the influx of investments into finance markets and the confidence of advertisers that advertising works. There are many uncertainties associated with advertising capital accumulation models, especially concerning users' privacy concerns, the use of ad-block technologies and other limits to advertising, and the question if targeted ads are effective or not. The possibility of investors' confidence dwindling after some trigger event and a resulting social media crisis cannot be ruled out because financialising and corporatising the Internet is accompanied by huge risks that both China and the West are facing.

Social media need to be understood in the context of capitalist accumulation, financialisation and crisis. But they also have cultural, political and ideological dimensions. One question that arises in the context of political crisis is what social media's role is in revolutions. Contemporary capitalism is shaped by both crises and political changes. It is no accident that protests and political change have intensified and accelerated in the time since the capitalism crisis started in 2008. Political changes have in the past years seen both progressive progress and new nationalism. Both have been reflected in the context of social media. The next section focuses on protests, while the following section provides an example of the rise of the far right.

Social media ideology #1: Twitter and Facebook revolutions

Times of economic crisis tend also to be times when the state is in crisis. In such situations, protests and revolutions do not necessarily emerge, but are more likely. In the course of the protests and revolutions that took place since 2008, the techno-determinist ideology that Twitter, Facebook and other social media caused such collective political action could often be heard. Even a *New York Times* writer stated that the "Egyptian revolution began on Facebook".[2]

There is very little serious empirical research about the actual role of social media in protests and revolutions. Most published academic works are speculative or big data analyses that can say nothing about how prevalent social media use was among actual activists who occupied squares.

The OccupyMedia! survey studied the role of social media in Occupy movements. I published its results in the book *OccupyMedia! The Occupy Movement and Social Media in Crisis Capitalism* (Fuchs, 2014c). The survey included 429 respondents who participated in the Occupy movement. One question was what the role of specific media was in protest mobilisation.

Activists use multiple media for mobilisation-oriented communication. These include classical interpersonal communication via phones, email, face-to-face and

TABLE 14.3 Frequency of usage per month of specific forms of communication in the mobilisation of protest

Form of communication	Infrequently (0 per month)	Medium (1–6 times per month)	Frequently (>6 times per month)
Face-to-face communication	15.0%	37.60%	47.40%
Email	29.8%	40.40%	29.80%
Phone	36.9%	39.50%	23.60%
SMS	49.7%	27.00%	23.30%
Email list	46.2%	29.90%	23.90%
Facebook	25.2%	32.40%	42.00%
Twitter	52.0%	15.90%	32.10%

Data source: Fuchs (2014c)

private social media profiles as well as more public forms of communication such as Facebook groups, Twitter and email lists. The data indicate that face-to-face communication, Facebook, email, phone, SMS and Twitter are the most important media that Occupy activists employed in trying to mobilise others for protests (see table 14.3).

I also conducted a correlation analysis of the variables that cover protest mobilisation communication (Fuchs, 2014c) and found that the frequency of activism tends to positively influence the frequency of media use for informing oneself about the movement, sharing user-generated content online, communicating between activists using various media and using media for protest mobilisation communication. The use of face-to-face communication and online communication tend to mutually reinforce each other. The use of various online media for information, the sharing of user-generated content and protest mobilisation also tend to mutually reinforce each other. We can therefore not say that online communication either determines protest or is unimportant. There is a *dialectic of online and offline protest communication*: Activists use multiple online and offline channels for obtaining information, discussing protests and trying to mobilise others. Online communication and face-to-face communication for these purposes tend to mutually reinforce each other.

The next section will show how right-wing ideology has in the contemporary crisis not just shaped society, but as a consequence also social media.

Social media ideology #2: red scare 2.0[3]

Anti-socialist ideology is at least as old as capitalism. After Marx's death, British right-wing media described *Das Kapital* as being "repellent in its cold formalism" and called Marx the "cold and methodical organiser of the International Association of Workers" (*The Morning Post*, March 19, 1883). The "English working men would not care to be identified with these principles [of communism] in their bald form" (*Leicester Chronicle and the Leicestershire Mercury*, March 24, 1883). *The Times* (January 18, 1919) wrote three days after Rosa Luxemburg and Karl Liebknecht had been assassinated: "Had power in Germany fallen into her [Luxemberg's] hands, she would have surpassed the reign of terror of the Russian Bolshevists". This statement indirectly welcomes Luxemburg's murder and implies that not her assassination was a form of terror, but that her politics were terroristic and that she therefore deserved to be killed.

In the 1980s, right-wing British news media characterised the Labour Party left and especially the Greater London Council, local London councils, Ken Livingstone and Tony Benn, as the 'Loony Left'. The term "combines two concepts, insanity and left-wing politics, with a subtext that suggests irrational authoritarianism" (Curran et al., 2005, p. 229). In respect to Tony Benn, the tabloid press spoke of "Dictatorship under Führer Benn" (*Daily Express*, 1 February 1975), "Benn The Dictator" (*Daily Express*, 28 May 1981), "Citizen Benn who shouts from the rooftops the debt we owe to a man called Joseph Stalin" (*News of the World*, 13 September 1981), "the Bennite monster" (*Daily Mail*, 16 January 1984), or wrote that "some say Tony Benn is raving bonkers" (Hollingsworth, 1986, p. 71). Jeremy Corbyn's win of the Labour leadership election in September 2015 was accompanied by the return of the 'Loony Left' and anti-socialist ideology.

I conducted an empirical ideology critique of tweets about Jeremy Corbyn during the leadership election. Data were collected with the help of Discovertext between 22 August 2015 and 13 September 2015, using keywords associated with the red scare. The result was a dataset consisting of 32,298 tweets. General opinions presented without arguments formed an important discourse topic in the dataset. One general bias that was frequently encountered in this respect was that Corbyn is a 'loony' left-winger:

> a wet handwringing leftie terrorist supporting anti Semite for Prime Minister ?? Corbyn will Drive Brit off a cliff
>
> *#242.*

> the radical extreme left wing lunacy of Jeremy left wing lunacy left wing loony lefty extreme radical Corbyn
>
> *#438.*

> Dangerous communist
>
> *#1228.*

> Bloody pinko
>
> *#1287.*

> Corbyn is satan
>
> *#4927.*

> socialist pig
>
> *#12741.*

> When will everyone realise that #Corbyn is a communist bastard? He's gonna fuck this country up if he gets in power #Labour
>
> *#17405.*

> Corbyn is a radical left wing idiot
>
> *#17528.*

> Corbyn is a left wing socialist scumbag
>
> *#20456.*

Single tweets even expressed the wish that Corbyn is killed because he is left-wing:

> Jeremy Corbyn. . . . . A communist fraud. . . . . . . hope he goes the way of Trotsky #Mexico1941 #NeverForget
>
> *#15440*

The sensationalist right-wing anti-Corbyn Twitter-discourse was not simply accepted, but instead was contested. There were various strategies that Corbyn supporters used for challenging anti-socialist ideology online. One strategy was that they associated Corbyn with positive general characteristics: "He seems to be about common sense and decency and so very normal/nice" (#422), "he is sensible, clear, knowledgeable & decent" (#606), and "In my view he just preaches common sense" (#22591).

A second strategy was to use the strategy of discursive dialectical reversal: the argument made in this strategy is that not Corbyn, but the Tories are extremist, radical, violent, hard-right, and dangerous. Figure 14.7 shows an example.

A third strategy was to use satire and humour to ridicule anti-socialist ideology. This was based on the insight that ideologies are often irrational and emotional. They are difficult to challenge by rational arguments. The hashtag #suggestacorbynsmear emerged on Twitter on August 31, 2015, and was used within 24 hours more than 11,000 times[4] is an example. Examples: "Jeremy Corbyn shares the letter 'n' with Stalin and Satan, and the letters 'e' and 'r' with Hitler! #suggestacorbynsmear" (#5229) and "Jeremy Corbyn was born in 1949. Stalin was alive in 1949. Coincidence? I think not. #suggestacorbynsmear" (5251).

Ideologies are semiotic structures that justify domination. Twitter limits linguistic expression to 140 characters. Twitter's brevity is an expression of high-speed capitalist consumer culture. User-generated ideology such as online redbaiting therefore has to compress ideology. User-generated ideology is the use of digital media for producing and spreading semiotic structures that justify domination by distorting reality, misrepresenting it or inventing false representations of reality. By making claims, insults and personal attacks without underlying arguments and justifications, users compress ideology on Twitter into 140 characters. A feature of many anti-socialist tweets was that they made claims about Corbyn without arguments and proof.

#Panorama cheap smear campaign against Corbyn tonight trying to link him to terrorist group short memory of this

RETWEETS FAVOURITES
116 52

FIGURE 14.7   A Twitter-critique of the BBC *Panorma* documentary on Corbyn that uses visual dialectical reversals by showing images of Gordon Brown and Tony Blair with Gaddafi, Blair with Assad, and Thatcher with Pinochet

Users are not the helpless victims of anti-socialist and other ideologies, but can contest, oppose and struggle against ideologies. Social media is a communication space where ideologies are expressed and challenged. Studying user-generated ideologies online therefore allows identifying and analysing the structure of anti-socialist and anti-Corbyn ideologies and how they can best be challenged.

Left-wing social media users have developed intelligent strategies of how to react to ideological smear campaigns. Studying counter-discourses to anti-socialist ideology can inform political campaigns at a time when redbaiting is again omnipresent in politics.

Conclusion

Society shapes and is shaped by communication technologies and society. There is a dialectic of media and society. In an antagonistic society, new information and communication technologies will therefore display an antagonistic logic. A critical theory and critique of the political economy of communications and the media tries to understand the contradictions of society and communications.

This chapter has investigated causes of the crisis of capitalism. This crisis is not a crisis of regulation, but a fundamental economic crisis that has emerged from capitalism's inherent contradictions. The economic crisis has also turned into political and cultural crises, for example a crisis of the European idea and European politics. On the level of communications, crises tend to manifest themselves in various ways. The focus of this chapter was social media in the context of capitalism's crisis: capitalism's crisis has favoured the expansion of targeted online advertising. In the realm of politics, social media communication and offline communication are two interacting forms of protest communication. The strengthening of rightwing extremism has resulted in various forms of far-right ideology and nationalism online (see Fuchs, 2016a, 2016b, for two detailed studies of ideology 2.0).

Social media are in complex ways embedded into the contradictions of capitalist society, economy, politics and ideology. As a consequence, social media are incompletely social and are shaped by the logic of instrumental reason that turns such communications into forms of domination and exploitation. Only social struggles can develop potentials of communications and society that communalise both society and the media so that social media and society can become truly social.

Notes

1 China's leading ad sellers to take 10% of the worldwide digital market this year. *eMarketer,* December 16, 2014.
2 Spring awakening. How an Egyptian revolution began on Facebook. *New York Times Online.* February 17, 2012. www.nytimes.com/2012/02/19/books/review/how-an-egyptian-revolution-began-on-facebook.html?pagewanted=all&_r=0
3 The following section is a short summary of some aspects presented in Fuchs (2016c).
4 www.telegraph.co.uk/news/politics/Jeremy_Corbyn/11836904/Twitters-funniest-smear-attacks-on-Jeremy-Corbyn-as-suggestacorbynsmear-goes-viral.html

References

Comscore. 2012. *The power of Like2: How social marketing works.* White Paper. Reston, VA: Comscore.
Curran, J., Petley, J., and Gaber, I. 2005. *Culture wars.* Edinburgh: Edinburgh University Press.
Fisher, E., and Fuchs, C., (eds.). 2015. *Reconsidering value and labour in the digital age.* Basingstoke: Palgrave Macmillan.
Forbes 2000. 2016. *Forbes 2016 Global 2000.* [online] Available at: http://www.forbes.com/global2000/ [Accessed 21st October 2016].
Fuchs, C. 2014a. *Digital labour and Karl Marx.* New York: Routledge.
Fuchs, C. 2014b. *Occupy media! The occupy movement and social media in crisis capitalism.* Winchester: Zero Books.
Fuchs, C. 2014c. *Social media: A critical introduction.* London: Sage.
Fuchs, C. 2015. *Culture and economy in the age of social media.* New York: Routledge.
Fuchs, C. 2016a. 'Racism, nationalism and right-wing extremism online: The Austrian presidential election 2016 on Facebook'. *Momentum Quarterly – Zeitschrift für sozialen Fortschritt (Journal for Societal Progress),* 5(3), pp. 172–196.
Fuchs, C. 2016b. *Reading Marx in the information age: A media and communication studies perspective on "Capital Volume I".* New York: Routledge.
Fuchs, C. 2016c. 'Red Scare 2.0: User-generated ideology in the age of Jeremy Corbyn and social media'. *Journal of Language and Politics,* 15(4), pp. 369–398.

Fuchs, C. 2017. 'Fascism 2.0: Twitter users' social media memories of Hitler on his 127th birthday'. *Fascism: Journal of Comparative Fascist Studies*, 6(2), pp. 228–263.

Fuchs, C., Boersma, K., Albrechtslund, A., and Sandoval, M., (eds.). 2012. *Internet and surveillance. The challenges of web 2.0 and social media*. New York: Routledge.

Fuchs, C., and Mosco, V., (eds.). 2016. *Marx in the age of digital capitalism: Studies in critical social sciences*, Volume 80. Leiden: Brill.

Fuchs, C., and Sandoval, M., (eds.). 2014. *Critique, social media and the information society*. New York: Routledge.

Hollingsworth, M. 1986. *The press and political dissent*. London: Pluto.

Marx, K. 1867. *Capital Volume 1*. London: Penguin.

Ofcom. 2014. *International communications marketreport 2014*. [online] Available at: http://stakeholders.ofcom.org.uk/binaries/research/cmr/cmr14/icmr/ICMR_2014.pdf [Accessed 21st October 2016].

Ofcom. 2015. *The communications market report 2015* [UK]. [online] Available at: http://stakeholders.ofcom.org.uk/binaries/research/cmr/cmr15/CMR_UK_2015.pdf [Accessed 21st October 2016].

Trottier, D., and Fuchs, C., (eds.). 2014. *Social media, politics and the state: Protests, revolutions, riots, crime and policing in the age of Facebook, Twitter and YouTube*. New York: Routledge.

15

NARRATIVE MEDIATION OF THE OCCUPY MOVEMENT

A case study of Stockholm and Latvia

Anne Kaun and Maria Francesca Murru

Introduction

The latest waves of protests that emerged in the context of the Euro crisis have spurred the question of how practices of activists intersect with (online) media usage. Economic crises are here considered as critical junctures not only in terms of the economic system as such, but also for the media system (McChesney, 2007), as protest movements employing different media technologies aim to fill the crisis-induced void with new meaning giving social change a specific direction. In the context of the 2008 financial crisis and the subsequent protests, social media were particularly emphasized by commentators (Castells, 2012). In that context, notions such as networks of protests and the connective action paradigm have been prevalent in the discussion (Castells, 2012; Bennett and Segerberg, 2013). While both notions have certainly value for understanding certain aspects of digital activism, their exclusive focus on the new organizational structures that are expected to result from digital-enabled peer production mechanisms, risks neglecting other dimensions of protests mobilization and identification that are equally important in contentious action in the context of economic crises. Following the representation of the Occupy Wall Street (OWS) movement and its local versions in Sweden (Occupy Stockholm, which was active roughly between October 2011 and July 2012) and Latvia (Occupy Latvia, which was mainly active on social networking sites in 2011/2012) in mainstream news media, the chapter advocates a narrative approach to the study of protest movements. In that way, the chapter relates to a large body of research engaging with the mediated representation of protest movements (for an overview see McCurdy, 2012) that has lately been overshadowed by the dominant focus on the role of digital and social media for mobilizations. While studies of mediated representations of protest movements have earlier focused on framing and discursive practices, we focus on narrative practices of mediation.

Considering particularly different narratives produced about this transnational protest movement, the chapter suggests that the analytical focus on narratives allows to follow the reshaping of protest movements through mainstream media coverage while broadening our understanding of the Euro crisis. At the same time, narrative analysis offers the possibility to focus on different layers of narrative mediation including self-narration and narratives by adversaries. However, the focus is here on narrative mediation by mainstream news media providing the material for sense-making of protest mobilizations by the public.

Narrative analysis of protest

In the context of this chapter, we consider narratives as essential components of the social construction of collective action. We study them as cultural constructs which mediate our experience of the social world in its most fundamental coordinates. We adopt this assumption from critical hermeneutics, and more specifically from Ricoeur (1984), according to whom every text implies a project of a world where it would be possible to live, a horizon of possible experience that contains the promise of transforming the *umwelt* of the reader – its immediate surroundings – into a *welt* – a world that can be symbolically inhabited. This is what he calls a process of symbolic mediation that each text exerts between a person and the world, between person and person, between a person and the self. Ricoeur proposes the narrative dimension as the cornerstone of this mediation, insofar as the acts of narrating and of living are linked by a relation of mutual implication. On the one hand, life needs stories to be comprehended. Action in fact can be understood as different from mere physical movement or physiological behaviour, only through a competent use of the *semantics of action,* a network of expressions and concepts that explain action in terms of aims, means and circumstances. In parallel, action, before being submitted to interpretation, is already readable thanks to those symbols that pre-interpret it in terms of which aspects of doing, of being-able to do, and of knowing how to do it embodies. On the other hand, narratives need a living receiver to be completed. Emplotment is the common work by the text and the reader insofar as the text is actualized in all its zones of indeterminacy and latent wealth of interpretation only when a reader puts into play their own horizon of expectations.

At the most superficial level, we can imagine social movements as bundles of stories (Fine, 1995) where personal, collective, internal and external as well as own and others' narratives co-exist and sometimes converge. Personal narratives are those stories which contain experiences and biographical fragments that will receive political resonance within the movement; but they can also be the participant's narrative that share emotions and feelings of being part of a collective endeavor. Collective narratives (Benford, 2002) are those stories that represent the purposes and the paths of actions of the movement. External narratives written by outsiders of the movement contextualize these same actions within the wider historical transformations of society and politics while reflecting at the movements' internal self-narration. Bruck (1992) focuses on codes and conventions of news media, and the way they reprocess the discourses provided through various sources. Through reassembling and rearranging information, they create their own ways of telling stories of different events. The rearrangements often reflect dominant ideologies and modes of representation (Kellner, 2012). However, Bruck (1992) argues that discourse can be changed by social movements. Hence, mainstream news media emerge as a site of struggle over the particular narration of social change.

Two main research paths are possible in the examination of narratives in social movements. The first one uses them as a method or means for exploring other aspects of the social life that animates collective action. The second one – which will be followed here – takes the narrative as an object of inquiry for its own sake. In this second path, narratives are studied as peculiar carriers of shared meaning, which inhabit potentialities in terms of constructing both identities and temporalities of and about collective action. At the same time, they are subject to certain cultural constraints concerning their expressive forms and conditions of performance. The study of narratives as objects can focus on either narratives produced by activists themselves or on narratives produced about their actions. Both approaches have received research attention earlier. We focus here on the latter and consider particularly narratives constructed by news media about the protest activities. Analyzing media representations of political activism has a long tradition. Previous research has highlighted the importance of mediated representations for forming ideas about social movements in the public as well as systematic biases that are produced by the news coverage (Gitlin, 2003; Weaver and Scacco, 2013). We propose that the analysis of narratives is not only fruitfully employed when it comes to activists' practices, but can also illuminate the process of contextualization of transnational protest movements by mainstream news media. In connection with critical discourse theory, the chapter focuses on mediating social practices and discerns narrative strategies in the representation of Occupy Stockholm and Occupy Latvia.

The financial crisis and the Occupy movement

The Occupy movement has been depicted as the most prominent example of protest related to the financial crisis (Pickerill and Krinsky, 2012; Graeber, 2013). However, the issues addressed by Occupy were much broader and more inclusive. The focus for the mobilizations changed according to the specific political and social context to which the Occupy narrative travelled (Kaun, 2017).

Although the Swedish and Latvian encampments and the mobilizations around the Occupy movement were not nearly as big as in the United States, they represent an interesting point in the case of transnational activism, which forms a global network, but which is very much rooted in local causes and previous activism. As Michael Gould-Wartofsky (2015) shows in his careful narration of OWS, the New York mobilization has a long history of local and international activism. Similarly, the activists in Sweden and Latvia have personal and collective histories of political activism. At the same time, Occupy Stockholm and Occupy Latvia, although small and sometimes including only a handful of activists, represent one of the

European responses to the economic crisis, addressing European institutions and hence serving as an entry point to looking at narratives generated by and around protest movements (Kaun, 2017). Furthermore, moving to the European periphery adds new insights to the study of the global Occupy movement, which has mainly been discussed from the perspective of the largest and most central encampments.

Occupy Latvia

According to the International Monetary Fund, the Baltic countries have suffered considerably from the financial crisis that peaked in 2008 (Purfield and Rosenberg, 2010). With the gross domestic product shrinking by 14.2 per cent in 2009, compared to the previous year, and an unemployment rate as high as 19.5 per cent in 2010, Latvia was, after a period of rapid growth, faced with an extreme economic situation (Eurostat, 2014a, 2014b). As in other EU member states, the crisis was tackled with a strategy of 'internal devaluation', including extensive cuts in wages and public spending. Despite these strong austerity measures, Anders Åslund[1] and Valdis Dombrovskis, the former prime minister of Latvia, argue in a 2011 book that the democratic institutions worked well. Therefore, they propose, there were only few protests and very little public criticism. The celebration of political institutions, however, silences accounts of social unrest that appeared. Latvia had seen crisis-related protest mobilizations already in 2008/2009. On 13 January 2009, for example, a protest against the government's and Europe's handling of the crisis was met with strong police action. Protesters, mainly students and youths, were calling for the resignation of the government. During the mobilization, several protesters tried to hinder MPs from entering parliament by camping in front of the main parliament building. After the resignation of the government, the protest quickly faded, as the activists seemed to have reached their goals. Additionally, in the autumn of 2009, a group of approximately 20 activists camped in front of the Cabinet of Ministers, the main Latvian government building. The encampment remained until the summer of 2010. The camp's activists put forward a broad range of demands directed at the Latvian government. Some of the main issues were unemployment and austerity measures. Despite these early occupations of different public spaces, Latvia has never seen an occupation connected to the global Occupy movement.

In contrast to the Swedish case, there were no physical occupations in Lativa. However, with the global spread of the Occupy movement, loose online networks linked to the movement appeared, discussing economic greed and politics in Latvia.

Occupy Stockholm

Compared to other European countries, Sweden has often been described as have been coping relatively well with the effects of the financial crisis. However, in Sweden, the economic stress indices reflected growing tensions in the markets in 2009, and the youth unemployment rate of more than 24 per cent, compared to the average rate of 8 per cent of unemployment, was the highest among Organisation for Economic Co-operation and Development (OECD) countries (UNRICs, 2012).

A local branch of the Occupy movement emerged in Stockholm in October 2011 and – with changing locations in the city centre and suburbs – kept an encampment until July 2012. Like other camps, Occupy Stockholm quickly diversified into several groups and committees working on specific issues; one of the largest was the media group, including several subdivisions working on its home page, Facebook, Twitter, YouTube, printed outlets and posters as well as graphics. Other divisions were dedicated to demonstrations and to a study group that met weekly between January and May 2012. As two informants involved with Occupy Stockholm have suggested, many first-time activists joined the group in the beginning. During the late summer of 2012, however, more and more members vanished, and with that, the actual occupation ended. A core group of five people remained and held regular general assemblies until October 2012, when they decided to dissolve Occupy Stockholm until the decision is taken to revive it.

The issues around which particular mobilizations evolved were broad and included homelessness, support for the demand to restrict the size of international banks, general Europe-wide protests against public debt and the Anti-Counterfeiting Trade Agreement (ACTA), World Environment Day, demonstrations against US war policies, support for the protest against European Stability Mechanism (ESM) funds, demonstrations against privatization and the financial system, Occupy May 1st, protests against weapons exports and the Data Retention Directive. Although Occupy Stockholm mobilized around specific European causes, this was not reflected in the reporting on the movement.

Swedish and Latvian Occupy narratives

In choosing Swedish and Latvian versions of the Occupy movement, the analysis builds on two heterogonous samples: Sweden, which had several Occupy encampments, and Latvia, which although it never saw an Occupy camp, the idea of Occupy resonated with alternative political voices and was invoked in different digital initiatives and offline mobilizations. Latvia and Sweden also represent historically different political activism contexts. As Kerstin Jacobsson and Steven Saxonberg show, post-Communist countries such as Latvia have often been considered as having weak civil societies, which is linked to their political history of state authoritarianism (Jacobsson and Saxonberg, 2013). However, the authors demonstrate that a broad variety of political activism exists in the post-Communist context, which, perforce, has not taken the same paths as in the West. Although we are not necessarily interested in reinforcing an East–West divide, the question of different historical contexts adds complexity to the analysis of protest movement narrations. At the same time, Latvia and Sweden share specific historical experiences such as the economic crisis – though to different degrees – which justifies a comparative perspective. The economic ties become particularly evident when looking at the three main banks in Latvia, which are all Swedish. Furthermore, Swedish media conglomerates such as Bonnier had been active in Latvia, which makes a comparison of mainstream media narratives especially interesting.[2]

Besides the comparative aspect, the material gathered for the analysis here emerged in different institutional settings. The sample of the mainstream news media consists of major Swedish and Latvian dailies reporting on Occupy. The choice of newspapers includes a broad spectrum of political positions (from liberal to conservative) as well as quality and tabloid. For the Latvian case, the sample includes the most important Russian-language daily newspapers, which are mainly read by the strong Russian-speaking minority (approximately 27 per cent of the Latvian population).

The material included all articles that referenced the Occupy movement from September to November 2011 in the following newspapers: the Swedish newspapers *Dagens Nyheter, Svenska Dagbladet, Aftonbladet* and *Expressen*; the Latvian newspapers *Diena, Neatkarīgā Rīta Avīze* and *Latvijas Avīze;* and the Russian-language newspapers *Chas* and *Vesti*. The period was chosen based on the main OWS activities. The Swedish sample consists of 63 articles in total, whereas during the same period, the Latvian newspapers published only 17 articles mentioning the Occupy movement. The first report in Sweden appeared on 29 September 2011 in *Svenska Dagbladet*; it was a fairly long article in the finance section. In Latvia, the earliest article on the Occupy movement was published on 3 October 2011.

Narrative mediation of protest

Analytically, we focus on the narrative mediation of protest as social practice and are only partly interested in the properties of media as mediating tools. According to Roger Silverstone (2002), mediation is a transformative process constructing the meaningfulness and value of things. In contrast, everyday life is characterized by ambiguity and messiness. Media are crucial for resolving a certain degree of ambiguity through the ordering that is implicated in their narratives and their scheduling capacity. Silverstone argues that the different modes of representation of the media – including news – in general meet the needs and desires for a certain degree of order. The process of mediation is however not completely even and frictionless. "Mediation . . . describes the fundamentally, but unevenly dialectical process in which instutionalised media of communication (the press, broadcast radio and television, and increasingly the world wide web) are involved in the general circulation of symbols in social life" (Silverstone, 2002, p. 762). Focusing on the narrative component of mediation allows us to trace specific strategies that are linked to the institutional context of mediation, but go beyond it. Stories and narratives are the concrete expressions of emplotment and the ordering function of narratives for all kinds of experiences in different contexts. At the most general level, narratives establish an order for all experiential elements in a contiguous plot. By way of ordering, the situational elements are given meaning; and in this way, a specific role in the plot and a temporal structure are established. At the micro level of stories, as well as at the more abstract discursive level, narratives establish some kind of coherence in a world of disorder.

Central to Silverstone's understanding of mediation is the narrative ordering that media provide. We suggest therefore to consider the Occupy movements both as object of narrative mediation and in terms of concrete narrative practices. For this we rely on narrative analysis – rooted in literature, history, anthropology, sociology and linguistics – that encompasses a variety of research practices and analytical strategies. In general, the notion of narrative may refer to an actual text or a more abstract discourse. Narrative analysis enables, therefore, the inclusion of individual voices and more abstract discourse. The inclusion of individual voices is of particular importance in the context of the Occupy movement, which was, and is, characterized by a broad diversity of political views and actors. Focusing on narratives allows us to follow the emplotment of individual and collective experiences, here in the sense of mediation (Van Leeuwen and Wodak, 1999; Van Leeuwen, 2007; Bennett, 2013). In line with van Leeuwen's framework, mediation considers all social practice as reformulated in talk and texts. Through discursive articulation, practices become meaningful from a specific point of view grounded in material, socioeconomic contexts. Van Leeuwen constructs a chain of recontextualization, moving from social to discursive signifying practices to discourse. Reisigl and Wodak (2009) suggest a number of several narrative strategies often employed in mediating social practices (Reisigl and Wodak, 2009; Wodak and Meyer, 2009). Based on the analysis of the material gathered for this project, we have identified the four major narrative strategies: nomination, predication, perspectivation and mitigation.[3]

Nomination refers to the discursive construction of social actors, objects, events and actions. In terms of nomination of causes for the emergence of the Occupy movement, the newspapers in both Latvia and Sweden focus on the greed of individual bankers and corporations, and make some mention of the growing inequality. However, as the following example from the Swedish *Expressen* illustrates, this is only justified and evidenced for the US and not the Swedish or Latvian context, and remains rather unspecific in terms of Occupy's criticisms suggested:

> The average income in the US has marginally increased the last 30 years. At the same time, the income of the richest part has exploded. The large productivity growth has not reached the middle class, however, the richest are paying ever less and the middle class ever more.
>
> *Expressen 22 October 2011*[4]

Predication, in contrast, pertains to the evaluation of the events, focusing on the discursive qualification of actors, objects, events and actions. In both contexts, Occupy is associated with other protest movements, such as the Global Justice Movement, Arab Spring and the Indignados, but also with WikiLeaks and Anonymous, as well as the Tea Party movement, as shown in *Diena*:

> The activists of *Occupy Wall Street* like to stress that they are a repercussion of the so-called Arab Spring protests. The internet edition of *International*

Business Times, however, rather links the American movement with the 15-M movement, which started in May in Madrid, followers of which are staying in the parks of the biggest cities for weeks and months, to demand that the government carries out social and political reforms. 15M can be proud of real achievements, because the socialist Prime Minister Jose Luis Zapatero announced extraordinary parliamentary elections in the summer.

Diena 14 October 2011[5]

There are, however, no links to traditional political organizations such as trade unions, although they have been supporting specific mobilizations of, for example, Occupy Stockholm. Through this kind of predication, the movement is ideologically depoliticized, especially as the comparison to all kinds of protest and social movements from the radical left to the right contextualizes the movement as ideologically and structurally arbitrary.

Perspectivation takes the writers' or speakers' point of view into consideration through expressing either involvement or distance. In terms of perspectivation, both Latvian and Swedish newspapers create only weak links between Occupy and the local/national context. The movement is largely considered in foreign news sections and as having little relevance for the local political and economic context:

Started as a rather marginal movement against the bankers of Wall Street, the protest campaign Occupy Wall Street concerns almost everybody in American society.

Latvijas Avīze 14 October 2011[6]

Lastly, mitigation refers to modification of "the illocutionary force and the epistemic or deontic status of utterances" (Reisigl and Wodak, 2009, p. 95). This category encompasses a meta-level of analysis and combines perspectivation, predication and nomination as concrete discursive practices to underlying strategies. Predication, perspectivation and nomination in the case of Occupy Stockholm and Occupy Lativa all point towards toning down and minimizing the act of protesting in public space itself. *Expressen* downplays the movement in the following way:

It is not true. 99 percent of the Swedes do not have to choose at all between paying for food *or* the rent. Of course the differences have increased during the last couple of years, but most parts of the Swedish population do not suffer economically.

Expressen 22 October 2011)[7]

In the Latvian context, the movement is mitigated by completely delinking it from the Latvian crisis experience while, in Sweden, commentators question the severity of the crisis and consequently the motivation of the local activists.

In general, the movement is depoliticized by disconnecting it from its initial cause of questioning and criticizing the global finance capitalism that led to the economic crisis on the national level. Furthermore, the movement is disconnected from other forms of critiquing or countering capitalist practices – for example, through institutionalized forms of political organization such as unions. Additionally, the causes of the movement are mitigated by delinking it from the crisis experience in the local context of both Sweden and Latvia. Hence, Occupy is largely constructed as foreign and less relevant in the North-European context. In terms of negotiating the global movement and the local context, mainstream news media in both Latvia and Sweden attribute more importance to the global level of the movement than to its local relevance, leading to a crude discrediting of the root causes for the emergence of the movement.

Conclusion: (de)contextualizing protest narratives

This chapter suggests narrative analysis of anti-austerity protests as an alternative approach. Instead of overemphasizing the role of digital networks and communication platforms, it has shifted the focus on the role of the discursive strategies of both mainstream news and activists.

The comparison of the dominant narrative mediation of the Occupy movement in Sweden and Latvia indicated that the mainstream newspaper articles share major discursive strategies in terms of nomination, predication, perspectivation and mitigation. In both the Swedish and Latvian context, the movement is, in general, depoliticized in terms of its ideology and motivations. The narratives constructed by major newspapers present weak links to the crisis of the economic system as a major source for the protests. Mainstream newspapers have reproduced the discourse of Latvia and Sweden respectively as 'success stories' considering the handling of the financial crisis. On the other hand, these success stories have been articulated differently. In the Swedish context, the discourse manifests the underlying idea that the situation is fundamentally different from the US experience. Compared to the structural inequality and the degree of the crisis in the United States, Sweden is much better off. In consequence, the protests and occupations are treated in a patronizing manner. They are playful and lack serious concerns. In the Latvian case, the underlying argument refers to the reoccurring hardship that the society has been suffering historically while always upholding the hope for a better future. Latvia has in that context been presented as a success story of how severe austerity measures enabled it to successfully endure the crisis (Åslund and Dombrovskis, 2011).

Notes

1 Anders Åslund is a Swedish economist who until 2009 was the economic advisor to Valdis Dombrovskis.
2 Bonnier sold its shares in *Diena* and *Dienas Bizness* in 2009.
3 Reisigl and Wodak (2009) as well as Wodak and Meyer (2009) identify additional discursive strategies, such as argumentation and self-perception. Here we have focused only on the strategies relevant to the analysed material.
4 Medelinkomsten i USA har nämligen knappt ökat alls på 30 år, samtidigt som den rikaste procentens inkomster exploderat. Den stora produktivitetsökning som skett har knappt alls kommit medelklassen till del, ändå har skattesystemet gjorts om så att de rikaste betalar allt mindre och medelklassen mer.

5 Kustības Occupy Wall Street aktīvistiem patīk uzsvērt, ka viņi ir tā sauktā Arābu pavasara protestu atskaņa. Interneta izdevums International Business Times amerikāņu kustību gan vairāk saista ar maijā Spānijas galvaspilsētā Madridē aisākušos kustību 15M, kuras sekotāji nedēļā un mēnešiem ilgi uzturas lielāko pilsētu centrālajos laukumos, lai pieprasītu valdībai politiskās un sociālās reformas. 15M var lepoties ar reāliem panākumiem, jo sociālistu premjerministrs Hosē Luiss Sapatero vasarā izsludināja ārkārtas parlamenta vēļēšanas.

6 Sākusies kā samērā margināla kustība pret Volstrītas baņķieriem, protesta akcija „Okupē Voltstrītu" vienaldzīgu neatstāj nevienu amerikāni.

7 Ändå skaver det i ögonen. Det är ju inte sant. 99 procent av svenskarna måste inte alls välja mellan att betala mat och hyra. Visst har klyftorna ökat på senare år, men de flesta svenskar har det ekonomiskt rätt bra.

References

Åslund, A., and Dombrovskis, V. 2011. *How Latvia came through the financial crisis.* Washington: Peter G. Peterson Institute for International Economics.

Benford, R. D. 2002. Controlling narratives and narratives as social control within social movements. In: Davis, J. E. (eds.), *Stories of change: Narrative and social movements.* Albany: SUNY Press.

Bennett, J. 2013. 'Moralising class: a discourse analysis of the mainstream political response to Occupy and the August 2011 British riots'. *Discourse and Society*, 24, pp. 27–45.

Bennett, L., and Segerberg, A. 2013. *The logic of connective action: Digital media and the personalization of contentious politics.* New York: Cambridge University Press.

Bruck, P. 1992. Discursive movements and social movements: The active negotiation of constraints. In: Wasko, J., and Mosco, V. (eds.), *Democratic communications in the information age.* Toronto: Garamond Press.

Castells, M. 2012. *Networks of outrage and hope: Social movements in the internet age.* Cambridge, MA: Polity Press.

Eurostat. 2014a. 'Real GDP rate – volume'. Available at http://ec.europa.eu/eurostat/tgm/table.do;jsessionid=9h6XkrKeNLyvnzyxy4YVnM6U_fBPY4h2E2REYG7cX7HEmbAwWD4!109820079?tab=table&plugin=1&language=en&pcode=tec00115. [Accessed 17 February 2015].

Eurostat. 2014b. 'Unemployment statistics'. Available at http://ec.europa.eu/eurostat/statistics-explained/index.php/Unemployment_statistics#Further_Eurostat_information. [Accessed 17 February 2015].

Fine, G. A. 1995. Public narration and group culture. In: Johnston, H. and Klandermans, B. (eds.), *Social movements and culture.* Minneapolis: University of Minnesota Press. pp. 127–143.

Gitlin, T. 2003. *The whole world is watching: Mass media in the making and unmaking of the new left.* Los Angeles, London: University of California Press.

Gould-Wartofsky, M. 2015. *The occupiers: the making of the 99 percent movement.* Oxford, New York: Oxford University Press.

Graeber, D. 2013. *The Democracy project. A history, a crises, a movement.* New York: Spiegel and Grau.

Jacobsson, K., and Saxonberg, S. (eds.) 2013. *Beyond NGO-ization: The Development of Social Movements in Central and Eastern Europe.* Farnham: Ashgate.

Kaun, A. 2017. Narrating protest: Silenced stories of Europe in Occupy Stockholm and Occupy Latvia. In: Fornäs, J. (ed.), *Europe faces Europe: Narratives from its Eastern half.* Bristol: Intellect, pp. 133–151.

Kellner, D. 2012. *Media spectacle and insurrection, 2011: From the Arab uprisings to Occupy everywhere.* London: Continuum.

McCurdy, P. 2012. 'Social movements, protest and mainstream media'. *Sociology Compass*, 6, pp. 244–255.

Pickerill, J., and Krinsky, J. 2012. 'Why does Occupy matter?' *Social Movement Studies: Journal of Social, Cultural and Political Protest*, 11, pp. 279–287.

Purfield, C. and Rosenberg, C.B. 2010. 'Adjustment under a Currency Peg: Estonia, Latvia and Lithuania during the Global Financial Crisis 2008–09'. *IMF Working Paper* [Online]. [Accessed 19 August 2013].

Reisigl, M., and Wodak, R. 2009. The discourse-historical approach. In: Wodak, R., and Meyer, M. (eds.). *Methods of critical discourse analysis*. London, Thousand Oaks: New Delhi, Singapore: Sage, pp. 87–91.

Ricoeur, P. 1984. *Time and narrative. Vol. 1*, Chicago: University of Chicago Press.

Silverstone, R. 2002. 'Complicity and Collusion in the Mediation of Everyday Life'. *New Literary History*, 33(4), pp. 761–780.

UNRIC 2012. *Sweden: Highest ratio of youth unemployment*. www.unric.org/en/youth-unemployment/27411-sweden-highest-ratio-of-youth-unemployment [Accessed 2 June 2017].

Van Leeuwen, T. 2007. 'Legitimation in discourse and communication'. *Discourse and Communication*, 1, pp. 91–112.

Van Leeuwen, T., and Wodak, R. 1999. Legitimizing immigration control: A discourse-historical analysis. *Discourse Studies*, 1, pp. 83–118.

Weaver, D. A., and Scacco, J. M. 2013. 'Revisiting the protest paradigm: The tea party as filtered through prime-time cable news'. *The International Journal of Press/Politics*, 18, pp. 61–84.

16

FACEBOOK AND THE POPULIST RIGHT

How populist politicians use social media to reimagine the news in Finland and the UK

Niko Hatakka

Populists reframing crisis news online

The inability to refinance national debts in Greece, Portugal, Ireland, Spain and Cyprus has led not only to deep economic distress but also to unprecedented institutional reforms for preventing further escalation of the crisis in the Eurozone. Journalistic news media along with political and financial elites have been central in framing the ongoing Euro crisis that started in late 2009. Quality newspapers' coverage on the crisis has been significantly elite-driven: using mostly high-level EU and national political actors and financial experts as sources, the news has framed the crisis predominantly as a European crisis with European-level solutions and few political alternatives (Herkman and Harjuniemi, 2015, pp. 224–9; Hubé et al., 2015, pp. 88–95; Picard, 2015).

The turmoil of economic and political crises tends to aid populist parties by providing them with discursive windows of opportunity. Populist actors can utilize crises especially for pointing out grievances within prevailing politics and for attributing blame to the political establishment while claiming to represent the pure will of the people (Taggart, 2004, p. 275; Pelinka, 2013; Jupskås, 2015, p. 23; Wodak, 2015). While there are significant regional and contextual differences in levels of support for European populist movements (Pappas and Kriesi, 2015), nationalist-populist parties with both hard and soft eurosceptic stances have enjoyed varying boosts in electoral support since the beginning of the Euro crisis. For example, in Northern Europe, where the economic effects of the Euro crisis have not been nearly as devastating as in the South, eurosceptic nationalist-populist parties such as the UK Independence Party (UKIP) and the Finns Party (Perussuomalaiset, or PS) have doubled or even tripled their support in national and European Parliament elections since the beginning of the crisis (Goodwin, 2015; Ylä-Anttila and Ylä-Anttila, 2015; see also Jungar, 2015; Jupskås, 2015, pp. 34–9).

Political scientists, sociologists and economists have revealed structural, economic and social factors that give us a general idea of why constituencies tend to turn to populist parties during economic recessions. Studies on financial news have suggested that the high salience of economic crisis affects people's actions as consumers and as voters, (Picard et al., 2014), while eurosceptic populist movements have not shied away from attempting to utilize the heightened sense of precariousness brought on by the Euro crisis in mobilizing potential supporters (Pappas, 2014, pp. 71–7; Jupskås, 2015, pp. 29–34; Ylä-Anttila and Ylä-Anttila, 2015). Still, the relationship between economic crises and the support for populist parties can be regarded as somewhat unclear (Pappas and Kriesi, 2015). In the end, we know quite little about how the mediated salience of economic recession or crisis – especially when coverage is highly elite-driven – can become reattributed to contribute to the resonance and appeal of populist political communication.

Concurrently, with the onset of the Euro crisis, the internet has become the second most important primary source of news on European political matters for EU citizens (Eurobarometer, 2014, p. 48). Horizontal online communication networks and professional news media have become inherently interconnected parts of the political public sphere. This has affected how news are disseminated and consumed. Andrew Chadwick (2013, pp. 62–4) has presented the idea that in the hybrid media system the political news cycle has transformed into the so-called political information cycle, in which non-elites have more ability to participate and to intervene in the mediation of political events via the use of digital media. Social media especially have been regarded as providing platforms for micro-level political struggles that provide meaning and signification to media events (Goode, 2009; Chadwick, 2011, 2013; Cushion, 2015). As the logics of older and newer media have become more converged, traditional news organizations, journalists and their sources cannot be regarded as the sole signifying agents behind the framing of news events. Therefore, personal mass communication taking place on social media must be taken into consideration when trying to understand the role of media in the relationship of economic crisis and the latest rise of populist movements.

This chapter explores the ideological perspectives of individuals' online news aggregation and distribution by analyzing how politicians of two eurosceptic populist parties have remediated Euro crisis journalism on Facebook. News media rely increasingly on the interpersonal networks of different audience communities to distribute their content (Villi et al., 2015). When individuals share and comment on news on social media, they partake in social news curation that also allows them to participate in shaping the news agenda. Online remediation and distribution of content can have not only journalistic (Villi, 2012) but also political consequences (Bolter and Grusin, 1999, pp. 73–5): When politicians share news on social media they consciously or unintentionally partake in reconfiguring the ideological wiring of the news flow, for example, by highlighting or challenging frames set by journalists and other commentators. This provides them with opportunities for politically motivated intervention, to present alternative interpretations of unfolding news events to their social networks. Analyzing populist politicians' online remediation of the news provides means for researching how nationalist-populist parties have tried to utilize economic crisis journalism to construct grievances, to attribute blame and causality, and to mobilize support.

The chapter raises the following questions: What kind of journalistic sources have populist politicians relied on in discussing the causes, repercussions, and remedies of the crisis? What kind of news frames and journalistic styles are more susceptible to being shared and discussed by populist politicians? What kind of strategies are populist politicians using when reframing the news flow on the crisis in an online environment?

Two countries and two contexts: Finland and the UK

The ideological aspects of politicians' online news curation are explored in the context of two European populist parties that have yielded great success from the Euro crisis and the political contestation of the EU: the Finns Party and UKIP. During 2010–2015 the parties had a combined total of 87 politicians (54 Finns Party, 33 UKIP) acting as members of European or national parliaments. In order to explore how populist parties have been able to incorporate the mediated salience of economic crisis in their efforts of mobilizing support, the chapter analyzes the parties' MPs' and MEPs' Facebook posts in which they shared and commented on news stories about the Euro crisis.

The success of both UKIP and the Finns Party derive from a combination of value conservatism, nationalism, anti-establishment and anti-immigration attitudes, euroscepticism fuelled by discontent brought upon by the post-2008 economic crises, and extensive dissatisfaction with established parties (Borg, 2012, pp. 201–3; Ford and Goodwin, 2014, p. 282). UKIP and the Finns Party are populist in the sense that they make clear distinctions between 'the pure people' and 'the corrupt elite', and argue that society should be organized according to the will of the people. Overall they present themselves as alternatives to the political establishment (see Canovan, 2005; Mudde, 2007; Mazzoleni, 2008). UKIP was originally founded to strive for the UK's exit from the EU, and it can be regarded as a hard-eurosceptic party (Taggart and Szczerbiak, 2008). The Finns Party has been the most fervent and consistent critic of European integration in Finland, but the party has demanded the country's exit from the EU and the Eurozone only in rhetoric (Raunio, 2011, p. 199; Ruostetsaari, 2011). Regardless, the high salience of the Euro crisis in the Finnish media and its resonance with the party's rhetoric have been interpreted as being among the main explanations for the party's rise to become a major parliamentary power in 2011 (Borg, 2012; Pernaa et al., 2012).

The cultures of contesting European integration in Finland and in the UK are, however, historically vastly different. After Finland joined the EU in 1995, openly eurosceptic voices were relatively marginal in the Finnish public sphere. Despite the fact that certain segments of the Finnish population have held fairly strong anti-EU attitudes and opinions, mainstream political parties have been either pro-EU or kept up pro-European appearances due to taking part in integration-minded governments. Partly because of this, the Finnish mainstream media have been mostly non-critical towards the EU (Raunio, 2007, 2011). Contrastingly, the UK has long traditions of euroscepticism both within mainstream political parties and the media (Forster, 2002; Daddow, 2012). Whereas UKIP (despite its popularity) remains firmly in the opposition without significant future prospects for obtaining governmental or even significant parliamentary power due to the first-past-the-post system, the Finns Party joined a coalition government in the spring of 2015. The accession to government has, to a certain extent, limited the party's possibilities of exerting overly critical rhetoric regarding European integration.

Methodology and research design

The study of political rhetoric and political communication is concerned with the production and exchange of meaning and signification in the public sphere, and how this affects distribution of power in society. According to Stuart Hall (1982), the power to signify – to give meaning to things – is not a force free of ideology. Significations affect the perceptions on conflicting social issues and hence affect their outcomes. The signification of societal phenomena is part of what has to be struggled over, for it is the means by which social understandings are created – and therefore signification is also the means of mobilizing consent for certain outcomes within societal negotiation. Essential in any signification struggle is framing: the rhetorical packaging of social phenomena in the pursuit of encouraging certain interpretations and discouraging others (Entman, 1993).

In this study, the populist politicians' online remediation and reframing of Euro crisis news is regarded as discursive construction of action frames. According to David Snow and Robert Benford, when creating action frames – the persuasive requisites for mobilization – political actors identify and define problems, attribute causality and blame explaining the prevailing circumstances, present alternatives or solutions to defined problems, and encourage taking action (Snow and Benford, 1988, pp. 199–202; Benford and Snow, 2000).

To describe how populist politicians incorporate online news remediation in their efforts to construct action frames, the two aforementioned parties' politicians' Facebook pages were subjected to analysis. The main analytical focus was on the comparison of frames in the Euro crisis news articles shared by the politicians and in the texts attached to the articles by the politicians. First, the shared news articles were analyzed from the perspectives of overall geopolitical frames, the main problem definition or impetus for covering the crisis, and possible short- and long-term remedies to the Euro crisis (see Picard, 2015). Then, the extent to which the populist parties' politicians accepted, highlighted or challenged the news articles' frames when sharing the news pieces was analyzed. This was done by carrying out a similar frame analysis on the texts the politicians applied to the shared news articles. This was complemented with further textual analysis on how the politicians discursively constructed the Euro crisis as a grievance, how they attributed blame to different actors, how they described the repercussions of the unfolding events and what kind of discursive mobilizing strategies they applied when garnering support or action.

The social media platform selected for the collection of the research material had to fulfill four requirements. First, the platform had to have been adopted at least to some extent by the researched politicians and used for news commentary ever since the onset of the Euro crisis in 2010. Second, the platform had to allow reliable discerning of partisan discussants. Third, the selected social media had to allow retroactive data collection dating several years back. Lastly, the platform had to allow analysis of the metadata attached to individual posts. The only social media platform that complied with all these requirements was Facebook. Out of the 87 researched politicians 71 were on Facebook during 2010–2015. During this period the politicians used three kinds of Facebook page formats: politician pages, community pages and personal profiles. This study focuses on the 43 MPs or MEPs (24 Finns Party, 19 UKIP) who had either a politician page or an official community page that was public and used for political communication with potential supporters. The data was collected from January 2010 to December 2015 using Netvizz, which is a non-commercial research tool allowing data extraction from public Facebook pages and groups (Rieder, 2013).

During the research period the selected politicians published a total of 18,817 posts (9,004 Finns Party; 9,813 UKIP) on their public Facebook pages. To discern posts related to the Euro crisis, first the posts without links to outside sources were filtered out of the sample. During six years, the researched politicians shared a total of 8,394 links. Strings of word searches in English and Finnish were applied to the posts and to the titles of the links shared. The word searches consisted of terminology pertinent to financial and monetary crisis, the names of the countries related to the crisis, and the most relevant institutional actors involved.[1] After the word searches to posts with attached links, the remaining 1,240 unique posts were browsed manually to confirm whether or not they were relevant for the study. After the manual filtering, the material consisted of 296 posts with external links directly related to the Euro crisis.

Results

Highlighting the salience of turmoil and distress

When discussing the Euro crisis on Facebook, the main type of sources for the populist parties' politicians was professional news journalism. Out of the 296 links shared, two thirds (61.2%, 181) were from professional news media. One fourth (25.7%, 76) were links to partisan blogs or party media. Just over one tenth (12.5%, 37) of the links led to other sources such as alternative online media, citizen initiatives or posts on other social media sites. In total, the politicians shared 181 news pieces on the Euro crisis from 54 different professional news media (28 Finns Party, 26 UKIP). In both countries the politicians relied largely on a few media when sharing news, but there were significant differences in the types of news organizations relied on by the two parties. The Finns Party's politicians utilized mainly non-partisan national quality media: nearly half of the shared stories (43.7 %) were either from the Finnish public service media *Yle* (28) and the largest daily, *Helsingin Sanomat* (17). In the UK, where the media landscape is more partisan, UKIP's sources were heavily weighed on two conservative papers, the *Telegraph* (24) and the tabloid *Daily Express* (17). Combined, the articles from the two papers made up more than half of the articles shared by UKIP politicians. As both of the parties relied heavily on national media, very few articles from international economic papers and European elite media (3.3%) or regional and local media (5.0%) were shared.

The politicians thus mainly relied on mainstream news – as opposed to 'alternative' sources – in discussing the Euro crisis, but not without putting their own spin to the news flow. The politicians from both parties shared news articles using three different strategies. The first strategy was to share the link by itself without providing further analysis or commentary on its contents; the second was to highlight ideologically affirmative aspects within the news stories; and the third was to actively challenge or attempt to realign political adversaries' political statements or journalistic representations of the Euro crisis. Roughly in half of the cases the politicians either shared the links as they were or reinforced certain frames in the articles. In the other half of the stories some aspects were pro-actively challenged or discursively re-aligned. By sharing stories as they were or by highlighting particular statements made in the stories, remediation served as a way of identifying and increasing the salience of significant problems within the Eurozone, especially regarding the attempted – and consistently inefficient – corrective procedures and national policies pertinent to the bailouts for the indebted southern countries. Reframing the stories via commenting was used mainly for explicating problems in the handling of the Euro crisis; domesticating the framing of the events to national contexts; attributing blame to southern countries and to the political establishment in the two countries; and providing remedies for both relieving their national economies and tackling the larger perceived problem related to the non-sovereignty of the people.

The politicians focused on sharing news that painted a drastically bleak picture of the ongoing crisis with strong emphases on the direness of the southern European countries' situation. The news shared without further reframing by the politicians portrayed the events of the Euro crisis in nearly all cases without too much optimism, regardless of the type of journalistic source. By sharing stories with titles such as "Finland to support Europe''s problem countries with billions" (*Yle,* 15 March 2013) or "Britain to pay 34bn to fill EU black hole" (*Daily Express,* 27 November 2014) the politicians did not have to discursively reframe the news at all to incorporate them to their grievance construction. Euro crisis journalism has predominantly applied frames which portray the crisis and its countermeasures using metaphors of war, disease or natural disaster (Joris et al., 2015). The selective incorporation of these metaphors, that to some extent cater to anxieties and are geared for emotional responses (e.g. Mazzoleni, 2008, pp. 53–5; Alvarez and

Dahlren, 2016, p. 54), was highly compliant with the populist politicians' online mobilization efforts. Emphasizing uncertainty brought on by the crisis, therefore, could be disseminated and made more salient both by selecting more negative stories from non-partisan media and by sourcing to politically inclined news media that already shared ideological resonance with the populists' preferred message.

When a piece of news contained multiple actors and offered a variety of views on the Euro crisis, the politicians had a tendency to highlight statements that were ideologically aligned with their own views – often dismissing contrasting or conflicting points of view. Regardless of the potentially varied and multi-voiced perspectives available on the crisis in the news coverage, the politicians could quote economists stating, for example, that "the Eurozone is a complete disaster and Britain needs to leave the EU" (Williams-Grut, 2015) or that "Greece will never pay back its debts" (Heiskanen, 2015). Selective quoting emphasized the hopelessness of the situation and indicated the flaws and moral dilemmas related to, for example, the shared responsibility over the indebted countries' past economic policies.

Realigning responsibility, assigning blame and suggesting remedies

By attaching their own commentary to the news flow the politicians were able to redefine what the crisis was about and how it should be handled. This was done through redefining the root causes, repercussions, and short- and long-term remedies of the Euro crisis. In journalism the predominant responsibility for remedying the crisis has most often been framed to belong to European institutions (Arrese and Vara, 2015, p. 166–167). In the populist politicians' commentary of the news, this framing was transformed to attribute responsibility mainly to indebted countries and financial institutions. The explanations for the onset and prolonging of the crisis were attributed especially to both the political choices made in the southern countries before the crisis and to national governments' participation in sustaining the policy of lending money, especially to Greece: "We're the ones taking the risks for other countries' and the banks' mistakes" (Lohela, 2013). Complementary to this, the politicians recurrently framed the continuation of the bailouts as a zero-sum game that prevented the remedying of other locally salient political problems such as poor education infrastructure or insufficient care for the elderly.

The politicians were active in realigning the geopolitical frames being portrayed as a common European crisis with European-level solutions and shared responsibility (see Mancini and Mazzoni, 2015, p. 187). In 90% of the shared stories in which the Euro crisis was framed as a European crisis, the politicians switched the geopolitical frame either to a foreign or a national one. In the foreign frame the politicians portrayed the Euro crisis as a matter for which their fellow taxpayers should not have to bear significant responsibility. Domestication of European frames took place by bridging stories to nationally salient political discussions.

Finns Party MPs especially linked the crisis with Finnish parliamentary dynamics by criticizing the two pre-2015 governments' participation in the bailouts for

Portugal and Greece: "We're being reminded of the governments' mistakes daily. It's good that the truth reveals itself before the election" (Terho, 2015). In the UK the national frame was not only used in criticizing 'europhilia' especially within the Labour party, but most importantly it was used as an argument for the necessity of a British referendum on EU membership: "Yet more proof we need a proper debate on our EU membership and a free and fair referendum on our own future" (Farage, 2012). The domestication of the stories was also evident in personifying criticism to national political elites, even though in the stories European leaders were also highly salient. Online remediation of the news, therefore, allowed the domestication of Europeanized news frames and the bridging of the actions of European level actors directly into the day-to-day politics salient in national public spheres.

Relatively few of the populist-party politicians' Facebook posts contained straightforward policy-related alternative solutions for the crisis. The informal online environment provided a chance for adopting ambivalent stances regarding both the short- and long-term responses to the crisis. Whereas continuing to lending money to especially Greece was actively framed as the worst option, simultaneously, the austerity measures targeting the Greek economy were framed as oppression carried out by international financial elites backed by national governments: "Many Greeks and indeed those from all over the world have been shocked at the sheer ruthlessness of the dictatorial Euro project" (Farage, 2015). More often than expressing policy-related problem solutions, the populist parties' politicians expressed the option of replacing the blameworthy national political elites with the populists themselves: "If [the Finns Party leader] Soini could take care of this without those morons, everything would be better for us" (Huhtasaari, 2015).

Discussion

By remediating news on the Euro crisis on Facebook, populist parties' politicians were able to present to their supporters an amplified version of economic crisis journalism on the one hand, and on the other, their alternative interpretation of the news flow. The story told by the remediated Euro crisis news was an affective continuation story of unsuccessful and misfortunate politics that needed to change. Especially news frames emphasizing the severity and the costs of the crisis were easily diffused into resonant populist rhetoric of corrupt elites needing to be dismantled. The Eurozone crisis was highlighted as a dire problem by focusing on sharing stories that painted an exceptionally bleak picture, by assigning clear-cut ones-to-blame, by bridging the highlighted problems to domestic grievances and by presenting solutions that mainly relied on ousting the political establishment. Thus remediation of the news allowed the populist parties' politicians to get more involved in the public contestation of the Euro crisis as it unfolded.

What does the populists' sharing and commenting of Euro crisis journalism tell us about the role of social media in the politicization of news? The internet and the birth of a web culture based on social interaction and user distribution of content have opened the way for parallel counterpublics that are intertwined with the traditional gate keepers of the professional news media. News on politics is not only being broadcasted, but it is also being shared, commented on and publicly re-interpreted by various actors. This not only reconfigures the ideological contents of the news flow but potentially emancipates alternative political movements communicating affective and populist messages. Certain journalistic conventions seem especially compatible with populist rhetoric; even minor sensationalist and grievance-driven news frames can become disproportionally utilized for populist purposes in online environments, as frames prone to populist and anti-establishment rhetoric are not only easily magnified but also bridged to support other political initiatives.

Politically motivated remediation of journalism can be regarded as redefining the power relations of political journalists, their sources and contentious political movements. For journalism and media research, the remediation and ideological reconfiguring of news content in multiple and overlapping online publics poses challenges for the relevance of using content and frame analyses of mainstream media sources as explanatory evidence for any political implications they might have. As available discourses have dislodged themselves from editorial offices only to become re-appropriated in fragmenting online publics, journalists could also begin to reflect critically on how, by whom and for what ends is their content being used. It is vital to acknowledge that not only 'fake' or 'alternative' news can be used to mobilize support for populist politics.

Note

1 Search terms used: ★the EU★, ★EU:★, euro★, ★union★, ★kreik★, ★greece★, ★greek★, ★portug★, ★ital★, ★espanj★, ★spain★, ★ECB, ★central bank★, ★EKP★, ★keskuspank★, ★IMF★, ★EMRV★, ★bailout, ★tukip★, ★debt★, ★velka★, ★commission★, ★komissio★, ★kommissio★, ★kriis★, ★crisis★.

References

Alvarez, C., and Dahlgren, P. 2016. 'Populism, extremism and media: Mapping an uncertain terrain'. *European Journal of Communication*, 31(1), pp. 46–57.

Arrese, Á., and Vara, A. 2015. Divergent perspectives? Financial newspapers and the general interest press. In: Picard R. G., (ed.), *The Euro crisis in the media: Journalistic coverage of economic crisis and European institutions.* London: I.B. Tauris, pp. 149–175.

Benford, R. and Snow, D. 2000 'Framing processes and Social Movements. An overview and assessment.' *Annual Review of Sociology*, 26, pp. 611–639.

Bolter, J., and Grusin, R. 1999. *Remediation: Understanding new media.* Cambridge: MIT Press.

Borg, S. 2012. Perussuomalaiset. In Borg, S., (ed.), *Muutosvaalit 2011.* Helsinki: Finnish Ministry of Justice, pp. 191–210.

Canovan, M. 2005. *The people.* Cambridge: Polity.

Chadwick, A. 2011. 'Britain's first live televised party leaders' debate: From the news Cycle to the political information cycle', *Parliamentary Affairs*, 61(1), pp. 24–44.

Chadwick, A. 2013. *The hybrid media system: Politics and power.* Oxford: Oxford University Press.

Cushion, S. 2015. *News and politics: the rise of live and interpretive journalism.* London: Routledge.

Daddow, O. 2012. 'The UK media and 'Europe': From permissive consensus to destructive dissent', *International Affairs*, 88(6), pp. 1219–1236.

Entman, R. 1993. 'Framing: Toward clarification of a fractured paradigm'. *Journal of Communication*, 43(4), pp. 51–58.

Eurobarometer. 2014. Standard Eurobarometer 83: Media use in the European Union. Report Autumn 2014. *European Commission*. Available at: http://ec.europa.eu/public_opinion/archives/eb/eb82/eb82_media_en.pdf [Accessed 18 December 2015].

Farage, N. 2012. *Yet more proof*, [Facebook], 10 August. Available at: www.facebook.com/nigelfarageofficial/posts/257288021055724 [Accessed 2 February 2016].

Farage, N. 2015. *Ruthlessness of the dictatorial Euro project*, [Facebook], 22 August. Available at: www.facebook.com/nigelfarageofficial/posts/894997570547847 [Accessed 6 February 2016].

Ford, R., and Goodwin, M. 2014. 'Understanding UKIP: Identity, social change and the left behind', *The Political Quarterly*, 58(3), pp. 227–284.

Forster, A. 2002. *Euroscepticism in contemporary British politics: Opposition to Europe in the British Conservative and Labour parties since 1945*. London: Routledge.

Goode, L. 2009. 'Social news, citizen journalism and democracy'. *New Media & Society*, 11(8), pp. 1287–1302.

Goodwin, M. 2015. The great recession and the rise of populist Euroscepticism in the United Kingdom. In: Kriesi, H., and Pappas, T., (eds.), *European populism in the shadow of the great recession*. Colchester: ECPR Press, pp. 273–286.

Hall, S. 1982. The rediscovery of ideology: Return to the repressed in media studies. In: Gurevitch, M. et al., (eds.), *Culture, society and the media*. London: Routledge, pp. 52–86.

Heiskanen, M. 2015. 'Kreikka ei tule maksamaan velkojaan', *Talouselämä*, 27 February [Online]. Available at: www.talouselama.fi/uutiset/kreikka-ei-tule-maksamaan-velkojaan-3472362 [Accessed 2 February 2016].

Herkman, J., and Harjuniemi, T. 2015. Unity or heteronegeneity: The promise of a European public sphere. In: Picard, R. G., (ed.), *The Euro crisis in the media: Journalistic coverage of Economic crisis and European institutions*. London: I. B. Tauris, pp. 221–236.

Hubé, N., Salgado, S., and Puustinen, L. 2015. The actors of the crisis: Between personalisation and Europeanisation. In: Picard R. G., (ed.), *The Euro crisis in the media: Journalistic coverage of economic crisis and European institutions*. London: I. B. Tauris, pp. 83–102.

Huhtasaari, L. 2015. *Jos Soini saisi ilman noita tunareita hoitaa homman*, [Facebook], 4 February 2015. Available at: www.facebook.com/www.laurahuhtasaari.fi/posts/602034759928406 [Accessed: 2 February 2016].

Joris, W., Puustinen, L., and Sobieraj, K. 2015. The battle for the Euro: Metaphors and frames in Euro crisis news In: Picard R. G. (ed.), *The Euro crisis in the media: Journalistic coverage of economic crisis and European institutions*. London: I. B. Tauris, pp. 125–147.

Jungar, A. C. 2015. Business as usual: Ideology and populist appeals of the Sweden Democrats. In: Kriesi, H., and Pappas, T., (eds.), *European populism in the shadow of the great recession*. Colchester: ECPR Press, pp. 58–80.

Jupskås, A. 2015. Institutionalised right-wing populism in times of economic crisis: A comparative study of the Norwegian Progress Party and the Danish People's Party. In: Kriesi, H., and Pappas, T. (eds.), *European populism in the shadow of the great recession*. Colchester: ECPR Press, pp. 23–40.

Lohela, M. 2013. *Suomen hallituksen puheet*, [Facebook], 20 August. Available at: www.facebook.com/permalink.php?story_fbid=544280702304894&id=108427315890237 [Accessed 2 February 2016].

Mancini, P. and Mazzoni, M. 2015. Countries still matter. In: Picard R. G., (ed.), *The Euro crisis in the media: Journalistic coverage of economic crisis and European institutions*. London: I.B. Tauris, pp. 177–194.

Mazzoleni, G. 2008. Populism and the media. In: Albertazzi, D., and McDonnel, D. (eds.), *Twenty-First century populism: The spectre of Western European democracy*. London: Palgrave Macmillan.

Mudde, C. 2007. *Populist radical right parties in Europe*. New York: Cambridge University Press.

Pappas, T. 2014. *Populism and crisis politics in Greece*. London: Palgrave Macmillan.

Pappas, T., and Kriesi, H. 2015. Populism and crisis: A fuzzy relationship. In: Kriesi, H., and Pappas, T., (eds.), *European populism in the shadow of the great recession*. Colchester: ECPR Press, pp. 303–326.

Pelinka, A. 2013. Right-Wing Populism: Concept and typology, In: Wodak, R. et al., (eds.), *Right-wing populism in Europe: Politics and discourse*. London: Bloomsbury Academic, pp. 3–22.

Pernaa, V., Hatakka, N., Niemi, M. K., Pitkänen, V., Railo, E., and Välimäki, M. 2012. Median vaaliagenda ja Jytky. In: Pernaa, V., and Railo, E., (eds.) *Jytky. Eduskuntavaalien 2011 media-julkisuus*. Turku: Kirja-Aurora, pp. 396–410.

Picard, R. G. 2015. Conclusions. In: Picard, R. G., (ed.) *The Euro crisis in the media: Journalistic coverage of economic crisis and European institutions*. London: I. B. Tauris, pp. 237–242.

Picard, R., Selva, M., and Bironzo, D. 2014. *Media coverage of banking and financial news*. Research report, Reuters institute. Available at: https://reutersinstitute.politics.ox.ac.uk/sites/default/files/Media%20Coverage%20of%20Banking%20and%20Financial%20News_0.pdf.

Raunio, T. 2007. 'Softening but persistent: Euroscepticism in the Nordic EU countries', *Acta Politica*, 42(2–3), pp. 191–210.

Raunio, T. 2011. Missä EU, siellä ongelma: Populistinen Eurooppa-vastaisuus Suomessa. In: Wiberg, M., (ed.) *Populismi: Kriittinen arvio*. Helsinki: Edita, pp. 197–220.

Rieder, B. 2013. 'Studying Facebook via data extraction: The netvizz application', *WebSci'*. 13, May 2–4, Available at: http://rieder.polsys.net/files/rieder_websci.pdf.

Ruostetsaari, I. 2011. Populistiset piirteet vennamolais-soinilaisen puolueen ohjelmissa. In: Wiberg, M., (ed.) *Populismi: Kriittinen arvio*. Helsinki: Edita, 94–146.

Snow, D., and Benford, D. 1988. 'Ideology, Frame Resonance, and Participant Mobilization', *International Social Movement Research*, 1, pp. 197–217.

Taggart, P. 2004. 'Populism and representative politics in contemporary Europe'. *Journal of Political Ideologies*, 9(3), pp. 269–288.

Taggart, P., and Szczerbiak, A. 2008 *Opposing Europe? The comparative party politics of Euroscepticism. Volume 1: Case Studies and Country Surveys*. Oxford: Oxford University Press.

Terho, S. 2015. *Muistutuksia kahden edellisen hallituksen virheistä*, [Facebook], 13 April. Available at: www.facebook.com/permalink.php?story_fbid=854026927969485&id=205004656205052 [Accessed 2 February 2016].

Villi, M. 2012. 'Social Curation in Audience communities: UDC (user-distributed content) in the networked media ecosystem'. *Participations: The International Journal of Audience and Reception Studies*, 9(2), pp. 614–632.

Villi, M., Matikainen, J., and Khaldarova, I. 2015. Recommend, Tweet, share: User-distributed Content (UDC) and the convergence of news media and social networks. In: Lugmayr, A., and Dal Zotto, C., (eds.) *Media convergence handbook 1. Journalism, broadcasting, and social media aspects of Convergence*. Heidelberg: Springer, pp. 289–306.

Williams-Grut, O. 2015. 'The Eurozone is a complete disaster and Britain needs to leave the EU', *Business Insider*, 14 May [Online]. Available at: www.businessinsider.com/capital-economics-roger-bootle-the-eurozone-is-a-complete-disaster-and-we-need-a-brexit-2015-5 [Accessed 2 February 2016]

Wodak, R. 2015. *The politics of fear: What right-wing populist discourses mean*. London: Sage.

Ylä-Anttila, T., and Ylä-Anttila, T. 2015. Exploiting the discursive opportunity of the Euro crisis: The rise of the Finns party. In: Kriesi, H., and Pappas, T., (eds.) *European populism in the shadow of the great recession*. Colchester: ECPR Press, pp. 57–73.

17

#THISISACOUP

The emergence of an anti-austerity hashtag across Europe's twittersphere

Max Hänska and Stefan Bauchowitz

Introduction and context

Since 2010 the fiscal and economic crisis has severely affected the fortunes of many Europeans, most of all in Greece, Spain, Ireland, and Portugal, all of which underwent harsh economic adjustments, often in exchange for bailouts organised by Eurozone countries, the International Monetary Fund (IMF), and the European Commission. Public services had to yield to the new orthodoxy of fiscal restraint, while governments propped up banks, outraging many and irking most citizens. The Eurozone's sovereign debt crisis is, of course, ongoing as we write. The prescription of austerity triggered protests around the world. From the Occupy movement, to the Spanish Indignados, Greek Aganaktismenoi, and Portugese Geração, people coalesced around messages of resistance. Many of these anti-austerity protests coincided with the mainstream adoption of social media, which are frequently hailed as a harbinger of empowerment, amplifying the voice of crowds, and extending their ability to organise. And so, Europe's austerity policies grabbed headlines as much as they featured on social feeds, activating citizens to engage in grassroots resistance to the mantra of fiscal restraint.

The high-water mark of pan-European anti-austerity protests came while Greece was negotiating its third bailout in 2015. The country had only recently elected Syriza, a left-wing party, on a platform of rejecting the punishing conditionalities of previous bailouts. Though assessing the parameters of the wider crisis is beyond this chapter's scope, it is important to set out the context of the disagreement in which protests emerged. The contention concerned the bailout's conditions. While the Greek government sought debt relief and a respite from creditor-imposed austerity measures, creditors wanted stricter conditionalities, and would – if at all – discuss debt relief only once further austerity measures had been agreed. Over the first half of 2015 both the Greek government and creditors had dug in their heels on the matter, unwilling to yield from their position. Successive pre-crisis governments had cooked the books, revelations of which triggered the need for the first bailout in 2010. Subsequent governments stood accused of lacking resolve when it came to implementing needed reforms. Trust between the Greek government and its creditors had all but vanished by the time circumstances necessitated a third bailout in five years. Having lost confidence in Greece, creditors used their credit line, on which Greece had become reliant, as leverage to extract what they deemed as necessary reforms. Yet neither bailouts nor economic adjustments have brought about the desired economic convalescence, though it is a matter of disagreement to what extent reforms have actually been implemented.

Greece's Syriza government blamed creditors (Germany and the IMF foremost amongst them) for imposing a bailout programme they claimed to be counter-productive and economically illiterate. The former Greek finance minister, Yannis Varoufakis, prominently espoused this view, colourfully describing the bailout programme as "economic asphyxiation" and "fiscal waterboarding" (Donnelly and Vlcek, 2017, p. 51). Instead, the Greek government demanded debt relief (the IMF and prominent economists have made similar demands) and more lenient terms. Yet creditors were reluctant to grant this wish, not only because they would lose the leverage they consider essential in getting the Greek government to implement reforms, but also because many of them would find it very hard to get their national parliaments to sign-off on debt relief for Greece. Some creditor countries pointed to the fact that they had to implement their own painful reforms, and that others are poorer than Greece or pay their citizens lower pensions. Wealthier countries like Finland, Germany, and the Netherlands would have found it similarly hard to find a parliamentary majority to approve debt relief. Indeed, in 2015 the Finnish government was close to collapse over its approval of the third Greek bailout.

We do not aim to adjudicate on the matter, but what should be clear is that political views on the Greek bailout diverged sharply, and the 2015 negotiations for a third bailout were amongst the most acrimonious and divisive to date. And so, amidst one of the deepest rift in the European Union's history, as the third bailout threatened to go the way of the previous two, and the Syriza government came under ever-greater pressure to adopt policies that it had been elected to reject, it called a referendum on the terms of the proposed bailout. On 5 July these conditions were rejected by 61% of the vote. Public resistance was mounting. Once again the streets of Athens swelled with protesters, as those of Madrid, Barcelona, and Lisbon had previously. Just days before the negotiations for the third bailout were concluded, on 12 July 2015, the hashtag #ThisIsACoup emerged and quickly went viral on Twitter. It criticised the creditors' demands and expressed support for the Greek government. How did it emerge? How did it diffuse across Europe's twitter-sphere? What impact did it have on wider public discourse? Was this a unified form of pan-European protest? These are the questions that this chapter will explore. It does so by examining a sample of tweets collected through Twitter's streaming API, and qualitative methods for textual analysis to examine a sample of prominent tweets and a sample of newspaper articles from across Europe.

Twitter, hashtags and connective action

Scholars have long taken an interest in the relationship between protests and media. Broadly speaking, one early strand of scholarship focused on the way protest movements were represented in the news media, noting that these often focused on the spectacle of protests in ways that tended to discredit them – what is sometimes referred to as the "protest paradigm" (Chan and Lee, 1984). A second strand focused on the relationship between protest movements and the media. Notably Gamson and Wolfsfeld (1993) distinguished between their relationship on a cultural level (who controlled the narrative, the meaning of protest events), and a structural level (how much did they need each other, as news sources, to mobilise, or reach a larger audience). With the mainstreaming of the Internet and the increasing ubiquity of social media platforms attention shifted from the role of mass media, to the role of online platforms in protests (McCurdy, 2012).

From the early 2000s onwards a sustained interest in the democratic, participatory potential of these new communication technologies emerged (Dahlgren, 2001; Dahlberg, 2004). Centring on the fundamental transformation in communicative affordances engendered by the Internet and social media, scholars considered their impact on political participation. Unlike mass media with its vertically integrated production structures and multiple gatekeepers, social media is networked, affording everyone with an Internet-enabled device the ability to publish a message that can potentially reach millions. The threshold for producing and disseminating media messages was radically reduced. But views on the impact of this communicative potential remained divided. While some saw little evidence that social media could catalyse deep political change (Gladwell, 2010), others were more optimistic about the transformative potential that social media could have on protests, political participation, and political change (Howard and Hussain, 2011).

Most research has focused on the role of social media in shaping protest behaviour. In particular, much attention has been focused on the role of social media as an organisational tool for mobilising and joining protests, and disseminating movement information. A range of studies has found that social media use is positively related to individual protest participation (Bennett and Segerberg, 2011; Gil de Zúñiga et al., 2012; Tufekci and Wilson, 2012). Others have focused on social media as a means of documenting protests and diffusing news about them (especially when they are not covered by the news media) (Hänska Ahy and Shapour, 2013). Indeed, social media may offer opportunities for protests to become less reliant on news media when seeking to reach wider audiences.

While the predominant focus has been on the role of social media in facilitating offline protests, social media also plays an important role as platforms for opinion expression. Moreover, platforms such as Twitter, Facebook, YouTube or Instagram can become sites of protest themselves. Providing immaterial, virtual sites for protests, they allow users to publicly signal their view on a matter by sharing a story, image, or video, using a hashtag or updating a profile image with an overlay that indicates support for a cause. While some have argued that this kind of slacktivism, clicktivism, or hashtag activism has no real impact on political life and is motivated by a personal desire to feel engaged (Morozov, 2009) others have argued that it has more potential. Though expressing one's view involves a lesser degree of engagement than physically participating in a protest, or even engaging in its long-term organisation, they argue that online opinion expression can catalyse conversations around an issue, and may even act as a gateway for more comprehensive forms of participation (Valenzuela, 2013). Perhaps more importantly, such individualised acts of online engagement can produce collective movements with macro-level coherence, which Bennett and Segerberg (2012) call "connective action".

Bennett and Segerberg's distinction between collective and connective action is elucidating – and helps to explain how collective action problems are sometimes overcome online. *Collective action* is what many scholars of protest movements consider most desirable. It gets people to participate in sustained movements, with clearly defined goals, but usually requires a deeper organisational structure and a shared identity that coalesces people into the movement. *Connective action* gets people to contribute to a cause without requiring a shared identity (it allows individualised forms of activism), and without relying on a permanent organisational structure to broker connections. This describes the kind of contentious actions that rapidly emerge through social media. Connective action usually manifests when people share protest artefacts through online social networks, for example hashtags (that can be shared easily, irrespective of your location, or embeddedness in a wider movement). Here social media platforms act as "stitching technologies", facilitating the emergence of macro-level organization from disparate individuals, groups, and organisations (Bennett et al., 2014).

On Twitter, a hashtag can be such an artefact through which connective actions emerge. Hashtags are keywords that allow users to label their messages in a way that clarifies a larger theme around which users coalesce. Hashtags allow users to share and tag relevant content, and thus to follow a particular issue, to learn about and engage with it (Gleason, 2013). Any word can become a hashtag (e.g. #Greece), but a hashtag such as #ThisIsACoup succinctly codifies the sentiment that Greece was being treated unfairly, and in that sense became a message in its own right. Hashtags as succinct messages expressing opinion, and indeed voicing protest, have grown in popularity. The hashtag #OccupyWallStreet was used in protests against social and economic inequalities after the 2008 financial crash and the subsequent public bailout of the financial industry (Tremayne, 2014). #BringBackOurGirls was started in the spring of 2014 by Nigerian activists to draw attention to 250 schoolgirls kidnapped by Boko Haram. #BlackLivesMatter was created by activists in 2013 after Trayvon Martin was killed in Florida. More recently Mexico's former President Vicente Fox Quesada popularised #FuckingWall in response to Donald Trump's efforts to build a border wall with Mexico. #ThisIsACoup is another instance of a unique word compound used to distil a message, in this instance expressing protest at the way Greece was treated by its creditors. Importantly, such social media activity can also shape the agenda of the news media (Hänska Ahy, 2016). Hashtag activism, after all, has frequently featured in the news as interesting phenomena in its own right.

In the context of Greece's bailout negotiations the emergence of #ThisIsACoup is also of interest because social media are transnational in scope, and while the bailout negotiations dominated public discourse in Greece, they were also politically salient in European creditor countries, and indeed internationally. As noted, there was mounting opposition to the bailout in Finland and Germany, but also in the Netherlands, Austria, Slovakia, and the Baltic states. The negotiations featured heavily in the news across Europe. Furthermore #ThisIsACoup became an international cause célèbre, as the bailout negotiations attracted much attention beyond Europe's shores. Unlike mass media, social media is not subject to the same kind of spatial constraints, in that communications can flow unhindered across national boundaries (Boyd, 2011). The transnational dimension of #ThisIsACoup is thus not only central to the protest, but also to its role in potentially facilitating a European public sphere. It should be noted that a longstanding area of research has studied the European public sphere, often lamenting its absence, as a pan-European communication space is deemed essential to address the European Union's democratic deficit (Koopmans and Statham, 2010; Hennen, 2016). Twitter may thus stitch together diverse groups from across Europe into pan-European connective actions, giving rise to a European online public sphere.

Data and methods

The findings presented in this chapter are based primarily on a set of tweets collected through Twitter's streaming API. Between 11 and 13 July 2015 we collected all tweets containing at least one of the following words: 'eurogroup', 'eurogruppe', 'eurogrupo', 'eurogruppo', 'eurogroupe', 'eurozone', 'grexit', and 'eurosummit', without limiting ourselves to hashtags. We collected 703,423 tweets relating to the bailout negotiations, serendipitously capturing the emergence and spread of the #ThisIsACoup hashtag. There are several methods for inferring location data from user profiles and tweets. While some users geo-tag their tweets, most do not (Hecht et al., 2011).[1] However, many users specify a location in their profile – and while users can enter any text, most use actual locations. We used a combination Google and Bing's geocoding services to infer quantitative location data from user-specified location fields. Feeding each tweet's user specified location fields into the geocode APIs, these return (possibly approximate) longitude and latitude. Of our sample, 434,590 tweets contained usable location data with 318,190 tweets originating in a EU country. Our enriched data allow us to map the geographic spread of the hashtag. As Twitter also facilitates interactions between users – for instance when one user retweets, quotes, or replies to a tweet – we are also able to map the geographic spread of the hashtag. For instance, if a Twitter user in Belgium tweets #ThisIsACoup, and another user in Greece retweets, replies, or quotes this tweet, we can take the four respective coordinates to trace the spatial and temporal spread of interactions that use the hashtag.

To investigate the content of tweets using the hashtag, we extracted the 50 most retweeted tweets originating in key Eurozone countries, including France,

Germany, Greece, Italy, Spain, and UK, plus the US, and conducted a thematic analysis of them to identify common and recurring themes. The aim was not so much a rigorous quantification of themes, but rather to gain insight into the ideas users sought to express through their use of the hashtag.

To investigate the impact of the hashtag on the international press, we conducted a search of the entire Factiva database for any article matching the keyword 'thisisacoup' between 12–25 July 2015. Because Greek newspapers are not indexed by Factiva, we also searched the databases of the leading centre-right *Kathimerini* and the leading centre-left *To Vima*, using the same parameter. The search yielded 739 hits on the Factiva database and 10 for the two Greek newspapers, for 749 in total. We carried out a thematic analysis of the 10 most relevant articles (relevance as ranked by Factiva) published in key Eurozone countries, including France, Germany, Greece, Italy, Spain, and UK, plus the US. The idea, as with tweets, was not quantification, but to get a sense of how the hashtag was thematised in the press.

Emergence and spread

Unsurprisingly the hashtag was most prominently used in Greece, as revealed in Figure 17.1, which shows its relative frequency by country. Furthermore, the timeline of its rise and decline shows how the hashtag emerged in Spain before it spread to Greece, as illustrated by Figure 17.2. This figure also demonstrates that the hashtag peaked on the day of its emergence and ebbed significantly thereafter. This is in line with prevailing accounts of connective action, because sharing a protest artefact through social media is the primary mechanism through which such macro phenomena of collective dissent emerge. This allows the network to scale quickly, but also means that engagement can tail off rapidly. Looking at the broader picture of the bailout negotiations, it becomes clear that the trigger for the emergence of the hashtag was a combination of events. A leaked 'Grexit' paper, which had

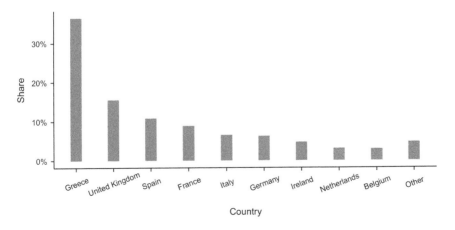

FIGURE 17.1 Relative frequency of hashtag by EU country

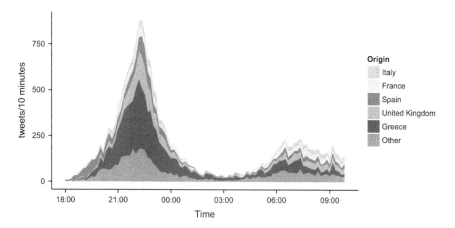

FIGURE 17.2   Frequency of hashtag use over time, stacked by country

emerged from the German finance ministry, proposed a temporary exit of Greece from the Eurozone. The paper, presumably designed to signal that the German government was not bluffing and would not back down on its demands, was thus interpreted as a quasi-coup d'état against the Greek people, who had only just rejected the bailout's terms in the July 5 referendum. News of this 'Grexit' paper had been making the rounds on Twitter the previous day (11 July).

The earliest use of the hashtag appears to be by Sandro Maccarrone, a mathematics and physics teacher from Barcelona, who tweeted at 6:01 PM GMT that "the Eurogroup's proposal is a disguised coup against the Greek people #ThisIsA-Coup #Grexit". His username (#UErgonya) is a play on the word *vergonya* ('shame' in Catalan) and European Union.

> "La propuesta del eurogrupo es un golpe estado encubierto contra el pueblo griego #ThisIsACoup #Grexit"
> — Sandro #UErgonya @smaccarrone, 6:01PM – 12 July 2015

Several newspapers reported that Maccarrone, when asked, noted that the hashtag was not his idea alone, but conceived by a group of activists (Ulrich and Schulz, 2015), and that it was pure chance that he was the first to use it. However, the hashtag did not gain much traction at first.

Only once it was used by the Catalan politician and mayor of Barcelona Ada Colau at 7:02 PM, an hour after Maccarrone first tweeted it, did #thisIsACoup take off. Colau's Twitter account acted as a node, brokering connections between different networks to amplify and rapidly scale the use of the hashtag. She tweeted "Greece wants to be in Europe, wants to pay its debt and negotiate. But it also wants respect, democracy and human rights. I'm with Greece #thisIsACoup."

"Grecia quiere estar en Europa, quiere pagar deuda y negociar. Pero quiere tb respeto, democracia y DDHH. Yo Estoy con Grecia #thisIsACoup"

– Ada Colau @AdaColau, 7:02PM – 12 July 2015

That the hashtag originated in Spain was also reported, amongst others, by the *Guardian* and *Süddeutsche Zeitung*. While a sizeable proportion of tweets using the hashtag originate in Spain, we have already established that the volume of tweets featuring the hashtag was much larger in Greece and the UK. To illustrate how the use of the hashtag spread across Europe we generated a series of plots at hourly intervals after Sandro Maccarrone first used the hashtag. Figure 17.3 maps the frequency distribution from Figure 17.2 onto a map of Europe, to illustrate where the hashtag was first used and how it spread across Europe. Between 18:00 and 20:00 the density of engagement is greatest in Spain, but with some significant engagement towards the end in the UK and Greece. Thereafter engagement with the hashtag is greatest in Greece, and the UK, before quieting down after midnight.

To understand how the hashtag spread across Europe, and indeed the world, we need to examine how it was first shared. To do so we mapped the cross-border retweets, replies, or quotes of tweets that used the hashtag. These kinds of cross-border interactions occur when a tweet published by a user in one country (e.g. Ada Colau's tweet using #ThisIsACoup) is retweeted, replied to, or quoted by a user in another country. We do this by aggregating interactions to the country level and visualising country links in a chord diagram where the frequency of interactions between countries (i.e. retweets, replies, or quotes) determine the width of a link (see Figure 17.4). What is revealed is that the most frequent cross-border

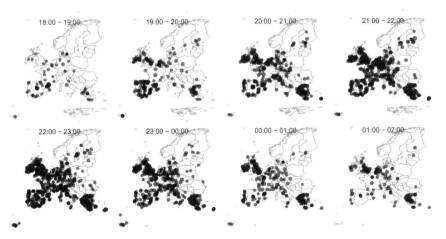

FIGURE 17.3 Geography of engagement with the hashtag over time

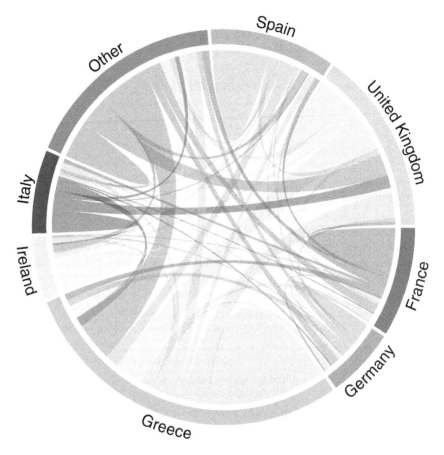

FIGURE 17.4 How those engaging with the hashtag interacted with each other across
borders

interactions occur between Greece and the UK, followed by Greece and Spain, and
then Greece and Belgium (included with 'Other' in the diagram). Figure 17.4 illustrates that direct cross-border interactions were crucial to the geographic spread of
the hashtag. Furthermore, it illustrates that connective action did not only involve
collective engagement with the hashtag, but also direct engagements between Twitter users in different European countries. Not only did people from across Europe
coalesce around the same hashtag, but they also interacted with each other across
borders on the issue.

What is noteworthy about social media platforms in general, and #ThisIsA-
Coup in particular, is the ease with which communications can spill across cultural,
linguistic, and political borders, especially in the European context where these
borders were often considered principal obstacles to the emergence of a European public sphere. Yet with #ThisIsACoup, a pan-European, indeed global, public
communication space opened up. The hashtag created a virtual site for citizens

from across Europe to come together in protest at the measures being imposed on Greece by its creditors. The sentiment the hashtag expressed was clear: seven years after the financial crash, here was another creditor forcing all the burden of adjustment on the narrowest of shoulders, while usurping its democratic right to self-determination. It took only four hours from the moment Maccarone posted the first tweet that used the hashtag until it was adopted by Twitter users across Europe, ensuring that the hashtag gained widespread popularity while the bailout negotiations were still ongoing. The hashtag's popularity also ensured its wider visibility, as the news media began reporting on this social media phenomenon.

Message and focus of tweets

A thematic analysis of top tweets yields the expected thematic pattern. Tweets using the #ThisIsACoup hashtag expressed solidarity with Greece, and opposition to what is viewed as the undemocratic, humiliating, or downright cruel treatment it received from its creditors. Spanish tweets indicated strong support for Greece and demanded respect for the outcome of the Greek referendum (which had rejected the terms of the bailout). French tweets similarly noted the "cruelty" and "humiliation" that Greece was forced to endure, noting that even the Germans agreed, referring to an article in *Der Spiegel* entitled "A Catalogue of Cruelties." Greek tweets seize on the "undemocratic" nature of the bailout. Italian tweets most frequently identify the Eurogroup as the culprit and displayed a strong sense of diffuse Euroscepticism. German top tweets are also unanimous in their criticism of the Eurogroup. While most countries have at least some top tweets critical of Germany, or less frequently of German finance minister Wolfgang Schäuble, in the sample we examined direct criticism of Germany is less prominent than we expected. The notable exception are top tweets originating from the UK, which more than any other point the finger at Germany. Articles and comments by the American Nobel Prize winning economist Paul Krugman, a vociferous critic of the bailout conditions, who called the Eurogroup's demands "madness", were also cited regularly in tweets from all countries. Overall, most of the tweets are clearly directed at creditors, calling on them to respect Greece and meet some of its demands.

Impact on the mass media

A powerful example of cross-media agenda-setting, the hashtag clearly impacted press reporting, with a total of 749 hits in our search that exactly matched 'thisisacoup'. Two Greek newspapers alone had 10 articles matching the search term, *Guardian* had 11, *Financial Times* 10, and *Süddeutsche Zeitung* 6, to name but a few.

International news coverage that mentioned the hashtag was to a very large extent descriptive, noting its use as a grassroots response to what is perceived as the technocratic usurpation of the Greek people's democratic mandate and a violation of Greek sovereignty. Newspapers generally link the hashtag to US economist Paul Krugman. German papers are similarly descriptive, with a *Süddeutsche Zeitung* article reporting on the group of Barcelona-based activists who hatched the idea for the social media campaign. It discusses how German politicians of the Green and Social Democratic parties have also been opposed to the harsh conditions of the bailout deal. But one of the perhaps most noteworthy aspects of German coverage is its account of how much anger is directed towards Germany, noting also the emergence of a counter campaign #ThisIsNotACoup. More generally, German newspaper coverage reflects concern over the damage done to Germany's reputation, and its international standing, particularly by Nazi comparisons.

The British press covered the hashtag's emergence too, noting the anti-German backlash and anti-German nature of many tweets. It also reports on an offshoot campaign that uses #boycottgermany to call on people to refrain from buying German products. Two prominent articles note that not all tweets echo this anti-German sentiment, and that there is indeed disagreement between Twitter users. Notably an article in the *Telegraph* argues that "This is not a coup" while an article in the *FT Magazine* ponders the emergence and significance of hashtags more generally, and how they have affected our communications and our thinking.

Spanish newspapers note that the international phenomenon was mostly very critical of Germany, though stopping short of editorialising, and criticised Nazi comparisons. Quoting tweets directly appears quite prominent in Spanish coverage, as well as discussions of the role and importance of Twitter. One article, for instance, discusses Twitter and notes how politicians participating in the summit use it to communicate the proceedings to the public.

The Greek press was the most forthrightly partisan. The centre-right *Kathimerini* was broadly critical of the hashtag campaign, calling it counter productive. One article was titled "This is not a coup". Nevertheless, this does not mean that the paper was not critical of the bailout agreement, but that its criticism was different in character to that revealed in Greek tweets. Much of its criticism was directed towards Greece's Syriza government. The centre-left *To Vima* reported that news coverage across Europe is discussing the destruction of European values at the hands of Germany, and notes that the hashtag is a global response thereto, as well as a rallying cry of support for the Greek government. *To Vima's* coverage was relatively closely aligned with sentiment expressed in Greek tweets. It also notes how Pablo Iglesias, head of Spain's left-wing Podemos party, used the hashtag in support of the Greek government.

Discussion and conclusion

The emergence of #ThisIsACoup is probably best described as a form of connective action (Bennett and Segerberg, 2012). It originated and was spread on Twitter. Through the hashtag, Twitter acted as a stitching technology, activating disparate, far-flung groups around a common grievance (Bennett et al., 2014). The hashtag connected people across the continent by providing them a succinct message around which to coalesce. The threshold to participate was low. People could engage with it on their own terms, without a shared focus, identity, or the kind of organisational bureaucracy that coordinating collective action requires. When people from across Europe started tweeting about #ThisIsACoup they gave rise to a macro-level phenomenon of pan-European dissent.

Like other instances of hashtag activism, it was a powerful way of making visible grassroots resistance to the bailout conditions that the creditors were seeking to impose on Greece. The rapid rise and geographic spread of #ThisIsACoup illustrates that national and linguistic boundaries are extremely porous on social media. Use of the hashtag scaled rapidly, as it spread from Spain to the rest of Europe in a matter of hours, rapidly gathering momentum in the interim. Without platforms such as Twitter, it seems unlikely that grassroots movements could have coordinated so rapidly to communicate their grievances.

But people did more than engage with a common hashtag; they also engaged with other Twitter users across national boundaries. It seems likely that people who participated in the Spanish Indignados, Greek Aganaktismenoi, and Portugese Geração were activated by and engaged with #ThisIsACoup, not least because these movements themselves mobilised through comparable connective actions (Theocharis, 2016). By stitching together people from across Europe, and facilitating engagement across boundaries, Twitter opened a transnational communications space, enabling this Europe-wide public display of resistance. It is hard to imagine how those who had serious misgivings about the bailout negotiations in Greece could have joined forces and signalled collective opposition with people from across Europe, and indeed the rest of the world, in the absence of such a stitching technology. The hashtag allowed people from across Europe with similar grievances to find each other, by coalescing around the same digital message, encapsulated by #ThisIsACoup, to synchronously express their grievance and dismay.

The effectiveness of connective action in opening up a pan-European public space for protest was amplified when the hashtag came to influence news media. Communications that started out on Twitter quickly spilled over into the press. In the two weeks following the hashtag's emergence, newspaper articles around the world mentioned the hashtag, mostly describing its emergence and the message it was communicating, but clearly acknowledging the grassroots nature of the protest. As such it managed to reach an audience well beyond active Twitter users and enter mainstream public discourse. It would have been hard for an attentive European audience to miss this pan-European expression of opposition to the bailout conditions demanded of Greece. However, #ThisIsACoup does not appear to have crossed the threshold into more sustained forms of collective action, with deeper organisational structures, a shared identity, and clear common goals. Attention to the hashtag, and the coalition that coalesced around it, did lend visibility to pan-European resistance, but engagement itself fizzled as fast as it scaled, absent organisational structures to sustain the coordination of this pan-European network.

As controversial austerity policies continue to be implemented in Europe, social media emerged as a potent means of connecting people from across the continent to voice their objection in concert. Importantly, it opened a transnational communication space that effortlessly traversed national, cultural, and linguistic boundaries, and extended the reach of the dissenting message by carrying it into news reports. The fact that people did more than engage with the hashtag, but interacted with others across the continent, illustrates that a genuine pan-European communication space opened up.

Note

1 Only around 0.2% of our tweets contained exact geographic location in the form of geographic coordinates.

References

Bennett, W. L., and Segerberg, A. 2011. 'Digital media and the personalization of collective action: Social technology and the organization of protests against the global economic crisis'. *Information, Communication & Society*, 14(6), pp. 770–799. Available from: http://dx.doi.org/10.1080/1369118X.2011.579141

Bennett, W. L., and Segerberg, A. 2012. 'The logic of connective action: Digital media and the personalization of contentious politics'. *Information, Communication & Society*, 15(5), pp. 739–768. Available from: http://dx.doi.org/10.1080/1369118X.2012.670661

Bennett, W. L., Segerberg, A., and Walker, S. 2014. 'Organization in the crowd: Peer production in large-scale networked protests'. *Information, Communication & Society*, 17(2), pp. 232–260. Available from: https://doi.org/10.1080/1369118X.2013.870379

boyd, d. 2011. Social network sites as networked publics: Affordances, dynamics and implications. In: Papacharissi, Z. (ed.), *A networked self: Identity, community and culture on social network sites*. London: Routledge, pp. 39–58.

Chan, J. M., and Lee, C.-C. 1984. Journalistic paradigms on civil protests: A case study of Hong Kong. In: Arno, A., and Dissanayake, W. (eds.), *The news media in national and international conflict*. Boulder, Co.: Westview Press, pp. 183–202.

Dahlberg, L. 2004. 'Net-public sphere research: Beyond the "first phase" '. *Javnost the Public*, 11(1), pp. 27–43. Available from: http://dx.doi.org/10.1080/13183222.2004.11008845.

Dahlgren, P. 2001. The public sphere and the net: Structure, space, and communication. In: Bennett, L., and Entman, R. M. (eds.), *Mediated politics: Communication in the future of democracy*. Cambridge: Cambridge University Press, pp. 33–55.

Donnelly, F. and Vlcek, W. 2017. 'Drowning the Greek economy: injurious speech and sovereign debt'. *Finance and Society*, 3(1), pp. 51–71.

Gamson, W., and Wolfsfeld, G. 1993. 'Movements and media as interacting systems'. *Annals of the American Academy of Political and Social Science*, 528, pp. 114–125.

Gil de Zúñiga, H., Jung, N., and Valenzuela, S. 2012. 'Social media use for news and individuals' social capital, civic engagement and political participation'. *Journal of Computer-Mediated Communication*, 17(3), pp. 319–336. Available from: http://dx.doi.org/10.1111/j.1083-6101.2012.01574.x

Gladwell, M. 2010. Small change: Why the revolution will not be tweeted. *The New Yorker*. pp. 42–49, 4 October. Available at: www.newyorker.com/reporting/2010/10/04/101004fa_fact_gladwell [Accessed 18th January 2016]

Gleason, B. (2013). '#Occupy Wall Street exploring informal learning about a social movement on Twitter'. *American Behavioral Scientist*, 57(7), pp. 966–982. Available from: https://doi.org/10.1177/0002764213479372

Hänska Ahy, M. 2016. 'Networked communication and the Arab Spring: Linking broadcast and social media'. *New Media & Society*, 18(1), pp. 99–116. Available from: https://doi.org/10.1177/1461444814538634.

Hänska Ahy, M., and Shapour, R. 2013. 'Who's reporting the protests? Converging practices of citizen journalists and two BBC World Service newsrooms, from Iran's election protests to the Arab Uprisings'. *Journalism Studies*, 14(1), pp. 29–45. Available from: https://doi.org/10.1080/1461670X.2012.657908.

Hecht, B., Hong, L., Suh, B., and Chi, E. H. 2011. 'Tweets from Justin Bieber's heart: The dynamics of the location field in user profiles'. In *Proceedings of the SIGCHI Conference on Human Factors in Computing Systems*, 7–12 May 2011, Vancouver, Canada. pp. 237–246.

Howard, P. N., and Hussain, M. M. 2011. 'The upheavals in Egypt and Tunisia: The role of digital media'. *Journal of Democracy*, 22(3), pp. 35–48. Available from: www.journalofdemocracy.org/upheavals-egypt-and-tunisia-role-digital-media.

Koopmans, R. and Statham, P. 2010. *The Making of a European Public Sphere: Media Discourse and Political Contention*. Cambridge: Cambridge University Press.

McCurdy, P. 2012. 'Social movements, protest and mainstream media'. *Sociology Compass*, 6(3), pp. 244–255. https://doi.org/10.1111/j.1751-9020.2011.00448.x

Morozov, E. 2009. 'Iran: Downside to the "Twitter Revolution"'. *Dissent*, 56(4), pp. 10–14. Available from: www.dissentmagazine.org/article/iran-downside-to-the-twitter-revolution

Theocharis, Y. 2016. Every crisis is a digital opportunity: The Aganaktismenoi movement's use of social media and the emergence of networked solidarity in Greece. In: Bruns, A., Enli, G., Skogerbo, E., Larsson, A. O., and Christensen, C. (eds.), *The Routledge companion to social media and politics*. New York: Routledge, pp. 184–197.

Tremayne, M. 2014. 'Anatomy of protest in the digital era: a network analysis of Twitter and Occupy Wall Street.' *Social Movement Studies*, 13(1), pp. 110–126.

Tufekci, Z., and Wilson, C. 2012. 'Social media and the decision to participate in political protest: Observations from Tahrir square'. *Journal of Communication*, 62(2), pp. 363–379. https://doi.org/10.1111/j.1460-2466.2012.01629.x.

Ulrich, S., and Schulz, J. 2015. Griechenland: Wer #ThisIsACoup erfand. *Süddeutsche Zeitung*, 14 July. Available at: www.sueddeutsche.de/wirtschaft/anti-deutsche-stimmung-zeichen-wut-1.2564318 [accessed 17th May 2017]

Valenzuela, S. 2013. 'Unpacking the use of social media for protest behavior the roles of information, opinion expression, and activism'. *American Behavioral Scientist*, 57(7), pp. 920–942. Available from: https://doi.org/10.1177/0002764213479375.

INDEX

Page numbers in *italics* indicate figures; **bold** indicates tables.